THE CHANGING AMERICAN VOTER

A TWENTIETH CENTURY FUND STUDY

The Twentieth Century Fund is a research foundation engaged in policy oriented studies of economic, political, and social issues and institutions. It was founded in 1919 by Edward A. Filene, who made a series of gifts that now constitute the Fund's assets.

THE CHANGING AMERICAN VOTER

Enlarged Edition

Norman H. Nie
Sidney Verba
John R. Petrocik

Harvard University Press
Cambridge, Massachusetts
and London, England
1979

Library of Congress Cataloging in Publication Data

Nie, Norman H.
    The changing American voter.

    "A Twentieth Century Fund study."
    Includes index.
    1.Elections—United States.   2. Voting—United
States.   3. Public opinion—United States.   I. Verba,
Sidney, joint author.   II. Petrocik, John R.,
1944–   joint author.   III. Title.
JK1976.N48   324′.2′0973   75-42429
ISBN 0-674-10830-2 (cloth)
ISBN 0-674-10835-3 (paper)

To
Angus Campbell,
Philip E. Converse,
Warren E. Miller,
and Donald E. Stokes

on whose coat-tails we ride.

Acknowledgments

Our analysis of the changing American voter is based on data from some fifteen separate national surveys conducted between 1939 and 1974. Collectively, these surveys contain information on the political attitudes, beliefs, and behavior of over 30,000 respondents. The management and statistical analysis of this large body of data could not have been accomplished without considerable assistance.

We wish to thank the Twentieth Century Fund for its sponsorship of this study. Lee Sigal, Selma Campbell, Carol Barker, and William Diaz at the Twentieth Century Fund worked closely with us. Wendy Mercer was patient and helpful with our incessant rebudgeting, and managed in the end to keep us both honest and solvent.

We would like to thank Professor Hans Daalder and Chris Haveman of the University of Leiden, where we began this research in 1972. The University of Leiden not only housed us and our research staff but also provided us with a substantial amount of computer time for the early stages of data preparation and analysis. A debt of gratitude is also owed to our own institutions—the National Opinion Research Center (NORC) of the University of Chicago and the Center for International Affairs at Harvard University. The Ford Foundation contributed support to the NORC 1973 survey, which is extensively used in the book.

Books based on complex survey analyses are often group products, with the group extending beyond the names found on the title page. Two people, Kristi Andersen and Goldie Shabad, played a particularly important role in the planning, design, and execution of our analyses. We are grateful to them for their significant intellectual contributions as well as their tireless efforts. The book could not have been done without them.

The tables and figures which form the basis of our arguments are the result of numerous hours of file preparation, variable construction, and computer analysis. What appears in this volume is often the fourth or fifth refinement of our original analysis. Several research assistants carried the main burden of these analyses. They were closest to the data and often suggested critical substantive or methodological insight which made a particular analysis work. Ioanna Crawford, Ester Fuchs, Bill McAllister, Jim Rabjohn, Carole Uhlaner, and Paul Warwick each made important contributions.

We also wish to express our thanks to Carol Lugtigheid, Jaap Rozema, and Jaap von Poelgeest, who helped us with the massive task of creating a unified data file out of the individual Michigan Survey Research Center election studies. To our colleague Jae-On Kim, whom we pester incessantly with our difficult research problems, we owe special thanks for his help in creating the index of political beliefs and for general advice at various points. Rachel Macurdy, Helen Parker, Eileen Petrohelos, and Narumi Ohara typed the numerous versions of the manuscript. They also drew and redrew the figures. Our friends and colleagues Philip E. Converse, James Davis, John Jackson, Benjamin Page, G. Bingham Powell, H. Douglas Price, and Kenneth Prewitt read and commented on various versions of the manuscript and offered important suggestions. Page and Powell drafted detailed critiques of the book. We greatly appreciate their assistance and labor.

We owe a special debt to Andrew Greeley, director of the Center for the Study of American Pluralism at NORC. He was our constant collaborator and critic.

Finally, our greatest debt is to the researchers at the Survey Research Center for Political Studies at the University of Michigan. The data they have gathered over two decades and their scholarly analyses of these data form the foundation for all electoral studies. Those scholars who use the Michigan election data form the largest, yet best-integrated, intellectual community in political science. Because the Michigan scholars have contributed so much, not only to social science but also to social science community-building, we have dedicated this book to them.

The 1979 enlarged edition has a new chapter on the 1976 election. In other respects, the book remains the same as the earlier edition.

Norman H. Nie, The University of Chicago and NORC
Sidney Verba, Harvard University
John R. Petrocik, University of California, Los Angeles

Contents

TABLES

FIGURES

Foreword

In 1971, the increasing political polarization of the American people was a controversial issue. The traumatic racial conflicts, debates and demonstrations over Vietnam, student unrest, and political assassinations of the 1960s had surely had their effect on the electorate, but the nature of that effect was unknown. In an attempt to go beyond the conflicting and impressionistic reports then in circulation, the Trustees of the Twentieth Century Fund sought to undertake a broad study of political and voting behavior. For this purpose, they commissioned the services of Norman Nie and Sidney Verba.

Nie and Verba are political scientists who had already written extensively and had individually established reputations for their insightful and sophisticated analyses of citizen attitudes and political behavior. They were later joined by John Petrocik, a young University of Chicago Ph.D., who was attracting the attention and respect of fellow scholars through his journal articles. The result of their collective efforts is a unique chronological portrait of the electorate that may well become a landmark in the study of domestic politics.

Drawing primarily on a series of surveys conducted by the University of Michigan's Survey Research Center from 1952 to 1972, Nie, Verba, and Petrocik depict a changing and increasingly dissatisfied and disillusioned citizenry. Voters today feel more and more alienated not only from the political parties but from the political process itself. Casual observation had previously suggested what these findings confirm, but the authors' careful documentation gives added weight to concerns about the future of American politics.

Their analysis contrasts sharply with the view of the American public presented in the now classic study, *The American Voter,* published in 1960. That view portrayed a largely passive citizenry, unaware of, and unconcerned about political issues, guided in its electoral choices primarily by party allegiance. But Nie, Verba, and Petrocik show that the contemporary voter is not only more aware of and sensitive to political issues but also far more likely to rely on his own issue position and to desert his party in making the voting decision.

Tracing these changes both to changes in the issues, which have become more divisive since the Eisenhower years, and to the entry of new voters into the electorate, the authors make a persuasive case that the electorate is undergoing a fundamental realignment, similar, in many respects to the realignment that occurred during the New Deal era. Nie, Verba, and Petrocik do not give the specifics of this realignment, but they do present a number of alternative futures—some of them bright, others less so—and indicate, through a series of mock elections, how the electorate might react in 1976 to various candidate choices.

Their book does not rest solely on its contemporary relevance. The way in which the authors have brought together a number of themes that have recently emerged in political science, their creative analyses and comprehensiveness may well make this study a major theoretical contribution to the understanding of electoral dynamics in America.

The Fund is grateful to the authors of this book for carrying out their assignment with care, diligence, and commitment. What they have to say should command the attention of all those concerned about American politics and its future.

M. J. Rossant, Director
The Twentieth Century Fund

THE CHANGING AMERICAN VOTER

1 Introduction

Nostalgia comes quickly these days. In the mid-seventies some are nostalgic for the fifties and others are already nostalgic for the sixties. It all reflects the rapidity of change. The seventies look different from the two previous decades; and the two previous decades could hardly be more different from each other.

Just as politics has changed, so has the public in response to that change. The American public in the mid-seventies differs in fundamental ways from the public of the fifties. In the 1950s the public was only mildly involved in politics, was relatively content with the political process, and had long-term commitments to one or the other of the major parties. Today it is more politically aroused, more detached from political parties than at any time in the past forty years, and deeply dissatisfied with the political process.

There are many reasons for these changes. We will focus on two: new issues and new people. The public has changed in response to the issues that have shocked the polity in the past two decades. Race, Vietnam, the urban crisis, Watergate, and the economic recession of the mid-seventies have had profound effects on the public, not only because they are important issues but also because they are issues that cut across the old alliance patterns of American politics. The part of the public on whom these issues have had the greatest impact is the new cohort of voters who have entered the electorate in the past two decades. As we hope to demonstrate, fundamental changes in the political alignment of the citizenry come from change in the composition of the electorate rather than from change in attitudes and behavior of those already in the electorate.

The changes that we shall document raise profound questions about the course of government in the United States and the responsiveness of the political process. The new issues are ones in relation to which the political process has not appeared responsive: the political parties have not been able to present clear alternatives, and with many of the issues a response to one group appears as lack of response to another. The issues are such that they have aroused the public and increased its political concern; the response is such that the public is left deeply dissatisfied.

This development raises another important question: Is the United States becoming ungovernable? Government, above all democratic government, depends on the support of the citizenry. It also depends on the ability and capacity of the political process to reconcile conflicting forces in the society. Today's public is a good deal less supportive than in the fifties; it has within it conflicting forces that are not easily reconciled. Americans have traditionally depended on the political party system to play a major role in the reconciliation of conflict in society—usually by building wide coalitions to contest elections. But the changes in the public over the past two decades have been such as to place greatest pressure on the parties. The divisions within the society are replicated within the parties—especially within the Democratic party. The result is that the withdrawal of support for the political process as a whole is accompanied by withdrawal of support for the political parties.

These opening comments sound apocalyptic. We are not, however, all that pessimistic. There is nothing in our evidence to suggest that the demise of the republic is imminent. The public may be dissatisfied with the government, but there is little evidence of a preference for antidemocratic alternatives. A substantial proportion of the public has withdrawn support for the major political parties; but they now respond to political issues more than in the past. We are entering a period of uncertainty as to how elections are going to be fought, not a period of uncertainty about the survival of the electoral process.

This book will trace the evolution of American public opinion in the past two decades. The responses of the American public are closely watched. Public opinion polls follow the reaction of the populace to the political events of the day. Surveys have chronicled the changes in public attitudes on busing, or in support for the war in Vietnam, or in the evaluation of President Johnson or President Nixon or President Ford. We know what proportions favored impeachment at various stages of Watergate and what proportions knew the meaning of impeachment. These data tell us a lot about how the public has reacted to the particular shocks of recent decades.

But the response of the American people to the events of the past decades has taken place on another level as well. The American people have changed in more fundamental ways, in their basic assumptions about the American polity and in the way in which they relate to that polity. They have changed not only in *what* they think about political matters, but in *how* they think about political matters.

We will chronicle that change and, beyond that, measure it as precisely as we can. A democratic polity, many have argued, rests on a set of public beliefs, commitments, and actions that keep democracy alive. Our task is to see how the basic political assumptions of the public have been affected by the turbulent years.

We base our analysis of change in the American public on a unique historical record: the periodic election surveys conducted over the past two decades by the Survey Research Center of the University of Michigan. These data provide detailed information on the political attitudes and behavior of the public. More important, the data are measured in a relatively standard way across the time period. Thus we can trace changes quite precisely. And we can trace relatively complex *patterns* of attitude and behavior, not simply how the public responds to this or that problem.

The baseline for our study of change will be the late Eisenhower years. We will begin from the "classic" portrait of the American electorate as presented in *The American Voter*,[1] a portrait drawn largely from a study of the 1956 presidential election, supplemented by a study of the 1952 presidential election and the 1958 congressional election.

National sample surveys of the American electorate, the prime requisite for the kind of political history we want to write, do not begin in 1956. There were more limited studies of the 1944 and 1948 presidential elections, the former by the National Opinion Research Center at the University of Chicago, the latter by the Survey Research Center at Michigan.[2] And, the Michi-

---

[1] Angus Campbell, Philip E. Converse, Warren E. Miller, and Donald E. Stokes, *The American Voter* (New York: Wiley, 1960).

[2] The 1944 NORC study is analyzed in Sheldon J. Korchin, "Psychological Variables in the Behavior of Voters," Ph.D. dissertation, Harvard University, 1946. The 1948 Michigan study is reported in Angus Campbell and Robert L. Kahn, *The People Elect a President* (Ann Arbor: University of Michigan, Survey Research Center Series #9, 1952).

gan group conducted a fairly complete study of the 1952 election. In addition, the Gallup Poll has, since the 1930s, tapped some aspects of the political activity and attachments of the American public[3] and there were two landmark studies of the American electorate in 1944 and in 1954 limited to specific localities.[4]

There are, however, good reasons to make the Eisenhower election our baseline. The main one is that the SRC 1956 study is the first major study of the American electorate with all baseline information we need, information that allows us to trace changes in the public in the following years. The 1952 study by the Michigan group does not contain all of the questions that became fairly standard fare in their studies from 1956 through 1972. Secondly, the 1956 study appears to have formed the major data base for the analysis that went into *The American Voter*. The data reported in that book come from the 1948, 1952, and 1956 studies, but most heavily from the 1956 election. This is particularly the case in relation to the analysis of the structure of political belief systems that is of particular interest to us.[5]

Is 1956 an unfortunate baseline, an atypical election year with few crucial and divisive political issues? In retrospect, 1956 may look calmer than it appeared at the time. But the placidity of the 1956 election year is certainly no illusion, especially when viewed from the perspective of what was to follow. The Korean war was over, the nation relatively prosperous, the administration in Washington relatively low-keyed. McCarthyism was perhaps the most divisive issue of the first Eisenhower administration, but by 1956, with the waning of Joseph McCarthy's fortunes, it had lost a good deal of its virulence. The major issues of the 1960s were waiting in the wings, but they were not yet recognized. During the first Eisenhower administration the Geneva Con-

---

[3] For results of the Gallup Poll see George Gallup, *The Gallup Poll 1935–1971* (New York: Random House, 1972).

[4] Paul F. Lazarsfeld, Bernard R. Berelson, and Hazel Gaudet, *The People's Choice* (New York: Duell, Sloan, and Pierce, 1944), and Bernard R. Berelson, Paul F. Lazarsfeld, and William N. McPhee, *Voting* (Chicago: University of Chicago Press, 1954).

[5] Of the tables and figures in *The American Voter* that report data from their surveys of the American public, 51 are based on the 1956 data alone, 37 are based on a combination of the 1952 and 1956 data, 4 are based on the 1952 data alone, and 29 more on more extensive data sets. The standard portrait of the American electorate that entered the literature in the early 1960s is largely a portrait of the public in 1956. Two of the most important analyses of the American public—the analysis of the "level of conceptualization" in *The American Voter,* and the analysis of mass political "ideologies" in Philip E. Converse's article on "The Nature of Belief Systems in Mass Publics" in David E. Apter, ed., *Ideology and Discontent* (New York: Free Press, 1964)—do not use the 1952 data. The "level of conceptualization" analysis draws on the 1956 study and the "mass belief" article draws on the 1956 study and the SRC's study of the 1958 and 1960 election. Chapters 9 and 10 of *The American Voter* that deal with these issues use only 1956 data.

ference "settled" the issue of Indochina, and the Supreme Court outlawed school segregation. Each event presaged what was to come, but neither was an issue in 1956.

The 1956 election is quite different from the ones that followed. The issue, though, is not which election is normal or typical. If 1956 is not a typical election, is 1960 typical? 1964? 1968? 1972? Was the calm of the 1950s abnormal and the present turbulence the norm for American politics, or was the Eisenhower period the time of normalcy? The answer is unclear and perhaps will always be so. What is important is that 1956 is the baseline from which much recent political analysis has begun. A comparison with later years reveals much about the permanence or impermanence of the characteristics of the public in 1956.

The American Voter was the dominant source of the classic portrayal of the electorate, but other major works appeared during the 1950s that helped form this description of the American populace. Berelson, Lazarsfeld, and McPhee's *Voting* appeared in 1954 and reported an earlier and highly significant study of the 1948 election.[6] Samuel Stouffer used an imaginative survey of citizens and community leaders to study the American responses to questions of loyalty and security (*Communism, Conformity and Civil Liberties,* 1955).[7] In a work published in the early 1960s but based on data collected in the 1950s Almond and Verba (*The Civic Culture,* 1963)[8] presented survey data from five nations of which the United States was one, and put the study of American political behavior in a comparative perspective. V.O. Key's monumental analysis *Public Opinion and American Democracy* was published in 1961 based on data of the 1950s.[9] Another influential work that added to the portrait of the American public was Dahl's *Who Governs?*[10] Although more a study of community decision-making than of citizen behavior, it used survey data from the city of New Haven to make a number of significant points about citizen activity.

The flowering of large-scale survey studies in the 1950s depended on the availability of scholars with training and inclinations in that direction, on the development of the technical apparatus needed for such studies, and on the willingness of foundations to supply the large sums of money required for such work. That the personnel, the technical apparatus, and the funding all came together during the Eisenhower years was fortuitous. But the fact that

---

[6] See n. 4.
[7] (New York: Wiley, 1955).
[8] (Princeton: Princeton University Press, 1963).
[9] (New York: Knopf, 1961).
[10] (New Haven: Yale University Press, 1961).

these pioneering studies of the American public were conducted at that time had a profound effect on the results and on the inferences that were drawn from them.

While this book is mainly about political attitudes and their relation to political events, it also is about social science and just how we know what we know about citizen beliefs. The twenty year period over which we trace changes in American political beliefs is also a period of revolution in political science. In fact, that revolution, which has been marked by periodic, systematic surveys of the American public, has made it possible to trace the changes in American political beliefs.

Several aspects of the change in political science are particularly relevant. Political science in the past two decades became more "scientific." The works cited above are the landmarks of that revolution. The discipline (or at least certain significant segments of it) turned away from the policy-oriented descriptive work that had characterized much previous political study to focus on more general, underlying patterns of political life. Political science was no longer to be the study of current events.

Another important fact is that political scientists turned away from the analysis of political institutions to the analysis of political behavior. The new approaches to political study stressed the sociological and psychological foundations of political life.

A third aspect was a methodological one. New techniques were applied to political studies, particularly techniques that enabled the quantitative study of political life. The most widely adopted technique was that of the sample survey which, coupled with the high-speed computer opened a new world of political research. Sample surveys changed radically the standard modes of political observation.

The main characteristics that differentiate sample surveys from other means of study of the mass public are the use of standardized instruments and systematic sampling of respondents. Previous studies of the public depended heavily on who the observer spoke to and what questions he asked. But one never knows how representative a group an observer has encountered. Even as careful an observer as Tocqueville, to whom we are indebted for the brilliant portrait of the American public in the early nineteenth century, obtained most of his information by talking to a limited set of local notables.

The new, more precise research techniques were used in the major studies of the American populace in the 1950s. The result was a description of the American electorate that conformed to some earlier impressions of that public but that was at variance with some other views. The new description was accepted, with considerable justification, as more accurate than earlier portraits of the public. Previous researchers may have thought they were studying the public at large, but the absence of a precise sample design often meant that they dealt with a rather narrow slice of the populace—the articulate few whom journalists, foreign aristocrats, or academic students of politics are likely to meet. Or generalizations about the mass public would be based on the even narrower group that leaves a written historical record. There is substantial evidence that the views of such groups differ sharply from those in the populace at large. The new survey studies of the public studied the articulate and the inarticulate.

The combination of these new research findings with a research orientaiton that sought for the explanation of such findings in underlying social and psychological forces had an interesting and significant result. It was assumed that a more accurate description of the American public was possible and that the data revealed a basic structure of political attitudes that was unlikely to change. New and more precise studies revealed attitudes and patterns of behavior that were presumed to have their origin in some fundamental social and psychological characteristics. The roots of the political attitudes were traced to early socialization in the family and school. Such attitudes were likely to persist throughout life. There was no evidence that public attitudes had ever been otherwise than what was revealed by these new studies. (If earlier studies did reveal a different picture they were, of course, not to be believed since their techniques were suspect.)

The problem was, however, that the patterns of public attitudes and public behavior revealed by the new research techniques may not have been as permanent as one imagined. The usual sample survey is a snapshot; it reveals political patterns at one moment of time. This is little problem if the snapshot is of a landscape that does not change from year to year. But if it is a snapshot of something that may look quite different next year from what it looks like today, one must use the snapshot with caution. If public attitudes—even those basic political attitudes which are supposed to originate in early life—are responsive to political events, then a pattern of political attitudes and behavior discovered at one point in time may differ substantially from that found at another point in time.

By considering the several election studies conducted from the 1950s to the 1970s, we hope to separate the timebound from the timeless in political attitudes. Donald T. Campbell describes how the British chemists Nicholson and Carlisle, in May 1800, used a new apparatus to analyze water in ways that had not been done before. They inserted two electrodes into a sample of London water and allowed an electric current to flow between them. "They obtained hydrogen gas at one electrode, oxygen at the other, and uninhibitedly generalized to all the water in all the world for all eternity."[11] Uncounted replications of the experiment, with other water from other times, have confirmed the result.

The social sciences differ from this natural science example. When a new apparatus—the systematic survey—was applied to the American public in the later 1950s, it revealed some components of political attitudes not observed before. But unlike the electrolysis experiments, the results found were somewhat idiosyncratic to the time and place. Later application of the same instrument would reveal something different.

The data we present will show some striking changes in the political assumptions of the populace in the past two decades. But the analysis ought not to imply a criticism of survey techniques—even if they do not reveal patterns as permanent as those in the natural sciences. Our ability to trace changes in American political attitudes and behavior since the early 1950s depends upon a series of such studies over time. If the danger of the precise techniques associated with survey research is that one may consider the results to be more stable than they in fact are, the advantage of such techniques is that they can be self-correcting. And in this way they can help us isolate the reasons why things change.

From this perspective, the series of studies conducted by the Michigan Survey Research Center is indeed valuable. In a field where most studies are conducted once, and never replicated, the repeated Michigan series is the exception. If things change substantially from one point in time to the next, their replicated surveys can locate and measure such changes, something that is much more difficult when less precise measurements are taken.

Furthermore, if the original studies led to the creation of a paradigm that no longer seems to be in full accord with the evidence, that does not imply criticism of the paradigm makers. Quite the contrary. It is the very precision of their data and the clarity of their analysis that allows one to observe changes from the baseline they give, and to understand some of the implications of those changes. Indeed, the notion that *The American Voter* established a fixed model of electoral behavior that could then be applied across subsequent elections without consideration of changing context is a notion more to be found among the readers of the writers of the fifties than among the writers themselves. As the authors of *The American Voter* clearly recognized—with a prescience for which their recent critics give them little credit—theirs was a book about the Eisenhower elections. "The data of a single four-

---

[11] Donald T. Campbell, "Prospective: Artifact and Control," in R. Rosenthal and R. L. Rosnow, eds., *Artifact in Behavioral Research* (New York: Academic Press, 1969), p. 361.

year period can suggest hypotheses; they can hardly supply their proof."[12] Recent work on changes in the American electorate (our work is but one example; the literature is voluminous) must be seen as attempting to test the suggested hypotheses.

As we shall see, the description of the electoral process of the late fifties no longer holds, and that change in the electoral process came in response to political events. Does this mean that all political processes are contingent on the events of the day and that generalization is impossible about political matters? The electrolysis instruments continue to produce hydrogen and oxygen decade after decade. The survey instruments produce different results now than they did a while back. Nevertheless, we remain convinced that generalization is possible, even about matters as volatile as politics. But the generalizations will have to take time into account. A modified paradigm of the electoral process (which we shall definitely *not* propose in this volume—though we hope our analyses will start us on the road to one) will have to deal systematically with the way in which the public responds to the political issues of the day.

A Note on Method

Intensive surveys at particular elections permitted political scientists to write a new kind of election analysis, one that dealt more precisely with the social and psychological roots of voting behavior. Similarly, the periodic surveys over a two decade period enable a new kind of political history, a history that traces in detail and with some precision the changing political views of the American public. The survey studies of elections have not replaced other forms of election analysis such as studies of campaign decisions or of the organization of the political parties. They form a key complement to these studies. Similarly, our history of changes in the American public seen through the instrument of the periodic surveys should not be regarded as a new political history to replace the old, but rather as an important complement to other historical accounts. The surveys have some advantage that other studies do not. They provide precise information about attitudes and their change that would not be otherwise available. They allow detailed comparisons among groups. Still they tell only part of the story. We will focus on the part of the story they tell. Although ours is not a general history of America in the past two decades, we shall try to connect these data to the more general trends in our society.

---

[12] *The American Voter,* p. 43; see also p. 12.

Our approach involves tracing the answers that the American public gave to *the same questions* asked at different points of time. The stress on the same questions is important, and worthy of some comment. Survey techniques depend on the fact that a large number of respondents are presented with the same stimulus—that is, are asked the same questions. If the stimulus is constant, one can effectively compare the responses of men and women, southerners and northerners, blacks and whites, Democrats and Republicans. But the comparison is obviously meaningless if different questions are asked. A question phrased one way will elicit one response, a seemingly similar question phrased another way may elicit a substantially different response. Often the difference in response is substantial even though the difference in the wording of the question is minimal. For example, the proportion favoring one or another position in some political controversy (escalate or de-escalate the war in Vietnam, impeach or not impeach, and so forth) is affected by which of the two alternatives is given first. (There is a slight tendency for respondents to favor the second alternative of any pair offered them.) Or, if respondents are given a neutral alternative ("Are you in favor of policy X or are you opposed or have you not made up your mind?"), there will be more neutral answers than if the "not made up your mind" is not given. More Americans describe themselves as Independents if they are asked something like, "Do you consider yourself a Democrat, a Republican, an Independent, or what?" than if asked, "Do you consider yourself a Democrat or a Republican?" The impact of question wording is not uniform across the population. Those with strong views on a subject are less likely to be affected by question wording than are those for whom the issue at hand is one that they have not previously considered. But in general one must be cautious about comparing responses to different questions.

If we are to trace changes in public attitudes over time it is important that we compare responses to the same stimuli. To find that the American public is less trusting of government officials today on the basis of one question than they were fifteen years ago on the basis of another question is to find something that is uninterpretable. Is the difference due to change in the amount of trust or to the change in the question wording?

We will, in our analysis, trace changes in answers to the same questions as they have been repeated in election studies by the Survey Research Center. The task, though, is not as straightforward as it may seem. For one thing, questions that are apparently the same sometimes undergo subtle changes in wording or format from election to election. In some cases, this has meant that we could not trace questions on a similar topic across time. But in many cases, we have been able to make one version of the question comparable with the other. At times, the difference is that more coding categories are used for the same question in one year than in another. In these cases, we can collapse the codes in one year to match those in another.

But there is a more complex problem. Even if the same question is asked at two different points of time, is it really the same question? The fact that times change may mean that the meaning of the question undergoes change. Consider several ways in which this happens. First, some periods of time are more intensely political than others. It is possible to compare answers to questions about political interest at the height of an election campaign with those asked in calmer political times if one is concerned with the question of the extent to which campaigns arouse interest in politics. But when looking at secular changes in interest, as we are, one cannot compare answers to questions asked in October 1968 with answers to questions asked in June 1971 to see if interest has gone up or down in the three-year period. This problem is not a severe one for our analysis. The studies with which we deal are largely election studies, conducted shortly before or after an election campaign. But for certain kinds of comparisons—levels of political interest or levels of political activity—it will be necessary to consider presidential and off-year elections separately since the former arouse more interest. Questions asked in one type of election are not directly comparable to those in the other type.

A more complicated problem is introduced by the fact that words change their meaning. Consider, for example, that at various times over the recent decades, the Gallup Poll has asked Americans whether they consider themselves liberals or conservatives. Over time the proportion calling themselves conservatives has grown, while the proportion calling themselves liberals has shrunk. But some other questions asked by the Gallup Poll indicate that the meaning of the term has changed as well. In the fifties, the terms referred to a person's general attitude on economic matters as well, perhaps, as his or her position on matters of civil liberties and civil rights. By the late 1960s the terms had, in part, a new content. Liberalism and conservatism, at least to some substantial portion of the population, referred to matters of sex, drugs, and general permissiveness. The point is that the person who was a liberal then and is conservative now may not have changed positions at all. He may have just changed his understanding of the issues to which the terms refer.

There are other examples. Questions about social welfare in the 1950s triggered off thoughts of social security and unemployment insurance; in the 1960s they triggered off thoughts of black welfare mothers. "Big government" in the 1950s meant New Deal type social reform programs. In the 1960s "big government" meant, for many citizens, American military might in Vietnam.

This problem is more difficult to deal with than the problem of changes in question wording. In some rare cases follow-up questions asking the respondent "What do you have in mind?" help interpret the meaning of answers. But such follow-up questions are costly to ask and are rarely found in surveys. There is no satisfactory solution to this problem. The measuring instrument itself changes and that makes it hard to identify the change. But we can, by seeing how attitudes relate to each other, get some insight into concepts that have lost one meaning and gained another. As we shall demonstrate, this is true of such concepts as "big government," "welfare," and even "interest in politics."

The examples thus far make clear that one cannot view the responses of individuals to survey questions as simply the verbal acts of isolated individuals. Rather the responses are the result of an interaction between the interviewer and the respondent and we must be sensitive to the fact that the nature of that interaction may change. The interviewer may ask a different question in one year from that asked in earlier years or he may ask the same question but the accepted meaning may have changed.

There is another fact to be kept in mind in interpreting change in citizens' attitudes over time. There is a third party to the interaction between interviewer and respondent: the real world of politics. The interviewer may ask the same question about politics in 1972 as was asked in 1956, but the question is about a different political reality. The point is obvious and is not a challenge to our analysis. Our main concern is the interaction between changes in the real political world and changes in the responses of citizens to that world. But it is a point worth making explicit and worth keeping in mind. As attention focuses on citizen attitudes, they sometimes seem to be disembodied patterns in people's minds: people become more trusting of political leaders or less; they become interested in politics or lose interest; they strengthen their commitment to the political parties or they loosen their affiliation. They do these things, and we shall trace how it happens. But the objects of their trust or interest or affiliation change as well. It is not simply that citizens become less trusting of government, it may be that government is less trustworthy. It is not simply that a particular group is less committed to the Democratic party in 1972 than it was in 1956; it may be that the party is itself substantially changed. It is not simply that citizens become more politically interested after 1956; it may be that politics has become more interesting.

In the following chapter we present the static picture of the American public as it was revealed in the studies of the late Eisenhower years. In subsequent chapters we convert this into a moving picture as we trace the evolution of the public's political views since then. Our basic approach is to take the measures we use in the static picture and follow them through the periodic election surveys up to 1972. In the main, our data are taken from the Michigan Survey Research Center's election surveys. The data in the next chapter are drawn from the 1956 presidential election study and the 1958 congressional study. In subsequent chapters we use these studies as well as those in 1964, 1968, 1970, and 1972. In addition we make some limited use of SRC congressional studies in 1962 and 1966, of studies conducted by the National Opinion Research Center of the University of Chicago in 1971 and 1973, and of some Gallup and Roper studies dating back into the 1930s. The various studies do not all contain the full panoply of items we want to trace. In most cases, the data begin with the SRC study of 1956, but in a few we have parallel data in the 1952 election survey and our trace of political attitudes begins there. In general, with the exception of 1952, the presidential election studies are the richest in terms of available information, but even these studies are not always complete from our point of view. Our use of pre-1950 studies will be even more limited. In the following, we shall present the fullest data series that we have.

2 | The American Public in the 1950s

The works based on the data of the 1950s differed in many respects. Dahl's *Who Governs?* was a study of community decision-making in one city; Stouffer's *Communism, Conformity, and Civil Liberties* was an analysis of the attitudes of citizens on civil liberties; Almond and Verba's *The Civic Culture* was a study of the "political culture of democracy" in which the United States figured as but one of five nations; *The American Voter* was an analysis of the social and psychological sources of the voting decision. Despite these differences, the works presented a consistent picture of the American electorate. In some instances the descriptions overlapped. But even where the works went off in different directions, the results were not contradictory.

What did these works find? In briefest summary they found an electorate that was only mildly involved in politics; that thought about politics in relatively simple and narrow terms; that was allied with one or the other of the major parties by ties that were more a matter of habit than of rational selection; and that was basically satisfied with the working of the political system. This combination of characteristics was the foundation for a general reinterpretation of the role of the citizen in democracy. In this chapter we will present the data on which the portrait of the electorate was based and explicate the reinterpretation. This will be familiar to students of recent political science. We present the data and their interpretation in order to provide the baseline from which we shall measure change. We shall present data from the various works of the era, but the bulk will be from *The American Voter* or from our reanalysis of the SRC's study of the 1956 election that went into *The American Voter*. These data are the most comprehensive and are followed up in subsequent election studies so that we can trace changes from the baseline.

The Average Citizen Was Involved in Political Life, But Not All That Involved

When Samuel Stouffer, at the height of the McCarthy era, asked a sample of the American public about what it was that "worried them," he found that most people responded with concerns from their personal and daily lives: their jobs, their families, their health. Relatively few (about 15 percent) mentioned things that could be thought of as involving the public issues of the day, and almost no one (about 1 percent) mentioned domestic communism.[1] In retrospect the result seems obvious. Of course people are likely to worry about job, family, and health, but at the time it seemed somewhat surprising. The issue of loyalty and security dominated the media and dominated the conversations of those with deep concern for politics—journalists, scholars, government officials. It would have been perfectly reasonable to expect, extrapolating from the media attention and from the dominant concerns of the most politically sophisticated and concerned citizens, that the average American did indeed check for communists under his bed each night.

The question that Stouffer asked and the response he received formed an important component of the emerging view of the ordinary citizen as a not-very-political animal. By asking an open-ended question ("What are you worried about?"), Stouffer measured the *salience* of political matters to the ordinary citizen. And he learned one important thing: one could not generalize from the experience of the politically active few to the public at large. For the public at large, politics was not central in their everyday concerns. Not that the public was completely apolitical. They had views on a number of issues that Stouffer asked about. But these were matters that were not at the center of their consciousness.

Almond and Verba's results were parallel. They asked people how they

---

[1] Samuel Stouffer, *Communism, Conformity and Civil Liberties* (New York: Wiley, 1955), chap. 3.

TABLE 2.1. Political interest in 1956

Percent who are:	
Very interested in the campaign	30
Not at all interested	31
Attentive to campaigns	
In newspapers	69
In magazines	31
On radio	45
On television	74
Very interested and follow campaigns in newspapers and magazines	14
Uninterested and do not follow campaigns in the written media	17

spent their free time (aside from work and family). Very few Americans (2 percent) mentioned anything that could be construed as political or civic activity.[2] Tocqueville, in his nineteenth century report on America, commented that the American deprived of his chance to take part in political matters would be "deprived of half his existence."[3] This clearly did not describe the Americans of the 1950s. (Whether it described the Americans of the nineteenth century is also a matter of debate.)

Some data from the 1956 election study parallel these findings. At the height of the election campaign, respondents were asked how interested they were in the campaign. The results can only be described as mixed; equal numbers said they were "very interested" and "not at all interested" with about the third of the sample expressing only moderate interest in the election (see table 2.1).[4] Similar things could be said about the amount of attention that the citizenry paid to the political campaign. Most citizens paid at least some attention to the campaign in the newspapers or on television, but only about three out of ten followed the campaign in magazines (a probable source of coverage in greater depth). The expressed interest in campaigns and the attention citizens reported to campaigns in the media can be combined to

[2] Gabriel Almond and Sidney Verba, *The Civic Culture* (Princeton: Princeton University Press, 1963), p. 263.

[3] Alexis de Tocqueville, *Democracy in America* (New York: Knopf, 1945), I, 250.

[4] As we shall see in a number of cases, there is no clear way to interpret data such as in table 2.1. Is there a lot of interest or a little? Is it that "as many as" one-third of the public says that it is not at all interested in the campaign, or is that "only" one-third is not at all interested (that is, two-thirds are interested)? There is no clear answer; it depends on one's expectations as to the level of citizen reference points for deciding if the data in table 2.1 represent a high or low level of interest.

TABLE 2.2. Campaign activity in 1956

Percent who:	
Reported voting for president	75
Reported voting for congressman	66
Talked to people and tried to show them how to vote	28
Displayed a campaign button or sticker	16
Gave money, bought tickets, or did anything to help the candidate	10
Attended a political meeting or rally	7
Belonged to a political club or organization	3
Did any other work for one of the parties or candidates	3

locate two kinds of citizens, the "involved" and the "uninvolved." The former are those who report they are very interested in the campaign and who follow it in both the newspapers and in magazines. They were 14 percent of the populace in 1956. The uninvolved, those who say they have no interest in the campaign and who follow it neither in newspapers nor in magazines, were a slightly larger 17 percent of the population.

More striking, perhaps, were the data on citizen activity. Almond and Verba found that only about one-quarter of the people they interviewed had ever attempted to influence a decision of the local government (and fewer yet had attempted to influence the national government). Dahl found similar levels of activity in his New Haven study.[5]

The most comprehensive data are in the SRC 1956 study. Most citizens, it was found, limited their political activity to the vote. When one looked beyond the vote, one found only a small proportion of the populace active. The most frequent political activity was that of "talking to people and trying to show them how to vote." This is an activity requiring no organization, it can take place anywhere, it requires no particular resources.[6] Yet only 28 percent of the populace reported being active in that way. And beyond that, the proportions fall precipitously: 16 percent had displayed a campaign button or sticker; 10 percent did anything to help a candidate; and only 3 percent belonged to a political club or organization.

---

[5] Almond and Verba, *The Civic Culture,* p. 188, and Robert A. Dahl, *Who Governs? Democracy and Power in an American City* (New Haven: Yale University Press, 1961), pp. 276–281.

[6] Angus Campbell and others, *The American Voter* (New York: Wiley, 1960), pp. 50–51.

The data on political activity are fairly consistent with those on interest and media exposure. The bulk of the American public was involved in the electoral process only in ways that did not reflect a great deal of time, effort, or commitment. About two-thirds of the public voted, about two-thirds followed the political campaign on the radio or in the newspapers, and about two-thirds expressed some interest in the campaign. But only in relation to such items did one find more than a majority of the populace giving positive responses. When it came to items that would appear to measure more intense involvement—to activity beyond the vote, to exposure to the campaign in magazines, to the expression of a great deal of interest in the campaign—only a small minority of the populace responded positively. And a minority of roughly equal size did not display even the marginal involvement found in the bulk of the population: they did not vote, they did not follow the campaign in the media, and they expressed no interest in the election generally.

The American Public Had a Remarkably Unsophisticated View of Political Matters Characterized by an Inability to Consider Such Matters in Broad Abstract Terms

No one expected the average American to be a political philosopher. Yet the gap between the way in which the ordinary citizen thought about political matters and the way in which those matters were conceived by the more politically sophisticated was larger than expected.

The Survey Research Center scholars developed an innovative set of questions for measuring the reasons people preferred one candidate over the other or one party over the other.[7] They asked, quite simply, what it was that the respondent liked and disliked about the Democratic party, and about the Republicans. Similar questions were asked about the major candidates for president. These questions allow the respondent to offer a variety of reasons for liking or disliking a party or candidate. He does not have to choose from a few alternatives offered by the researcher. The respondent expresses *his* reasons (or lack of them) rather than his evaluation of the researcher's list of reasons. The responses to these questions can be used to understand the nature of the images that voters have of the candidates or to estimate the impact on the vote of preferences for one candidate over another. The authors of *The American Voter* also used these questions to evaluate the "level of conceptualization" of the American public. By this they referred to the sophistication of the conceptual scheme used by an individual in relation to

---

[7] Ibid., chap. 10.

politics. Did the respondent place political matters into the kind of broad, ideological categories used by political philosophers? Did he think in more concrete issue terms? Or did he have a rather vague view of political matters? The authors of *The American Voter* coded the responses to the like-dislike questions in a very careful and sensitive way. They found that only a very small handful of the American public (2½ percent of the public at large, 3½ percent of the voters) could be thought of as responding to political matters in terms of a political ideology, that is, in terms of broad political principles such as liberalism or conservatism. This small group did not necessarily espouse a full political philosophy. The authors of *The American Voter* were rather generous in categorizing as "ideologues" those who displayed any ability to think about politics in abstract terms and to connect those abstractions to particular candidates or parties. It did not take a very high level of sophistication to be placed in the ideologue category, yet only 2½ percent fell in it. Even if one considers only those with some college education, one finds only 10 percent so categorized.

In addition to the small number of ideologues, *The American Voter* found a somewhat larger group (about 9 percent of the sample) who could be categorized as "near ideologues." Near ideologues used some of the more general concepts of political ideology but in ways that left doubt about whether they appreciated their meaning. The rest of the populace thought about politics in more concrete terms. A large proportion evaluated candidates and parties in terms of the favorable or unfavorable treatment that one could expect for social groups. Another large group spoke vaguely about the "nature of the times"; one party or one candidate was preferred because of the association with good or bad times, with prosperity or depression, with war or peace. And a last group—ten times as large as the ideologue group— had almost no issue content in their evaluations of candidates or parties; they expressed habitual party loyalty, and they focused on candidate personality.

We cannot reproduce the detailed discussion in *The American Voter* of the levels of conceptualization of their sample. The examples presented there of citizens at the various levels of conceptualization will make it quite clear that even the ideologues view politics in rather simple terms.

As with the other measures of political attitude and political behavior, we would like to trace the levels of conceptualization over time. But unlike the other measures, we cannot replicate the way in which the answers of respondents in the 1956 study were categorized. The answers to the like-dislike questions were coded by a small group of researchers at the SRC who read the entire set of answers for a respondent and placed the respondent in one of the categories. Such coding has not been done for other studies by the

SRC and the effort required to replicate that measure in the seven studies where the questions were asked is prohibitive.[8]

The original SRC measure is based on evaluation of the parties and of the candidates. It represents a "global" decision about what the respondent's answers indicate about his or her level of conceptualization. We have created an alternative measure of level of conceptualization, using the like-dislike questions for the parties and candidates. The master codes have several hundred categories for coding the answers to these questions. While the categories do not capture the nuances of the responses that were used to allocate citizens to one or the other of the level of conceptualization in *The American Voter,* they allow one roughly to approximate those categorizations. The measures we have built cannot be directly compared with the SRC measure, but they tap, we believe, the same dimension. Because they are standardized measures that can be applied to all the election studies, they allow us to trace the level of conceptualization of the American public across time (see Chapter 7 and, for a full description of our measure, Appendix 2C). The responses were coded into seven categories, as follows:

1. Explicitly ideological: candidates or parties are referred to as socialist, liberal, conservative, or other ideological terms.

2. Implicitly ideological: parties or candidates are evaluated by some comprehensive standard which embraces several individual issues—for example, social reform, individual liberty, states' rights, or government intervention.

3. Policy referent: the respondent evaluates the parties or candidates by referring to their positions on specific issues—communism, unemployment, civil rights, strikes, law and order, and the like.

4. Group referent: the respondent evaluates the party or candidates in terms of policy toward or treatment of a particular social group.

5. Nature of the times: the parties or candidates are held responsible for the general "goodness" or "badness" of the times, prosperity, peace, and so on.

6. Party responses: along the lines of, "I've always been a Democrat."

7. Nonpolitical responses: including references to the personal qualities of the candidates, personal influence on the respondent, and such vague statements as, "They do a good job."

We counted for each respondent the number of evaluations falling into each of these categories. Candidate and party evaluations were counted separately because there are some interesting differences between the two. Only

---

[8] There have been, however, several attempts to replicate the kind of coding done for *The American Voter* for later elections (see our Chapter 7).

the first three answers were used. The pattern of responses found among these types of evaluations were the basis for the creation of ideological types.

Table 2.3 illustrates the differences between our categorization and that of the SRC. Our most sophisticated category contains those respondents who refer to politics in broad ideological terms (liberal, conservative, socialist, capitalist) but who also refer to particular issues or to particular group benefits. The fact that each respondent is permitted to express several likes and dislikes gives ample opportunity to offer ideological expressions—that is, to use abstract, general concepts—as well as to have more specific issue references. Eleven percent of the 1956 sample fell in the ideological category in relation to the parties, 1 percent in relation to the candidates. We have placed this group at a higher level of conceptualization than those who merely use general or abstract ideological terms with no specific referent (6 percent of

TABLE 2.3. Levels of conceptualization in 1956 (proportion of total sample)

SRC measure		Our parallel measure			
Evaluation of parties and candidates			Evaluation of parties	Evaluation of candidates	Combined evaluation
Ideology	2½	Ideological words plus issue or group conflict	11	1	12
Near-ideology	9	Ideological words only	6	2	6
Group benefits	42	Group benefits and issues	16	7	19
Nature of times	24	Issues alone	11	25	21
No issue content	22½	Group benefits	20	9	17
	100	Party references	16	40	18
		Nature of times, nonpolitical	20	16	8
			100	100	101[a]

[a] On this and some subsequent tables percentages do not add to 100 percent due to rounding errors.

the sample in relation to parties, 2 percent in relation to candidates). The latter may be using the ideological terms as slogans which have little or no content. A third category contains respondents who referred to group benefits and issues (16 percent in relation to parties, 7 percent in relation to candidates). Eleven percent spoke of issues alone in relation to parties, 25 percent in relation to candidates. Twenty percent spoke of group benefits alone in relation to parties; 9 percent in relation to candidates. In addition, some respondents referred to parties in party terms—that is they liked a party because it "was their party," they "had always been Democrats," and so forth. Sixteen percent gave this rather redundant response as an evaluation of the parties. A much larger proportion—40 percent—used the party affiliation of one or both of the candidates as a standard of evaluation (a less redundant use of party as a criterion for evaluation). And similar percentages (20 and 16 respectively) gave vague or contentless answers.

Our categorization places a larger number of respondents in the more sophisticated "ideological" categories than does the categorization used in *The American Voter*—at least this is the case in relation to the evaluation of parties.[9]

Some differences between the evaluations of the parties and the candidates (in our coding scheme) are worth noting. The parties are more likely to be evaluated in ideological terms than are the candidates. The parties are also evaluated in terms of group benefits more than are the candidates, while the latter are connected more frequently in the minds of respondents with particular issues. This is, of course, not unexpected. The parties are associated in the minds of the public with particular groups; candidates are more likely to be associated with the specific issues in a particular race.

Lastly one ought to note the large proportion of the population that evaluates one or both of the candidates in party terms—they like or dislike them because of the party with which they are associated. That proportion appears particularly large in comparison with the meager proportion that thinks of candidates in ideological terms or the somewhat more substantial but nevertheless small proportions who evaluate the candidates in terms of issue position or group benefit. This underscores a point made earlier: party affiliation served as an anchor point for the citizen.

Our measure of the level of conceptualization of citizens in 1956 is not fully comparable to that developed by the SRC researchers. Yet it tells a story

---

[9] But since a respondent was rated as having a high level of conceptualization in the SRC categorization if he used ideological terms to evaluate either the parties or the candidates, our location of a larger number of ideologues in relation to the parties means that we have more ideologues than was found by the SRC despite the smaller number who use such terms to evaluate the candidates.

similar to theirs: citizens did not conceive of politics in sophisticated ways. And evaluations in partisan terms were frequent.

Citizens Had Inconsistent Views When One Looked Across a Range of Issues

If the American public did not conceptualize politics in the same abstract terms that one would expect from a citizenry with a clear political ideology, neither did their political beliefs manifest another characteristic that one would associate with a well-structured political ideology. Their attitudes on various political matters did not exhibit what Philip Converse labeled "constraint." By constraint, Converse refers to the ability we would have to predict a person's position on one issue from his position on another.[10] If citizens had clear and consistent political ideologies we should have quite a bit of success predicting one position from another. A liberal favoring greater welfare spending would be likely to favor a bigger and more active government, would be favorable to racial integration, and would be an internationalist and not a militant anticommunist in foreign affairs. A conservative would be expected to hold the opposite positions. With either person, if you know his position on one issue you should know them on all issues.

However, Converse demonstrated that there is little constraint among political attitudes in the mass public. If you know a person's position on one issue that is not much help in predicting where he will stand on other issues. Consider the interrelationship among political attitudes as they existed in 1956. We will not present data on all issues which were asked about in that year. We will focus on those issues which can be traced in later years because questions about them were repeated. Questions covering five issue areas are available on all of the presidential election surveys from 1956 to 1972 and also on the 1958 congressional election study.[11]

The five issue areas for which we have comparable data over the entire time period are:

1. *Social welfare.* The questions elicit the respondent's attitudes on the

---

[10] See Philip E. Converse, "The Nature of Belief Systems in Mass Publics," in David E. Apter, ed., *Ideology and Discontent* (New York: Free Press, 1964).

[11] The data was report are slightly different from those presented by Converse, who uses data from 1956 and 1958. We will use the 1956 data as our baseline. As we shall see, 1956 and 1958 are virtually identical. Also, we focus on those attitudes we can trace beyond 1958. But our picture of 1956 is quite consistent with Converse's portrait of mass belief systems based on the 1956 and 1958 data. This analysis and its extension in Chapter 8 draws on Norman H. Nie with Kristi Andersen, "Mass Belief Systems Revisited: Political Change and Attitude Structure," *Journal of Politics,* 36 (September 1974), 541–591.

federal government's responsibility to provide welfare programs in the areas of employment, education, and medical care. We define liberal answers as those favoring such welfare measures; conservative answers oppose such measures.

2. *Welfare measures specific for blacks.* Respondents were asked whether they thought the federal government should provide special welfare programs for blacks in the areas of jobs and housing. Liberals are in favor of these programs.

3. *The size of government.* From 1956 through 1960 respondents were asked whether they thought that it was best if the federal government were kept out of areas such as housing and electric power generation that were traditionally handled by private industry. From 1964 through 1972, respondents were asked whether they thought the federal government was already too big and involved in too many areas. Liberals support a large and active government.

4. *Racial integration in the schools.* The questions asked whether the federal government ought to enforce school integration or stay completely out of that problem. Liberals support efforts by the federal government to enforce integration in the schools.

5. *The cold war.* These questions vary from period to period with changes in America's relations with communist countries; but they are all concerned with the "toughness" of the U.S. stance toward communism and the desirability of military opposition to communism. In 1956, 1958, and 1960 respondents were asked whether they thought the government ought to send soldiers abroad to aid countries fighting communism. The 1964, 1968, and 1972 cold war measures use the responses to questions which asked whether the United States should have gotten involved in Vietnam and what the country should do given the involvement. Liberals took the less anticommunist and less aggressive posture.

Table 2.4 presents the intercorrelations between pairs of issues. The statistic is gamma, which can be interpreted as a measure of consistency among attitudes. Positive values for the gamma relationship between measurements of attitudes on two issues mean that respondents who answer the question about one issue in a liberal direction are likely to answer the question about the other issue in a liberal direction. Similarly conservatives on one issue are likely to be conservative on another. The higher the gamma, the larger the proportion giving consistent responses across the issues. Thus, positive correlations indicate the presence of at least some liberal-conservative opinion consistency. Zero or low correlations indicate an absence of liberal-conservative consistency, while negative coefficients signify that those giving

TABLE 2.4. Level of attitude constraint in 1956 (average gammas)

Average gammas between and	Attitudes on welfare	Attitudes on size of govern- ment	Attitudes on inte- gration	Attitudes on black welfare
Attitudes on size of govern- ment	.19			
Attitudes on inte- gration	.11	.24		
Attitudes on black welfare	.38	.12	.46	
Attitudes on the cold war	−.16	.15	.08	−.09

liberal responses to questions within one issue area are more likely to give conservative responses to questions in the other.[12]

The relatively low level of liberal-conservative attitude consistency in 1956 is quite apparent. All but three of the coefficients in this year are below .25 and two of the ten are slightly negative. In a few cases, where the issues are both domestic issues and are fairly close (attitudes on welfare for blacks and attitudes on integration, or attitudes on welfare for blacks and attitudes on welfare in general), the interrelationship among the attitudes is moderately high. To know someone favors greater welfare for blacks is to know that he or she is more likely to favor more rapid integration.

But beyond that, there is little relationship among the items. To know an individual's position on general welfare issues provides little information about that person's position on the size of the government; and to know someone's position on racial integration provides equally little information about his position on welfare. Finally, someone's position on domestic issues

---

[12] For those issue areas where there is more than one question available—namely social welfare and the cold war—the correlations presented are an average of the gammas between each of the questions in that issue area and the question or questions in the other area. In those cases where there is only one question for each of the two issue areas the simple correlation between those two questions is presented.

tells little if anything about an individual's attitude toward American policy toward communist countries.[13]

As with many of the statistics we report, it is difficult to evaluate just how much constraint there is between the various political attitudes. One does not expect perfect relationships, but how much constraint is reflected in a gamma of, say .19? Fortunately, Converse had some data to provide a benchmark. In 1958 a similar set of attitude questions was asked of a sample of candidates for seats in the House of Representatives (incumbents and challengers). This group offers a nice comparison with the general population, since the candidates for the House are clearly a set of political elites for whom politics is a salient matter and among whom one would expect a more constrained set of political attitudes.

As table 2.5 makes clear, this is exactly what Converse found. Table 2.5 reports the average interrelationship (gamma) between attitudes for the elites. Further, it compares them with the interrelationships for the mass public. The constraint among political attitudes is much stronger for the elites. For domestic issues, the elite group has an average gamma of .38; the parallel figure for the mass sample is .25. Indeed, the interrelationship across the domestic and foreign fields (where the relationships are expected to be weaker) is stronger for the political elites than is the level of constraint within the domestic sphere for the nonelites. The elite data provide a good benchmark for what things could be like for the mass sample if there were fairly high constraint among political attitudes.[14]

There are a number of ways one can explain such low intercorrelations among political issues. For one thing, low intercorrelations do not necessarily indicate inconsistency or irrationality. One can quite reasonably be "left" on the issue of integration but "right" when it comes to welfare. Indeed, such pairing of attitudes for a substantial portion of the populace would be convincing evidence that political attitudes did not all fall on some single left-right continuum. It is more likely, though, that the low correlations do not reflect a carefully reasoned choice of political positions. The low correlations probably indicate one (or all) of the following:

1. Citizens are not guided in their political views by an overarching

---

[13] Attitudes on welfare correlate negatively with a liberal position on relations with communist countries. But in the 1950s the liberal position may in fact have been the reverse of the liberal position in the 1960s: we code the dovish position during Vietnam as liberal. But "liberal interventionism" was a common view in the Eisenhower (and Kennedy) years. The −.16 may represent not mild inconsistency but mild consistency. However, the main point is the weakness of the relationship.

[14] Again, we have used our measures and the 1956 mass baseline rather than Converse's specific measures, but table 2.5 is compatible with his findings.

TABLE 2.5. Attitude constraint: mass and elite compared (average gammas)

Average coefficients	Mass public (1956)	Political elites (1958)
Between domestic issues	.24	.38
Between domestic and foreign issues	−.01	.25
Overall index of consistency	.14	.31

political ideology—conservatism, liberalism, socialism, or any ideology that would provide an interrelated set of answers to the various issue questions. They could, of course, be guided by an ideology from which one could deduce a conservative position on one issue, a liberal position on another. But we know of no such articulated ideologies that are likely to have had much popular notice.

2. Politics is of such low salience to citizens that possible inconsistencies among their various answers would not be very apparent to them.

3. Many of the answers they give about issues to the survey researcher represent superficial responses on matters to which they have given little previous thought.

The summary in *The American Voter* is apt:

When we examine the attitudes and beliefs of the electorate as a whole over a broad range of policy questions—welfare legislation, foreign policy, federal economic programs, minority rights, civil liberties—we do not find coherent patterns of belief. The common tendency to characterize large blocs of the electorate in such terms as "liberal" or "conservative" greatly exaggerates the actual amount of consistent patterning one finds. Our failure to locate more than a trace of "ideological" thinking in the protocols of our surveys emphasizes the general impoverishment of political thought in a large proportion of the electorate.

It is also apparent from these protocols that there is a great deal of uncertainty and confusion in the public mind as to what specific policies the election of one party over the other would imply. Very few of our respondents have shown a sensitive understanding of the positions of the parties on current policy issues. Even among those people who are relatively familiar with the issues presented in our surveys—and our test of familiarity has been an easy one—there is little agreement as to where the two parties stand. This fact reflects the similarity of party positions on many issues, as well as the range of opinion within parties. But it also reflects how little attention even the relatively informed part of the electorate gives the specifics of public policy formation.

We have, then, the portrait of an electorate almost wholly without detailed information about decision making in government. A substantial portion of the public is able to respond in a discrete manner to issues that *might* be the subject of legislative or administrative action. Yet it knows little about what government has done on these issues or what the parties propose to do. It is almost completely unable to judge the rationality of government actions; knowing little of particular policies and what has led to them, the mass electorate is not able to appraise either its goals or the appropriateness of the means chosen to serve these goals.[15]

The low level of constraint among political attitudes had significant consequences for American politics. It meant that the ability of either of the political parties (or of some new political party or movement) to appeal to a large segment of the populace on the basis of a consistent set of political positions from the right or from the left was severely limited. The party or movement dependent for support on citizens with consistent left or right attitudes would find few such citizens.

If the population does not neatly divide up into citizens on the left and citizens on the right, each with a coherent set of attitudes across a number of issues, political parties looking to maximize their vote must look elsewhere than to an appeal based on the issues. They certainly cannot rely upon an issue appeal based on a clearly staked out liberal or conservative position. Instead they would do better to depend on the personality of a candidate or on issues that fall outside of the ordinary left-right dimensions. From this perspective, the Republican nomination of the war hero Eisenhower in 1952, rather than the more consistently conservative Robert Taft, coupled with the slogan of "Communism, Corruption and Korea," represented the most effective electoral strategy.

Most Americans Had Strong, Long-term Commitments to One of the Major Political Parties, and This Commitment Served as a Guide to Their Political Behavior

In a book published in 1959, Herbert Hyman examined political socialization literature concerning the impact of early learning on political attitudes and behavior. He found that attitudes about political issues were imperfectly

---

[15] *The American Voter,* p. 543.

transferred from generation to generation; one knew relatively little about the position of an individual on an issue by knowing the position of the parent. But one fundamental political orientation appeared to be transmitted fairly often from generation to generation: party affiliation. If one wanted to guess the party affiliation of an individual, one could hardly find more useful information than knowledge of the affiliation of his or her parents.[16] For instance, 74 percent of those in the 1958 SRC study whose parents supported a party supported the same party.[17]

Hyman's interpretation was intriguing: issues come and issues go, but the political parties are with us permanently. One could hardly expect one generation to have the same issue positions as the previous one. The nature of issues changes; the way they relate to particular population groups changes. But partisan affiliation can be a guide for political choice from one generation to the next. In part it can serve this function because the parties change. If they once were aligned with a particular social group on an issue, they may still be close to that social group in the next generation, though on the basis of another issue. Parties may follow their constituencies from generation to generation as the preferences and problems of the constituency change. Though issues have changed, the party of one's parents still is closest to one's own position.

But given the low issue concern of many citizens, another interpretation comes to mind. Party affiliation is transmitted from generation to generation not because parties adjust to suit the issue preferences of social groups but because the attachment to parties is a habitual, somewhat sentimental attachment, not unlike the religious preferences that most citizens inherit from their parents. Party attachment is a form of social identity. It is probably much more common for the voter to develop issue positions characteristic of his party than to select his party on the basis of his issue positions. The party is the anchor point of the individual's political position.

The discovery of the importance of party affiliation in the socialization literature was consistent with data on the role of party in the 1950s. Most individuals had a partisan commitment and the commitment tended to be long-term. One might defect by voting for a candidate of the other party (as many Democrats switched to vote for Eisenhower), but the voter remained Democrat or Republican and party affiliation remained the key to the voting decision.

Let us consider the partisan profile of the American public in 1956. The

---

16 Herbert H. Hyman, *Political Socialization* (Glencoe: Free Press, 1959).
17 *The American Voter*, p. 147 (computed from table 7–1).

TABLE 2.6 Party identification in 1956 (percentages)

Democrats	45
Republicans	30
Independents	24
("Pure" Independents 9)	
Proportion of Democrats with strong identification	47
Proportion of Republicans with strong identification	51

Survey Research Center interviewers asked respondents about their party affiliation: did they consider themselves Democrats, Republicans, or what? As table 2.6 shows, about three quarters of the populace identified with one or the other of the parties. And in each of the party groupings, about half identified themselves as "strong" supporters of their political party. This left about one-fourth of the public with no affiliation. But when they were asked whether they leaned toward one party or another, more than half of that group (15 percent out of the 24 percent) indicated at least some party preference. The remainder can be considered "pure" Independents—they express no party preferences even when offered the opportunity to express a preference indicating only limited commitment.

Eisenhower presented himself as someone above political party, and his electoral success depended on the willingness of many Democrats to vote for him. But the switching of Democrats to Eisenhower illustrated the long-term commitment to party: those Democrats who voted for him did not cease to consider themselves Democrats—even after voting for him in 1952 and 1956, as many did. The continuing commitment of a majority to the Democratic party reasserted itself in congressional elections where the results were generally Democratic during the Eisenhower years.[18]

Furthermore, even though there was a lot of switching of Democrats to Eisenhower, the bulk of the voters in 1956 voted in ways consistent with their party affiliation. As table 2.7 shows, only 17 percent of those identified with one of the major parties voted for the opposite party's candidate for the presidency in that year. In other words, more than four out of five of those with a partisan affiliation voted consistently with that affiliation. When it came to House and Senate races, defection from one's party was even less frequent. The defection rate was somewhat larger in state and local offices. The higher

[18] Ibid., pp. 10–11.

TABLE 2.7.

A. Proportion of party identifiers voting for candidate
of the other party, 1956

Presidential vote	17
Senate vote	11
House vote	9
State and local offices[a]	28

B. Pearson correlations of party identification and the
vote, 1956[b]

Party identification and the presidential vote	.68
Party identification and the Senate vote	.71
Party identification and the House vote	.75
Party identification and state and local vote	.74

[a] At least one defection from straight ticket voting.
[b] Calculated with Independents in the center category.

proportion of voters who report some switching derives from the fact that the opportunities are greater since there are many state and local offices (and we categorize as a "switcher" anyone who crosses the line on any office to vote for the opposing party). In general, the data show that most voters vote according to their party affiliation.

Another bit of data helps round out our portrait of the partisanship of the American electorate. As we pointed out earlier, respondents were asked what they liked or disliked about each of the parties. To each of the four questions (what they like about the Democratic party, dislike about the Democratic party; what they like about the Republican party, dislike about it) they could give a number of replies. We counted the number of times they said positive, negative, or neutral things about each party. This allowed us to categorize the respondents in terms of their views of their own party and of the opposition.

Table 2.8 reports the results of this categorization. Most of the respondents could be categorized as "partisans" of one or the other party. This means they said more good things than bad things about their own party and were neutral or, on balance, negative about the opposition. Thirty-six percent of the sample could be considered Democratic partisans, 26 percent Republican partisans. In addition, 9 percent of the respondents had, on balance, good

TABLE 2.8. Positive and negative evaluations of parties, 1956 (percentages)

Democratic partisan evaluation	36	
Republican partisan evaluation	26	
Positive evaluation of both parties	9	
Total positive partisans		71
Alienated (negative evaluation of each party)	12	
Parochial (no opinion of either party)	14	
Neutral (balanced evaluations)	3	
Total negative or neutral to parties		29

things to say (that is, more positive than negative remarks) about both parties. These three kinds of citizens, who have a generally positive attachment to one or both of the parties, form 71 percent of the sample. The rest of the sample was more negative or neutral to the parties. Those categorized as "alienated" said, on balance, negative things about both parties. A similar sized group is "parochial"; they have little to say about either party. And a small residual group comes out with equal negative and positive responses about the parties. We call them neutrals.

The important point is that the latter three groups together are less than a third of our sample. Most Americans manifested, on the whole, favorable views of the political parties.

The stability and centrality of partisan affiliation was in sharp contrast to the seeming inconsistency of political beliefs. Converse compared the stability of partisan identification with the stability of attitudes on specific issues by using a panel study. Respondents interviewed in 1958 were reinterviewed two years later. He found that correlations between issue positions at the two points of time were moderate or low. Correlation between one's party affiliation at the two points of time was substantially higher (see figure 2.1).

The relative importance of party affiliation and issue position can be seen most dramatically if we compare the correlation of each with the vote (table 2.9). All of the correlations in the first column are substantial. The correlation between party affiliation and state and local voting is higher than that between party and vote for national office. This is not inconsistent with the data on the proportion who switch in the various races, for, though many more switch to vote for at least one opposite party candidate at the state and local level than abandon their party in relation to the national offices, there are many more opportunities to vote consistently with one's party affiliation.

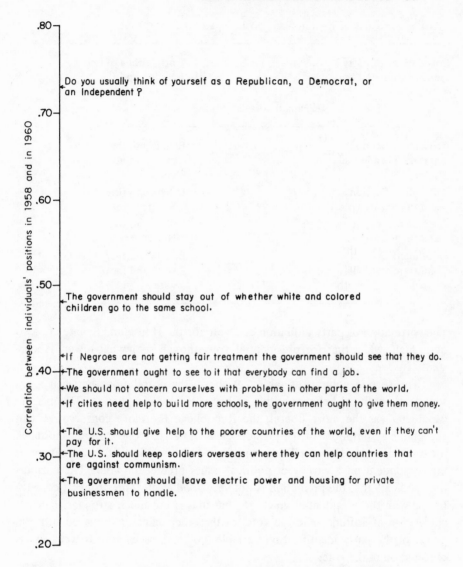

FIGURE 2.1. Temporal stability of different belief elements for individuals, 1958–1960

Source: Adapted from Philip E. Converse, "The Nature of Belief Systems in Mass Publics," in David E. Apter, ed., *Ideology and Discontent* (New York: Free Press, 1964), p. 240.

TABLE 2.9. Party affiliation, issue position, and the vote, 1956

Correlations of party identification and the vote		Correlations of issue position and the vote	
(Pearson correlations)			
Party identification and the presidential vote	.68	Beliefs and the presidential vote	.18
Party identification and the Senate vote	.71	Beliefs and the Senate vote	.12
Party identification and the House vote	.75	Beliefs and the House vote	.14
Party identification and state and local vote	.74	Beliefs and the state and local vote	.12

The correlation of party affiliation and vote for the House and Senate are also quite high, while that for presidential vote, though somewhat lower, is substantial as well.

The second column of table 2.9 shows the correlations between a respondent's political beliefs and his or her vote. Assume that the Democratic candidate was the more liberal, the Republican the more conservative (an acceptable assumption for the presidency, a less certain one for the candidates for other offices). How well does the degree of liberalism or conservatism of the respondent on a variety of political issues predict the vote? The correlations indicate that the prediction is not very good at all. The strongest correlation is with the presidential vote, .18; but that is not much stronger than the correlation of attitudes and the vote for the other offices. Compared with the power of the party identification variable, political issues appear weak as an explanation of the vote.

The power of party identification in relation to the vote coupled with apparent long-term commitment that citizens had to their party led to the development of the notion of the "normal" vote. A normal vote was based on one's party identification. Normal votes were then modified in an election by "short-term forces." The latter could be the issues of the day. But as one might expect from the low level of citizen information about issues, the low level at which they conceptualized issues, and the relative inconsistency of issue positions, the short-term forces were likely to be the personal appeal of a particular candidate. In the elections of 1952 and 1956, millions of Democrats deserted their party's candidate to vote for a Republican. The best evidence is that they did so because of the personal appeal of Eisenhower, not because of preference for his issue positions.[19]

Citizens Felt Relatively Satisfied with the Political System and Relatively Efficacious

If citizens were not as active as Tocqueville found (or thought he found) Americans in the nineteenth century, if they did not calculate voting decisions the way "rational" citizens should, they were by no means dissatisfied with their lot. The data of the 1950s indicated that the average American was fairly satisfied with the government and with the political parties. Almond and Verba found a higher proportion of Americans proud of the political system than was true in any other country they studied. And though Americans had fairly strong identifications with their own party, they were by no means hostile to the supporters of the other party; partisanship was strong but open. Furthermore, Americans felt relatively efficacious compared with people elsewhere. If they did not actively participate in political affairs, they felt that they could do so if they wanted to.

In addition the American people viewed their government with a healthy mixture of trust and skepticism. Our characterization of the American public in terms of its level of trust in the government and political leaders is a tenuous one, especially if we stick to the data of one year. Trust is measured by a series of questions such as, "Would you say that the government is run by a few big interests looking out for themselves or that it is run for the benefit of all the people?" Depending upon the specific question, one finds high proportions replying with answers indicating trust or indicating distrust. There is little sense of the depth or intensity of the feeling. Also the great variation in the proportion giving trusting or distrusting answers suggests a great deal of susceptibility to the nuances of the wording.

We report the answers to a variety of questions having to do with trust in government in table 2.10. The data are for 1958 since these questions on trust do not appear in the SRC studies until that year. But in most respects, 1958 and 1956 are similar. And since these items are then carried forward in other studies, we shall have the opportunity to trace changes in them. Indeed, it is the tracing of these items over time that will give greater meaning to them (see Chapter 9). For 1958, note that the proportion of the population giving

---

[19] Ibid., p. 526.

TABLE 2.10. Trust and confidence in the government, 1958

	Trusting answers		Distrusting answers[a]	
		(percent)		
How much tax does the government waste?[b]	Not much	11	A lot	45
Do you trust the government to do what is right?	Always	17	Hardly ever	24
How much dishonesty is there in government?	Hardly any	28	A lot	26
Do public officials care what people think?[c]	Yes	64	No	36
Is the government run for the benefit of all or the benefit of a few?	For all	80	A few	19

[a] Other respondents, not listed on this table, took positions in between.
[b] Questions paraphrased.
[c] Data from 1956.

trusting answers varied from a low of 11 percent to a high of 80 percent. In between, we find roughly equal proportions of the populace saying that there is "hardly any" dishonesty in the government and saying that there is "a lot" of dishonesty. One could speculate as to why some questions trigger off distrusting responses. But the speculation would not get us very far. Rather, it is best to sum up the responses in table 2.10 as reflecting a mixture of confidence and skepticism. We are then in a position to see what happens.

The Citizen of the 1950s and Democratic Theory

The works we have cited were not limited to a description of the American public. Rather, these works tried, in one way or another, to link the patterns of attitudes and behavior they found to the way in which democracy operated. Again the works vary. Almond and Verba were mostly concerned with democratic stability, Dahl with the way in which citizens control leaders, the authors of *The American Voter* with the way in which individual voting behavior affects electoral outcome, Stouffer with the role of citizen support for civil liberties. But the works have running through them some common views about democratic government.

The Source of Political Attitudes

One conclusion common to the various works was that basic political attitudes are not closely linked to passing political events but, rather, have their roots in more permanent sociological and psychological factors. This gives the American political system a certain stability. A citizen's sense of political efficacy, Almond and Verba found, begins to develop within the family and school. Even if, in later years, the individual does not engage much in politics, the basic sense of his ability to do so makes him a potential activist if things go badly.[20] Similarly the belief in democratic practices, as Dahl points out, is maintained "by a variety of powerful social forces," beginning in the schools and carried on throughout life.[21] This stable commitment to a democratic creed is important, even if, as the Dahl and Almond and Verba works show, the creed is in part a myth. That citizens believe in the creed makes it more likely that they will act to live up to it (that they will take part in politics, that they will favor democratic institutions). Leaders, in turn, whether they believe in the creed or not (and as these works showed, they were more likely to adhere to it than ordinary citizens—at least verbally), must justify their activities in its terms. Robert Dahl, after demonstrating that citizens did not in fact always live up to democratic norms, nevertheless argued the importance of this long-run belief in them:

> Even if universal belief in a democratic creed does not guarantee the stability of a democratic system, a substantial decline in the popular consensus would greatly increase the chance of serious instability. How the professionals act, what they advocate, what they are likely to believe, are all constrained by the wide adherence to the creed that exists throughout the community. If a substantial segment of the electorate begins to doubt the creed, professionals will quickly come forth to fan that doubt. The nature and course of an appeal to the populace will change. What today is a question of applying the fundamental norms of democracy will become tomorrow an inquiry into the validity of these norms.[22]

If commitment to the democratic creed had its roots in early socialization and educational experiences, so did the other characteristics of citizen

---

[20] Almond and Verba, *The Civic Culture,* chap. 12.
[21] Dahl, *Who Governs?* p. 317.
[22] Ibid., p. 325.

attitudes and behavior—especially the relatively low level at which citizens conceptualized politics and the relative lack of consistency among political attitudes. These characteristics derived from two sources: "political involvement" and "cognitive capacities." Political involvement referred to the amount of attention paid to political events; cognitive capacities referred to the ability of the individual to think abstractly about politics—an ability linked to educational level. The data in *The American Voter* indicated that both factors were important in relation to an individual's level of conceptualization.[23]

The level of conceptualization of politics might change, therefore, if the issues of politics change. If the political issues of the day were such as to catch the attention of the public—more than the issues of the Eisenhower years did—citizen conceptualization of politics would likely become more sophisticated. But the fundamental limitations on the cognitive capacity of the less well educated implied that many citizens would not reach high levels of conceptualization. "Whatever the depth of a person's political involvement, there are rather basic limitations on cognitive capacities which are likely to make certain of the most sophisticated types of content remain inaccessible to the poorly endowed observer."[24]

The most important anchor point for citizen political behavior was, as we have seen, partisan identification. This too was a long-term commitment. Its roots were in the family; citizens tended to follow the partisanship of their parents. Party identification, once adopted by the individual, remained a permanent commitment throughout the life cycle. These commitments were not easily affected by the events of the day. Quite the contrary. At least in the Eisenhower period, the events of the day were more likely to be interpreted in the light of enduring partisan commitments than were the latter commitments to be modified by reactions to the particular issues of the moment. As *The American Voter* put it,

> In the period of our studies the influence of party identification on attitudes toward the perceived elements of politics has been far more important than the influence of these attitudes on party identification itself. We are convinced that the relationships in our data reflect primarily the role of enduring partisan commitments on shaping attitudes toward political objects. We know that persons who identify with one of the parties typically have held the same partisan tie for all, or almost all, of their adult lives. But within their experience since coming of voting age many of the elements of politics have changed. Yet the reactions to the

---

[23] *The American Voter*, p. 252, table 10–3.
[24] Ibid., p. 255.

personalities of Eisenhower and Stevenson, to the issues of the Far Eastern war, and to the probity of the Democratic administration differed markedly according to the individual's party allegiance. If we are to trust the evidence on the stability of party identification, these differences must be attributed to the capacity of a general partisan orientation to color responses to particular political objects.[25]

The Consequences of Citizen Attitudes

The particular contours of citizen attitudes and behavior patterns as well as the fact that they were based on early experiences and on the individual's level of education has consequences for the operation of the American political system. For one thing, the moderate degree of political involvement and political activity of the American public, though it did not accord with some ideal models of democracy, had some beneficial effects on democratic government. It gave leaders flexibility in the making of public polity, and it allowed the governors to govern. As the authors of *The Civic Culture* put it, "nonelites cannot themselves rule. If a political system is to be effective—if it is to be able to initiate and carry out policies, adjust to new situations, meet internal and external challenges—there must be mechanisms whereby government officials are endowed with the power to make authoritative decisions."[26] Citizen unconcern with political matters helps give public officials that flexibility. Furthermore, the fact that the voting decision of the average citizen is not based on a close review of public policy means "that the electoral decision gives great freedom to those who must frame the policies of government."[27]

This is not to argue that democracy flourishes when leaders are uncontrolled by the populace. The fact that citizens have an ingrained belief that they can intervene in politics and that the political system will respond makes them potential activists. And this potential activity checks—albeit negatively—political leaders.[28] This kind of negative control is exemplified in the electoral system. As V. O. Key and the authors of *The American Voter* argue, the public does not choose on the basis of clear policy alternatives for the future. It responds to perceptions of success or failure of past administrations. This gives little precise policy guidance to political leaders, but it does keep them generally concerned about the need to satisfy the populace.

The facts about the stratification of the American populace also led to some positive evaluations of the moderate political involvement of the public

---

[25] Ibid., p. 135.
[26] Almond and Verba, *The Civic Culture*, p. 341.
[27] *The American Voter*, p. 544.
[28] Almond and Verba, *The Civic Culture,* chap. 15.

at large. Those who were more educated were more active, and these educated activists appeared to have several attractive features. They were better informed and "more rational" in political decisions. They were more satisfied with the polity, felt more efficacious, and were more committed to democratic norms. In short, as one moves from the relatively apathetic mass of the citizenry to the more active and involved citizens, one finds a "higher quality" citizen who is more likely to support and participate actively in the politics of democracy. Any regret that one might have had that more were not politically active was tempered by the consideration that those who stayed out of politics were less concerned with preserving civil liberties and less likely to act rationally when they voted.

The pattern of political attitudes found in the American electorate had significant implications for the way in which elections were conducted. Partisan attachments, rather than the issues of the day, appeared to govern the voting behavior of the citizenry. This was clearest in the 1948 election which the authors of *The American Voter* labeled a "maintaining" election. In such an election, the basic partisan commitments of the electorate guide the vote. In 1948, those commitments were the result of the New Deal realignment. The 1948 election was essentially a New Deal election, with FDR's vice-president as the incumbent running against FDR's opponent of 1944. According to *The American Voter,* the electorate responded in that year in terms of their partisan commitments, not in terms of the issues.

> It is likely, then, that in 1948 the electorate responded to current elements in politics very much in terms of its existing partisan loyalties. Apparently very little of the political landscape attracted strong feeling in that year. But what feeling there was seemed to be governed largely by antecedent attachments to one of the two major parties.[29]

The Eisenhower elections would, at first glance, appear to violate the rule that citizens vote their long-term partisan commitments. Though the Democratic identifiers were a majority of the population, Eisenhower won easily in 1952 and 1956. However, the evidence indicates that there was little abandonment of party affiliation except in the short-term sense, and that abandonment was in reaction not to a set of issues but to the personality of the candidate. These elections were "deviating" elections. The outcome was different from that which would be predicted on the basis of party affiliation, but the implication was that once the short-term force that dominated those elections—the personal appeal of Eisenhower—faded, the system would return to normal.

---

[29] *The American Voter,* p. 532.

The definition we have given of a deviating election implies that in such an election more people than usual will cross party lines in casting their votes. As a result, events of a deviating election can easily suggest that traditional party loyalties have become less important. To be sure, they have—in an immediate sense. But if our view of the motivational basis of voting is correct, a deviating election should not be taken as evidence of a secular decline in the importance of party identification.[30]

The depth and longevity of partisan commitments gave the political system a level of stability it would not otherwise have had. Students of comparative politics compared societies in which such commitments existed to others where there were less fully formed affiliations. Where the bulk of the citizenry has a long-term and stable commitment to one party or another, momentary changes in the political world are likely to be muted. The reaction of the citizenry to changing events is mediated by the positions taken by the established parties. Where there are no such established parties or where the citizenry has not established commitment to the parties, electoral competition is less predictable. "Flash" parties are likely to appear in times of crisis and the citizenry is more likely to turn to undemocratic parties.[31] In short, political parties to which citizens have continuing commitments provide an important degree of stability to the political process.

Furthermore, the nature of citizen attitudes has serious consequences for the way in which elections are conducted. The strategies of political parties reflect the ways in which citizens come to the voting choice: parties do not attempt to win votes by staking out clear positions along some ideological dimension; rather they attempt to find a candidate and a set of issues that have broad appeal.

The difference in these strategic outlooks expresses much of the difference in what the Taft and Eisenhower forces urged the Republican Party to do in the convention of 1952. The Taft view was that the party should

---

[30] Ibid.

[31] Philip E. Converse, "Of Time and Partisan Stability," *Comparative Political Studies*, 2 (July 1969), 141–142. The whole notion of flash parties rests on the assumption that a considerable portion of the electorate lacks a firm commitment to a party. Maurice Duverger's *Political Parties* (New York: Wiley, 1963) is the most widely cited source of the notion of flash parties. The relatively low commitment of the electorate to any of the parties of Weimar Germany is frequently used to explain the rapid success of the Nazi party; see Seymour M. Lipset, *Political Man* (New York: Vintage Press, 1960), chap. 5; see also W. Philips Shiveley, "Party Identification, Party Choice and Voting Stability: The Weimar Case," *American Political Science Review*, 56 (December 1972), 1203–1225 for a more recent study of the Nazi rise. A clever experiment to test for the extent of demogogic appeal in a nonparty election is in Dean Jaros and W. Mason, "Party Choice and Support for Demogogues: An Experimental Examination," *American Political Science Review*, 63 (March 1975), 100–110.

take a plainly conservative position on the left-right dimension that had emerged out of the struggle over the New Deal by nominating a candidate whose conservative stand was unquestioned. The belief that such a course would lead to majority support at the polls was based on the assumptions that the electorate was moving to the right and that the party had previously failed to attract its full potential vote because of non-voting among those who felt it was aping the Democrats. The strategic view that implicitly was endorsed by a majority of the Republican convention was that the party should exploit quite different dimensions of opinion, especially by nominating a war hero of enormous popular appeal. The slogan "Corruption, Korea and Communism," with which the Republican Party went into the campaign, suggests nicely the free-wheeling character of this strategy. Each of the elements of the slogan referred to a subject of public concern, real or imagined, that was relatively new and transitory, and none of the three bore much relation to the others, except for an alliterative one.[32]

An election based on this type of calculation might not offer a clear-cut choice to the American public, but it prevents a polarization of the American electorate into militantly opposed party groups. Such a polarization was, in any case, impeded by the fact that the public did not fall into clearly opposed groups; political attitudes were too unstructured to allow that. The parties, by their choice of candidates and electoral strategies, reinforced those public characteristics.

In sum, the characteristics of the public were such as to provide a firm base for a stable polity.

---

[32] *The American Voter*, p. 551.

3 | The Pattern Changes:
From the 1950s to the 1970s

To call the set of data and ideas that have just been sketched out a dominant paradigm for the understanding of politics in America is perhaps something of an exaggeration. The various works are not always consistent one with another, nor were their conclusions presented as unchanging truths. Yet these works, because they combined systematic data with sophisticated theorizing, did provide a set of ideas that guided much of the thinking and research on American politics.

Hardly had the studies of the 1950s been published when the 1960s exploded. There was little in the works of the 1950s that predicted the politics of the 1960s. None of the works paid much attention to blacks and none predicted the development of a more militant civil rights movement. These works could not be expected to say anything about or predict Vietnam, but there was not too much in them that helped predict the response to Vietnam. The same could be said for student unrest, the development of the women's rights movement, ecology, or anything else one wants to add to the list of political problems that emerged in the 1960s. The voting studies of the 1950s explain why the Republicans in 1952 chose Eisenhower over Taft, but in 1964 the Republicans chose Goldwater and in 1972 the Democrats chose McGovern.

One possible reason for the seeming incongruity between the data of the 1950s and subsequent events is that the former were not about the latter. The survey studies of the 1950s dealt with basic political attitudes. The events of the 1960s had their sources in things other than those basic attitudes. The more militant turn of the civil rights movement and the urban violence that accompanied it derived from the acts of a small segment of society that perhaps had been outside the mainstream. The same could be said for the militant student movement. And, of course, the war in Vietnam was the product of governmental actions, not anything that could be predicted on the basis of the attitudes of the American public.

Perhaps the events of the 1960s are not incongruent with the data of the 1950s. But the events provide an excellent opportunity for a reconsideration of those data. What impact, if any, might the events have on those basic political attitudes? The works of the 1950s uncovered what appeared to be long-term, not easily changeable attitudes. Commitment to democratic values and a sense of political efficacy developed early, at home and in the school. Party affiliation had roots in family tradition. The low level of conceptualization of political issues rested on the inherent complexity of these issues and that complexity made it unlikely that citizens could achieve better structure to their political attitudes. If this were the case, one would expect substantial stability in the pattern of public attitudes. Or if there were a change, it would likely be limited to the new, younger cohorts entering the political arena.

On the other hand, perhaps what appeared to be permanent was more timebound than had been thought; perhaps new events could have a profound effect on basic attitudes. If this were the case, one should see sharp changes in American attitudes as the 1960s unfolded. And the changes ought not to be limited to those for whom the 1960s represented the first adult exposure to politics. Perhaps attitudes of the 1950s were less the cause than the consequence of the particular blandness of the Eisenhower politics.

In the succeeding chapters of this book we will trace a variety of changes in the American electorate. In relation to some characteristics of the electorate we will demonstrate that a remarkable degree of change has taken place since the late Eisenhower years. When we consider some other characteristics we will find a good deal of stability. The data will also suggest a reinterpretation of the underlying dynamics of citizen attitudes and how those attitudes relate to the political process.[1] It may be useful to sketch the com-

---

[1] A number of recent works have been considering changes in the American electorate using the Michigan data sets. We shall refer to them where relevant. Some general works considering a range of issues rather than one or two include: Gerald Pomper, *Voters'*

ponents of that reinterpretation in order to give some overview of the large and complex body of data we shall present, the overall meaning of which may at times be obscured by the mass of the data.

The dynamics of the electoral system depends, we argue, on the interplay of long-term partisan commitments and the political issues facing the nation. But we assign somewhat more weight to political issues in structuring citizen political behavior than is the case in the "normal vote" model of the Michigan researchers.

The evidence, as we shall see, strongly confirms the Michigan contention that party identification is a long-term commitment, established early in life and usually maintained after that. The fact that the number of citizens with no such commitment has risen substantially in recent years as more and more citizens identify themselves as independents, modifies but does not contradict that contention. However, partisan commitments interact with the issues of the day. How this happens can be seen if we consider the system that was discovered in the studies of the 1950s. That decade, as the Michigan researchers pointed out, was still in many ways dominated by the partisan alignments that had grown up in response to the political issues of the New Deal. The partisan commitments that had been formed at that time remained dominant during those years, despite the fact that the issues on the basis of which they had been formed were no longer as salient as they once had been.

Though the New Deal issues were no longer as important, they had not been replaced by any new issues that were of deep concern to the electorate. As we shall see below, the issues of the Eisenhower years were relatively distant ones for the public. Under these circumstances, there was little to disturb the previously formed partisan commitment. The new voters who came of age during the fifties had not themselves experienced the political conflicts of the New Deal nor the trauma of the depression that confirmed the partisan commitments of the New Deal generation. Yet there was nothing to impede their inheritance of the partisan commitments of their parents, since no new issues pulled them in other directions. Thus the previous set of issues no longer played a significant role, but they had not been replaced by a new set of issues. The partisan commitments based on the earlier issues remained, however, and, in the absence or other forces, were transmitted to the next generation. Under the circumstances, party seemed all-important, issues unimportant.

Choice: Varieties of American Electoral Behavior (New York: Dodd Mead, 1975), and Philip E. Converse, "Change in the American Electorate," in Angus Campbell and Philip Converse, eds. *The Human Meaning of Social Change* (New York: Russell Sage, 1972).

The new issues that come along in the 1960s upset this system. These issues—Vietnam, but especially race—cut deeply into the consciousness of the public. They were not the sort to reconfirm the partisan commitments of the New Deal era. The positions of the citizenry and the positions of the parties (insofar as they could be said to have identifiable positions on these issues) cut across the partisan divisions associated with the economic issues of the New Deal. These new issues had a greater impact on the electorate. But—and here the Michigan model holds up remarkably well—the impact was most complete on those who were least exposed to the earlier party system. It was among the new generation of voters that the new issues resulted in loss of partisan identification—or, more precisely, the failure to adopt one when one entered the electorate. Not that those who had already entered the electorate and formed party ties before the new issues of the 1960s emerged were unaffected by the changes. But the effect was not as great as that on those who had no previous party commitment. The older voters began to abandon their party more frequently to vote for the opposition candidate. But they did maintain, with little weakening, their self-identification with one or the other of the parties.

In short, partisan commitments, when they are formed, appear to be affected by the issues of the day. But once a commitment is fixed, it tends to be long lasting even if the older issues fade and potent issues arise. Furthermore, in the absence of potent new issues, the partisan commitments based on earlier potent issues can be transferred to new members of the electorate even if the earlier issues no longer apply. But when one has the combination of the weakening of the older issues, the rise of potent new issues, and a new generation of voters, the stability of party commitments is shattered. Intergenerational transmission in the mid-1970s no longer works as well, and the new populace is ready for party change.

In Chapters 4 through 11 we shall trace the changes in the American electorate from the baseline presented in Chapter 2. Most of the data come from the 1952–1972 SRC studies, but we shall use other data (as well as the SRC data) to look backward to the pre-Eisenhower years. Chapters 12 through 14 consider some ways in which the party coalitions have changed in the past two decades. Chapter 15 tries to tie together a number of the changes. In Chapters 16 through 19, we look more closely at the changing structure of American elections to see how the recent changes are likely to affect future elections.

4 | The Decline of Partisanship

Perhaps the most dramatic political change in the American public over the past two decades has been the decline of partisanship. As we have seen party affiliation was the central thread running through interpretations of American politics in the 1950s and 1960s. Citizen attitudes on issues appeared to be only slightly related one to another, and they were unstable enough over time to suggest that a high proportion of citizens had no meaningful issue positions. But party affiliation was a stable characteristic of the individual: it was likely to be inherited, it was likely to remain steady throughout the citizen's political life, and it was likely to grow in strength during that lifetime.[1]

---

[1] See Angus Campbell, Gerald Gurin, Warren Miller, *The Voter Decides* (Evanston: Row Peterson, 1954); Angus Campbell and others, *The American Voter* (New York: Wiley, 1960); Angus Campbell and others, *Elections and the Political Order* (New York: Wiley, 1966); Philip E. Converse, "Of Time and Partisan Stability," *Comparative Political Studies*, 2 (July 1969), 139–171; Philip E. Converse, "The Nature of Belief Systems in Mass Publics," in David E. Apter, ed., *Ideology and Discontent* (New York: Free Press, 1964), 206–261, especially 238–240 where the stability of party preference is compared to the stability of other political attitudes; Herbert H. Hyman, *Political Socialization* (Glencoe: Free Press, 1959); M. Kent Jennings and Richard G. Niemi, "The Transmission of Political Values from Parent to Child," *American Political Science Review*, 62 (March 1968), 169–184.

Even more important, party affiliation was connected to other political phenomena. For the citizen, his sense of identification with a party was a guide to behavior; citizens voted for their party's candidates. It was a guide to understanding the political universe; candidates and issues were evaluated in party terms. Parties were objects of affective attachment; citizens expressed positive feelings about their parties. And those citizens with partisan affiliation were the most active and involved citizens; partisanship appeared to be a force mobilizing citizens into political life. Partisanship gave continuity and direction to the political behavior of citizens and to American electoral life.[2]

The weakening of partisanship has been documented many times in the works of political scientists such as Gerald Pomper, Walter Dean Burnham, and Jack Dennis.[3] Much of the data we present in this chapter parallels theirs and will not be new to the student of the subject. It is, however, important to lay out the variety of ways in which the decline of partisanship has been manifested in order to connect these varied changes with other trends we shall discuss. The situation can be summarized as follows: (1.) Fewer citizens have steady and strong psychological identification with a party. (2.) Party affiliation is less of a guide to electoral choice. (3.) Parties are less frequently used as standards of evaluation. (4.) Parties are less frequently objects of positive feelings on the part of citizens. (5.) Partisanship is less likely to be transferred from generation to generation.

Some Data on Partisanship

Party Identification

Figure 4.1 traces over time the proportion of the population that strongly identifies with one of the political parties, the proportion that weakly identifies with a party, and the proportion that professes independence of the parties.

---

[2] The concept of party identification and the linkages between that identification and electoral behavior was first systematically elaborated by George Belknap and Angus Campbell, "Political Party Identification and Attitudes toward Foreign Policy," *Public Opinion Quarterly,* 15 (Winter 1952), 601–623. The utility and power of the concept of psychological attachment to political parties as a property separate from voting or voting intentions was fully elaborated in Campbell and others, *The Voter Decides* and *The American Voter.* In Campbell and others, *Elections and the Political Order,* the authors demonstrate how this variable, along with actual voting patterns, can be used to understand the nature of elections and the flow of the voting in American society. For the centrality of party identification as a systemic as well as individual concept in American politics see Kenneth Prewitt and Norman H. Nie, "Election Studies of the Survey Research Center," *British Journal of Politics,* 1 (October 1971), 479–502.

[3] For excellent overviews, parallel to our own, see Jack Dennis, "Trends in Support for the American Party System," *British Journal of Political Science,* 5 (April 1975), 187–230; and Gerald Pomper, *Voters' Choice: Varieties of American Behavior* (New

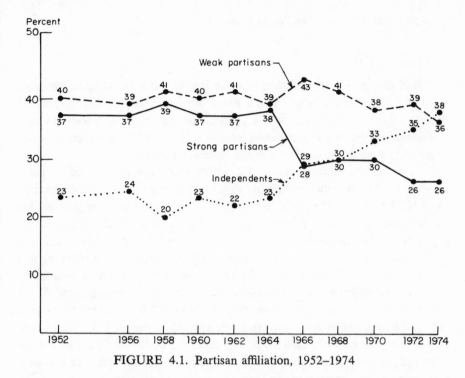

FIGURE 4.1. Partisan affiliation, 1952–1974

From 1952 to 1964 the proportions remain remarkably stable: a little more than a third of the populace is strongly partisan and a slightly larger group is weakly partisan. The remaining fifth of the population is Independent. The stability of these figures through 1964—despite the wide swings in popular vote from the strong Eisenhower victory of 1956, through the close 1960 race, to the Johnson sweep in 1964—represent convincing evidence of the continuity of partisanship.

From 1964 through 1974, however, the situation changes. The proportion of strong identifiers drops while the proportion of Independents rises. By 1974 only about one out of four Americans can be considered a strong partisan while 38 percent are Independent. Note also that among those who identify with a political party from 1952 through 1964, about equal numbers consider themselves weak and strong partisans. By the 1970s those who consider themselves partisans are more likely to be weak than strong partisans. The figures indicate a clear erosion of the strength of party affiliation in the American public.[4]

York: Dodd Mead, 1975), chap. 2. The decline of partisanship is presented in historical perspective in Walter Dean Burnham, *Critical Elections and the Mainsprings of American Politics* (New York: Norton, 1970).

[4] This overview of national trends conceals many variations hidden within the data—the South differs from the North, young from old, and so on. We deal with these differences below.

Party and the Vote

In 1956 party identification was the key to the vote. Despite the large number of Democrats who crossed party lines to vote for Eisenhower, 83 percent of those Americans with a party identification voted consistent with that identification in the presidential election; about 90 percent voted consistent with that identification in the congressional elections.

Consider the data in figure 4.2 which show the proportion of party identifiers who did not vote for the candidate of their party in the elections from 1952 to 1972. The proportion defecting from their party in presidential elections was quite similar from 1952 to 1964, again a stability worth stressing given the heterogeneity of those elections. The defection rate in 1968 was substantially higher (largely a reflection of George Wallace's candidacy) and stayed high in 1972. In 1968 and 1972, more than one out of four party identifiers voted for the presidential candidate of the opposition party. If the group of identifiers who abandoned their party in 1972 to vote for the opposing presidential candidate (they are 17 percent of all voters[5]) is added to the 34 percent who are Independents in that year, one finds that 51 percent of the voting population are not guided by a party affiliation. They either vote against their own party's candidate, or they are Independent with no party ties to guide them.

Presidential voting figures, however, are hard to interpret since they are heavily dependent on the noncomparable exigencies of the particular race. The extent to which the division of the vote is influenced by the characteristics and appeal of the presidential candidates, for example, is well known. The defection rates in other races, therefore, may be essential to interpreting the erosion of party support. The proportion of defectors in both House and Senate elections also rises, especially toward the end of the period. There tends to be somewhat more defection in presidential years because of the pull of the presidential candidates and because the electorate is larger and contains more voters with weak party ties.[6] For this reason, off-year elections may provide clearer data on the role of party. We have plotted the off-year elections separately, and they show a pattern of change similar to that of the presidential elections. Compare 1958 with 1974, for instance. The defection rate in Senate and House elections almost doubles.[7]

---

[5] That is, they are 27 percent of the party identifiers, but only 17 percent of the voters.

[6] Angus Campbell, "Surge and Decline: A Study of Electoral Change," *Public Opinion Quarterly*, 24 (Fall 1960), 397–418.

[7] For an analysis of the declining importance of party in Senate elections see Warren Lee Kostroski, "Party and Incumbency in Post-War Senate Elections: Trends, Patterns, and Models," *American Political Science Review*, 67 (December 1973), 1213–1234.

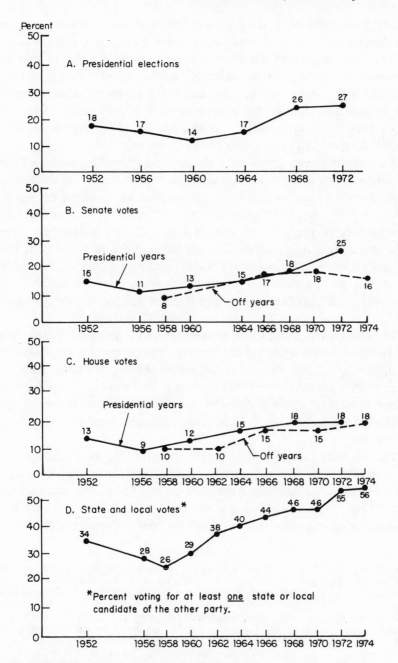

FIGURE 4.2. Proportion of party identifiers voting for candidate of other party, 1952–1972

Lastly we can look at the defection rates for state and local elections. The defection rates are in general higher in these races since we consider a voter to be a defector if he did not vote the straight party ticket in state and local elections—that is, even one defecting vote for one of the many offices in the election makes one a defector. The number of voters not voting a straight ticket in state and local elections remains more or less steady from 1952 through 1960. From then on, it rises sharply. By 1974 more than half of those voting report abandoning their party at least once.

The data for the nonpresidential elections are compelling evidence of the weakening of party ties. Presidential elections depend heavily on the particular candidates. In congressional and local elections where candidates are less well known, party should be more important.[8] Yet there is a clear decline in the importance of party on all political levels. Clearly, citizens no longer depend as heavily as they once did on party labels in deciding their vote. They more easily switch to the candidate of the opposition party. To look at the data another way, in 1956 the correlation between party identification and House vote was .72; between party identification and Senate vote it was .68. By 1972 these correlations had fallen to .55 and .47, respectively.[9]

The data on split ticket voting are summarized in figure 4.3, which shows the proportion of the population that reports voting a straight party ticket and the proportion that reports split ticket voting. Among the latter group we distinguish between those who vote a straight ticket except for the presidential vote and those who report some ticket splitting at the subpresidential level since the latter form of ticket splitting may represent a more significant break in partisanship.

There is little variation in the proportion who split their ballot only on the presidential vote. The proportion remains small throughout the period. What does change substantially is the proportion of voters who vote a straight ticket. Of course this change is reflected in the proportion who split their ballots below the presidential level. The high points of straight ticket voting

---

[8] On the other hand, it is not obviously wrong to assume that the factor of personal recognition does play a considerable role in voting for lower level offices. The "friends-and-neighbors" factor in local voting can be a significant determinant of the outcome of local elections. In a lower level election an individual's reputation can be more important to many voters than his party. The invulnerability of some public officials in otherwise competitive states, counties, and cities can only be attributed to the recognition and positive personal evaluations these officials enjoy. Certainly this is one of the factors which go into giving incumbent politicians an advantage. For some illustrations of the variable importance of party see Donald E. Stokes and Warren E. Miller, "Party Government and the Saliency of Congress," *Public Opinion Quarterly,* 26 (Winter 1962), 531–546.

[9] The correlations reported here are Pearson product moment correlations.

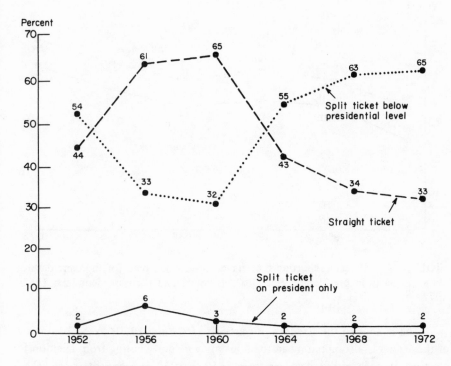

FIGURE 4.3. Straight and split ticket voting, 1952–1972

are 1956 and 1960. Split ticket voting was greater in 1952 and returns to that level in 1964; in 1968 and 1972 it increases even further. The data summarize what has been shown thus far: the 1956 and 1960 elections were high points of party attachment.

The data are particularly striking when one remembers that these are defection rates for those who profess affiliation with a party. Over time the proportion with such self-identification has fallen. One would think that those who remain attached to one or the other of the parties would be those whose commitment was stronger, the less committed having moved into the Independent ranks. Yet even among the increasingly smaller group of party identifiers one finds party affiliation playing a smaller role in determining the vote.[10]

---

[10] There is little evidence that weak partisans have become Independents over the preceding years. Our conclusions about this party change rest upon data which show that most of the change in party identification depends upon the introduction of new populations into the electorate in the last twenty years. Since there does seem to be some small abandonment of party affiliation, however, remaining strong partisans constitute a

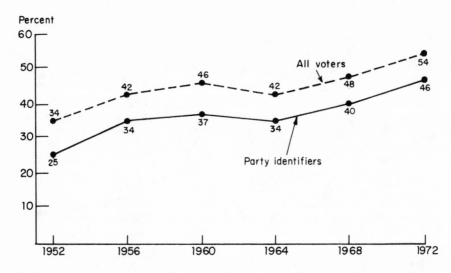

FIGURE 4.4. Percent reporting they have not always voted for the candidate of the same party in presidential elections: all voters and partisan identifiers, 1952–1972

The change in the strength of party ties from the 1950s to the beginning of the 1970s is also apparent in the constancy of party voting from election to election. In each of the elections from 1952 to 1972, respondents were asked whether they always voted for the same party in presidential elections. In 1952, one-third of the voters reported that they had not always voted for presidential candidates of the same party. By 1972, the situation had changed drastically. Over half of the voters reported that their presidential vote had not been constant in party terms (figure 4.4, dotted line).

The proportion of citizens who are inconstant in their vote—sometimes voting for the presidential candidate of one party, sometimes for the other—can be expected to rise with the rise in the proportion of Independents in the population. Their votes are more likely to move from party to party. But even those who still consider themselves to be partisans are more likely to switch their votes from party to party. The solid line in figure 4.4 reports the proportion of inconstant presidential voters only for those with a party affiliation. The inconstancy of presidential voting has increased even among those who have maintained their affiliation. In 1952, only one out of four party iden-

---

group which has not relinquished their party loyalties in spite of the relatively great disfavor into which parties have fallen.

tifiers reported inconstancy in the vote. By 1972, almost one out of two identifiers said that they did not always vote for the same party.

The identifiers in the later years—1968 and 1972—ought to be a "hard-core" of partisans since so many of the weaker partisans have taken to considering themselves Independents. But even the hard-core group is weakening in the steadiness with which it follows the party line when it comes to the presidential vote.

Party and Candidate Evaluation

It is clear from these data that citizens are less frequently guided by partisan affiliation in the choice of the candidate for whom they will vote. One can observe this in a somewhat different way by considering what it is that respondents like or dislike about the candidates in presidential races.[11] As noted earlier, almost half of the electorate mention the party affiliation of the candidate as one reason for liking or disliking a candidate: "He is a good Democrat," and so forth. Figure 4.5 shows the proportion that use partisanship as an evaluative standard for candidates from 1952 to 1972. In 1952, 46 percent of the voters cite a party reason for candidate preference. The percentage goes down in 1964 but up again in 1968. By 1972, that figure has dropped to 24 percent. And the proportion of citizens who evaluate both candidates in party terms—they like their own candidate because of his party and dislike the opponent because he is affiliated with the opposition—had fallen even more precipitously, form 12 percent to 2 percent.[12]

The decline in the use of party as an evaluative standard is not merely a function of the larger proportion of the populace who have no party ties. The frequency with which candidates are preferred or rejected because of their party ties has declined, even among those who identify with one of the parties (see figure 4.6).

---

[11] For early demonstrations of the importance of these feelings see *The Voter Decides; The American Voter;* Angus Campbell and Donald E. Stokes, "Partisan Attitudes and the Presidential Vote" in Eugene Burdick and Arthur J. Brodbeck, eds., *American Voting Behavior* (Glencoe: Free Press, 1959), 353–371; Donald E. Stokes, Angus Campbell, and Warren E. Miller, "Components of Electoral Decision," *American Political Science Review,* 52 (June 1958), 367–387; Donald E. Stokes, "Some Dynamic Elements of Contests for the Presidency," *American Political Science Review,* 60 (March 1966), 19–28. More recent use of these measures to account for voting choice include David E. Repass, "Issue Salience and Party Choice," *American Political Science Review,* 60 (June 1971), 389–400; Stanley Kelley and Thad W. Miner, "The Simple Act of Voting," *American Political Science Review,* 68 (June 1974), 572–591.

[12] The decline between 1968 and 1972 may be partly attributable to a change in coding for the 1972 study, but the decline through 1968 leads us to believe that it cannot be completely attributed to coding.

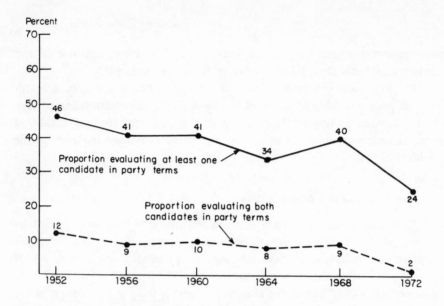

FIGURE 4.5. Proportion of citizens mentioning the candidate's party affiliation as a reason for liking or disliking him, 1952–1972

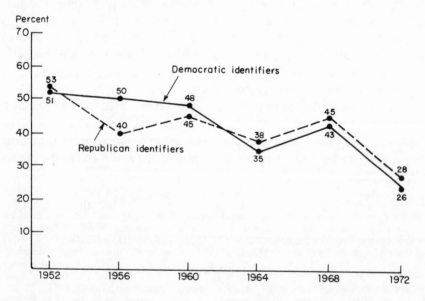

FIGURE 4.6. Proportion of Democratic and Republican identifiers mentioning the candidate's party affiliation as a reason for liking or disliking him, 1952–1972

The data on the use of partisan characteristics of the candidate as a basis for evaluations of the candidate add an important separate confirmation of the erosion of the importance of party. The candidate evaluation questions are open-ended. They elicit whatever standards of evaluation the respondent has in his mind. When party is mentioned it is mentioned spontaneously. The fact that the frequency of such spontaneous mentions declines so rapidly is further evidence that the political centrality of the political party has declined.

Citizen Affection for the Parties

Perhaps the clearest evidence of the erosion of support for the parties is found in figure 4.7. In each of the election years, the SRC has asked respondents what they like and what they dislike about each of the parties. Earlier, answers to these questions were used to assign respondents to one or another level of conceptualization. These responses can also be used to measure the extent to which respondents have positive or negative views about the parties. Respondents can mention a number of things they like about each party and a number of things they dislike. We compared the rate of positive and negative references. In 1952 we find that most respondents fall in a category we called "partisans": they say on balance more positive than negative things about their own party and on balance are either negative or neutral about the opposition. Sixty-four percent of the population falls into this category. An additional 5 percent says positive things about both parties. The remaining 31 percent of respondents are considered nonsupporters of the party system: they are either negative about both parties, negative about one and neutral about the other, or have no opinion about either.

Figure 4.7 shows what happens to the proportion of these various types of party supporters. The small group that likes both parties remains low throughout the period. More striking is the decline in the partisans and the rise in the nonsupporters. In the elections of the 1950s those who were positive about their own party and combined that with negative or neutral views about the opposition outnumbered those who supported neither party by more than two to one. By 1972 more Americans were either hostile or neutral toward the political parties than were supporters of one or the other parties.

In sum, the data show a dramatic decline of partisanship during the two decades we have been tracing. The decline is apparent across a wide range of measures. Citizens are less likely to identify with a party, to feel positively about a party, or to be guided in their voting behavior by partisan cues.

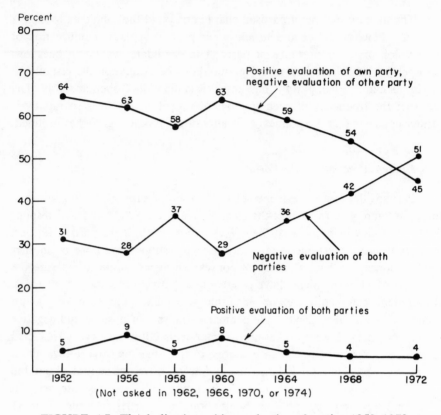

FIGURE 4.7. The decline in positive evaluation of parties, 1952–1972

The loosening of party ties, however, is not manifested in a switch of allegiance from one of the major parties to the other. In the SRC studies, respondents are asked if they have switched parties. Table 4.1 shows the proportions who report switching allegiance from one party to the other in the previous four years. As one can see, the proportion is small and remains small even during the period of rapid erosion of partisanship in the late 1960s and early 1970s.[13] The trend appears to be away from parties, not from one party to another.

---

[13] The data on recalled switch of parties is quite consistent with a more direct measure of party switching derived from the panel study of voters conducted by the SRC in 1956, 1958, and 1960. If one cross tabulates the party allegiance of voters in 1956 with their allegiance in 1960, one finds that 4 percent report allegiance to one party in 1956 and to the other in 1960. Computed from data in John C. Pierce and Douglas D. Rose, "Non-Attitudes and American Public Opinion," *American Political Science Review,* 68 (June 1974), 633. For a fuller discussion of the panel data and some recent analyses that seem to contradict this point see Appendix 4.

TABLE 4.1. Proportion of partisan identifiers who report changing their party identification during the previous four years, 1952–1974

1952	1956	1958	1960	1964	1968	1970	1972	1974
3	5	2	3	4	3	3	5	4

Sources of the Decline of Partisanship

Partisanship is a habit, the strength of which grows with the length of time one has had the habit. This is one of the main findings of analyses of partisanship across the citizen's life cycle.[14] Older citizens should be more firmly attached to one of the political parties. They have had more exposure to the electoral process and, therefore, more time to acquire and confirm their party attachment. The surge of Independents, this suggests, may come from new entrants into the political system rather than from those who have abandoned already-established party ties. The data in table 4.2 support this expectation. Table 4.2 presents the proportion of Independents who report having abandoned a party identification in the previous four years. The data are for those Independents who are over twenty-five years of age and who have been

TABLE 4.2. Proportion of Independents over 25 years of age who have abandoned party identification during the previous four years, 1956–1972[a]

1956	1958	1960	1964	1968	1970	1972
8	13	3	8	8	11	10

[a] Question not asked in 1952; asked in a noncomparable form in 1974.

---

[14] See *The American Voter*, chap. 7; Converse, "Of Time and Partisan Stability"; David Butler and Donald E. Stokes, *Political Change in Britain* (New York: St. Martins Press, 1969). Other item specific analyses of the relationship between aging, political preference, and political involvement can be found in Norval D. Glenn, "Aging, Disengagement and Opinionation," *Public Opinion Quarterly*, 33 (Spring 1969), 17–34; Neal E. Cutler, "Generation, Maturation and Party Affiliation: A Cohort Analysis," *Public Opinion Quarterly*, 33 (Winter 1969), 583–588; and Norval D. Glenn and Michael Grimes, "Aging, Voting, and Political Interest," *American Sociological Review*, 33 (September 1968), pp. 563–575. See also Norman Ryder, "The Cohort as a Concept in the Study of Social Change," *American Sociological Review*, 30 (December 1965), 848, and William Klecka, "Applying Political Generation to the Study of Political Behavior: A Cohort Analysis," *Public Opinion Quarterly*, 35 (Fall 1971), 358–373.

in the electorate for the previous four years. As one can see, the proportion who have abandoned a party preference is small in each of the years. More important, the proportions show very little rise in the period of erosion of party ties. In most years, only about 10 percent of the Independents report having had previous party ties. Clearly, the increase in Independents is not attributable in any large part to an abandonment of partisanship by those already in the electorate. The alternative explanation may lie in the replacement of the older electorate with a new one. The young voters who enter the electorate are less likely to have party attachment.

Thus, the source of the rise of independence is found by considering age differences. Table 4.3 presents the proportion of Independents found in different age groups in each of the presidential years. The data are consistent with the view that the strength of party affiliation grows with age. In each year one finds a larger percentage of the young falling into the category of Independents and a smaller percentage of the older age groups with no party attachment.

The fact of stronger partisan ties among older citizens appears consistently in the various election years, but there is a clear change in magnitude across the years. In the earlier period there is much less difference among the age groups than in the later period. In 1952, the youngest group differs from

TABLE 4.3. Proportion Independents by age, 1952–1974

Age	1952	1956	1960	1964	1968	1972[a]	1974[a]
21–25	25	37	39	33	53	51	53
26–30	32	31	26	29	41	50	42
31–40	23	26	27	26	29	40	39
41–50	26	21	25	24	31	30	37
51–65	19	24	21	18	24	26	32
66+	20	13	13	14	15	19	23
Average percent Independent among those over 30	22	22	22	21	26	28	34
Difference between youngest and over 30	3	15	17	12	27	23	19

[a] For 1972 and 1974 the youngest age group is 18 to 25.

the over-thirty years of age population by only 3 percentage points in terms of the proportions of Independents. Twenty-five percent of the youngest group and 22 percent of the over-thirty group are Independent. By 1974, there is a 19 percentage point difference between the two age groups; 53 percent of the youngest group is Independent compared with 34 percent of the over-thirty population. The data strongly suggest that the change in the direction of partisan independence comes largely among the younger citizens.[15]

The situation can be made clearer by considering changes in some age cohorts over time. The cohorts we compare are:

1. The established voters of 1952. These are the citizens who were twenty-five years of age or older in 1952. In 1956, they are the group that is twenty-nine years and older, and so on until 1974 when they are at least forty-seven years of age. By following their degree of partisanship, we can see what happens to a group that was exposed to the electoral process during the era when partisan tie were stable and firm.

2. The new voters of 1952. This is the age group that enters the electorate between 1949 and 1953. They are twenty-one to twenty-four years of age in our 1952 study; forty-three to forty-five years of age in 1974. They, too, have long exposure to the party system by the time the late 1960s come around, though, on the average, not as long as the established voters of 1952.

3. The new voters of 1960. These are the voters who enter the electorate between the 1956 elections and 1961. They do not appear in our 1952 data, of course. They are the twenty-one to twenty-four years of age in 1960, and they are thirty-five to thirty-eight years of age in the 1974 data.

4. The new voters of 1964. This group enters the electorate by the time of the 1964 election, but not by the 1960 election. Members of this group range in age from thirty-one to thirty-four years of age in 1974.

---

[15] Education changes in the past twenty years have frequently been used to explain changes in the social and cultural values of the young, but they cannot explain these changes. The increase in Independents is unrelated to the increasing educational advantages of the young.
Increase in percent of Independents from 1952 to 1974:

25 years or under	+21	points
Did not finish high school	+20	points
Finished high school	+26	points
At least some college	+23	points
26 to 30 years	+18	points
Did not finish high school	+20	points
Finished high school	+15	points
At least some college	+12	points

5. The post-1964 voters. They enter the electorate between 1956 and 1973. They are eighteen to thirty years of age in 1974.[16]

Party Identification

Figure 4.8 compares these age cohorts in terms of the proportion Independent across the two decades. Because sample sizes become quite small when one looks at specific age groups, we average the data for pairs of elections—that is, we report the average for the 1956 and 1958 elections, the 1960 and 1962 elections, and so on.[17] The data allow us to examine the relationship between the close and stable partisan ties that characterized the electorate in the 1950s and the forces making for the erosion of such ties in the late 1960s. If the hypothesis that such ties become stronger the longer they exist is correct, we should find differences among the cohorts in the way they react to the challenges to the party system in the late 1960s. The data in figure 4.8 support the proposition that partisanship solidifies with exposure to the party system. The data also suggest a relationship between long-term commitments to a party and the specific historical events that loosened party ties in the late 1960s. Party affiliation appears harder to shake the longer it has existed. However, such attachment can loosen among those whose party commitment has had less time to become well rooted. More important, the events which erode partisanship seem to have their largest impact on the newest cohort of voters.

Consider the group that was well established in the electorate by 1952: the established voters of 1952. When the challenges to the party system begin in the late 1960s, this group does not respond with an increase in party independence. By the time the parties come under challenge, this cohort has had at least twenty and in most cases many more years to acquire an affiliation. When they first appear on our figure in 1952, 23 percent are Independent. Twenty years later the proportion of Independents among them has risen by only 4 percent.

---

[16] The average age of these cohorts in the different years is presented here.

	1952	1956	1960	1964	1968	1972
Established 1952	43.4	47.5	51.6	54.4	57.3	60.6
New 1952	22.4	26.5	30.5	34.5	38.5	42.4
New 1960			22.7	26.6	30.3	34.4
New 1964				22.5	26.3	30.3
Post–1964					22.4	23.4

[17] For example, the proportion Independent that is reported for the new voters of 1960 for the 1960–1962 data point is the average of the proportion of Independents among those 21 to 24 in 1960 and those 23 to 26 in 1962.

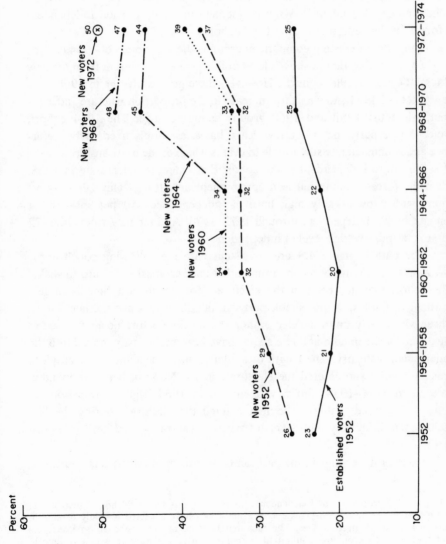

FIGURE 4.8. Proportion of Independents by age cohorts, 1952–1972

The next cohort to consider is that of the new voters of 1952. When partisanship comes under challenge in the late 1960s, they too have been in the electorate for a long time (about sixteen years), but not as long as those voters who were "established" in 1952. This cohort is not immune from the impact of the challenges to the parties. The proportion who are Independents grows by 11 percentage points over the two decades. At the beginning of the time period, this group was only 3 percentage points more Independent than the established voters of 1952. By the end of the time period they are 10 points more Independent.[18] A similar increase in the proportion Independent is found for the new voters of the 1960 cohort.

The more interesting comparison group is the new voters of 1964 cohort. In 1964–1966 they do not show a level of independence different from the new voters of 1952 or 1960 cohorts. However, these groups diverge in 1968. The new voters of 1964 show a sharp increase in the proportion who are Independent, while the 1952 and 1960 groups do not change. The 1964 cohort, attached to a party for only a few years, has a less firmly fixed party preference and is immediately susceptible to events which erode partisanship.

Still more Independent is the cohort that enters the electorate in 1968, when the forces eroding partisan commitment are strong. This 1968 cohort enters with a remarkably high level of independence—50 percent—and it remains highly Independent through 1972–1974. And the new voters of 1972 enter at a similarly high level of independence.

The data in figure 4.8 are consistent with the following conclusions: Partisanship is a long-term commitment that once established is hard to shake. The cohort that has been in the electorate for the longest time is largely resistant to the forces that shook partisan identification since the late 1960s. Those who have been in the electorate a shorter time before being exposed to the events of the middle and late sixties have been more easily moved into the Independent category. The length of affiliation has a delaying effect on party erosion. Those who entered the electorate in 1952 do not begin to abandon party until 1972–1974; those who entered in 1964 begin their exodus in 1968–1970. Finally, those who first entered the electorate during the late 1960s come in at very high levels of partisan neutrality, and have remained there.

Much of the change in the partisan commitment of Americans appears to

---

[18] The 1972 proportion of Independents for this group is markedly higher than it was in 1968. If the aging hypothesis is correct, one would have expected a steady decline in Independents as this group ages. The fact that they do not change over time suggests that they may be even less committed to political parties than one would ordinarily expect.

come from those new voters who enter the electorate in the late 1960s. Their impact is made greater by the fact that young voters have been an increasing proportion of the electorate. In 1952, 8 percent of our sample was between twenty-one and twenty-four; twenty years later 12 percent of the sample falls in that age group (and if one adds the eighteen to twenty year olds, one has an electorate in 1972 in which 17 percent of its members was not eligible to vote in the previous election). The combination of the fact that the new voters are a larger proportion of the electorate and the fact of their greater independence makes clear that these new voters contribute disproportionately to the decay of partisanship.

Changing Strength of Commitment

The members of the cohort who entered the electorate in 1952 tended to maintain their party preference; but does the preference weaken over time? We can answer this question by looking at some of the indicators of strength of partisan commitment among those who are partisans. Figure 4.9 deals with strength of identification. The percentages are the proportion of those who identify with a party who report that they are strong identifiers. As we have seen earlier, that proportion has been falling over time. But as figure 4.9 indicates, those cohorts who had entered the electorate by the time of the 1952 election have, in general, remained strong partisans. The established voters of 1952 cohort (those who were twenty-four and over in 1952) does not change. About one-half of the identifiers consider themselves strong identifiers in each election during the two decades. The same is true for the new voters of 1952. They also remain relatively steadfast in terms of the proportion of identifiers who have strong identification.

The source of the weakened identification among those who are party identifiers is found in the new cohorts who enter the electorate in the 1960s. Only about one-third of the party identifiers enter the electorate with strong identifications. But unlike the situation in relation to partisan independence, one finds little evidence of decay of partisan strength after the cohort enters.

When one compares figures 4.8 and 4.9, one observes two different ways in which partisanship erodes. The new cohorts of 1960 and 1964 enter the electorate looking like the older cohorts in terms of partisan identification. In succeeding years their partisanship decays. But they enter the electorate with a *strength* of party affiliation already below that of the earlier cohorts—and the strength of identification remains constant. The change in strength of identification appears to result from the replacement of one age group with another.

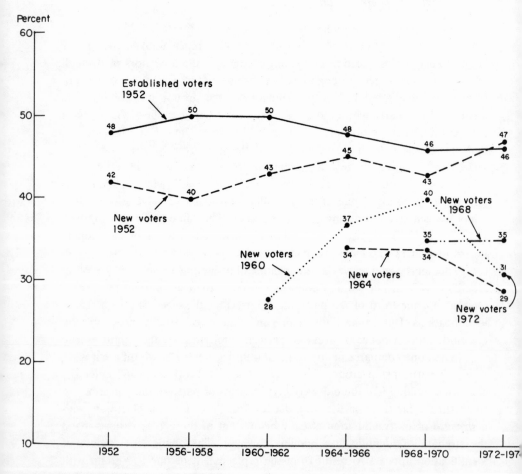

FIGURE 4.9. Strength of party affiliation by age cohorts: percent of identifiers with strong identi-fication, 1952–1974

Partisanship and the Vote

Not all manifestations of weakened partisanship, however, are due to the entrance of new voters. The role of partisanship as a guide to the vote has eroded in a very different way. As we have seen, the proportion of voters who vote a straight party ticket has fallen substantially since 1956 and 1960—the high points of party regularity for the two decades we are studying. Figure 4.10 has data on the proportions of the various age cohorts who vote a straight ticket in presidential years. The data offer a quite different picture

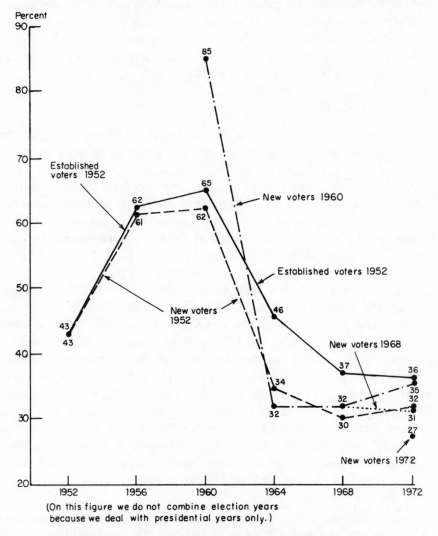

FIGURE 4.10. Straight ticket voters by age cohorts, 1952–1972

from that in relation to party identification and the strength of that identification. The various cohorts—those who were in the electorate in 1952 as well
as the later cohorts—appear quite similar in the proportion who vote a
straight ticket at each point in time.

The new and the established voters of 1952 behave identically from
1952 to 1960. In addition, the new cohort that enters in 1960 looks quite
similar to the older groups. As straight ticket voting begins to decline after
1960, it declines for each cohort. When the newer cohorts enter the electorate
in 1968 and 1972, they show frequencies of straight ticket voting as low—*but
not lower*—than the older groups. Clearly the commitment to political parties
that kept the older cohorts constant in their strong identification does not
impede them from following the general tendency toward split ticket voting.
The rise of split ticket voting appears to be more a function of the pressures
of the period than the generation of the voter.

Party Evaluations

A similar story is told by the data in figure 4.11. There we report the
proportions of the various age groups who give positive evaluation of one or
both of the political parties. As reported earlier, the proportion of the population with generally positive things to say about one or both of the parties falls
substantially during the period we have been tracing. At the beginning of our
period, more than two out of three Americans had a generally favorable
evaluation of at least one of the parties. By 1972, the proportion making such
positive evaluations had fallen to less than half.

As figure 4.11 indicates, positive evaluations of parties fall for all age
cohorts, including those who were in the electorate in 1952. The younger
groups who enter in 1968 and 1972 are the most negative toward the
parties.[19] But the older groups change substantially as well. The established
voters of 1952 cohort falls from 72 percent who can be considered positive
partisans to 56 percent; and the new voters of 1952 cohort changes even
more, from 70 percent positive to 47 percent. The 1952 cohort does not wind
up as negative about the parties as are the newer cohorts, but the decline in
their affection is substantial. The measure of party evaluation appears to fall
between that of frequency of independence and that of split ticket voting.
Long-term party attachment has an effect in dampening the decline in affection (as it dampened the rise of independence) but there is still some movement with the times for the established voters.

---

[19] The data in figure 4.11 are for both identifiers and Independents. If one eliminated
the Independents (who are half of the younger cohorts), the younger age cohorts would
not look as different.

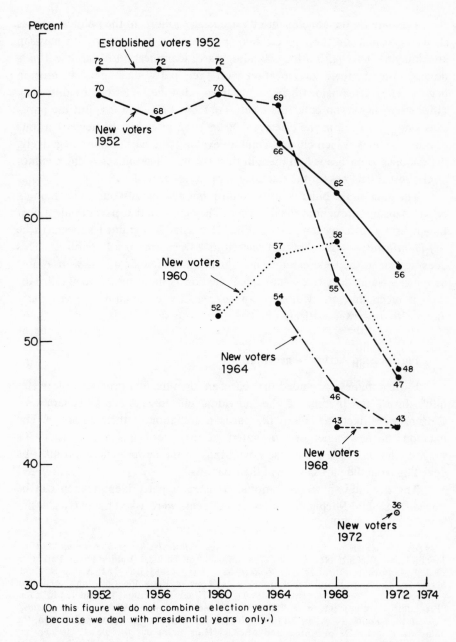

FIGURE 4.11. Proportion of positive partisan evaluators by age cohort, 1952–1972

The data on the attachment of various age cohorts to the political parties sheds some light on the impact of long association with a party on partisan attachment. Those with a long-standing party identification in the late 1960s do not falter in their identification with their party when partisan erosion begins. They remain identifiers, and strong identifiers at that. In this, they differ from those who enter the electorate from 1960 onward. But the partisans who have been in the electorate since 1952 resemble the newer entrants in other respects. When citizens come to evaluate the parties more negatively, the established partisans join them in this. When straight ticket voting declines after 1960, it declines for the established partisans as well.

The data on the older cohorts confirm but also modify our understanding of partisanship throughout the life cycle. They confirm that partisan identification is firmly fixed by long association. But what is ingrained appears to be *self-identification*—one thinks of oneself as a Democrat or a Republican. This does not mean that one cannot vote against that identification—with almost as much ease as does one whose identification is more newly acquired. Nor does it mean that one will not express negative evaluation of one's party along with the newer partisans.

Partisanship Across Generations

Earlier studies concluded that partisan identification produced party stability during the lifetime of the individual citizen and across generations. Citizens were likely to inherit the partisan affiliation of their parents.[20] The data on the new generation of voters of the late 1960s and early 1970s suggests that this is less the case now. Many in the newer generation must be deviating from the partisan ties of their parents.

The decline in intergenerational transfer of party identification can be traced. In several Michigan studies, respondents were asked the party identifi-

---

[20] See *The American Voter;* Butler and Stokes, *Political Change in Britain;* M. Kent Jennings and Richard Neimi, "The Transmission of Political Values From Parent to Child," *American Political Science Review,* 62 (March 1968), 169–184; Arthur S. Goldberg, "Social Determinism and Rationality as Bases of Party Identification," *American Political Science Review,* 63 (March 1969), 5–25; Jack Dennis and Donald J. McCrone, "Pre-Adult Development of Political Party Identification in Western Democracies," *Comparative Political Studies,* 3 (July 1970), 243–263. Although not very thorough, the data presented by David Knoke and Michael Hunt point out the clearly greater importance of parental party preference in the development of party affiliation, "Social and Demographic Factors in American Party Affiliation: 1952–1972," *American Sociological Review,* 39 (October 1974), 700–713. See also Philip Converse and Georges Dupeux, "The Politicization of the Electorate in France and the United States," in Campbell and others, *Elections and the Political Order,* and Donald D. Searing and others, "The Structuring Principle: Political Socialization and Belief Systems," *American Political Science Review,* 67 (June 1973), 415–432.

cation of their parents during the years when the respondent was growing up. By taking those that came from families with an unambiguous partisan affiliation—eliminating those who could not remember the affiliation of their parents, those whose parents were unaffiliated, and those who parents did not agree on party affiliation—one can isolate those respondents who had clear Democratic or Republican family backgrounds.

Figure 4.12 examines the current party ties of these respondents. We separate the respondents into those with Democratic family backgrounds and those with Republican backgrounds, and divide each of these groups into those over thirty at the time of the survey and those under thirty. Consider those respondents who were over thirty and had a Democratic family background (in the upper left graph). For the first three years for which we have data (1952, 1958, and 1964) about three out of four of those with a Democratic family are Democratic identifiers. The proportion falls about 10 percent during the next decade. Intergenerational transfer of partisan identity is clearly weakening a bit among the over-thirty voters in the early 1970s. But the loss of intergenerational stability does not imply much transfer of the electorate from the Democrats to the Republicans. The decline in the proportion conforming to the partisan ties of their parents is matched by a rise in the proportion of voters from a Democratic family who are Independent. But the proportion that switches to the opposite party does not change.

The data for the younger Democrats are more striking than those for the older. In the first three election years, younger Democrats resemble the over-thirty group—over 70 percent remain constant to the partisan ties of their parents. But starting in 1968, the proportion falls substantially. In 1968 and the following years, almost one in two respondents who report a Democratic family background are not Democratic identifiers. Those who have abandoned the affiliation of their parents have become Independents. The proportion that switch to the Republican party remains small throughout the period. It shows no rise during the later years when defection from parental affiliation is high.

Republicans are similar. Among the over-thirty group, the proportion that maintains the affiliation of their parents remains relatively constant over the time period. If there is any breakdown in the transfer of party allegiance, the result is an increase in the proportion of Independents, not a rise in the number of Democrats. The weakness of intergenerational transfer among Republicans is most extreme among the younger Republicans in the late 1960s. The proportion following in the partisan footsteps of their parents falls to under 50 percent. In general, Republicans transfer party affiliation some what less effectively than do the Democrats.

The data confirm the decline of partisanship as a stable and long-term

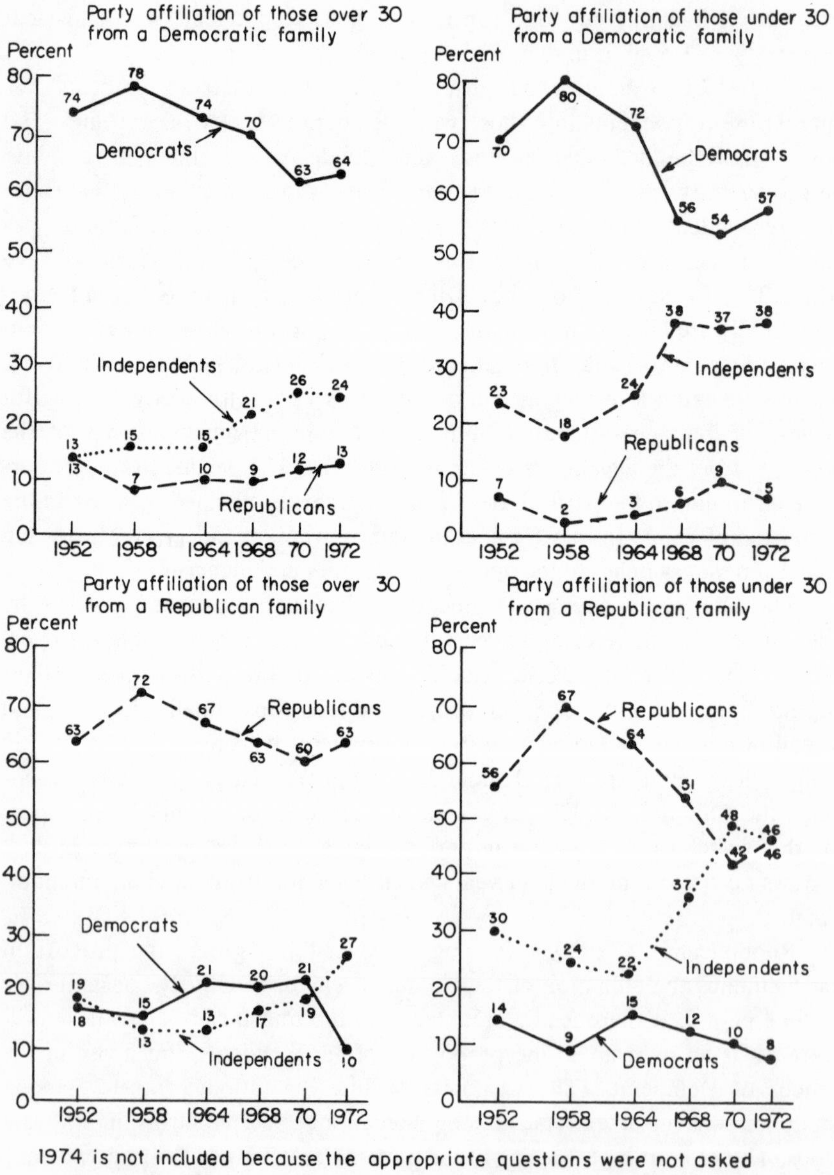
Party affiliation of those over 30 from a Democratic family
Percent
Democrats
Independents
Republicans
Party affiliation of those under 30 from a Democratic family
Percent
Democrats
Independents
Republicans
Party affiliation of those over 30 from a Republican family
Percent
Republicans
Democrats
Independents
Party affiliation of those under 30 from a Republican family
Percent
Republicans
Independents
Democrats
1952 1958 1964 1968 70 1972
1974 is not included because the appropriate questions were not asked

FIGURE 4.12. Intergenerational party transmission, 1952–1972

commitment of citizens. Among the new voters entering the electorate at the end of the 1960s, the partisan ties of their parents are not much of a guide. About half have abandoned those ties. But when they do, it is to become Independents, not to switch to the opposition party.

Conclusion

Citizen affiliation with the major political parties has been looked at from a number of perspectives: party as a psychological identification, as a guide to electoral choice and candidate evaluation, and as an object of affection. In each case, the data confirm a decline in the attachment of the citizenry to the political parties. Party affiliation, once the central thread connecting the citizen and the political process, is a thread that has certainly been frayed.

However, these changes in the depth and stability of partisan attachment have confirmed one of the conclusions of the early studies that stressed the centrality of partisanship. Partisanship does appear to be a long-term, habitual commitment of individuals. For those in the late 1960s with fully developed and long-term partisan identifications, the erosion of party support is not nearly as dramatic as it is for those with a less firmly rooted party attachment. The data on recent changes make clear that some political events can interfere with the development through the life cycle of that long-term commitment. Such events seem to have been powerful in recent years because they have not only retarded the acquisition or development of a party preference, but they have also reduced the significance of party affiliation for those who remain identified with a party. Citizens who identified with a party are less guided by their affiliation in the seventies than they were in the fifties.

5 Generation, Partisan Shift, and Realignment: A Glance Back to the New Deal

Kristi Andersen

The fact that partisanship has declined for the population as a whole while little change occurs among established voters led us to look back at the last major partisan realignment during the New Deal to see if the process was similar. This consideration of the 1930s represents something of a detour in our exposition. But it has two purposes: we want to see if what we have learned about partisanship from recent studies can, when applied to the 1930s, illuminate the New Deal realignment; and we want, in turn, to use what we learn from the 1930s to highlight the current situation.

The literature dealing with the New Deal realignment—largely based on aggregate voting data—conveys an image of party switching by individuals on a grand scale. The emphasis of these studies is often on *a* critical election rather than on a longer-term *process* of realignment; change takes place through crisis-induced shifts in individual party loyalties. For example, James Sundquist writes that "the millions of voters who switched from the Republican to the Democratic party . . . made the latter the clear majority party for the first time in eight years." The urban, predominately ethnic voters who became the backbone of this new Democratic majority were converted from Republicans to Democrats between 1928 and 1936 "and stayed switched."[1]

The data appear to support this interpretation. The Democrats received only 35 percent of the two-party presidential vote in 1920 and 1924. (In the latter year they received only 29 percent of the total vote.) The dramatic and rapid increase in the Democrats' share of the vote to 59 percent in 1932 and 62 percent in 1936 would seem to require a massive conversion of Republicans. Such conversions would appear to contradict what recent survey-based studies tell us about partisanship. It is possible, nevertheless, that partisan ties were less stable in the early period. Voters then may have been more willing to make permanent changes in partisanship. We would argue, however, that the nature of partisan attachment—in particular the habitual and unchanging character of party identification for the majority of citizens—was not significantly different in the 1920s and 1930s from what it is today. The shift to a Democratic majority occurred largely through the entry of new groups into the active electorate between 1920 and 1936. These new entrants consisted of young voters entering the electorate and older (largely immigrant or second generation) Americans voting for the first time. The conversion of long-time Republicans played a far less significant role.

Our interpretation is consistent with the generalization that established

---

[1] James L. Sundquist, *Dynamics of the Party System* (Washington: Brookings Institute, 1973), p. 200. Similarly, Burnham defines a "critical realignment" as an event in which "majority parties become minorities; politics which was once competitive becomes noncompetitive, [because] large blocks of the active electorate—minorities, to be sure, but perhaps involving as much as a fifth to a third of the voters—shift their partisan allegiance." Walter Dean Burnham, *Critical Elections and the Mainsprings of American Politics* (New York: W. W. Norton, 1970). See also Angus Campbell and others, *Elections and the Political Order* (New York: Wiley, 1966), p. 61. In short, as Key and Munger put it, "the cumulation of individual shifts in partisanship" is virtually the only explanation given for the massive realignment which took place in the 1920s and 1930s. V. O. Key and F. Munger, "Social Determinism and Electoral Decisions: The Case of Indiana," in Eugene Burdick and Arthur J. Brodbeck, *The American Voting Behavior* (New York: Free Press, 1959). See also W. Philip Shively, "A Reinterpretation of the New Deal Realignment," *Public Opinion Quarterly*, 34 (1971–72), 621–624; Jerome Clubb and Howard Allen, "The Cities and the Election of 1928: Partisan Realignment?" *American Historical Review*, 74 (1969), 1205–1220; V. O. Key, "Secular Realignment and the Party System," *Journal of Politics*, 21 (1959), 198–210. Sundquist describes these presumed converts more specifically: "The millions who switched parties between 1928 and 1936 and stayed switched can be identified most readily by place of residence. They were concentrated in the great industrial cities of the North . . . Within the cities, the Republicans-turned-Democrats were predominantly of the working class" (pp. 200, 202). According to both election returns and early surveys, after 1932 (or 1936) Catholics, Jews, various immigrant groups, and the urban working class were more homogeneously Democratic than ever before, or, in some cases, predominantly Democratic for the first time. This has been taken to imply that many individuals belonging to these groups discarded their Republican attachments and became Democrats during the political crisis.

party ties do not change. We suggest that replacement of the electorate rather than conversion plays the major role. Others have suggested a similar interpretation, though there has been little analysis to support it. The authors of *The American Voter,* for example, state that "our inquiries into the political histories of our respondents lead us to believe that a larger proportion of the [Democratic] gain came from young voters entering the electorate and older people who had previously failed to vote."[2] V. O. Key makes the same point in a footnote to his "Theory of Critical Elections," and Charles Sellers argues in a somewhat more definite and more generally applicable way that "realignment seems not to be caused mainly by permanent changes on the part of people with established party identification (though a good number of voters may shift for one or more elections before returning to the party with which they identify), but rather by a strong shift to the disadvantaged party by younger people and other new voters still in the process of forming their identification."[3]

The electoral replacement hypothesis is consistent with what we know of the political volatility of the young and other politically inexperienced groups. McPhee and Ferguson have used the concept of political "immunization" to refer to the notion that political experience—usually in the form of voting—establishes and reinforces one's commitment to a party. Older voters (or more precisely, those who have voted more often regardless of their age) are less likely to be affected by short-term political stimuli. The greatest source of political instability for an established party system is the arrival of individuals who have little experience or sympathy with the divisions of that party system.[4]

The electorate in the 1920s contained a high proportion of inexperienced and "available" citizens. Just as the present electorate contains a large proportion of people who have no personal memory of the conflicts which

---

[2] Angus Campbell and others, *The American Voter* (New York: Wiley, 1960), p. 153.

[3] V. O. Key, "A Theory of Critical Elections," *Journal of Politics,* 17 (1955), 16–17; Charles Sellers, "The Equilibrium Cycle in Two-Party Politics," *Public Opinion Quarterly,* 29 (1965), 25–26. See also Samuel Lubell, "Revolt of the City," and Carl N. Degler, "American Political Parties and the Rise of the City: An Interpretation," both in Jerome M. Clubb and Howard Allen, *Electoral Change and Stability in American Political History* (New York: Free Press, 1971). A recent discussion that anticipates our analysis is in Philip Converse, "Public Opinion and Voting Behavior," in Fred A. Greenstein and Nelson Polsby, *The Handbook of Political Science* (Reading, Mass.: Addison-Wesley, 1975), pp. 136–144.

[4] William McPhee and Jack Ferguson, "Political Immunization," in William McPhee and Nathan Glaser, *Public Opinion and Congressional Elections* (New York: Free Press, 1966). See also Walter D. Burnham, "Confessionalism and Political Immunization," *Journal of Contemporary History,* 3 (Summer 1972), pp. 1–30, and David Butler and Donald Stokes, *Political Change in Britain* (New York: St. Martins Press, 1969), pp. 44–45.

generated the current Democratic and Republican coalitions, the period of the 1920s was peopled by a good number of citizens who had not been around at the last major party reshuffling at the end of the nineteenth century. Furthermore, voting turnout in the early 1920s was particularly low: only about 44 percent of the voting-age population went to the polls in the presidential elections of 1920 and 1924. The pool of nonimmunized, that is, electorally inexperienced, citizens was unusually large.

Several factors contributed to this large pool of available citizens. Suffrage was extended to women in 1920, but many women, in particular those of foreign stock, did not immediately take advantage of this newly won right.[5] A second factor, not as significant numerically, was immigration. The major wave of southern and eastern European immigration crested in the first decade of the century, but it has been estimated that the process of naturalization took an average of ten to twelve years. Thus many immigrants became U.S. citizens in the 1920s. Third, and perhaps most important, a large cohort of children of the turn of the century immigrants was coming of age during this period.[6] These people were doubly nonimmunized, as they had no personal political experience and had not inherited a party identification from their immigrant parents.

In short, there was in the 1920s an unusually large pool of nonvoting, politically inexperienced, and uncommitted individuals available for mobilization. The young (in particular the children of immigrants), newly naturalized citizens, and women all contributed to the pool of nonimmunized citizens which the Democratic party was able to mobilize in the space of several elections. The Smith candidacy in 1928, the depression, and Roosevelt's New Deal policies gave the Democrats an appeal among these groups which was translated into votes and into a persisting Democratic majority. It was this mobilization of new populations, rather than conversion of Republicans, which we believe constituted the substance of the realignment.

Reconstruction Party Identification

The SRC data, around which most of this book has been written, can be used to assess the relative validity of the conversion and electoral replacement

---

[5] Burnham estimated that the sex differential in turnout in Chicago in the presidential elections of 1916 and 1920 and the mayoral elections of 1915 and 1919 ranged between 20 and 30 percent. Walter Dean Burnham, "Theory and Voting Research," *American Political Science Review*, 68 (September 1974), p. 1013. Even those women who did begin voting in the early 1920s would have been less strongly committed to a particular party (if one accepts the "immunization" argument) than their male counterparts who had been voting for years.

[6] J. B. Tauber and C. Tauber, *People of the U.S.*, Bureau of the Census, 1971, pp. 445 and 116. See also Lubell, "Revolt of the City," pp. 3–8.

models. How is this possible? The 1952 survey, the earliest in our series, was conducted a full sixteen years after the New Deal realignment had been completed, and twenty to thirty years after the crucial pre-realignment period of the 1920s. But the surveys contain some relevant data. In eight election studies between 1952 and 1972, almost 15,000 citizens have been interviewed.[7] Many of these people lived through the era we are interested in analyzing. Indeed, of the total number of respondents about 1,800 were of voting age in 1920, and an additional 3,000 had entered the electorate by 1936. Respondents in these surveys were asked not only their current party identification (that is, whether they thought of themselves as Democrats, Republicans, or Independents) but also whether this identification had changed, and if so, when. In short, the 1952–1972 surveys include the right people and the right questions; it is simply a matter of utilizing this information in a way which will enable us to talk about aggregate changes in partisanship during the twenties and thirties.

To this end the eight surveys can be combined so that all respondents are analyzed together as one data set, ignoring the actual years in which they were interviewed. The data on past and present party identification, combined with the respondent's year of birth, enable us to estimate the party preference of an individual in any year since that individual became a voter. For example, let us say a fifty year old respondent interviewed in 1958 says that she is currently a Republican but used to be a Democrat, and reports having made that change in 1934. She would be categorized as a Democrat if the year we were interested in was 1930, but a Republican if we wanted her party identification in 1938. Most people, of course (about 80 percent of our pooled samples), report never having changed their party identification and can be assigned their current party identification at all points in time.[8]

We can aggregate the party identifications of all respondents who were over twenty in a particular year to estimate the distribution of identifications for the population in that year. We must, however, take account of the fact that the age distribution of the population shifts over time. An age cohort which in 1936 constituted 15 percent of the adult population might, twenty years later when a sample is drawn for a survey, constitute only 10 percent. We need to know the distribution of age groups in the population in the year for which we want to describe the country's partisan makeup. We can then

---

[7] The 1962 and 1966 data sets were not used, since questions on past party identification were not asked in those years.

[8] People who say they are supporters of a party and have never changed are not probed to see if they were ever Independents. Some "always Democrats" or "always Republicans" may have considered themselves Independents when they first entered the electorate.

TABLE 5.1. Sample reconstruction of party identification: percentage Democratic of the 1940 population

(A) Age groups: years of birth	(B) Age groups: ages in 1940	(C) Proportion of population in each age group, 1940	(D) Percentage Democratic in each age group, 1940	(E) Contribution of each group to percent Democratic (C × D)
1916–1919	21–24	.109	.581	.075
1911–1915	25–29	.131	.588	.077
1906–1910	30–34	.133	.536	.071
1901–1905	35–39	.113	.543	.061
1896–1900	40–44	.104	.507	.053
1891–1895	45–49	.097	.478	.046
1886–1890	50–54	.085	.491	.042
1881–1885	55–59	.068	.503	.034
1876–1880	60–65	.056	.495	.028
pre–1876	over 65	.106	.445	.047

Reconstructed percent Democratic in 1940 = 52.2

weigh the age cohorts in our pooled sample by the proportion they were of the population in that earlier year.

Table 5.1 is an example of the method by which the party identification of the population can be reconstructed for any given year. In this example, the proportion Democratic for the year 1940 is calculated. The respondents who were in the electorate at that time are first divided into eleven age groups; their years of birth are given in column A, their ages in 1940 in column B. Column C reports the proportion of the population each of these age groups was, according to the 1940 census.[9] Each respondent is assigned a party identification for 1940. This is done by assigning a respondent his current party identification if he reports never changing, and by assigning "changers" to the party that their date of change tells us they supported in 1940. The resultant percentage of Democrats in each age group is reported in column D. To take into account both the extent to which the group identified with the Democrats and the group's relative size in 1940, the proportion Democratic (D) is mulitplied by the group's size (C). The result, in column E, is the

---

[9] Age distributions are from the *1970 Census of Population*, vol. 1, part 1, table 51. For intercensal years, the population in each age group was interpolated; this is the method used by the Census Bureau for such estimations until the late 1940s.

group's contribution to the total amount of Democratic support. For example, the group which was 30 to 34 in 1940 was 13.3 percent of the adult population in 1940. According to the retrospective questions, 53.6 percent of the group were Democrats in 1940. The product of these percentages is the contribution to the Democrats of this age cohort. Summing the entries in column E for all the age cohorts gives the reconstructed proportion of Democratic identifiers in the population in 1940, 52.2 percent.

Some Tests of the Validity of the Reconstruction

There are a number of reasons why we might be uneasy about such retrospective reconstruction. For one thing, people's memories may be inaccurate. This would be particularly devastating for our estimates if there were systematic distortion—for instance, more remember early support for the Democrats than was actually the case because that party is currently favored. Another weakness of the method has to do with death rates. Our weighting procedure deals with overall mortality rates, but it does not deal with the possibility that the supporters of one party may live longer than supporters of the other, thereby leaving us in later years with a biased sample of those who lived in earlier decades.[10]

There are several ways, however, of checking the accuracy of our technique of estimation. First, we can use the SRC data themselves as a standard against which to measure our reconstructed party identifications. Data gathered in 1968, 1970, and 1972 can be used to calculate the citizenry's partisan preferences in 1952 and 1956. The 1952 and 1956 surveys then give us a contemporary measure against which to check our estimates. Table 5.2 compares our reconstruction of partisanship in these two years on the basis of the 1968 through 1972 surveys, with the responses actually obtained in 1952 and 1956.

As can be seen from this table, the estimates are very similar to the actual distributions of party identification in the earlier years. The differences between the reconstruction and the earlier data, in fact, are no larger than the differences between the SRC and Gallup Poll results for party identification in those years (from surveys conducted within three months of one another).[11]

---

[10] See Butler and Stokes, *Political Change,* pp. 263–274; David Segal and others, "Mortality and Political Partisanship: A Test of the Butler-Stokes Hypothesis," *Comparative Politics,* 5 (July 1973), 601–610.

[11] The Gallup differences are in the opposite direction from the SRC data, that is, they report fewer Democrats. Meuller suggests that at least until 1952 and possibly later, Gallup's sample consistently underrepresented lower-class persons and, therefore, Democrats. John E. Mueller, *War, Presidents, and Public Opinion* (New York: Wiley, 1973).

TABLE 5.2. Reconstruction of 1952 and 1956 party identification compared with SRC party identification (percentages)

1952	Democratic	Independent	Republican
Estimate based on our reconstruction from later data	51	18	31
Actual data from SRC 1952 study	49	23	28

1956	Democratic	Independent	Republican
Estimate based on our reconstruction from later data	51	20	29
Actual data from SRC 1956 study	45	24	30

The slight underestimation of Independents is to be expected, since the one partisan shift we cannot tap adequately through our reconstructions is from Independent to Democrat or Republican. Thus a few individuals who may have been independent in 1952 or 1956 but who were, for example, moved to identify with the Democrats during the Kennedy era, would be counted as having always been Democrats.[12] The slight discrepancy between the reconstruction and the contemporary data, which shows a smaller Democratic advantage, especially in 1956, is also explainable. Party identification if asked close to election time may reflect the vote intentions of some respondents rather than their underlying party loyalty, and 1952 and 1956 were, of course, Republican presidential victories.

We can also compare our reconstruction with some earlier data. The earliest questions on party identification were asked in 1937 by the Gallup organization. Table 5.3 compares our reconstruction for 1937 with the party identification data from the Gallup study of that year. The figures are remarkably similar; the reconstruction concurs almost completely with the proportion Democratic, Republican, and Independent reported by Gallup in 1937.

Finally, we can deal more directly with the possibilities of systematic

---

12 We assume that those who report never changing their identification acquired that identification upon entering the electorate. We will modify that assumption shortly.

TABLE 5.3. Reconstruction of 1937 party identification compared with Gallup 1937 party identification (percentages)

	Democratic	Independent	Republican
Reconstruction based on later data	53	12	34
Gallup 1937	53	16	32

memory distortion and unequal mortality rates between the two parties. This can be done by reconstructing the 1937 party identification twice: once with the surveys conducted in 1952, 1956, and 1958, and once with the surveys conducted in 1968, 1970, and 1972. If either systematic bias exists—biased memory or differential death rates—the reconstruction based on the earlier surveys should be more accurate.

Table 5.4 presents the Gallup 1937 data on party identification; a reconstruction of the 1937 electorate based on the surveys conducted in 1952, 1956, and 1958; and a reconstruction based on the 1968, 1970, and 1972 surveys. The differences between the two reconstructions are minimal. If there is any tendency for Republicans to outlive Democrats, using a group of relatively elderly people (as is done with the 1968–70–72 data) to reconstruct party identification at an earlier time would produce a distortion in a Republican direction. The fact that the estimate of 1937 party identification using the 1952–56–58 data is in fact more Republican than the estimate using the 1968–70–72 data indicates that this kind of distortion is not taking place. The same logic leads to a rejection of the hypothesis of systematic bias in memory. Any such bias would be more apparent in the later surveys.

TABLE 5.4. Reconstruction of 1937 party identification based on 1951–1956–1958 data and on 1968–1970–1972 data, compared with Gallup 1937 party identification (percentages)

	Democratic	Independent	Republican
Reconstruction (1952–58 data)	53	12	35
Reconstruction (1968–72 data)	54	14	32
Gallup 1937	53	16	32

Changes in Party Identification, 1920–1974

The memory data appear accurate. We can now present the reconstruction of party identification based on them. Figure 5.1 presents the reconstructed party identification of Americans from 1920 through 1948 and the party identification reported by respondents in the SRC election studies from 1952 through 1972 and in a Market Opinion Research study of 1974. It documents clearly the dramatic changes in the party system during the past sixty years. In contrast to the strong two-party system of 1920, the United States party system now has as many Independents as Democrats, while the Republicans claim the loyalty of less than 20 percent of the population. The change can be divided into several periods.

Period 1: Realignment, 1920–1936. In 1920 each party, according to our reconstruction, claimed almost the same number of identifiers, and less

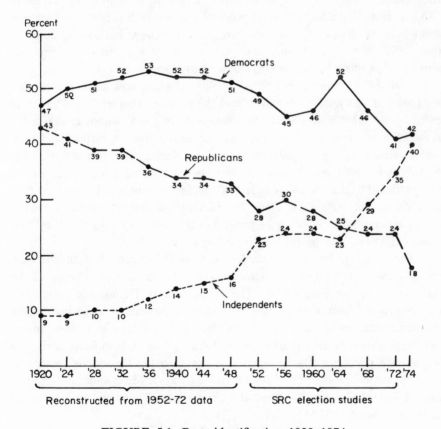

FIGURE 5.1. Party identification, 1920–1974

than 10 percent of the population was Independent. Over the next sixteen years the proportion of Independents remained basically stable, while the Democrats gained ground steadily at the expense of the Republicans. By 1936, the reconstruction estimates the population to have become 53 percent Democratic, 36 percent Republican, and 12 percent Independent—a thirteen percentage point redistribution in the strength of the two major parties.

Period 2: Stabilization, 1936–1952. In the next period Democratic support declined slightly. The proportion of Republicans also continued to decline, though not as precipitously as in the preceding period. In fact, the Republican share of the electorate remained fairly stable from 1936 to 1948, which accords with Sundquist's description of the "aftershocks" of the New Deal realignment, during which Republicans as well as the Democrats made gains in some areas.[13] Perhaps the most interesting point to be made about this era is that once the realignment had been accomplished, the number of Independents began to grow, rising from 12 percent in 1936 to 23 percent in 1952. It is as if the highly potent political issues which produce the realignment polarize the population into two partisan camps, but having done so, their salience wanes. The partisan pull is less strong, and once again the number of people who are loyal to neither party grows.

Period 3: No net change, 1952–1964. We are now back to the contemporary data which are familiar from the previous chapter. The 1950s and early 1960s show a decline of the Democrats in the Eisenhower era and a resurgence at the time of the Kennedy administration. A further slight decrease occurs in the proportion of the population who identify with the Republicans, but there is no major alteration in the relative strength of the two parties. The proportion of Independents in the population remains stable. It is during this essentially static period that the first and most influential survey-based voting studies were produced. It is not surprising that they concluded that party attachment was a life-long commitment.

Period 4: Decline of the parties, 1964–1974. Since 1964 the partisan composition of the population has undergone the most rapid change of the sixty years we are considering. The proportion of Democratic supporters dropped from a high of 52 percent in 1964 to 42 percent ten years later, while the Republican party suffered a six percentage point drop in support in the two Watergate-saturated years between 1972 and 1974 (proportionately, the Republican decline was a little more severe than the Democrats', since the Republicans began the period with a smaller base). Meanwhile, the proportion of Independents in the population grew from 23 percent to 40 percent between 1964 and 1974.

---

[13] Sundquist, *Dynamics,* chap. 17.

The Role of New Cohorts in the New Deal Realignment

We have hypothesized that the New Deal realignment represented a gradual process of consolidation of Democratic support based on the mobilization of new voters rather than on the permanent conversion of Republicans.[14] Our data allow us to estimate the impact on the aggregate changes of various age cohorts. We can use the retrospective questions to calculate the party identification distribution of a particular four-year age cohort when that cohort was twenty-one to twenty-four years old. Since our concern is with one age cohort at a time, no weights need be involved. Figure 5.2 displays the party preferences of entering cohorts—based on contemporary surveys from 1952 onward, and on the respondents' recollections for the earlier years. The data show, for example, that the age cohort which was first able to vote in 1948 was 51 percent Democratic, 30 percent Republican, and 15 percent Independent. This figure demonstrates the responsiveness of the young to the political temper of the times.[15] The entering cohort of 1920 is the most Republican of any cohort; the entering cohort of 1936 is the most Democratic.

Let us look more closely at the cohorts who entered the electorate around the time of the New Deal realignment. Table 5.5 compares the youngest voters in each election year between 1920 and 1940 with the total

---

[14] Many observers have commented on the significance of "political generations." Butler and Stokes, for example, who attribute the phenomenon to "the fact that those who are young in a given period are exposed to common political influences," point out that the distribution of party support in Britain in the mid-1960s "can be accounted for in terms of the impress of early political forces on the young and the preservation of these forces in the hardening allegiances of later years. We must ask not how old the elector is but when it was that he was young." *Political Change,* pp. 61 and 51. See also Philip Converse, "Of Time and Partisan Stability," *Comparative Political Studies,* 2 (July 1969), 139–171; Herbert H. Hyman, *Political Socialization* (Glencoe: Free Press, 1959), pp. 125–126; Ronald Inglehart, "The Silent Revolution in Europe: Intergenerational Change in Post-Industrial Societies," *American Political Science Review,* 65 (1971), 991–1107.

[15] Our main interest in figure 5.2 is what it tells us about the New Deal period. But figure 5.2 also highlights the impact that new voters may have on the shape of the electorate at various points in time. For example, the decreasing frequency with which the Democrats during the last two Roosevelt administrations recruited new young voters, and the concomitant resurgence of the Republican party among the same group, contributed to the decline in Democratic support from 1948 to 1956 and the stability of Republican support in the fifties. Similarly, the group that entered the electorate in 1964 was 39 percent Independent—11 percentage points more Independent than the group that first voted in 1960, and 14 percentage points more so than the population. This marked increase in Independents among a group that was at the time 9 percent of the adult population is in good part responsible for the subsequent growth in the proportion of Independents in the population as a whole. In addition, it is obvious from figure 5.2 that the Republicans' continuing inability to win new voters to their side has had a cumulative, damaging effect on Republican Strength over the years.

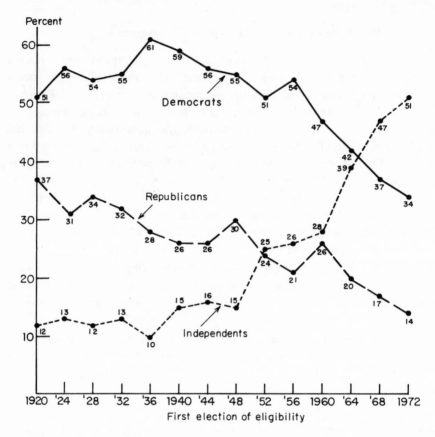

FIGURE 5.2. Party identification of age cohorts at entrance into electorate, 1920–1972

electorate as we have reconstructed its party identification. The youngest age groups during the entire era were around five percentage points more Democratic than the population as a whole. Sixty-one percent of those who were twenty-one to twenty-four in 1936, for example, recall being Democrats at that time, while the population at that time was only 53 percent Democratic. What is more surprising, the groups which entered the electorate in 1920, 1924, and 1928—at a time when the Republican party should have been most successful in recruiting young citizens—were also substantially more Democratic than the population.

If the young citizens during the twenties and thirties had entered the electorate with the same partisan makeup as the rest of the citizenry, substantial conversion of Republicans would have been necessary to effect the redistribution of party support which occurred between 1920 and 1936. Instead,

TABLE 5.5. Reconstructed percent Democratic of
21–24 year olds and population, 1920–1940

| Year | Percent Democratic | |
	21–24	Population
1920	51	47
1924	56	50
1928	54	51
1932	55	52
1936	61	53
1940	59	52

each successive group which came of age in the twenties was different (more Democratic, less Republican) than the populace which it joined. This consistent Democratic bias in the partisanship of the young had the cumulative effect of changing the partisan balance from a relatively even division to a clear Democratic majority.[16]

The voting behavior of the young during the realignment era also supports the notion of a youthful surge toward the Democrats as a prime contributory factor to the realignment. Data on respondents' recalled first vote are in table 5.6. It shows that of those who cast their first presidential vote in 1932, and were twenty-eight or under at the time, 80 percent voted for Roosevelt.[17] In 1936, while FDR received 62 percent of the two-party vote nationally, the under-twenty-eight first voters gave him an extraordinary majority of 85 percent.

The data in table 5.6 pose a puzzle, however. In contrast to the voters coming of age in the New Deal period, young voters who came of age in the twenties remember giving proportionately fewer votes to the Democratic

---

[16] One can easily, if crudely, estimate the amount of partisan redistribution accounted for by the bias of the young rather than by conversion. By starting with the partisan split we estimate for 1920, applying the appropriate mortality rates to both Democrats and non-Democrats, and adding to the population entering cohorts who are proportionately Democratic and non-Democratic (see figure 5.2), one can produce over 60 percent of the increase in Democratic strength which occurred according to the reconstruction. This is a conservative estimate, however, of the role of the young, since the mortality rates for Republicans, a generally older group, are bound to have been higher than for Democrats.

[17] These figures and subsequent data on respondents' first vote are based on answers to questions asked, unfortunately, only in the 1952 election study: "Do you remember who you voted for the first time you voted for president?" and "Do you remember what year that was?"

TABLE 5.6. Recalled first vote of voters 28 or under, 1920–1940, compared with national vote

	Percent Democratic among first voters[a]	Percent Democratic of national two-party vote
1920	30	36
1924	28	35
1928	47	41
1932	80	59
1936	85	62
1940	66	55

[a] Data from SRC 1952 election study.

presidential candidates than did the population as a whole. This seems inconsistent with the high proportion of Democratic identifiers that we found among those who were young in the twenties. A similar discrepancy occurs when the general population is considered. Our party identification reconstruction in figure 5.1 shows a Democratic majority as early as 1920, yet the Democrats did not win a majority of the presidential or congressional vote until 1932. Let us consider these apparent contradictions.

Realignment as the Mobilization of Potential Democrats

There is a gap in the data on which the reconstruction of party identification is based. Democrats are asked whether they ever considered themselves Republicans; Republicans are asked whether they ever considered themselves Democrats; and Independents are asked if they were ever Republicans or Democrats. Those who presently identify with a party are not, however, asked whether they used to be Independents. Nor are party identifiers asked (and perhaps this would be an impossible question) when they began to regard themselves as Democrats or Republicans. The fact that a Democrat says he has "never changed" his party identification can have varied meanings. On the one hand, it can mean that his parents were Democrats, that he has always considered himself a Democrat, and that he began voting for Democrats as soon as he was legally able to do so. On the other hand, it could mean that he has never identified with the Republican party, but did not come to think of himself as a Democrat until age thirty or forty. If this person had been queried about his party affiliation at age twenty-five, he would probably have said Independent or no party rather than Democrat.[18]

Suppose we assume that a person who reports never switching party identification assumed that identification, not when he came of voting age, but when he cast his first vote. This changes our estimate of party identification in the 1920s substantially. Nonvoting was especially high in the 1920s, and it is very likely that these nonvoters were disproportionately citizens who had recently become of voting age. The voting turnout of newly enfranchised women was very low in the twenties. Only about one-third of the women who had received the franchise in 1920 report voting in that year (according to the data from the 1952 study where questions about early voting behavior are asked). Many (24 percent of those who did eventually participate in a presidential election) waited until the 1928, 1932, or 1936 elections to cast their first ballot.[19] In general, the majority of people who came of age in the 1920s did not vote until much later. Of those who came of age between 1920 and 1928, 39 percent did not vote until at least the third election in which they were eligible.

The question asked in 1952 on respondents' first vote can be used to calculate the proportion of each entering cohort between 1920 and 1940 who voted in the first election in which they were eligible. Figure 5.3 presents these data for respondents who in 1952 categorized themselves as Republicans or Democrats who had never switched. This figure shows clearly that the "never switched" Democrats comprised the majority of the youthful nonvoters in the 1920s. Of the people who came into the electorate between 1924 and 1928, for example, 39 percent were "never switched" Democrats who did not vote in the 1924 election, while only 10 percent were "never switched" Republicans who did not vote. The young Republicans who voted in 1924 outnumbered their Democratic contemporaries. The higher Republican participation holds true for the entire decade; it explains the discrepancy between the large proportion of Democrats we seem to find among the young of the 1920s and the predominantly Republican voting behavior of the "first voters" of that era.

---

[18] This does not alter the important fact that this person was never a Republican. He may have identified with the Democrats ever since he came of age, or he may have been mobilized to support the Democrats after having been Independent or apolitical for many years. But he is not a Democrat who switched from the Republican side.

[19] Burner's data support this: "Part of the explanation for Smith's strength in the immigrant cities," he contends, "was an apparent rise in voting among Roman Catholic women." He describes heavily Italian precincts in Boston where female registration rose by 29 percent in 1928, and Irish precincts where the rise in female voting was comparable. David Burner, *The Politics of Provincialism: The Democratic Party in Transition, 1918–1932* (New York: Knopf, 1968), p. 299.

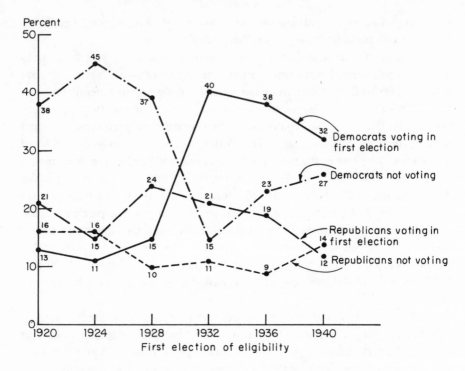

FIGURE 5.3. Voting behavior of Democrats and Republicans at age of entry into electorate, 1920–1940

The voting behavior of "never switched" Democrats who enter the electorate changes after 1932: they voted as soon as they were able. Over 70 percent of those who were twenty-one to twenty-four and who are "never switched" Democrats voted in 1932. In both 1932 and 1936, there were twice as many voting Democrats as voting Republicans among the youngest citizens.

Let us return to our assumption that an individual who reports he has always supported a party and has never switched took on that partisan identification not when he entered the electorate but at the time of his first vote. The data just presented would mean that a large number of people came of political age in the 1920s but did not take on a party identification because they did not vote. When they were mobilized to vote in 1928 or 1932 or 1936, most voted Democratic and also took on a Democratic identification which they never dropped. (This is why they appear in the later surveys as people who have always been Democrats.) In addition, another large group of voters come of age between 1928 and 1936. They voted as soon as they were legally able and most of these people also became Democrats. The surge in the Democratic vote in 1932 and 1936 comes from these two newly mobilized groups. They were young, substantially female, urban, working class, and foreign stock.[20]

Party Identification and Voting: Another Look at the Reconstruction

We can now revise our estimate of past party identification in the light of this argument by using responses to the 1952 question on first vote. In 1928, for example, we have estimated that the population was 51 percent Democratic, 39 percent Republican, and 10 percent Independent. But many of these people had never voted in a presidential election. The 1952 survey tells us when Democrats and Republicans of a particular age began to vote. We know, for example, that in 1928, 28 percent of the Democrats just eligible to vote did so. And only 40 percent of the Democrats aged forty to forty-four in 1928 had voted in a presidential election in that year or previously. In this way we can arrive at the proportion of nonvoting and voting Democrats (and Republicans) in each of the age groups we used to reconstruct party identification for 1928. The same method of weighting each age group according to its share of the 1928 population is followed to derive an estimate of the proportion of voting and nonvoting Democrats or Republicans in that year. In this case, we estimate that 39 percent of the 1928 Democrats had voted in a presidential election at some time, but 61 percent had not done so. The nonvoters can be labeled "potential" Democrats, as we know they will eventually think of themselves as Democrats. But in 1928 they are likely to have been apolitical. In the same way, we calculate that 33 percent of the 1928

---

[20] Aggregate data as well as survey data support this interpretation. It was precisely in the urban, highly foreign-stock areas that the increase in voter turnout, and corresponding Democratic gains, are most apparent. In eight poor, predominantly foreign-stock wards in Pittsburgh, for example, turnout in presidential elections in the twenties averaged 36 percent of the eligible voters. This figure changed to 54 percent in the years 1932–1944. The proportion of the total population voting Republican in these wards remained stable during the entire period, from 1920 to 1944, but the Democrats' portion of that population increased from 8 percent in 1920 to a high of 52 percent in 1940. The same trend can be seen in native stock and other wards in Pittsburgh, but it is most pronounced in poor, foreign-stock, and black areas. David Prindle, "Mobilization and Realignment in Pittsburgh, 1920–1924," unpublished manuscript, Massachusetts Institute of Technology, 1975. Similar results obtain in Chicago ethnic precincts. The number of Republican votes cast in lower-middle-class and working-class Polish, Czechoslovakian, Lithuanian, Yugoslavian, and Italian neighborhoods remained steady between 1920 and 1936. The total number of votes cast in presidential elections, however, increased by 94 percent during this period, despite a decline in the number of eligible voters. The Democratic share of the electorate grew accordingly. Though there were undoubtedly some Republican-to-Democratic switches in these neighborhoods, the data indicate that the increasingly Democratic character of their vote resulted primarily from the mobilization of those who had not previously voted. Kristi Andersen, "Political Generations and Partisan Change," Ph.D. dissertation, University of Chicago, 1976.

Republicans were potential Republicans who had not yet voted. Thus the 1928 population is broken down in the following manner: 20 percent Democrats; 26 percent Republicans; 32 percent potential Democrats; 13 percent potential Republicans; 10 percent Independents.

In figure 5.4 we present a reconstruction of the electorate into these categories across all the years since 1920. The data account quite well for the changes that took place in the party alignment during that period. At the beginning of the time period in 1920, a mere 14 percent of the population consisted of Democrats who had voted in presidential elections. 34 percent were potential Democrats who did not vote. The number of potential Republicans was also greater in 1920 than the number of voting Republicans. In all we estimate that in 1920, 34 percent of the citizens were voters, 57 percent were nonvoters, and 9 percent were Independents. This agrees roughly with Burnham's characterization of the twenties as a decade in which "hardly more than one-third of the eligible adults were . . . core voters. Another one-sixth were peripheral voters and fully one-half remained outside the active voting universe altogether."[21]

By 1940, the Democrats' position had completely reversed itself, with 34 percent of the population classed as voting Democrats and only 14 percent as potential Democrats. Nonvoting among Republicans had decreased at about the same rate as nonvoting among Democrats. However, since the number of Republicans in the population had decreased (from 43 percent to 34 percent), the proportion of voting Republicans increased only six percentage points between 1920 and 1940 compared with the 20 percent growth among Democrats.

In summary, the changes in party identification and voting behavior which took place between 1920 and 1940 are the following: The proportion of Independents remains stable during the twenties, but increases from 10 percent to 14 percent between 1932 and 1940. Voting Republicans are also a relatively stable segment of the population, varying between 20 and 27 percent and averaging 24 percent during the twenty years. The greatest increase in this group occurred between 1924 and 1928, which corresponds to the particularly large Republican presidential vote cast in 1928. In contrast to the stability shown by the voting Republican identifiers, Democratic voters more than doubled in these years, from 14 percent to 35 percent of the population. The largest increment was between 1928 and 1932, though it was not until 1936, according to this estimate, that Democratic voters outnumbered Republican voters. (A high Republican defection rate, as well as a highly Demo-

---

[21] Walter Dean Burnham, "The Changing Shape of the American Political Universe," *American Political Science Review,* 59 (March 1965), 23.

Percent of
Population

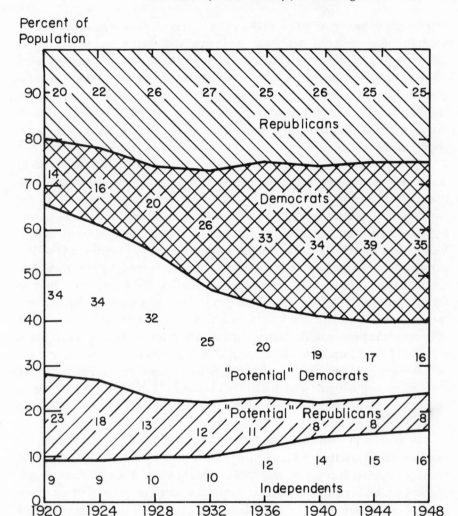

FIGURE 5.4. Party identification and voting in the electorate, 1920–1940

cratic Independent vote, in the 1932 election may have accounted for much of Roosevelt's margin of victory. In the 1936 election 20 percent of FDR's total vote, according to a 1937 Gallup poll, came from Republicans and Independents.)

Available Voters, Then and Now

A major source of the surge of Democratic votes in the thirties was the group of potential Democrats who had been such a large proportion of the electorate in the 1920s. They were an available pool that was mobilized to

vote by Smith and more so by FDR. (The "delayed" first voters who partici-
pated in the elections of 1932 and 1936 gave Roosevelt nearly 90 percent of
their vote in each year.) In addition, the new cohorts who came of age after
1928 promptly began voting and voted largely Democratic. These changes
propelled the Democrats into their majority position. Contrary to many past
interpretations of the New Deal realignment, our analysis shows that conversion of those with established Republican loyalties was not a significant component of the realignment.

The central role played by the young and by other nonimmunized or
nonparticipant citizens in the New Deal realignment raises interesting questions about the similarities between the 1920s and the present era. In the
earlier period, our reconstruction locates a large number of nonvoters, mostly
highly concentrated among those who later supported the Democratic party.
Voting data from the twenties confirms our survey-based impressions of low
participation: turnout in both presidential and congressional elections was
substantially lower than in previous years and, by and large, lower than in
subsequent years. The rate of nonvoting in recent years is not as high as in the
twenties, though turnout for both presidential and congressional contests has
been somewhat lower in the sixties than it was in the fifties, and 1972 saw a
substantial drop in presidential turnout. The gap between the young and the
rest of the population in terms of voting is large, however: 66 percent of the
over thirty population voted in 1972, but only 47 percent of eighteen to
twenty year olds and 50 percent of twenty-one to twenty-four year olds did
so.[22]

A more important similarity between the twenties and the present is the
low level of attachment to the parties in each period. In 1974, 40 percent of
the U.S. population could be regarded as Independent. Many of these people
are, in fact, nonimmunized citizens: they are young (nearly half of the Independents in 1974 were under thirty-five) and have no sustained experience of
support for one or the other party. Our data do not allow us to determine the
extent to which the huge numbers of nonvoters in the twenties considered
themselves Independents. But if even half the nonvoters of 1920 are added to
the 9 percent of the population which we estimate to have been Independent
then, the proportion of Independents in the population rises to 38 percent,
approximately the present level. Then, as now, a large pool of nonimmunized
citizens were available for mobilization to new partisan commitments.

Along with the nonpartisanship which the electorates of the 1920s and
the 1970s have in common, they share also a certain electoral volatility. In

---

[22] *Statistical Abstract of the U.S.,* 1974, p. 437.

the late 1960s and the 1970s even those citizens who still considered themselves supporters—even strong supporters—of one of the major parties were
far more willing to defect from their party in their vote than were party
supporters in the 1950s. This situation is highly reminiscent of the 1920–1930
period as Burnham has described it, with its high incidence of split ticket
voting and partisan swing from election to election.[23]

But the two periods differ as well. The party balance in the 1970s is
vastly different from what it was in the 1920s. If, again, we assume that half
the nonvoters of the twenties could be considered "true" Independents, and
assign the remainder to the Democrats and Republicans, the result approaches a 50/50 split among identifiers. The New Deal, acting on this partisan division, created a new, dominant majority party. But the Republican
party was able to maintain itself as a substantial opposition party. Currently,
Democratic identifiers are 70 percent of all identifiers. A realignment which
moved the unaffiliated to the Democrats would leave the Republicans in an
unprecedentedly weak position. We would have, at best, a one and a half
party system.

Another difference between the two periods is that the Independents of
the 1970s are not the same as those of the 1920s. Though both groups are
predominantly young, the current crop of Independents is better educated and
more likely to be politically sophisticated. Whereas in the twenties one has the
impression of a mass of apathetic citizens to whom either of the parties might
have plausibly appealed, in the seventies there appears to be a more prin-
cipled rejection of parties. This may make the capture of the unaffiliated by
one of the major parties exceedingly difficult.

Our retrospect of the New Deal realignment highlights some features of
the present time when a large available population exists. We shall return to
this theme in our conclusion when we consider some alternative futures for
the party system.

---

[23] Burnham, *Critical Elections and the Mainsprings of American Politics,* chap. 5.

6 | New Issues

For the public of the late fifties, party was the guide to political behavior. It no longer is. What, if anything, guides the political behavior of the individual? In this chapter and in the following three, we want to explore the role of political issues, as an alternative to party, as a guide to political behavior. In the fifties, citizens thought of political issues in the crudest of terms; they had inconsistent sets of issue positions, and their issue positions were relatively unrelated to the vote.

As party has declined, issues have become important to the voter. The reasons are simple: new issues have appeared and the meaning of old issues has changed. This in turn has affected the ways citizens think about politics—not what issue positions individuals hold, but the way in which they conceptualize such issues, the coherence of their issue positions, and the extent to which they are guided in their vote by their issue positions.

Can we show that modes of thinking change in response to changing political problems and issues? Such a demonstration, plausible though the connection may seem, is not easy. In effect, we are trying to explain changes we observe in the data on citizen attitudes and behavior on the basis of changes not measured and recorded within that data set—on the basis of changes in the external world of politics.

But it is worth trying to locate the connection, for if such a connection exists it has important implications for the nature of mass belief systems. It means that the ways in which the citizenry thinks about politics—the categories used, the calculations that go into political choices—are quite flexible and more sensitive to the real world of politics than interpretations of citizen attitudes as rooted in long-term social and psychological characteristics would lead one to expect.

The Changing Issues

The fact that the first major interpretations of American politics on the basis of systematic surveys took place in the Eisenhower years is, as we have suggested, fortuitous. The studies began then for reasons independent of the particular political configuration of the time. The timing of the research was probably due to the intellectual interests of certain scholars, the willingness of foundations to support such work, and the development in previous years of survey research technology. But the fact that those studies took place at that particular moment had profound implications for the results of those studies. The late Eisenhower years were—as the authors of *The American Voter* were aware[1]—a period of comparative political blandness. There were few issues of consequence. And Eisenhower's leadership style was such as to mute whatever issues did exist. With few significant issues, one cannot expect issue coherence or a close relation of issues and the vote.

In contrast, the issues that emerge in the 1960s foster coherence in citizen attitudes and a greater use of issue positions as criteria for political evaluations. The characteristics of the new issues are: (1.) they are issues that catch the attention of the public; (2.) they are issues that penetrate into the personal lives of citizens; (3.) they are issues that cluster together. (Why they cluster is somewhat uncertain. The various issues are not always logically connected one to another. Rather, they may come to the citizen as issue bundles because someone has packaged them that way; either the political parties or candidates take more coherent stands on the issues, or the media present the issues in such a way that connections across them can be seen.)

The Rise of New Issues

The issues that emerge in the 1960s are well known. But it may be helpful to see the rise of new issues through the eyes of the American public.

---

[1] Angus Campbell and others, *The American Voter* (New York: Wiley, 1960), p. 12.

From the late 1940s to the present, the Gallup Poll has asked its respondents what they consider to be the most important problem facing the nation. The question is not an ideal way of obtaining information on the political problems that most disturb people. The question catches whatever is on the top of a citizen's mind. One does not know how seriously he or she takes the particular problem that is mentioned. Furthermore, the fact that a problem is not mentioned does not mean that it does not exist. If a particularly exciting issue breaks into the media it will be cited by many as the most important problem, but earlier problems may remain as important as they had been previously.

Nevertheless, that disadvantage of the question is, from another perspective, an advantage. The question allows the citizen spontaneously to tell what is on his mind; he is offered no suggestions. The answer should give some idea of changes in issue focus.

The data on the "most important problem" are in table 6.1. The problem cited by most citizens in each year is in boldface. There is quite a bit of volatility in the issue that is considered most important, but some general patterns appear:

1949–1950: In the years before the Eisenhower administration, domestic economic issues and issues of foreign policy dominate, sometimes one being more important, sometimes the other.

The Eisenhower years: The data for the Eisenhower years confirm the relative political blandness of that period. The most important issues throughout the period tend to be issues of foreign policy—war, the threat of (foreign) communism, the atomic bomb. These are, of course, important issues but they are, we believe, the kinds of issues to which citizens react as spectators. They are not issues that cut deeply into one's daily life. Nor are they the kinds of issues that clearly divide party from party or one group of citizens from another. Rather such issues tend to unify the public—especially when the president is as popular a figure as Eisenhower with a reputation for effectiveness in international affairs.

It is interesting, furthermore, that the one potentially divisive issue of the 1950s—the issue of domestic communism—fades from the scene during the first Eisenhower administration. In the first years of the Eisenhower incumbency, close to one out of five Americans mention this problem; by Eisenhower's second term—at the time of our basepoint—it was gone. Issues of the domestic economy, on the other hand, remain a steady but secondary source of concern throughout the period.[2]

---

[2] As *The American Voter* (p. 526, figure 19–1) indicates, the "attitudinal force" of domestic issues was roughly equal to that of foreign issues in the 1952 election (the

From Kennedy to Johnson, 1960–1964: We have no data for 1960 and 1961, but we do have measurements in 1962, 1963, and 1964. This is a particularly crucial period for our analysis, for it is the time when we see the rise in the level of issue coherence among the public. What is most striking during this period is the sharp jump upward in the salience of the race issue. The change takes place between the measurements taken in March and September of 1963. In the March 1963 survey 4 percent of the population mention race-related problems as being the most salient for the nation, a figure similar to measurements taken previously. In the September 1963 survey 52 percent mention race. (One need only look at the headlines for the late spring of 1963 to see the source of this sudden surge of concern—the Birmingham riots in April and May; Governor Wallace confronting the Kennedy administration "at the schoolhouse door"; the assassination of Medgar Evers.) The proportion mentioning race as the most important problem stays high until it is pushed from top place by Vietnam. (And one would guess that its replacement by Vietnam as the most important problem does not represent a decline in its importance in the public mind.)

The Johnson years, 1964–1968: Vietnam becomes the major issue. Race issues are generally salient as well, though they fluctuate in importance. These two issues crowd out the issue of domestic economy.

The first Nixon administration: Vietnam and race issues fade somewhat from the top position as we see the rise of new issues—crime, drugs, problems of youth. And during this period, the more traditional economic issues begin to come back to the top of the list.

We cannot link the changing salience of issues directly to our various measures of change in the American electorate. But it is clear that these changes parallel the other changes in the electorate. Though it requires a willingness to speculate, we can, we believe, speak of four different kinds of issue—each coming to the fore at a different period of time.

The Traditional Economic Issues

These were most salient in the late Truman years. They are the standard economic issues of welfare, of business versus labor (the Taft-Hartley act was one of the major controversies of the period), of government intervention in the economy. When issues of this sort are at the forefront, they are likely to have the following consequences for citizen attitudes and behavior: They tend to reinforce party ties since the two major parties—at least since the New

---

former having a pro-Democratic impact, the latter a pro-Republican impact). By 1956 the force coming from domestic issues had shrunk substantially while that for foreign issues was as strong (both still pushing in the same directions).

TABLE 6.1. Gallup Poll: What do you think is the most important problem facing the American people today?

Problem	Date	Late Truman years					
		9/ 49	11/ 49	2/ 50	3/ 50	6/ 50	9/ 50
War, communism (abroad), foreign policy, atom bomb		27	29		46	30	56
Economy: unemployment, taxes, cost of living, strikes, labor-management		33	45	59	29	29	24
Civil rights, integration				4		3	
Vietnam, Indochina							
"Communists" (in U.S.)		7	3		8		
Social problems: crime, riots, juvenile delinquency							1
Drugs, youth							

	First Eisenhower term							Second Eisenhower term								
3/ 3	3/ 54	5/ 54	7/ 54	6/ 55	10/ 55	9/ 56	10/ 56	5/ 57	8/ 57	10/ 57	1/ 58	3/ 58	9/ 58	2/ 59	4/ 59	9/ 59
1	39	33	21	50	44	48	48	40	43	39	50	27	44	42	44	51
8	40	17	31	14	22	22	23	21	26	14	18	40	19	28	25	21
1		1	4	4	2	18	12	10		29	4	4	9	10	7	5
		18														
	17	16	4	6	5	3										
	2					2		4		4						

(*continued*)

TABLE 6.1. Gallup Poll: What do you think is the most important problem facing the American people today? (*continued*)

Problem	Date	Kennedy to Johnson					
		4/ 62	3/ 63	9/ 63	4/ 64	6/ 64	8/ 64
War, communism (abroad), foreign policy, atom bomb		63	63	25	41	35	51
Economy: unemployment, taxes, cost of living, strikes, labor-management		18	18	13	14	9	7
Civil rights, integration		6	4	52	41	47	40
Vietnam, Indochina							
"Communists" (in U.S.)							
Social problems: crime, riots, juvenile delinquency		3					
Drugs, youth							

	Johnson administration									First Nixon term							
5/65	9/65	10/65	11/65	5/66	8/67	10/67	5/68	6/68	1/69	3/70	3/71	6/71	8/71	10/71	6/72	9/72
29	26	26	25	15					14	12	7	5		8	8	10
9	8	8	7	20	16	16	12	12	12	10	29	27	51	41	30	30
23	27	17	19	9	24	21	25	13	16	13	16	13	7	7	7	6
25	19	37	33	45	56	50	42	52	40	22	28	33	25	15	32	27
3			2													
2	5	2					15	29	17	8	7	7	12	10	6	8
	2	2							4	30	6	18	6	8	13	11

Deal—have been on opposite sides of the fence on these issues. They lead to political conflict among groups, but—except in times of severe economic depression—not to virulent conflict. The reason is that economic issues, though important, are fundamentally bargainable. They divide class from class, but the classes in the United States do not see themselves as fundamentally opposed one to the other. Furthermore, much of the conflict associated with economic issues is settled outside of the political arena, through collective bargaining between employer and employees, for instance.

The Unifying Issues of Foreign Policy

At the top of the list during the Eisenhower administration and during the Kennedy years (until the outbreak of the race issue) were issues of the cold war, of foreign policy, of arms control and nuclear war. One cannot tell from the Gallup question how deeply citizens were concerned about these issues—even if they perceived them as the most important facing the nation. Other studies have suggested that foreign issues—with the rare exception of an issue like Vietnam that cuts deeply into domestic political life—rarely generate the depth of personal concern that is generated by issues closer to the daily lives of the citizenry. Furthermore, no matter how deep citizen concerns were over this issue, it is not an issue that tends to divide the populace into contending groups. (As table 6.1 shows, few citizens mentioned domestic communism during the Eisenhower years; and, after 1956, it disappears completely.) In general foreign issues, involving as they do the United States versus others, tend to blur or reduce differences domestically.

The Polarizing Issue of Race

Race is probably the most polarizing issue of American politics of the post World War II era. It is a deeply felt issue among blacks. And among whites as well it tends to generate strong and stable attitudes. Converse found that the overtime stability of race attitudes was greater than that for other attitudes.[3] Furthermore, racial issues are divisive. Unlike the boundaries between social classes—which are somewhat unclear and thereby serve to reduce the sharpness of conflict—the race boundaries are clear. Traditional economic issues concern the relative share of the national income that goes to various groups. These can be settled, at least in part, outside of the govern-

---

[3] Philip Converse, "The Nature of Belief Systems in the Mass Public," in David E. Apter, ed., *Ideology and Discontent* (New York: Free Press, 1964).

mental arena. Race issues as they emerged in the 1960s tended to require governmental intervention for their solution. And this increases their virulence.

Lastly, the race issue differs from the standard economic issues in that it does not clearly divide the society along party lines. Blacks, it is true, are heavily involved with the Democratic party, and their involvement grows during the period we are tracing. But the Democratic party also contains a large proportion of whites whose position on racial matters is the polar opposite of the black position. The traditional economic issues divide the population into opposing issue groups and at the same time reinforce party attachment. The race issue divides the population more deeply into opposing issue groups. But it cuts across party ties.

The Issues of Discontent

In the late Johnson years and the Nixon years we find a new set of issues coming to the fore—Vietnam, crime, drugs, and, finally, inflation. These issues are quite different one from another. But they have some important characteristics in common. They do not clearly divide the population into opposing groups: the positions that citizens take on these issues do not clearly coincide with major demographic groupings in the population. Nor do the political parties take sharply opposing views on these issues. They are negative "valence" issues. Most Americans are united in being unhappy about the issues and unhappy with the performance of the government in relation to them. Few citizens favor crime, drugs, inflation, or the war in Vietnam, but they are divided on what to do about these issues. However, the division on what to do about these issues is less clear and based on less intense feeling than is the discontent about the issues.[4] Issues of this sort are likely to generate unhappiness with the government. And they are likely to weaken party ties—simply because neither party is seen as responsive to the issue. They do not generate clear group conflict but they do help create a climate of discontent in which other conflicts can become more intense.

The Number of Issues

The movement from one dominant issue to another over the years is fairly clear. But there is another change revealed on table 6.1 that is worth

---

[4] For data on this point in relation to the war in Vietnam, see Milton Rosenberg, Sidney Verba, and Philip Converse, *Vietnam and the Silent Majority* (New York: Harper and Row, 1970).

noting. The number of different issues cited by the public rises substantially over the years. Up to the beginning of the full Johnson term in 1965, one finds that usually three and sometimes four of the categories of issues are filled on table 6.1. After that, the range of issues widens as is evidenced by the number of coding categories in which responses appear. In the Johnson years and more so in the Nixon years, issues of crime, juvenile delinquency, drugs, youth, and urban disorders join economic issues, race, and Vietnam as worries of the American public. Not only do the issues change but there are more of them.

The Penetration of Issues into the Life Space of the Citizenry

Perhaps more important than the changing substance of political issues is the fact that they have come to have a more direct impact on daily life. The Gallup question on the most important problem facing the nation does not necessarily tell which problems actually penetrate the life space of the citizen. The question focuses attention on the nation and not on the citizen's own personal concerns. Not all national political issues intrude equally into the lives of citizens.

In studies based on the work of Hadley Cantril, however, we do have some better measures of the penetration of political matters into the lives of citizens. In 1959, 1964, and 1971 samples of the public were asked to describe their most important hopes and fears for the future in relation to *their own personal lives.*[5] The questions focus on the life space of the citizen. Thus, we can observe whether citizens see political matters as penetrating into their private lives. Furthermore, the three time points straddle the period in which we are interested.

Table 6.2 reports the responses received to these questions in the three time periods. It is not completely certain what from the list on table 6.2 ought to be considered a political hope or fear and what ought to be considered a purely private hope or fear. But it is possible to isolate some hopes and fears that seem predominantly private ones and some that are clearly political. We have categorized as political those hopes that can be realized or those fears that can be avoided only through some intervention of the government. There is clear indication of the growth in the relevance of political matters to personal life. Most of the categories of hopes that reflect essentially private concerns (good health, aspirations for children, a happy family life, better

---

[5] Albert H. Cantril and Charles W. Roll, Jr., *Hopes and Fears of the American People* (New York: Universe Books, 1971), p. 19.

TABLE 6.2. Personal hopes and fears, 1959, 1964, 1971

Personal hope	1959	1964	1971
Good health for self	40	29	29
Better standard of living	38	40	27
Peace in the world	9	17	19
Achievement of aspirations for children	29	35	17
Happy family life	18	18	14
Good family life	16	25	13
Own house or live in better one	24	12	11
Peace of mind; emotional maturity	5	9	8
Having wealth	2	5	7
Having leisure time	11	5	6
Happy old age	10	8	6
Good job; congenial work	7	9	6
Employment	5	8	6
Freedom from inflation	1	2	6
Other concerns for family	7	4	5

Personal fear	1959	1964	1971
Ill health for self	40	25	28
Lower standard of living	23	19	18
War	21	29	17
Ill health for family	25	27	16
Unemployment	10	14	13
Inflation	1	3	11
Unhappy children	12	10	8
Drugs problem in family	—	—	7
Pollution	—	—	7
Political instability	1	2	5
No fears at all	12	10	5
Crime	—	—	5

Source: Albert H. Cantril and Charles W. Roll, Jr., *Hopes and Fears of the American People* (New York: Universe Books, 1971), p. 19.

house, leisure time, and so forth) diminish somewhat in size as do the categories of essentially private fears (ill health, unhappiness of children). Of course, some of the hopes and fears that seem relatively private—health, a better home, even happy children—may involve governmental intervention to achieve the hopes and avoid the fears. But they tend to be largely private.

In contrast, politically relevant hopes and fears are easier to identify

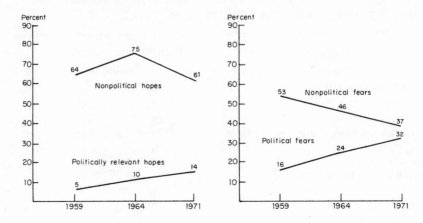

FIGURE 6.1. Personal hopes and fears

Source: Based on table 6.2, above, from Albert H. Cantril and Charles W. Roll, Jr., *Hopes and Fears of the American People* (New York: Universe Books, 1971), p. 19.

than purely private ones. There are two categories of hope that clearly require intervention of the government if they are to be realized: peace in the world and freedom from inflation. Reference to each increases. There are several categories of fear that would require governmental intervention if that which is feared is to be avoided: war, inflation, crime, pollution, and political instability. References to inflation increase. Reference to war as a fear rises from 1959 to 1964, through it falls again somewhat in 1971.[6] And crime, pollution, and political instability appear for the first time in 1971.

The degree to which political concerns have penetrated the private lives of citizens is summed up in figure 6.1. For the three years for which we have data, we plot the proportion of "citizen hopes" that is nonpolitical and the proportion that is political. And we do the same for "citizen fears."[7] Nonpolitical hopes do not change much as a proportion of all hopes, but political

---

[6] We suggested above that citizen mentions of war and foreign problems as the major national problems—a phenomenon we found in the Eisenhower years—did not imply deep concern or worry for the average citizen. This interpretation is supported by the data in table 6.2. In 1959, the Gallup Poll consistently found that matters of war, peace, and foreign affairs were cited as the main problem facing the nation. But in that year, fewer people mention such problems as cause of concern in their personal lives than mention such problems in 1964 or 1971, when such problems had fallen substantially in the frequency with which they were mentioned as national problems.

[7] The figures are the proportions of the number of *answers* that fall in the private and political categories since we do not know the proportion of respondents who gave such answers (the data in table 6.2 from Cantril and Roll, *Hopes and Fears,* reports multiple responses).

hopes rise substantially from 5 percent in 1969 to 14 percent in 1971. The bigger change, though, is on the fear side—as one might expect in a period of general discontent. The proportion of fears that can be considered relatively nonpolitical falls from 53 percent to 37 percent, while the politically relevant fears double from 16 percent to 32 percent.

In sum, the nature of the issues facing the American public has changed substantially since the fifties. The data in this chapter merely document the obvious fact that the public has come to focus on a new set of issues; the new set covers a wider range and those that draw most attention are ones of particular intensity and divisiveness. More important, perhaps, is the fact that political issues have come to "intrude" into the personal lives of citizens. As we shall document in the following chapters, the way the public thinks about issues has changed as well.

7 | The Level of Conceptualization

The authors of *The American Voter,* as we have seen, found few Americans who conceptualized the political world in sophisticated terms. Although they used quite generous standards to define political sophistication, they could characterize only 2½ percent of their sample as ideologues in 1956. Almost half the sample talked in vague nature-of-the-times terms or had no political content in their answers to the open-ended questions on party and candidate evaluations. Among those with grade school education over half fell in these lower reaches of the level of conceptualization scale, and even among those with some college education almost one-third fell in this category.[1]

The level of conceptualization is a characteristic of the public that one would ordinarily expect to be quite stable over time, especially if one explains the low levels at which citizens conceptualize politics in terms of cognitive limitations of large proportions of the mass public. A large segment of the public, according to this view, has neither an adequate educational background, nor contextual knowledge, nor the ability to manipulate the abstract political

---

[1] Angus Campbell and others, *The American Voter* (New York: Wiley, 1960), pp. 249–250.

concepts that give order and structure to the myriad details of politics. As *The American Voter* argues, the problem of adequate comprehension of politics goes "a good deal beyond limitations of time and information . . . Once below the higher deciles of the population, there are major barriers to understanding that disrupt the processing of even that information about public policy to which the person attends. To some degree these barriers are the product of an inadequate backlog of information. In some measure too they reflect the incapacity to handle abstractions that permit the individual to maintain an ordered view of remote events."[2]

There is, however, an alternative explanation for the 1956 distribution of citizens on the levels of conceptualization hierarchy. As the authors of *The American Voter* also note, the conceptualizations that citizens use may be in part situational—that is, dependent on the content of political debate. "There are periods in which the heat of partisan debate slackens and becomes almost perfunctory, and the positions of the parties become relatively indistinct on basic issues. In times such as these even the person sensitive to a range of political philosophies may not feel this knowledge to be helpful in an evaluation of current politics, and hence may fail to receive proper assignment in a level of conceptualization."[3] If level of conceptualization depended on political content, one would expect movement across levels as the content of politics changed, though the movement might still be inhibited by cognitive limitations.

The change in political discourse after 1956 provided a test of the relative importance of cognitive limitations and political content in determining levels of conceptualization. The appearance of the Goldwater candidacy in 1964, with its strong ideological cues, led John O. Field and Ronald E. Anderson to attempt a replication of the levels of conceptualization analysis (though they, as we have done after them, used the coding categories rather than a broad reading of the protocols to assign respondents to levels). They found a substantial increase in the proportion who could be categorized as using some form of political ideology when evaluating candidates and parties.[4]

We can extend that analysis across the full range of presidential elections from 1952 to 1972. As we have pointed out, we have not replicated the coding of the original study. But we have used the master codes to isolate two groups that may approach the "ideologues" and "near-ideologues" of *The*

---

2 Ibid., p. 253.
3 Ibid., p. 256.
4 John O. Field and Ronald E. Anderson, "Ideology in the Public's Conception of the 1964 Election," *Public Opinion Quarterly,* 33 (Fall 1969), 380–398.

American Voter in sophistication. (See above, Chapter 2, for a discussion, and Appendix 2C, for details on our categorization.) Our ideologues are those categorized in our most sophisticated category, that is, those who use broad ideological terms as well as specific issue reference in evaluating the parties. Near-ideologues are those who use the broad ideological terms alone and do not link them to issues. Figure 7.1 traces the proportions falling into these two categories in their evaluation of parties from 1952 to 1972. The categorization "ideologues and near-ideologues" combines all those who use ideological terms in describing the parties (whether or not they mention issues) and is a somewhat less stringent measure of ideological sophistication.

Consider the line for ideologues. In 1956 we were able to place 11 percent of the respondents in that category. But it would appear that 1956 represents a low point in the proportion that can be so categorized. Starting in 1956 there is a steady increase in the proportion using a combination of ideological terms and issue reference to evaluate one or both of the parties. By 1972 the proportion making such evaluations has doubled to 22 percent.

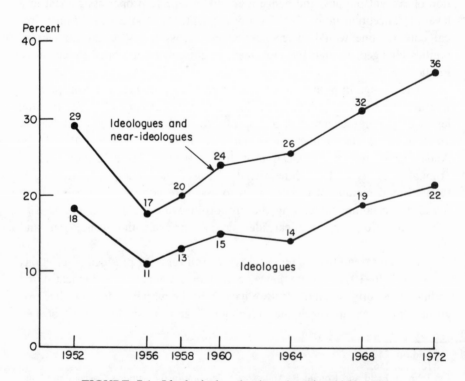

FIGURE 7.1. Ideological evaluation of parties, 1952–1972

And if we look back from our base-year of 1956, we see a substantially higher proportion making such sophisticated evaluations in 1952.

The upper line based on a looser criterion of ideological sophistication (any use of an ideological term whether or not it is coupled to issue reference) shows a similar change. Ideological terminology was quite frequent in 1952, falls to a lower level in 1956 and 1958, and then rises steadily to 1972. By 1972 the proportion using ideological terms is up to 36 percent, about double that in 1956.

The data in figure 7.2 show an even more dramatic change in the levels of conceptualization of the American public. There we plot the proportions who can be considered ideologues and near-ideologues on the basis of the way in which they evaluate the candidates in the various presidential races. This separation out of candidate evaluations from party ones is, we believe, important, since it is the changing candidates rather than the parties that provide the major change in political content. Consider the line reflecting the proportion of ideologues—that is, the proportiton that uses both ideological terminology and specific issue reference in relation to one or both of the candi-

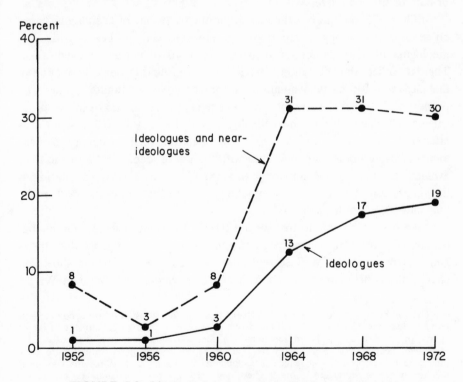

FIGURE 7.2. Ideological evaluation of candidates, 1952–1972

dates. In the elections of the 1950s—the two Eisenhower-Stevenson races— only a handful of respondents evaluate the candidates in these terms. In 1960 the percentage rises to 3 percent. But after 1960, the percentage of respondents using both general ideological terms and issue reference to describe candidates climbs sharply. In 1964, 13 percent of the population is in this category—still not a large percentage in an absolute sense, but a substantial rise from the three previous elections. This change in 1964 is consistent with the findings of Anderson and Field. But note how the proportion using such terms continues to rise until 1972, when almost one out of five Americans could be categorized as ideologues.

The change is similar if we use the less stringent criterion of the use of ideological terms to describe candidates even in the absence of specific issue reference. In this case, 1956 is seen to be a particularly low point. In the presidential elections preceding and following that in 1956, we find somewhat larger proportions using such terms. But all three elections from 1952 to 1960 differ substantially from those from 1964 on. In the latter elections almost one out of three Americans uses some ideological term to describe one or both of the candidates.

Figure 7.3 summarizes the changes in the frequency of evaluations based on issues and ideology. It reports the proportions who can be categorized as ideologues or near-ideologues in their evaluations of parties *or* candidates.[5] The data reflect the substantial changes we have found in our examination of the measures for party evaluation or for candidate evaluation alone. The proportion in either the strictly defined category of ideologues or in the looser category of ideologues and near-ideologues falls from 1952 to 1956, but rises after that. By 1972 a third of the respondents fall in the category of ideologues; they combine issue reference with the use of ideological terms in their evaluations of candidates and/or parties. And if we use the looser criterion of the simple use of ideological terminology, we find that about one-half of the respondents fall in this category.

We cannot be certain that we are tracing the same phenomenon as that captured by the SRC categorizations. Our coding is more gross than theirs and it is possible that a close replication of their analysis would show less change than the figures we report. Hans Klingemann and William Wright

---

[5] The combined measure is somewhat looser than the measures based on candidate and party evaluations. If a respondent is an ideologue on one of the two component variables (party or candidate) he is an ideologue on the combined measure. The categories ideologue, near-ideologue, issue referent, group referent, and party referent are considered to be hierarchical—in effect, a respondent is assigned a value for the combined measure which is equivalent to his "highest" value for the party or candidate evaluation measures.

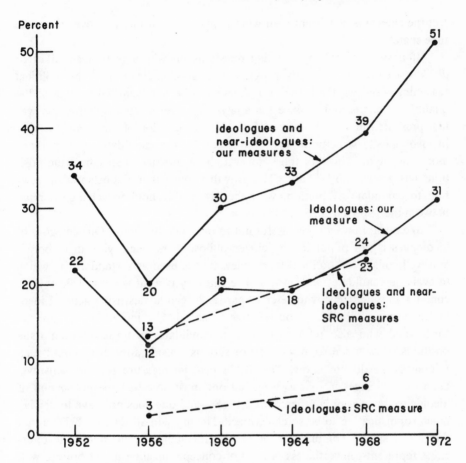

FIGURE 7.3. Ideological evaluation of candidates and parties, 1952–1972 (our measure and SRC measure compared)

replicated for the 1968 election the intensive "global" coding carried out on the 1956 interviews. Their goal was to apply the exact criteria for categorizing respondents used in 1956. We plot their findings on figure 7.3. In general, their more stringent criteria locate fewer ideologues and near-ideologues. But the change they find between 1956 and 1968 parallels ours. In 1968 they found that the proportion of ideologues (using the SRC's definition discussed in Chapter 3) had risen to 6 percent of the voters, a figure that is about double the percentage found in 1956. The combined proportion of ideologues and near-ideologues goes from 13 percent to 23 percent of the population. The proportionate changes are somewhat less great than those we found. Their figures double; ours increase by a factor of about two and a half.

But the change is consistent with what happens to our measure over the same time span.[6]

If answers to the open-ended questions on why a respondent likes or dislikes a candidate or party provide some good indications of his political reasoning—and we think they do—there has been substantial change in the quality of that reasoning since the analysis of level of conceptualization was first presented in *The American Voter.* The proportion of citizens who think in ideologically structured ways about parties and candidates and, perhaps more important, who link those general characteristics to specific issue positions has grown substantially. The growth is particularly substantial in relation to candidate evaluation, with the major threshold for change coming between the 1960 and 1964 elections.

We must, however, be careful not to overstate the point. Our category of ideologues is not populated by citizen-philosophers, each with an elaborate and well-considered political world view that is used as a standard by which to evaluate candidates and parties. The category is what we have said it is: it contains those citizens who refer to parties or candidates using general ideological terms—"liberal," "conservative," "socialist," "individualist," and so forth—and who also refer to parties or candidates in terms of their issue positions. How much sophistication or serious consideration lies behind such references we do not know. The SRC's original measure is more sensitive. Data show changes in that as well, but one must note that the proportion of ideologues reaches only 6 percent by 1968—and one does not have to display much sophistication to be so categorized. Having said all this, we believe that the use of such a combination of general ideological terms and issue references represents, nevertheless, a level of conceptualization about politics well beyond that of citizens who evaluate parties or candidates in vague "temper of the times" terms, or who simply prefer a party or candidate because of habitual party attachment.

The data, as presented in figures 7.1, 7.2, and 7.3 blur the distinction between references to broad ideological terms and to specific issues. It is interesting to ask which—reference to ideological terms or reference to issues—has grown most in the past two decades. Figure 7.4 sorts this out. In Part A we plot the references to parties, in Part B the references to candidates, and in each we plot separately the proportion that refers only to issues but

---

[6] The data are reported in Philip Converse, "Public Opinion and Voting Behavior," in Fred A. Greenstein and Nelson Polsby, eds., *The Handbook of Political Science* (Reading, Mass.: Addison-Wesley, 1975). See also John C. Pierce, "Party Identification and the Changing Role of Ideology in American Politics," *Midwest Journal of Political Science,* February 14, 1970, p. 35. Pierce's data are similar to ours.

does not use ideological terms, the proportion that uses ideological terms but does not refer to specific issues, and the proportion that does both (our ideologue category).

The pattern is the same for party evaluations and candidate evaluations: the proportion that uses ideological terms alone as well as the proportion that uses such terms in combination with issue reference rises, but the proportion that mentions issues alone does not change. As we have pointed out, more respondents refer to candidates in issue terms that refer to parties in such terms, but in each case the line indicating reference to issues alone is remarkably flat across the years.

This of course does not imply that the total amount of issue reference is unchanging. The proportion mentioning issues rises substantially as one can see by adding the figures for those mentioning issues alone and for those mentioning issues and ideology. But the rise in issue reference comes from citizens who combine reference to a specific issue with some more general ideological terminology. In addition, ideological terminology unlinked to specific issues rises. It is hard to read the data in figure 7.4 as saying anything other than that there has been a substantial change in the ways in which citizens conceptualize political matters between the mid-Eisenhower years and the early 1970s.

We have, thus far, considered changes in the proportion of the electorate falling in the upper reaches of the levels of conceptualization measure. Cognitive limitations do not seem to have prevented some citizens from moving into the upper categories of the scale (a moderately large proportion moves if one uses our categorization; a smaller proportion if one uses the SRC measures). But such limitations might inhibit citizens from moving out of the lower reaches of the scale. Indeed, the notion of cognitive limitations may more appropriately apply to the lower half of the levels of conceptualization scale than to the upper. The replication of the SRC measures by Klingemann and Wright support the view that movement on the scale is limited to movement from the middle to the upper categories. The proportion falling in the lower categories (nature-of-the-times or nonpolitical) does not change at all between 1956 and 1968.[7] Our measure shows somewhat more change, but the change is neither as clear nor as great as that at the top of the scale. In 1956, we categorized 16 percent as falling in the nature-of-the-times or nonpolitical categories. The proportion rises to 18 percent in 1960, but falls to 12 and 10

---

[7] Converse, "Public Opinion and Voting Behavior," p. 102. Converse has recently indicated that the notion of cognitive limitations in *The American Voter* was intended to apply only to the bottom of the levels of conceptualization scale (personal communication).

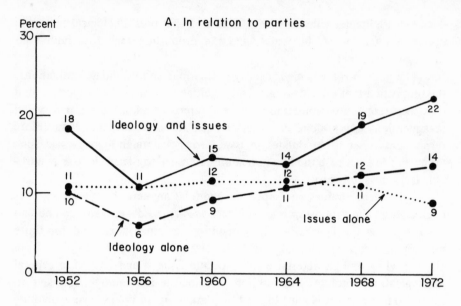

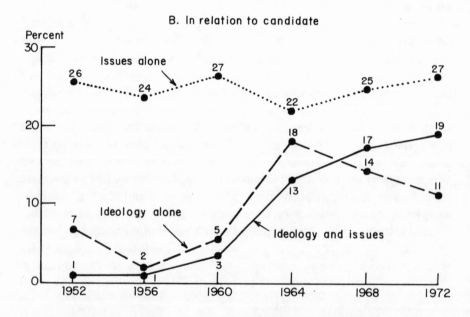

FIGURE 7.4. Issue reference and ideological reference, 1952–1972

percent respectively in 1964 and 1968. However, by 1972 it is up again at 15 percent. The proportions in the bottom section of our levels of conceptualization scale do erode somewhat in 1964 and 1968, but the general pattern for our measure is not inconsistent with the Klingemann and Wright finding that change comes at the top of scale more than at the bottom.

The data suggest that position on the levels of conceptualization measure is sensitive to changes in the content of political discourse, though the small amount of movement across the scale—particularly in the lower reaches of the scale—is not inconsistent with the existence of long-term cognitive limitations. We can obtain a better sense of the relative importance of these two factors by comparing educational groups. The movement of the electorate on the levels of conceptualization scale might be explained—in a way that would be completely consistent with a cognitive limitations hypothesis—by an upgrading of the population in educational terms. The ability to understand and manipulate highly abstract concepts and to absorb and utilize contextual knowledge are associated with levels of education. As *The American Voter* puts it, "a rising level of education may permit a slow upgrading in the level of conceptualization."[8]

The period we have been considering is one in which there has been a general increase in the educational level of the electorate. Figure 7.5 illustrates this. In the sixteen years from 1956 to 1972 the portion of the population most likely to have the capacity for ideological thinking—those with at least some college training—has increased from less than 20 percent to almost 30 percent of the population. At the same time, those with less than a complete high school education have decreased from 52 percent of the population in 1956 to 38 percent in 1972.

It is interesting to note that substantial changes at both ends of the education ladder take place after 1960, precisely when levels of conceptualization rose most significantly.[9] In short, in terms of both magnitude and timing, it seems possible that the rise in conceptual level within the mass public is the consequence of an increasingly educated and thus more knowledgeable and sophisticated public.

But the data on changing levels of conceptualization in figures 7.1 and 7.2 suggest that the changes have been more substantial than one would

---

[8] *The American Voter*, p. 255.

[9] There are two related reasons why the educational shifts cumulate after 1960. First, 1964 is the first year in which large numbers of the war-baby population enter the electorate. Second, this group not only is very large but also has received an unprecedented amount of educational training. In short, because these young adults represent a big portion of the population who are highly educated, they have a major effect on the overall proportions of the population at various levels of educational attainment.

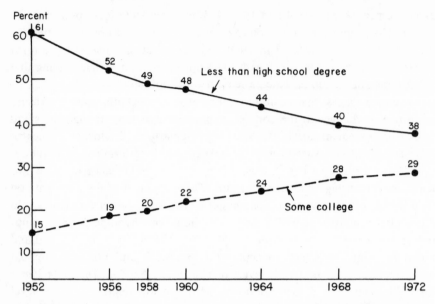

FIGURE 7.5. Changes in level of educational achievement, 1952–1972

expect from the slower and steadier change in educational attainment during the same years. We can look at this more directly by controlling for education when we consider the rise in the proportion of the population using ideological and issue reference to evaluate candidates. If the rise in frequency of the more sophisticated political evaluations is a function of the rising educational level of the population, we should find the proportion making such evaluations to be unchanging after we have controlled for education.

In figure 7.6 we plot the proportions over time who use ideological terms and issue references in evaluating candidates and parties by educational levels. As one can see, there is a difference across the educational groups. At each time point, those with higher levels of education are more likely to make ideological/issue evaluations. But the important point is that the frequency of such evaluations increases in a similar manner for each of the educational levels. If one starts at the low point of 1956, one finds a growth in frequency of ideological/issue evaluations of approximately 20 percentage points in each of the educational levels. The percentage growth is least in the lowest educational category—there is an increase of 17 percentage points between 1956 and 1972 for that group compared with 20 and 22 percentage points for the two higher educational groups. But in terms of proportionate gain, the change is most dramatic among those with less than a high school degree. The proportion using the more sophisticated terminology more than triples from

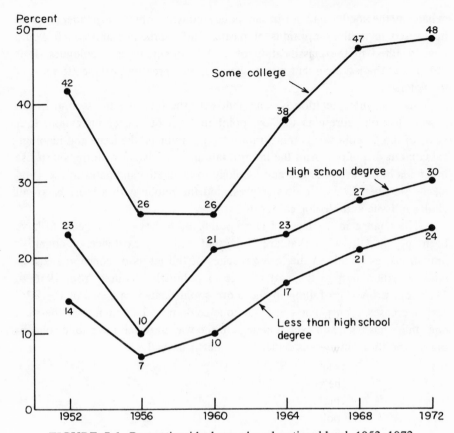

FIGURE 7.6. Proportion ideologues by educational level, 1952–1972

1956 to 1972. In fact, by 1972 about as large a proportion of those who have not finished high school are found in our ideologue category as was found among the college educated in 1956 and 1960. At the lower reaches of the levels of conceptualization scale, however, we find less movement. The proportion of those with less than a high school degree in the category that combines nature-of-the-times responses and nonpolitical ones was 21 percent in 1956. It falls to 14 percent in 1964 and 1968, but is back at 21 percent in 1972.

In general, the data on levels of conceptualization do support the hypothesis that the way in which citizens conceptualize the political realm is dependent on the political content to which they are exposed. The year 1956 was one in which the issues were so indistinct and Eisenhower so capable of establishing a position above controversy that there was little in the election that could be conceived of in ideological terms. It is not so much that political debate in the media had no broad policy content which respondents could have used in their descriptions of parties and candidates and which would have resulted in the classification of such respondents as ideologues. It is rather that the issue content was probably not of great importance to most of the voters.

Such an interpretation is consistent with the fact that the second Eisenhower election represents the low point in level of conceptualization, four years of the Eisenhower administration having reduced the issue and ideological content of politics. And the interpretation is consistent with the sharp rise one finds in the use of issues and ideology to evaluate candidates in the 1964 election—when Barry Goldwater presented the public with a more clear-cut choice in issue and ideological terms.

The change in the level of conceptualization, however, appears to have been inhibited in ways that are consistent with the existence of cognitive limitations, especially in the lower reaches of the levels of conceptualization scale. Further, despite the vast change in political discourse from 1956 to 1968, the proportion falling in the more sophisticated category of the SRC scale increases to only 6 percent. Our conclusion must be a middle-of-the-road one: there has been substantial change in the way in which the public conceptualizes politics, yet there is evidence for inertia as well.

8 The Rise of Issue Consistency

We can now turn to another characteristic of citizen belief systems. The American public in the Eisenhower years was found to have political opinions with little coherent structure —citizens' attitudes in one issue area were not related to attitudes in other issue areas.[1] We shall demonstrate in this chapter that there has been a major increase in the level of attitude consistency within the mass public. Not only has constraint increased among traditional attitudes but also as new issues have merged in the 1960s, they have been incorporated by the mass public into what now appears to be a broad liberal/conservative ideology. Liberals on traditional issues tend to be more liberal on new issues; conservatives are more conservative on these issues.[2]

---

[1] For an extensive discussion of the level of attitude consistency which actually characterized the fifties see Philip E. Converse, "Attitudes and Non-Attitudes: Continuation of a Dialogue," in Edward Tufte, ed. *The Quantitative Study of Politics* (New York: Addison-Wesley, 1971), and Philip E. Converse, "The Nature of Belief Systems in Mass Publics," in David E. Apter, ed. *Ideology and Discontent* (New York: Free Press, 1964). See also John C. Pierce and Douglas D. Rose, "Non-Attitudes and American Public Opinion: The Examination of a Thesis," *American Political Science Review* 68 (June 1974), 626–649, and the "Comment" by Converse and the "Rejoinder" by Pierce and Rose in the same issue.

[2] Throughout, we use the terms "attitude consistency," "attitude coherence," and "attitude constraint" interchangeably. The terms imply that liberal-conservative attitudes are predictable across issue areas.

Table 8.1 repeats the data from our earlier chapter on the interrelationship among political attitudes in 1956 and traces those interrelationships across time to 1973. As we did in Chapter 2, we report the average interrelation (gamma) for pairs of questions across issue areas. The five issue areas are: size of government, welfare, integration, welfare for blacks, and the cold war. The data come, as usual, from the SRC election studies but we add data from two studies we conducted at the National Opinion Research Center of the University of Chicago in 1971 and 1973. These studies give us two more data points and also allow us to consider the relationship among political attitudes in nonpresidential years. The NORC studies and the 1958 SRC study should be particularly useful since these studies are uncontaminated by short-term forces specific to presidential election years.

The changes shown in table 8.1 are striking. There appears to have been a sharp shift upward in the level of issue constraint between 1960 and 1964. Relatively low levels of issue constraint are found in 1956, 1958, and 1960,

TABLE 8.1. Levels of attitude constraint, 1956–1973
(average gammas between issue spheres)

Issue	1956	1958	1960	1964	1968	1971a	1972	1973
Welfare/
black welfare	.39	.34	.38	.48	.51	.49	.42	.36
Welfare/
integration	.11	.16	.19	.26	.49	.42	.33	.38
Welfare/
size of government	.16	.05	.14	.52	.47	—	.02	.46
Welfare/
cold war	−.16	−.16	−.12	.26	.18	.25	.26	.16
Black welfare/
integration	.46	.64	.53	.71	.73	.63	.73	.63
Black welfare/
size of government	.11	.03	.05	.51	.40	—	.15	.35
Black welfare/
cold war	−.09	−.14	−.15	.29	.26	.24	.28	.20
Integration/
size of government	.23	.16	.17	.46	.44	—	.09	.40
Integration/
cold war	.08	−.01	.05	.20	.27	.24	.27	.12
Size of government/
cold war	.15	.04	.08	.42	.20	—	.11	.11

a Data for 1971 come from the NORC National Survey. No question on size of government is available in that survey.

but the correlation among issue positions moves upward in 1964 across almost all issue areas. The relationship between the domestic economic issues —welfare and size of government—increases. In addition, cold war issues become increasingly tied to attitudes on domestic policies. Integration and black welfare, the only issues which were substantially related to each other prior to 1964, are now related at an even higher level. In general, issues involving race began to be strongly related both to other domestic and to cold war issues in 1964, were more strongly related in 1968, and fall off slightly thereafter.

There are small fluctuations in the correlations (perhaps due to sampling error or to short-term forces acting on specific issues). But we can clearly observe two periods. There was a very low level of attitude consistency from 1956 through 1960, followed by a rapid growth of constraint at some point between 1960 and 1964 that moves the correlation among attitudes to a high level which remains at each subsequent point through 1973. The only exception is the weakening of the relationship between size of government and all other issues between 1968 and 1972.[3] (We shall consider that in a moment.)

There is little to suggest that individual presidential elections or other specific events exert significant *short-term* influences on general levels of constraint. If, for example, the Goldwater-Johnson presidential election acted as a catalyst for the emergence of issue constraint within the mass public (a hypothesis which would not be inconsistent with the timing of the increase in constraint), the changes it helped bring about have persisted. The independence of levels of attitude coherence from the events of specific elections is underlined by the data from 1958, 1971, and 1973. In the latter two years no national elections took place; 1958 was a congressional election year. Even though these three time points are at considerable distance from the excitation of presidential campaigns, the level of constraint at each point fits precisely on the expected trend line based on the presidential years. Thus in 1958 coherence of attitudes was low and at the same level as found in 1956 and 1960; in 1971 and 1973 levels of attitude consistency are virtually identical to the high levels found in the presidential years of 1964, 1968, and 1972.

The Size of Government Issue: A Puzzle

The one deviation from the general pattern of increasing consistency is found in the set of relationships between questions on the size of government and other items in 1972. These relationships had all risen with the other pairs

---

[3] Unfortunately, the 1962 election study does not have sufficient attitude measures to allow us to use it in this analysis.

of relationships in 1964. But in 1972 the relationships between attitudes on size of government and other subjects fall close to zero. Indeed, they become smaller than they were at the beginning of the time period. However, we do not believe this reflects a weakening of political consistency; rather it is an example of new meaning being given to an old question. It may be worth a small digression to illustrate how this can happen.

Attitudes on the size of government have traditionally divided liberals and conservatives. "That government is best which governs least" has been a central conservative position, while American liberalism has favored a government active in trying to rectify social and economic injustices.

The size of government questions tap this distinction with varying effectiveness. In the years up to 1960, the question the SRC asked in this issue area focused specifically on big government as an instrument of domestic economic reform: respondents were asked whether they favored government ownership of public utilities and government involvement in housing. After 1964, the question changes and becomes more general: citizens are asked whether the government has become "too powerful for the good of the county and the individual citizen." Despite the new and more general wording, we believe that the question continued, in the early 1960s, to tap attitudes toward the government as an agency for domestic reform. But the more general and vague nature of the question allowed it to receive new content after 1968. From 1968 to 1972, the question appears to take on a mixed meaning. Big and powerful government no longer appears to refer only to the economic interventionist governments of the New Deal; it comes to connote as well a government involved in the Vietnam war and in the harassment of protesters. Such a change in meaning would create opponents of "big and powerful" government on both the left and right.

The data support such an interpretation of the change in the meaning of the "big government" question. This can be seen by examining the change over the past eight years of the positions of liberals and conservatives on the size of government issues. From 1964 onward, the SRC asked respondents to place several groups, including liberals and conservatives, on a scale which measured their feelings toward the groups. On the basis of these questions we were able to classify respondents as liberals, moderates, and conservatives. Figure 8.1 presents the proportion of each of these groups who state that the government is too big and powerful. The data are for 1964, 1968, and 1972.

In 1964 the size of government issue split the population as expected along liberal/conservative lines. Only 25 percent of the liberals said that government was too big, while 40 percent of the moderates and fully 71 percent of the conservatives took this position. While the direction of the relationship remained the same in 1968, it had clearly begun to decrease, with

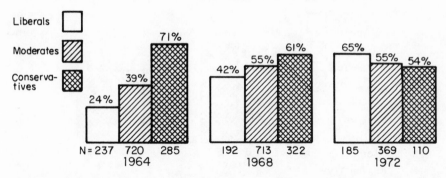

FIGURE 8.1. Proportion saying the government is too big among liberals, moderates, and conservatives, 1964, 1968, 1972

a substantial increase in the proportion of liberals agreeing with the conservatives that government had become too big and powerful. By 1972 liberals were more opposed to big government than were conservatives. We cannot be sure of why the question is redefined, but the reasons mentioned above—from Vietnam to the fact that an active conservative administration was in power in 1972—seem plausible.

To test whether our interpretation was correct—that "big government" no longer suggested "reformist government" to many citizens—we devised a new size of government question in our 1973 NORC study. The new question focused exclusively on domestic issues and on government as a "solver" of our country's problems.[4] We also repeated the SRC version that had become standard after 1960. Our version of the question seems to recapture the earlier New Deal component of the government size item. In figure 8.2 we compare the two question versions in terms of their relationship to liberal/conservative self-identification. It is clear that the NORC measure is closely related to liberalism/conservatism; the SRC measure is not.

This digression allows us to make sense of the pattern found in table 8.1. The relationships between our 1973 size of government question and the other issue areas return to roughly the same level as in 1964. For example, the correlation between welfare items and the size of government item is .52 in 1964 and .47 in 1968. It falls to .02 in 1972. Using the NORC measure, the relationship is .46 in 1973, approximately what it is in 1964 and 1968. Similar patterns are seen in the relationship of the size of government to the other two domestic issues—black welfare and integration.

---

[4] The question asked the respondent to choose between two positions: "Some people think that the government in Washington is trying to do too many things that should be left to individuals and private business. Others think that the government should do even more to solve our country's problems."

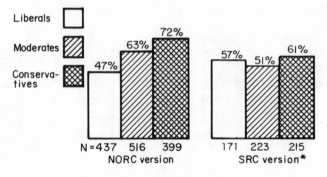

*Asked of only a subsample.

FIGURE 8.2. Government size and liberalism-conservatism, 1973: percent saying government is too big on SRC item and NORC item by self-identification as liberal or conservative

Only in relation to the correlation between the size of government and cold war items do we *not* find a return to the level of relationship found before 1972. But this confirms our interpretation that the new big government question has recaptured the domestic component of that attitude.

Summarizing the Growth of Ideological Consistency

The timing as well as the scope and magnitude of the growth of attitude consistency can be seen more clearly in the summary measures presented in figure 8.3. Plotted through time in this figure are three measures of attitude consistency—the overall index of constraint (a simple average of the ten correlations in each column of table 8.1); an index of domestic attitude consistency (the average correlations among the four domestic issues); and an index of consistency between domestic and foreign issues (computed by taking the average for each year of the correlation of the four domestic issues with attitudes on the cold war).[5]

The difference between the studies done in 1956, 1958 and 1960 and

---

[5] We calculate the averages in 1972 without the "size of government" item for reasons discussed above. Given the wording of the question and the changed meaning of "big and powerful government," the item in 1972 cannot be expected to fit into the liberal/conservative space. The item is therefore excluded in all subsequent summary indices for 1972.

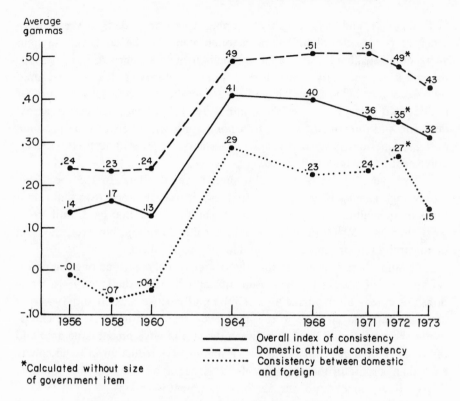

FIGURE 8.3. Changes in attitude consistency, 1956–1973

those from 1964 onward is striking. Consider the relations among domestic issues. In the 1956–1960 period the average gamma hovers around .23. In 1964 it jumps to .49. It remains consistently at that level through 1972. In 1973 it has fallen a bit, but it remains well above the pre-1964 level.

The pattern with regard to the index of the relationship between attitudes on domestic issues and positions on the cold war indicates an equally dramatic and similarly timed increase in issue constraint. In 1956, just a few years after the end of the Korean war, the average relationship between a liberal/conservative attitude on domestic issues and the desirability of a tough stand against an international communist threat was almost zero. Domestic liberals were no less in favor of a tough international stance than conservatives. In 1964 and thereafter, on the other hand, the correlation between domestic attitudes and a tough stance abroad rose to about .29. The questions in 1968, 1971, and 1972 are about keeping American soldiers in Vietnam. In other years they are about taking a tough stand on the cold war. In later years, domestic liberals favor a more conciliatory policy abroad. In contrast to the mid-fifties and early sixties, foreign policy attitudes (at least as measured by position on the cold war) have increasingly become connected with other political attitudes in the public's mind. In 1973, the relationship across domestic and foreign issues falls to a point somewhere between the pre- and post-1964 periods. This is perhaps understandable given that direct U.S. involvement in Vietnam had ended.

The overall index of constraint summarizes the data. In 1956 to 1960, the average gamma is around .15. In 1964, it soars to about two and a half times the magnitude of previous years. It stays at about that level until 1973, when there is a downturn to .32. Even after this downturn, however, the level of constraint remains twice that found in the pre-1960 era.

In sum, there is evidence that the degree of coherence among the political attitudes of citizens has increased substantially since the late 1950s. Relationships among all five issue areas grew rapidly between 1960 and 1964 and have generally stayed close to the high levels displayed in 1964. One exception is the relationship in 1972 between the size of government issue area and the other issue areas. But this is less a matter of a reduction in issue coherence than a shift in the meaning of the issue. If we consider the domestic intervention component of the size of government issue—as we do in 1973—we find relationships with other issue areas about as robust as those in the years of 1964 to 1968. In regard to the five issue areas we can trace from the mid-1950s, the evidence of increasing attitudinal constraint is convincing.

The strength of citizen attitude consistency has clearly grown since the mid- and late 1950s. There is evidence that the scope of that attitude consistency has grown as well. By this we mean that other issues have come to be linked with the five basic issue areas we have been tracing. To test for the increasing scope of issue consistency we will consider two more issue areas. First we will examine the issue of the civil liberties of political dissenters—an issue that was connected with McCarthyism during our base period in the 1950s and that reemerged during the protests of the late 1960s. We shall than turn to the new "social issues" of the late 1960s.

Liberal/Conservative Constraint and Attitudes on the Civil Liberties of Dissenters

Traditional liberal ideology in the United States involves not only attitudes on social welfare, minority rights, and governmental control over the

economy, but a concern about civil liberties and the rights of political dissenters as well. It has often been noted, however, that there is little relationship between attitudes on economic or racial issues and attitudes on civil
liberties. Indeed, this fact has been cited as prime evidence that liberalism and
conservatism as coherent patterns of belief do not exist among the mass
public. Commitment to free speech and to the other freedoms of the Bill of
Rights was more likely to be found among the educated and affluent segments
of the society, even though these groups were often quite conservative on
economic matters. On the other hand, the working classes favored liberal
economic and welfare policies, but their commitment to civil liberties was by
no means strong.[6]

If something approaching a liberal/conservative ideology has emerged in
the mass public, it ought to encompass these issues as well. Although comparable data for attitudes on civil liberties do not exist for the entire period
we are examining, several questions on attitudes toward political dissenters
are available in the beginning and toward the end of the time period.

In the 1956 election study—at the conclusion of the McCarthy era—the
Survey Research Center asked the citizenry whether they thought a government worker suspected of being a communist ought to be fired even though
his communist affiliation had not been proved. The 1971 NORC study included equivalent questions on the rights of political dissenters: (1) Should
the government have the right to spy on radical groups even though they may
not have violated any law? (2) Should the government have the right to enter
and search the meeting places of such groups without a warrant? and
(3) Should the government have the right to hold without bail individuals
who stand accused of incitement to riot? The first of these items also appears
on the 1973 NORC study. In 1972, a related question was asked on amnesty
for those who dissented from government policy by refusing to participate in
the war in Vietnam. In addition, we have in the SRC 1968 and 1972 studies
and in the NORC 1971 study a common set of questions on attitudes toward
civil protest and demonstrations: whether or not there are any circumstances
that make sit-ins and peaceful demonstrations tolerable.

Table 8.2 presents the relationships of these civil liberties attitudes to
attitudes on our basic set of issues. The first column contains the data from
1956. The other columns contain the data from the later studies. The pattern
in 1956 once again confirms the general absence of attitude constraint in the

---

[6] For a particularly good discussion of this point, see V. O. Key, *Public Opinion and
American Democracy* (New York: Knopf, 1961), pp. 171–172. See also James W.
Prothro and C. W. Grigg, "Fundamental Principles of Democracy: Basis of Agreement
and Disagreement," *Journal of Politics* 22 (May 1960), 276–294.

mid-1950s. All of the correlations are low, and there is no discernible pattern. The data on "rights of radicals" from 1971 and 1973 offer perhaps the best comparison with the 1956 data. They indicate considerably greater attitude consistency between positions on the protection of civil liberties of radical activists and attitudes in the core issue areas. The relationships between the other issue areas and whether or not to grant amnesty to those refusing to serve in the military during the Vietnam war are even stronger.

In sum, the average gammas between attitude on firing government workers and other issues was .01 in 1956. In 1971 and 1973 the average correlation between the core issue areas and position on rights of radicals had risen to .28 and .24, respectively, while the average correlation with attitudes on amnesty was a striking .51.

The average correlation between attitudes on tolerance for sit-ins and protest demonstrations and the other issues is also substantial. The data for 1968, 1971, and 1972 are strikingly similar. Those who believed that under certain circumstances individuals "have the right to stop the government from engaging in its usual activities through protest and demonstrations" also tend to be those giving a liberal response in each of the other issue areas. All of the

TABLE 8.2. Relationship between attitudes on the civil liberties of dissenters and attitudes on the domestic and cold war issues, 1956–1973

(average gammas)

	Firing government workers suspected of communist affiliation	Rights of radicals		Amnesty for those who refused the draft	Acceptability of protests and peaceful demonstrations		
	1956	1971	1973	1972	1968	1971	1972
Welfare	−.14	.22	.25	.43	.28	.25	.25
Black welfare	.07	.33	.29	.41	.38	.31	.33
Integration	.14	.32	.22	.50	.29	.21	.29
Size of government	−.04	—a	.18	—b	.23	—a	—b
Cold war	.04	.23	.27	.70	.28	.18	.27
Average gammas	.01	.28	.24	.51	.29	.26	.29

a Not available.
b Not used in calculations.

correlations are consistent on this point, and they range from moderate to moderately high in comparison to others we have viewed.

A generalized liberal/conservative ideology would seem to imply a consistent set of beliefs in the areas of race, welfare, economics, and foreign policy, as well as consistency between these areas and attitudes toward civil liberties. Our data indicate that this consistency did not exist in 1956. It had come into being by 1968 and has persisted through 1973.

Liberal/Conservative Constraint and Attitudes on the Social Issues

The data thus far presented show a growth in the coherence of citizen attitudes across a wide range of traditional political issues. But the late 1960s saw the rise of a new set of "social issues." This term has been used to refer to some of the civil liberties issues we discussed in the previous section, particularly attitudes about political radicals; to the growing concern with violence and safety; and to changes in morals and values among the young. The new issues do not easily fit into the ordinary polarities of American politics. Richard Scammon and Ben Wattenberg, for instance, claim that these new social issues are independent of the more traditional issues that divided liberals from conservatives.[7]

We have divided the social issues into two components: issues involving crime and urban unrest and issues involving drugs and alternative life styles. In the various studies of the late 1960s we have several questions on these matters. They can be related (using our usual technique) to the five issue areas we have been tracing. The data on crime and urban unrest are reported in table 8.3. In the first column, we present the relationship between our various issue areas and a question on the proper way to deal with urban unrest: Is it done through the use of force or by attempting to cure the underlying social ills? As one can see, the relationship between this issue and the other five issue areas is fairly close and generally consistent across the various issue areas.

The next three columns of table 8.3 report similar data from the 1971, 1972, and 1973 studies. In these studies there were two questions that fall under the rubric of crime and urban unrest. One is the question just described from the 1968 study, and the other is a question on the importance of the rights of accused criminals. The average gammas between these two questions

---

[7] See Richard M. Scammon and Ben J. Wattenberg, *The Real Majority: An Extraordinary Examination of the American Electorate* (New York: Coward, McCann and Geoghegan, 1970).

TABLE 8.3. Relationship between the attitudes on crime and urban unrest and attitudes on the domestic and cold war issues, 1968–1973
(average gammas)

	Urban unrest	Urban unrest and rights of criminals		
	1968	1971	1972	1973
Welfare	.32	.32	.24	.34
Black welfare	.31	.41	.24	.35
Integration	.38	.37	.29	.38
Size of government	.22	—a	—b	.41
Cold war	.32	.29	.26	.19
Average gammas	.31	.35	.26	.33

a Not available.
b Not used in calculations.

and the five issue areas are consistent with those found in 1968. The average gamma between the unrest/crime dimension and the other five issue areas is a bit higher in 1971 than it was in 1968; it falls in 1972 but rises to a level between the 1968 and 1971 levels in 1973. The data support the position that these new issues are at least moderately related to the other more traditional political issues in the minds of the public.

Table 8.4 presents the correlations between our standard five issue areas and questions about drugs and life styles. In 1971, questions were asked about attitudes toward "hippies" and toward the legalization of marijuana. In the 1972 and 1973 studies, the marijuana question was repeated. The data from 1971 are quite similar to the data we have seen in relation to the dimension of crime and urban unrest. The life style issues relate moderately strongly to the other issue areas, the average gamma of .29 being similar to those found when we related crime and urban unrest issues to the five stand-ard issue areas. But the data for 1972 and 1973 suggest a weakening of that relationship. We cannot be sure how to interpret the change; the time span of the studies is too narrow. But the fact that the relationships so closely parallel other relationships in 1971, then fade somewhat in 1972 and remain at the lower 1972 levels in 1973, suggest that these life style issues are relatively ephemeral. They were originally part of a package of new issues that became linked to more traditional issues in the minds of the public. As time passes,

TABLE 8.4. Relationship between attitudes on life style issues
and attitudes on domestic and cold war issues, 1971–1973
(average gammas)

	Hippies, marijuana	Marijuana	
	1971	1972	1973
Welfare	.21	.09	.17
Black welfare	.34	.15	.24
Integration	.36	.19	.25
Size of government	—[a]	—[b]	.11
Cold war	.25	.27	.22

[a] Not available.
[b] Not used in calculations.

however, these life style issues may lose much of their political meaning and salience in the minds of citizens. With this decline in importance would come a decline in their connection with other issues.

In short, by 1972 we find substantial correlations among domestic and cold war issues, strong relationships between positions on these issues and attitudes on the civil liberties of dissenters, and a moderate to strong relationship between all these issues and the new social issues—indicating a striking growth in the scope and strength of issue coherence among the mass public.

Attitude Consistency in Mass and Elite

The data we have presented ought not to be taken to imply that the average citizen now has a fully coherent and logical political ideology where every specific issue polition is deduceable from some set of general principles. The attitude consistency we have uncovered is a weaker phenomenon. But we can obtain some notion of the extent to which the correlations we find after 1964 represent meaningful consistency by looking back at the comparison made in 1958 between the mass public and congressional candidates. The latter is a useful criterion group—an "elite" political group for whom politics is a major preoccupation, a group well informed and more politically thoughtful than is the average citizen.

As we have shown in Chapter 2, congressional candidates in 1958, when asked the same set of questions, responded with policy positions indicating

TABLE 8.5. Comparison of levels of attitude consistency between elites and the mass public

		Index of attitude consistency within domestic issues	Index of consistency between domestic and foreign	Overall index of attitude consistency
Congressional candidates	1958	.38	.25	.31
Mass public	1956	.24	−.01	.14
	1958	.23	−.07	.17
	1960	.24	−.04	.13
	1964	.49	.29	.41
	1968	.51	.23	.40
	1971	.51	.24	.38
	1972	.49	.27	.38
	1973	.43	.15	.32

substantially more consistency among positions than was found in the mass public. Table 8.5 reports the data on the level of consistency among the congressional candidates in 1958 and compares their consistency with that in the mass public as that public has changed since the late 1950s.[8] In the earlier years, the congressional candidates did indeed show substantially more consistency among political positions than did the mass public. But by 1964, the level of consistency among the public was reflected in a correlation of .49, substantially above the level shown by congressional candidates in 1958.

A similar situation holds for the interrelationship between domestic and foreign attitudes. In 1956, 1958 and 1960, there was no relationship across these issues among the mass public, compared with a 1958 index of .25 among the candidates. But by 1964, citizens displayed an index of consistency at the level of the candidates in 1958. The summary index shows a similar

---

[8] Specifically, questions in four major areas were utilized: social welfare, size of government, government role in aiding blacks, and attitudes toward the cold war. The responses to the questions in each of these areas were trichotomized to conform to the specifications developed for handling the mass public surveys. The computational procedures were also identical to those employed in the cross-section analysis.

The figures presented in table 8.5 and those presented in Converse's essay (see "The Nature of Belief Systems," pp. 228–229) are somewhat different. There are a few differences in the items employed (particularly in the foreign policy sphere) but the biggest differences stem from the fact that he includes the correlations among attitudes within issue spheres as well as across issue spheres, while our analysis concentrates exclusively on the latter relationships.

rise between 1960 and 1964, and even when the measures of domestic consistency and overall consistency fall in 1973, they remain at or above the 1958 elite level.

This is not to say that the mass citizenry now has patterns of attitude consistency equal to that of a group of political elites such as the congressional candidates. We do not have data on the interrelationship of attitudes among a comparable elite population during the later period. It is possible that elite consistency has risen as has consistency among the mass public. This could mean that in the post-1964 years a gap would still exist between elite and mass in this respect.[9] But that would not change the main thrust of our argument. Congressional candidates in 1958 were used as a criterion group to illustrate what attitude consistency might look like if the American public were fully involved in and sophisticated about political matters. Six years later, the views of the average citizen had reached a level of coherence higher than that of the criterion group. If we use the level of attitude consistency of these candidates as a criterion for a generalized liberal/conservative political ideology, it would seem that we must conclude that a similar level of ideology now exists among the citizenry at large.

Issue Consistency: What Does It Mean?

It is easier to document that something significant has happened to citizen political attitudes than it is to be certain about what such a change means. We have seen a rise in issue consistency, but it is important to be clear as to what exactly we have measured. The increase in the consistency across issues means that individuals who answer a question on one topic in a liberal direction are now more likely to answer liberally on another topic, and vice versa for conservative answers. To some extent this is an arbitrary definition of consistency: a respondent who favors faster school integration and also favors more welfare spending is consistent because we have placed both answers at the same end of liberal/conservative dimension. Similarly, a respondent who was a dove on Vietnam and a supporter of welfare for blacks is

---

[9] A recent study by Jerrold Schneider, "Measuring Political Forces in Congress," paper presented at the Annual Meeting of the American Political Science Association, San Francisco, September 1975, does suggest that there has been a substantial increase in the coherence of attitudes of congressmen during the same time period. His data are based on congressmen alone, not all candidates, and are derived from different interview questions and in part from roll-call analysis. They are not directly comparable to the 1958 data used by Converse. But they suggest that consistency is roughly twice as great in the early 1970s as it was in the late 1950s. This would make the increase comparable in magnitude to that in the mass public, and the result would be an elite group that remains quite different from the mass public.

consistent simply because we assign both of those answers to the same end of a liberal/conservative dimension.

As we have pointed out, there is no logical connection across these issues. We might accuse someone of inconsistency who believed that "all races should be treated equally" yet also favored discrimination against blacks, but one can certainly oppose school integration yet favor increased welfare without being accused of inconsistency. It is important to remember what our measures in fact measure, for otherwise one tends to reify and over-interpret the findings.

Does this mean that the change we trace is an artifact of our arbitrary categorization? If there is no logical necessity that places a pro-welfare, a pro-integration, and an anti–cold war attitude at the same (liberal) end of the issue continuum, perhaps consistency has not increased. In the years before 1964 political attitudes may have been constrained, but in directions different from those we have assigned: one could predict one attitude as well from another but what we would call a liberal attitude on one issue would predict what we would call a conservative attitude on another. There is certainly an identifiable ideology in the United States that links support for welfare measures such as minimun wage laws or medical care programs with opposition to civil rights. Our categories make someone with such a position inconsistent. Perhaps the person holding such a position is being consistent in ways we do not recognize.

The counterargument is plausible and compelling. It reminds us that there may be many categorized by us as having inconsistent political attitudes who have well thought out positions that have a coherence of their own, and a coherence no more or less intrinsically valid than that of our consistent liberals or consistent conservatives. As the works of scholars such as Robert Lane remind us, popular beliefs can have a much more complex structure than that summarized on our particular measures.[10]

On the other hand, there is good reason to believe that the change is more than a reflection of our arbitrary categorization. For one thing, the categorization is not all that arbitrary. Though one can identify meaningful positions that "criss-cross" our categorization, the general tendency in American politics is for issues to line up together as we have categorized them.

Furthermore, if there were substantial numbers of the citizens in the earlier years who held a consistent set of attitudes that criss-crossed our categorization, we should have found a negative relationship across issue areas, rather than the zero relationship we do find. The zero relationship in

---

[10] Robert Lane, *Political Ideology* (New York: Free Press, 1962).

the earlier years indicates an absence of coherence, not the presence of an alternative coherence.[11] Thus we feel confident that there has been a real change in citizen attitudes in the direction of more meaningful structure. (And, as we shall show in the next chapter, change in our measure of consistency is paralleled by other changes of a similar sort.)

The rise in issue consistency does not imply that the citizen now has a well-developed philosophy of politics, which she or he constantly reexamines so its various parts will hold together logically. Our measures do not indicate that the populace has become more "sophisticated" (if the possession of a logically coherent set of political beliefs is taken as an indicator of sophistication). Increased issue consistency can result from changes in the stimuli the citizen receives from the political world or from changes in the way he or she processes these stimuli.

1. In the first instance, there may be changes in the way issues line up with each other in the political world. An individual may be opposed to blacks and in favor of welfare. At some point, a variety of new programs is introduced that results in a high proportion of welfare spending going as aid to black families. He decides welfare is a bad thing. Our measures would find him moving from an inconsistent to a consistent position. It is not necessary for the issues themselves to change for the stimuli to change. What may be more likely is that the way issues are presented will change. If a candidate comes along who presents a new "bundle" of issue positions, a citizen who accepts the bundle may wind up with a more (or less, depending on how the items in the bundle fit into our liberal-conservative categorization) consistent position. As we will try to demonstrate in Chapters 11 and 17, a good deal of the change in issue consistency derives from changes in the kinds of issue bundles presented to the citizenry.

2. Issue consistency can also rise because citizens process the stimuli they receive differently. They may become more sensitive to the consistencies or inconsistencies in their positions and respond by bringing their attitudes into line with each other. As we shall show in the next chapter, this process has been taking place as well. But even this change in the way citizens process stimuli is not unrelated to changes in the stimuli themselves. As we shall try to

---

[11] Of course, there is another alternative. In the earlier years one might have had two sets of citizens with coherent attitudes: some whose attitudes cohere along the liberal-conservative continuum we have postulated, and others who have coherent attitudes of the criss-cross variety. Using our measures, we would have a positive relationship across issue areas for the former group, a negative relationship for the latter group. This would then average out to zero. We cannot eliminate this possibility completely, but in close examination of subgroupings of the population we have uncovered no division of the population that would create this result.

show, the greater consistency in citizen attitudes is, in part, a response to the changes in the political stimuli they have been receiving—in particular to the heightened intensity of political issues in the 1960s.

Whether issue consistency results from changes in political stimuli or from changes in the way stimuli are processed (it clearly results from a combination of the two), its appearance has significant implications for the political process. It affects the kinds of political coalitions that can be formed and the basis on which such coalitions can be held together. This becomes particularly important as the ties of party affiliation weaken. We shall return to this theme in Chapter 10 and Chapters 16–19.

An Index of Attitude Consistency

We have based our analysis on the gamma statistic in order to compare our findings to previous work on attitude constraint. But it would be useful to have a more flexible index of consistency. Such an index would allow us to estimate changes in the proportion of the citizenry that can be considered to have consistent liberal or conservative attitudes at different points in time. It would also provide us with a single measure of consistency that could be easily related to other variables that might either be the causes or the consequences of that consistency.[12]

In order to create such a summary index of liberal-conservative attitude consistency that would be comparable across time and reflect only changes in the degree to which the attitudes of the citizenry were consistent across the issues, we took the following steps.

(1) We standardized the distribution of each of the items in each year, so that (a) the items in each of the five issue spheres would have a comparable metric, and (b) changes in the distribution of responses due to changes in question wording, the number of response categories, or changes in the actual proportion of the population having liberal or conservative attitudes on the issues would not affect the degree of consistency observed. The standardization process produces a set of measures which are comparable across issue spheres and across time.

---

[12] A summary index is also necessary if we are to examine changes in consistency among subgroups of the population. For certain groups, attitudes on the individual items are skewed in a left or right direction. In such cases, the lack of variance on individual issues produced degenerate correlations; correlations between such skewed items and other issues become useless as a means for describing levels of consistency. A subgroup may be united in a liberal direction on two issue areas, but the correlation across issue areas will be low. This is particularly the case for some of the most interesting population groups such as blacks and southern whites, groups that have come to be very consistently left or right. Finally, a summary measure is desirable for gauging directional change—that is, to see which groups are becoming more left, more right, or more polarized.

(2) These standardized items were then added together. This produces an index with a mean of zero in each year. Because of the standardization, the variance around the mean in any one year is a function of the degree of attitude consistency; that is, a function of intercorrelation among the items. In those years where attitude consistency is low, most citizens will obtain a summary score near zero, because their liberal position on some issues will cancel out their conservative attitudes on others. In years when attitude consistency is higher, the variation around the mean will grow, with more respondents having extreme positive or negative scores, reflecting the fact that all or most of their responses were consistently liberal or conservative.

(3) We add one additional step, which increases the precision of the measures. Prior to summing the standardized items, they were subjected in each year to a principle component analysis. This variety of factor analysis produces a loading for each item which reflects its degree of correlation with all other items in the set. These loadings were then used as weights in summing the items. In years when attitude consistency is relatively low, the weights are generally small; in those years when attitude consistency is relatively high, the larger interitem correlations yield larger factor weights. The weighting highlights the differences across the years without affecting the basic pattern.

The distributions of this index for all the years were then combined, yielding an average distribution from 1956 through 1972. Using the distribution of scale scores for all the years combined we establish cutting points which divide the population into consistent and inconsistent proportions. We break the population into five groups that approximate a bell-shaped normal distribution. Those who fall in the left-most sixth of the attitude scale are our leftists; those in the right-most sixth are the rightists. The next sixth of the distribution on the scale as one moves toward the center gives us our moderate leftists and moderate rightists. The remaining one-third of the population that is in the middle of the scale are our centrists. Thus, if an individual is assigned to one of those categories it is because his own score puts him into that category compared with respondents across all the years. Because the cutting points on the scale are based on the distribution of the scores across all years, the proportion in each of these categories varies from year to year depending on the amount of consistency present in that year. Thus the scale can be used to tell us how many citizens are consistent in any year compared with the average situation across the two decades.[13]

Figure 8.4 traces changes in the proportion of citizens with consistent attitudes over the seventeen year period. It displays the proportion of the

---

[13] See Appendix 2B for a full discussion.

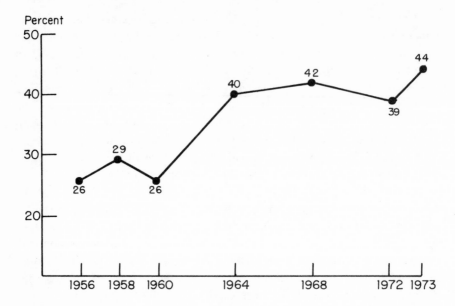

FIGURE 8.4. The rise of political consistency: percent of the population with consistent attitudes, 1956–1973

population in each year who fall into the left-most or the right-most sixths of the aggregated attitude scale. By combining the left and right consistents we have a group that falls in the top third in terms of consistency based on the average level of consistency across the entire time period. The choice of the one-third criterion is arbitrary; we could have isolated the 20 percent most consistent or the 10 percent who were most consistent. What matters is how the proportion in that consistent category changes. If there were no change in the amount of political consistency, one would find 33 percent falling at the extremes of the consistency scale at each time point. But as figure 8.4 indicates, there is a sharp change in the proportion of the population with consistent attitudes. In 1956, about one in four citizens falls in the extremes of the attitude consistency scale. The proportion remains between 25 percent and 30 percent through 1960. As is to be expected from our earlier analysis, there is a sharp change between 1960 and 1964. The proportion holding consistent attitudes increases to 40 percent of the population, and the proportion remains at this higher level through 1973.

The Shape of Public Attitudes, 1956 to 1973

The increased consistency among political attitudes on the part of the *individual citizen* means that the "shape" of the attitudes of the American

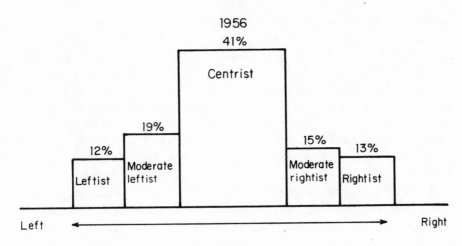

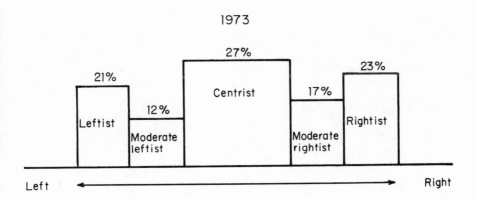

FIGURE 8.5. Distribution of population on political beliefs, 1956 and 1973

public *as a whole* has changed. We can see this by comparing the distribution of citizens along our overall liberalism-conservatism continuum in 1956 with the distribution in 1973. Such a comparison will make clear how different is the public in these later years from what it was at an earlier time.

Our scale of attitude consistency allows us to compare 1956 with 1973 in terms of the overall attitude distribution for the population. Figure 8.5 displays the attitude distribution for those two years using the five categories: the left-most sixth of the population, the moderate left sixth; the middle third, the moderate right sixth, and the right-most sixth. In 1956 the bulk of the public was close to the middle because a lack of attitude coherence meant that a liberal position on some issues cancelled out a conservative one on others. The fact that the distribution of attitudes in 1956 closely approximates a bell-shaped distribution underscores the lack of structure of political opinion that period.[14] The distribution of left-right opinion in 1973 is very different indeed. Only 27 percent of the population is in the centrist category, far fewer than the number in 1956. Concomitantly, we find a large growth in the proportion of citizens taking consistently left or right views across all five issue spheres, with 21 percent in the far-left category and 23 percent in the far right. We contrast the 1956 pattern with the data from 1973 because these two years represent the first and last years for which we have a complete measurement of attitudes across all five issue areas. However, 1958 and 1960 look very much like 1956, and the years from 1964 onward take on a shape very similar to that found in 1973. The clear contrast in degree of polarization and attitude coherence is one between the pre- and post-1964 periods. Thus, from 1964 onward one finds a more polarized electorate, with large numbers of people on both the left and the right. Figure 8.5 illustrates how much the "shape" of the public has changed.

---

[14] There is another way in which people could fall in the center position on our scale. They could consistently choose the middle choice on each of the issue questions. There is, however, no evidence that the greater proportion of centrists in the mid-fifties was due to a greater frequency of consistently centrist attitudes.

9

Issue Consistency: A Closer Look

We wish to extend our consideration of issue consistency by considering some other ways in which it is manifested and by exploring some of the possible sources for its rise.

Have Issues Grown in Importance?

That issues grow in consistency does not mean that they matter more to the individual, though one can make the argument that they are likely to matter more if they have some coherent pattern. We can, however, find independent evidence for an increase in issue importance that comes at the same time as the sharp step upward in issue consistency. This is seen in figure 9.1. We repeat the data from the previous chapter on the proportion who have consistent political attitudes, and plot, as well, the proportion who mention political issues when asked what they like or dislike about the presidential candidates of that year. The two measures move in the same way: both show a major increase after 1960. The frequency with which issues are mentioned peaks in 1964 and falls somewhat in the succeeding election, but returns in 1972 to the peak level of 1964.

The two measures, it should be stressed, are quite independent of and different from each other. The measure of issue consistency depends on the intercorrelation among

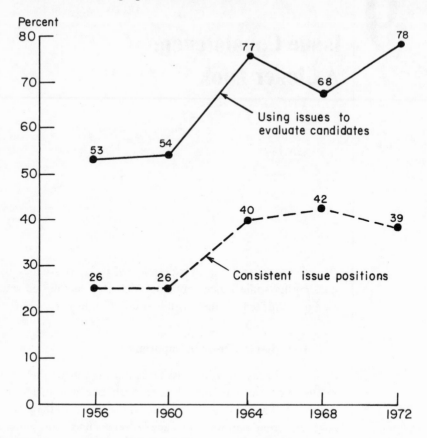

FIGURE 9.1. Proportion consistent in attitudes and proportion referring to issues to evaluate candidates, 1956–1972

answers to a number of specific issue questions. The measure of the use of issues in evaluating candidates is based on answers to open-ended questions about the candidates. That two measures, based on such different questions, produce such similar results adds a good deal of credence to the evidence for a substantial change in the ways in which citizens think about political matters.

Futhermore, there is evidence that these two changes in the role of issues—the growth in consistency and the growth in their use in evaluating candidates—are related. From the answers to the open-ended questions on likes and dislikes of candidates, we constructed a measure of the issue-based evaluation of candidates. The measure tells us whether those who mention issues mention them in a way that favors one candidate over another.[1] This

---

[1] The number of times issues were mentioned as a reason for liking the Democratic candidate was substracted from the number of times issues were mentioned as a reason

TABLE 9.1. Pearson correlations of candidate evaluation on the issues, with index of issue consistency

1956	1960	1964	1968	1972
.14	.25	.51	.43	.40

measure was then correlated with our belief scale. A high correlation would indicate that those whose issue evaluation favored the Democratic candidate were also liberal on our left-right issue scale, those whose issue evaluation favored the Republican would be on the right on the issue continuum. A low correlation would mean that there was no link between the use of issue evaluation and the coherence of one's attitudes.

The results are in table 9.1. In 1956 and 1960 there is almost no relationship between these evaluations and the citizenry's positions on the issues as measured by our belief scale. Once again, this points to the almost random nature of issue responses in the fifties and early sixties. From 1964 onward, however, these evaluations become highly correlated with the citizenry's general positions on the left-right belief index. Over the period, this correlation increases substantially, peaking (as did the frequency of issue mention) in 1964, but remaining well above the pre-1964 level thereafter. Thus, citizens are more likely now to hold consistent views on the issues and to use these views as criteria when considering their electoral choices.

Furthermore, the change in the relationship between the measure of issue consistency and the measure of the issue evaluation of the candidates occurs at the same time as the increase in the level of issue consistency and the change in the frequency of the evaluative use of issues. These data support our contention that a significant and systematic change in the way in which the American public thinks about political matters took place between 1960 and 1964.

We do not want to exaggerate the nature of this change. It does not mean, necessarily, that the United States is now divided into two polarized ideological camps, one with a conservative world view, the other with a liberal one. The "extremists" on our scale of political attitudes are now only about 40 percent of the public, and they are not all that extreme in their positions.

---

for liking the Republicans. In addition, the number of times issues were the reason for disliking the Republicans was subtracted from the number of times issues were the reason for disliking the Democrats. The two figures were added, giving a score reflecting the degree to which issue references favor one candidate over the other. Those who mention no issues are omitted from the calculation.

But the data in figure 9.1 suggest that something important has happened to the American public. Using any criterion of measurement, it has changed substantially from 1956. Issue positions are more coherent and more important.

A More Educated and Cognitively Competent Public

When the absence of issue consistency in the mass public was first noted in the 1950s, great stress was put upon some differences between the better educated and the less well educated. Converse found attitude consistency in the mass public to be generally low, but the consistency among those with higher levels of education was substantially higher than among those with more limited education. If we use our measure of consistency in the 1956 and 1958 studies, we find an average gamma of .10 for all issues among those who did not finish high school compared with an average gamma of .19 for those with at least some college education.[2] If we consider the correlations among domestic issues we find an average gamma of .16 for those with less than a high school degree compared with .34 among those with some college. The difference is substantial enough to lead one to suspect that the changes in the amount of issue consistency in the mass public that we have observed over time may be a function of increased levels of education.

As we saw in Chapter 7, the educational level of the public has risen substantially since the late 1950s. When we sought the explanation of the rising level of conceptualization of the American public in these educational changes, we did not find it. The change in the level of conceptualization appeared to be much greater in magnitude than would be explicable by educational changes, and we found that among those with lower education, there was an even larger increase than among the college educated in the use of ideological and issue terms to evaluate candidates and parties.

Can we explain the rise in attitude consistency by educational changes? The data indicate that we cannot. Figure 9.2 presents over-time data on levels of attitude consistency for two educational groups—those with less than a complete high school education and those who have at least some college training. We present two separate summary measures of the degree of issue constraint—the overall summary measure (average gammas) that takes into account the relationship among all the core issues, both domestic and foreign (top graph) and the average degrees of constraint considering only the relationships among the domestic issues (bottom graph).

---

2 The data are based on averages across both of the years.

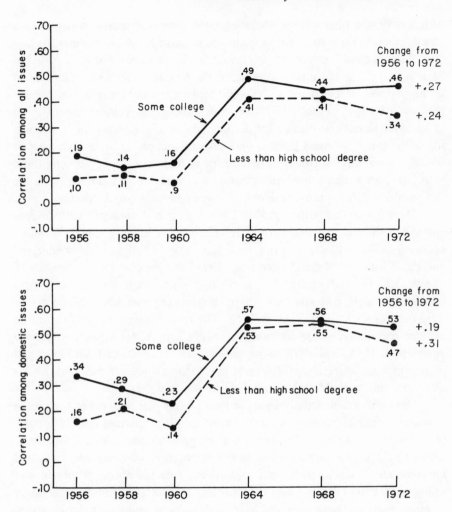

FIGURE 9.2. Comparison of levels of attitude consistency through time for two educational groups, 1956–1972

The data on overall levels of attitude consistency across both domestic and foreign issues make it quite clear that educational shifts have had little if any impact on the changes in the structure of mass beliefs that we have encountered. While those with some college education manifest higher levels of consistency throughout the period, both the educated and less-educated groups have shown increases in consistency which are far greater than the differences between the groups at any point in time. More important, those with less than a high school education have shown increases in consistency almost equal in magnitude to the increases shown for the college educated.

When we concentrate on the core domestic issues, we find that there has been a decline in the disparity between the less and the better-educated in terms of level of consistency. Though consistency on these issues has increased for those at both levels of educational achievement, increases in consistency have been greater for the low educational group—those, according to the theory of mass beliefs, who have least capacity for a high level of liberal/conservative ideology. The level of attitude consistency among those with less than a high school education has increased by 31 points, while the comparable figure for those with at least some college is only 19 points.

Most important, with regard to both overall and domestic attitude consistency, is the fact that the sharp increase in level of attitude constraint which occurred between 1960 and 1964, took place among both the highly educated and those with little formal education. The sharp increase in the consistency of attitudes among those with less than a high school degree can be seen most dramatically if we compare that group with the congressional candidates who were used as a criterion group in 1958. The congressional candidates had an average correlation of .38 for domestic issues and .31 for all issues. For the years 1964, 1968, and 1972, those ordinary citizens who had not completed high school have average correlations of .52 for domestic issues and .39 for all issues: substantially higher than the criterion "elite" group!

The implication of the findings in figure 9.2 is that the growth of attitude consistency within the mass public is not the result of increases in the population's cognitive capacities brought about by gains in educational attainment. These findings raise the question of the importance of permanent personal characteristics such as ideational sophistication or the ability to obtain and utilize contextual knowledge as determinants of levels of attitude consistency in mass publics. Those with the lowest educational attainment have experienced the largest increases in consistency on the core domestic issues. The difference in issue consistency between the two educational groups is small in comparison to the importance of the increase in consistency which each group has experienced. It is unlikely that those who have not completed high school are as capable of manipulating abstract concepts as those who have some college training. Yet, if factors such as these place limits on the level of attitudinal consistency among the masses, we would not now find that those at the educational extremes display relatively equal and high levels of attitude consistency. The year 1956 appears to have been a moment when there was an unusually large gap between the levels of consistency across educational groups. But the gap appears to be smaller in later periods.

Entrance of New Populations Into the Electorate

There is another plausible explanation of the growth in consistency among political views: that issue consistency has been brought into the political process by the new voters who have come of age during the late 1960s. As we saw in relation to party identification, most of the growth in partisan independence was attributable to these new entrants.

Perhaps the new mode of political thinking also comes with the entrance of new cohorts. Some of the same forces which may have led the new voters to be politically independent may also have led them to view politics in more ideologically consistent terms. However, our detailed examination of the attitude consistency of age cohorts over time reveals that this is not the case. The coherence of attitudes rises for those in all age groups and does so at almost equal rates. There is no appreciable difference among age groups in the degree of attitude consistency at any point in the time period we are investigating.[3]

Citizen Attitudes and the World of Politics

Increased cognitive capacity does not appear to explain the increase in attitude consistency. Citizens at all educational levels have developed more coherent attitudes. Similarly we found earlier that citizens at all educational levels have begun to conceptualize politics in issue and ideological terms. To understand the source of these changes, it may be better to look outside of the individual citizen to the real would of politics. The way in which people think about the political world is not merely the result of their social and psychological characteristics—the education they have or their cognitive capacities. The way people think about politics is also a reflection of the stimuli offered to them by the political world: the nature of issues, the salience of these issues, and the way in which issues are presented. We have seen this in relation to levels of conceptualization.

The simple explanation for increased issue consistency may be that politics have changed. Issues have become more salient to citizens and they have been presented to citizens as meaningful bundles of issues. This contrasts with the situation in the 1950s when there were no important political issues and when the leading political figure—Dwight Eisenhower—presented a political image above the issues.

---

[3] There are some important differences, however, in the *direction* of the political views of the new age cohorts (see Chapter 14).

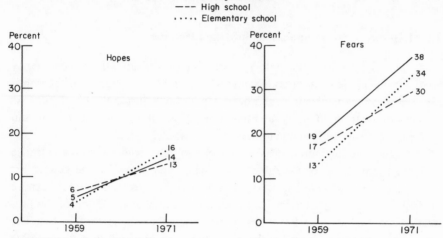

FIGURE 9.3. Political hopes and fears in personal life by education, 1959 and 1971

We saw in Chapter 6 that the issues on which citizens focus have changed since the Eisenhower years and, what may be more important, these political issues now penetrate into the personal hopes and fears of the citizens. Nor is this greater awareness of the impact of political matters on one's day-to-day life a function of cognitive competence—that is, a better educated and, hence, more sophisticated citizenry. Consider the data in figure 9.3. It reports the proportions of citizens at three different educational levels who express politically relevant hopes and fears in 1959 compared with the proportions who so report in 1971.[4] The increase in the penetration of politics into the personal lives of citizens has taken place for citizens at all levels of education. These data are consistent with our interpretation of the changes that have taken place from the Eisenhower years until recently. The increased awareness of politics affects citizens at all levels of cognitive competence (assuming education measures that). It is not that citizens are better educated and therefore see a closer connection between their own life space and the political world. If greater political sophistication were the explanation, one would expect more frequent political reference among the upper educated and/or a greater change in that frequency among those citizens with higher levels of education. Rather the data suggest that the world of politics impinges on the lives of all citizens. If the political world has become more salient, it is

[4] The 1959 data are from Hadley Cantril, *The Pattern of Human Concerns* (New Brunswick, N.J.: Rutgers University Press, 1965); the 1971 data are from Hadley Cantril and Charles W. Roll, *Hopes and Fears of the American People* (New York: Universe Books, 1971). We could not locate educational breakdowns for the 1964 data.

because political matters have intruded into private lives. And that intrusion affects lower and upper educated citizens.

Can this increase in the salience of politics that we find across all educational groups explain the rise in issue consistency? There is good reason to expect this. A repeated finding from social-psychological research on attitude change and attitude structure is that inconsistent or dissonant beliefs are frequently held in areas of people's lives distant from their daily concerns.[5] However, these studies indicate that when the salience or centrality of the psychological object is heightened, pressures are brought on individuals to force their inconsistent beliefs into harmony. Our data show that political events after the late 1950s have caused citizens to perceive politics as increasingly central to their lives. If we are correct about this increased salience, then the social-psychological theories of attitude change represent a possible explanation for the observed increases in issue consistency.

As we shall see in Chapter 15 there has been a substantial rise in political interest since 1960. We can test for the relationship between interest and attitude consistency. As was the case with the hypothesis that education leads to consistency, we need to examine the levels of attitude consistency over time among the interested and uninterested. This we do in figure 9.4, where we plot the levels of attitude consistency for those who are highly interested in the campaigns and for those who report no interest at all, first on all of the issues, and then on the core domestic issues.

We can see that the growth of interest alone does not account for the rise of liberal/conservative ideology; consistency has gone up among the interested and uninterested alike. This is similar to the situation in relation to education: consistency went up among both the educated and less educated. However, while increased educational attainment appeared to play almost no role in the growth of attitude consistency, increases in political interest (or the salience of politics) appears to play a very significant role.

Between 1960 and 1968, it is among the growing group of interested citizens that one finds the largest increase in attitude consistency. When we compared education groups we found a diminishing difference over time in the degree of issue consistency between the more and less well educated. In relation to political interest we find the opposite: that there is a much greater gap in constraint between the more and less interested in 1964 and 1968 than

---

[5] See Leon Festinger, *A Theory of Cognitive Dissonance* (Stanford: Stanford University Press, 1968). Various types of empirical evidence confirming the proposition that increased salience leads to increased attitude constraint can be found in Milton J. Rosenberg and others, *Attitude Organization and Change* (New Haven: Yale Studies in Attitude Communication, vol. 3, 1960).

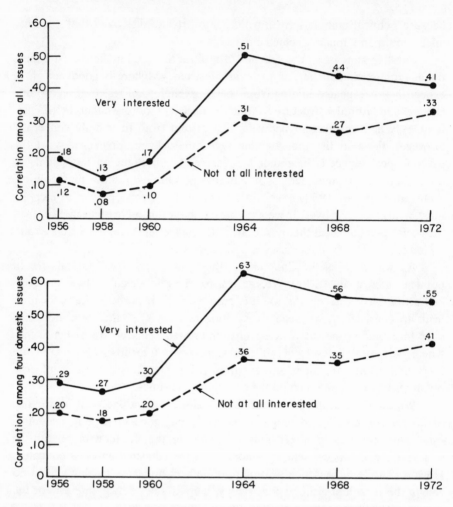

FIGURE 9.4. Comparison of levels of attitude consistency through time for the interested and uninterested in presidential campaigns, 1956–1972

in the pre-1964 period. Between 1956 and 1968, the gammas reflecting overall consistency (including domestic and foreign issues) among those with no interest increase only 15 points, while for the highly interested the average gammas among the same issues grow 26 points. The pattern is the same for the average correlations among the core domestic issues.[6]

---

[6] The important role of political interest is consistent with the data in *The American Voter*. Education was found to be a less important explanation of the consistent line-up of issue position with party affiliation than was a measure of political involvement. See *The American Voter*, p. 208.

Furthermore, the relative size of the interested group undergoes an increase just before the rise in consistency, from about 30 to about 40 percent of the population (see below, figure 15.2). The combined impact of the rise in attitude consistency among those interested in politics and the increase in the numbers of such citizens accounts for a major proportion of the observed growth of ideological constraint in the population as a whole. It is exposure to politics, not attainment of higher levels of education and its accompanying cognitive capacity, that seems to lead to the greater coherence of citizen attitudes.

10 The Rise of Issue Voting

The role of party has declined as a guide to the vote. And, as party has declined in importance, the role of issues appears to have risen. These changes are not independent of each other. The following abstract analysis, into which we later place some data, helps us understand some of the dynamics of party- and issue-guided voting.

Party Voting

The main rule of party voting is simple: when there is a choice between the candidate of the party with which you identify and the opposition party, vote for your party's candidate. Party voting therefore requires that:

1. A voter have a party identification. He or she must prefer one or the other of the two parties. This preference must be a relatively long-term preference; one that extends across elections. In some countries, party identification appears to be coterminus with voting intention; if a person is going to vote for or has just voted for the candidate of a party he will almost always say he identifies with that party.[1] But

---

[1] See David Butler and Donald E. Stokes, *Political Change in Britain* (New York: St. Martins Press, 1969). This presumption that in most other countries voting and party preference is identical may be a result of an insensitivity to the different meaning assigned to similar phrases in different countries. It is at least possible that asking people if they

for there to be party voting, it must also be possible to vote in a way that deviates from the party; it must be meaningful to say "I am a Democrat, but I voted for a Republican."

2. The candidates must be from different parties, otherwise one cannot choose on the basis of party. There is no party vote in the Democratic primary.

3. The individual must use the party affiliation as the criterion (or at least as a major criterion) for choice. It is not always easy to tell whether this is the case. If someone who calls himself a Democrat votes for the Democratic candidate, that does not necessarily indicate that he voted that way for party reasons—he might have flipped a coin. But we can use the voting behavior of an aggregate of people who identify with the Democratic party to see if their behavior is consistent with the hypothesis that they vote on the basis of party. And we can go further and ask them why they voted as they did; or, as the SRC does, ask them why they like a candidate and record whether they mention his party.

The notion of a party vote also implies that:

4. A voter with no party identification cannot vote on the basis of party. Thus the growth in the number of Independents automatically reduces the number who can give a party vote.

5. A candidate not identified with one of the major parties cannot receive a party vote. This is an oversimplification, of course. Someone who has a long-term identification with the Socialist party and votes for the Socialist candidate gives a party vote. Furthermore, a candidate without the official nomination of one of the main parties may still be perceived by voters to be the candidate of that party. One can argue, as does Schneider, that Wallace in 1968 was perceived by many southern Democrats as the mainstream Democratic candidate, though this was not the case with northern democrats.[2] But for our purposes, a party vote will be considered to be a vote for one of the major party candidates.

Issue Voting

Issue voting is analogous to party voting, but somewhat more complicated. The main rule of issue voting is similar to that for party voting: if there

---

are Conservative or Labour identifiers in Britain is not the equivalent of asking party identification in the United States. In the United States the party preference questions appear to inquire about whether the respondent prefers a party, while in England it may appear that the party identification questions are asking about formal membership in a party. The confusion between party identification and membership in a party can arise because dues paying membership in a party is as common to most party systems as it is infrequent in the United States.

[2] William Schneider, "Issues, Voting, and Cleavages," *American Behavioral Scientist,* 18 (September 1974), 111–146.

is an issue A and two positions on that issue (A_1 and A_2), the voter who prefers one of the two positions will vote for the candidate who holds that same position. Issue voting therefore requires:

1. That the individual have a preference for either A_1 or A_2 (just as he had to have a party identification for a party vote). Furthermore, just as party identification has to be more than a mere reflection of how one intends to vote or had just voted, so the issue preference of the individual must be more than a mere reflection of his preference for one candidate over the other. If the voter adopts an issue position because his preferred candidate adopts it, he will appear to cast an issue vote but it will not in fact be one.

2. The candidates must offer a choice on the issues. One candidate must support A_1, the other A_2; or one must support one of the positions and the other be neutral. If a candidate supports A_1 and the other takes no position, voters with issue positions can still vote on that basis: voters who prefer A_1 will vote for the candidate who also prefers it, and those who prefer position A_2 will vote for the neutral candidate. But if both candidates support the same position or are both neutral, issue voting is impossible.[3]

Issue voting, however, offers a number of complexities not found in party voting. For one thing, issues do not always offer clear dichotomous choices of A_1 versus A_2 as is the choice between the Republican and Democratic parties. There may be many possible positions on the issue. Sometimes the issue positions can be thought of as points along a continuum: the amount we ought to spend for defense can range from zero dollars to the total GNP, and we can imagine citizens with preferences somewhere along the continuum that runs from one point to the other. If there were such a continuum, we could change the general rule of issue voting to read: vote for the candidate whose position on the continuum is closest to your own. In figure 10.1, voter *a* votes for candidate 1; voter *c* for candidate 2. Voter *b* is close to an indifference point (he cannot make an issue vote if he is equidistant between the two candidates), but he is a touch closer to candidate 1 and an issue vote would go to him. Note the important point: a voter has to be closer to one candidate than another to make an issue vote. The closer the two candidates are to each other, the more difficult is it to make such a vote. If the candidates do not differ, issue voting is impossible.

A second complexity is that issue positions may not always line up along a continuum. What whould we do if there is an embargo on oil shipments by OPEC? Invade the persian Gulf? Drastically reduce our energy consumption?

---

[3] This is the critical assumption of all studies of issue voting. See Anthony Downs, *An Economic Theory of Democracy* (New York: Harper & Row, 1957).

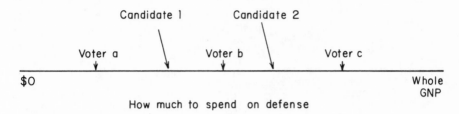

FIGURE 10.1. Hypothetical issue continuum

Stop our support to Israel in the hope that OPEC will resume oil shipments? The three positions do not form a neat continuum, nor are they mutually exclusive. Casting an issue vote becomes more complicated under these circumstances, but it is still possible: vote for the candidate whose mix of positions is closest to your own.

Third, a more complicated situation arises when there is more than one relevant issue. Assume that there are two issues in an election, and each is equally salient to a voter. An issue voter would vote for the candidate who was closer to him on the two-dimensional plane defined by the two issues. Consider figure 10.2. Voter *a* should vote for candidate 1 if he casts an issue vote. Though he is closer to candidate 2 on issue A (candidate 1 is more liberal than voter *a* on that) he is further from candidate 2 on issue B than he is from candidate 1 on issue A. Voter *b*, on the other hand, is closer to candidate 2 on both issues and should vote for him if he casts an issue vote. The two-issue case can be extended to the three- or four-issue case. For our purposes what is important is the illustration this gives as to why issue consistency increases the potential for issue voting.

Issue consistency converts the two-dimensional space defined by the two-issue continuum into one dimension. This is illustrated in figure 10.3. If citizens take consistent positions across two issues, it means that they are found in the upper left (consistent liberal) and lower right (consistent conservative) positions. The greater the proportion of the citizenry with consistent positions, the more the issue space can be accurately simplified by the heavy line joining those two positions. As our analysis of issue consistency has shown, more citizens fall on that line after 1964 than before. (In Chapter 8 we showed that the variance in attitudes that is explained by a hypothesized single liberal-conservative dimension rises substantially between 1960 and 1964.)

Let us assume that candidates as well fall somewhere along the heavy line of issue consistency—that is, that they are likely to be consistent liberals, consistent middle of the roaders, or consistent conservatives. For the purpose of our argument, it is not necessary that they fall exactly on the line, but

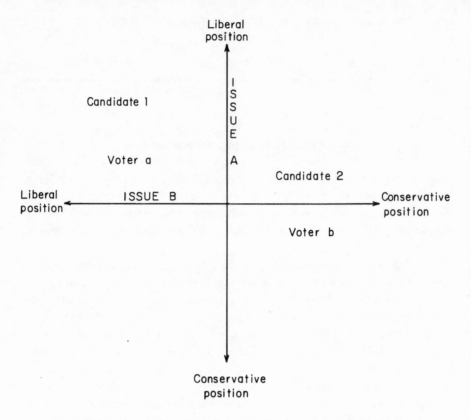

FIGURE 10.2. Hypothetical issue continuum involving two issues

simply that they be closer to the line than is the average citizen (that is, that there is more "constraint" in their issue positions than there is on the part of the citizenry).

If candidates fall on that line, the proportion of citizens who give an issue vote (who are unambiguously closer to one candidate than another) will increase the more citizens there are on that line. For example, suppose candidate 1 is running against candidate 4 (a consistently liberal candidate versus a consistently conservative one—see figure 10.3). Citizens at either end of the liberal-conservative continuum have unambiguous issue choices. Consistent liberals will vote for candidate 1; consistent conservatives will vote for candidate 4. If there are some citizens who take a middle of the road position on both issues, they will not be able to choose between candidates 1 and 4 on the issues. They are equidistant between the two candidates. This is true as well for those citizens who have strong but "criss-cross" positions on the issues—that is, they are liberal on one issue and conservative on the other. Citizens in

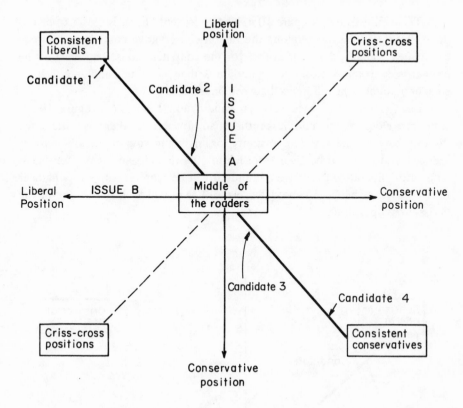

FIGURE 10.3. Voters and candidates on a two-issue space

those positions (in the lower left and upper right of figure 10.3) are equidistant between the candidates 1 and 4 and cannot cast an issue vote.

As another example, suppose consistently liberal candidate 1 runs against candidate 3 who is a middle of the roader a touch to the right of center. Again the choice for the consistent liberals and consistent conservatives is fairly clear. In this case, the middle of the roaders have an issue choice as well—they are closer to candidate 3. The criss-crossed voter is also somewhat closer to candidate 3 but the distinction between candidate 3 and candidate 1 in terms of closeness is not as great as is the case for citizens on the liberal-conservative continuum. The citizen who is liberal on issue B but conservative on issue A likes candidate 1's position on the former, and dislikes his position on the latter. He is fairly indifferent to candidate 3's position on both issues. The situation is by no means as clear to him as it is to almost all citizens on the liberal-conservative continuum—especially to those at the ends of the continuum.

This is illustrated in figure 10.4. The consistent liberal is closer to candidate 1 by the full distance along the liberal-conservative continuum between candidates 1 and 3, the same is true for the consistent conservatives. But the criss-crossed voter is closer to candidate 3 than he is to candidate 1 by a smaller amount—the difference between lines x and y.

Lastly, consider a race between candidates 2 and 3 (on figure 10.3). Both are close to the middle of the road. Insofar as there is little issue distance between them, the opportunity for anyone to vote on an issue basis is reduced. But it should be clear from figure 10.4 that citizens at the consistent ends of the liberal-conservative continuum will be more sensitive to whatever difference exists between candidates 2 and 3 than will a citizen at one of the "criss-cross" positions.

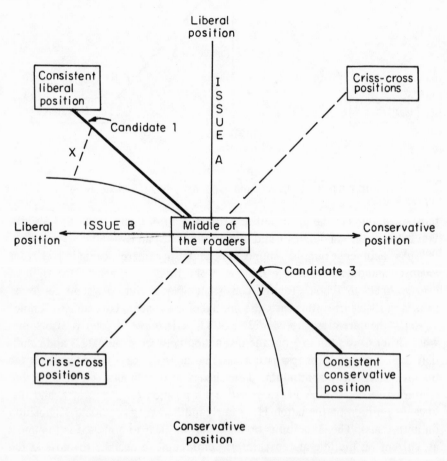

FIGURE 10.4. Issue consistency and issue distance

In sum, issue consistency has a potentially important impact on the voting decision. It simplifies the issue space for the voter and makes it easier for him to choose on the basis of his issue position. Voters with consistent issue positions will be more sensitive to the issue positions of candidates.

We have not paid much attention to issue salience. Another way in which a multiplicity of issues can be simplified is when one issue is overriding. In such a case, one has really returned to a single issue space for the voter who has an overriding issue.[4] There are, of course, many mixed circumstances—where one has multiple issues of varying salience and with varying degrees of consistency among them. These are important complexities, but ones we shall not explore.

One final complexity for issue voting: a good deal depends on the location of the candidates on the issues. Citizens with issue positions cannot vote those positions unless they are given a choice (consider the difficulty of issue voting when candidate 2 opposes candidate 3 as in figure 10.3). In this respect, issue voting differs from party voting.

The party affiliation of candidates is fairly clear and unambiguous. The major party candidates may fudge their party affiliation somewhat. They may make nonpartisan appeals or in other ways try to lower the salience of their party affiliation. However, in each of the elections since 1964 at least one candidate has taken a consistently liberal or conservative position: Goldwater in 1964; Wallace (as the third party candidate) in 1968; and McGovern in 1972. Thus, at least in these elections, the existence of a candidate with a position on the liberal-conservative continuum that is both unambiguous and fairly far from the center has facilitated issue voting.[5]

Lastly, there is some evidence that respondents consider candidates to have more consistent positions across a range of issues than the respondents themselves have. In the 1968 and 1972 election studies, respondents placed themselves on issue scales in connection with a number of issues. They also placed candidates on the same scales. We can measure the consistency of an

---

4 On this see Sidney Verba and Norman H. Nie, *Participation in America* (New York: Harper and Row, 1972), chap. 7.

5 Unambiguous issue positions among candidates and voters is the essential element for issue voting. In addition to Downs, *An Economic Theory of Democracy,* and Black, *The Theory of Committees and Elections,* a recent deductive model of voter choice is Otto Davis, Melvin H. Hinch, and Peter C. Ordershook, "An Expository Development of a Mathematical Model of the Electoral Process," *American Political Science Review,* 64 (June 1970), 426–448. A more plausible empirical analysis is in M. J. Shapiro, "Rational Political Man, A Synthesis of Economic and Social Psychological Perspectives," *American Political Science Review,* 63 (December 1969), 1106–1119. The most sophisticated discussion of candidate positions in relation to voter choice is found in Benjamin I. Page, *Choices and Echoes in Presidential Elections,* forthcoming.

individual's position across two issues by the "distance" between the positions he assigns himself on those two issues.[6] This can be compared with the distance between the positions he assigns to a candidate on the same pair of issues.

In all cases, respondents assign the candidates to more consistent positions than they choose for themselves. This applies to those candidates perceived as being at one or the other ends of the issue continuum—McGovern and Wallace. But it also applies to a candidate such as Nixon. He is placed a bit to the right of center by voters, on a number of issues. His position is thus that of a slightly right *consistent* middle of the roader. Thus he too would fall on the main diagonal on figure 10.3.

Data on Issue Voting and Party Voting

Decline in party voting comes about in two ways: (1) the proportion of the electorate with no party affiliation has risen and, therefore, the proportion that can cast a party vote has fallen and (2) even among those who have a partisan identity, the proportion voting for the opposition party has grown. We have also seen (in Chapter 8) the rise in the number of citizens who can cast issue votes because they have consistent issue positions. As numerous analyses have demonstrated in recent years, there is a concomitant rise in the likelihood that they will vote in accord with their issue position.[7]

Figure 10.5 compares two correlations: the correlation between our summary index of attitudes and the direction of the presidential vote and the correlation between party identification and the vote.[8] Our concern is with

---

[6] The scales have to be adjusted so that the liberal answer is always at the same end of the scale.

[7] There is a considerable amount of research literature which attempts an estimate of issue voting. The bibliography in John Kessel, "Comment: The Issues in Issue Voting," *American Political Science Review*, 66 (June 1972), 459–465, is as complete a list as one will find, and Kessel offers some worthy observations on the topic. The assessment of issue voting versus party voting is cleverly done in Richard W. Boyd, "Popular Control of Public Policy: A Normal Vote Analysis of the 1968 Election," *American Political Science Review*, 66 (June 1972), 429–449. Although the published research is too voluminous to cite here, special attention might be paid to assessments of issue voting following the themes developed by David E. Repass, "Issue Salience and Party Choice," *American Political Science Review*, 65 (June 1971), 389–400, and David G. Lawrence, *Issue Voting and Demand Failure in American Presidential Elections: 1952–1968*, Ph.D. dissertation, University of Chicago, 1975. An excellent treatment is in Pomper, *The Voter's Choice*, chap. 8.

[8] We assume that the Democratic candidate is on the left, the Republican candidate on the right. Thus a positive correlation means that citizens on the liberal end of the issue scale are more likely to vote for the Democratic candidate, citizens at the conservative end more likely to vote Republican. The assumption of the position of the major party candidates since 1956 is, we believe, a realistic one, and is confirmed by all data we can find on the perception of citizens of the issue location of candidates.

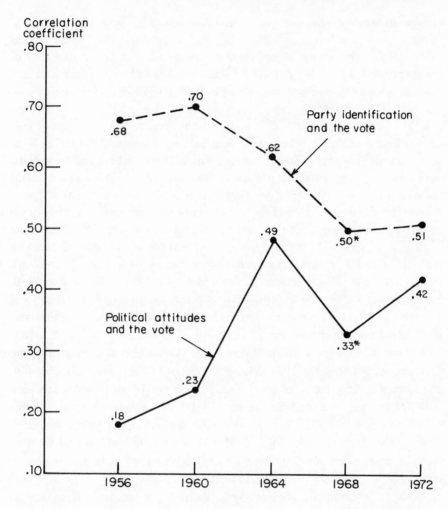

Correlation coefficient

FIGURE 10.5. Pearson correlations between party identification and the presidential vote and between the summary measure of political beliefs and the presidential vote, 1956–1972

* Weighted average of the correlation between attitudes and a Nixon/Humphrey choice, a Nixon/Wallace choice, and a Humphrey/Wallace choice.

In 1968, there is the complexity of the Wallace candidacy. In general, we have treated him as a candidate to the right of Nixon. The correlation between issue position and the vote for 1968, reported in figure 10.5, is an average of three correlations between issue position on the one hand and a Humphrey/Nixon, Humphrey/Wallace, and Nixon/Wallace choice, with the second-named candidate the conservative candidate in each pair.

changes in these correlations over time. The relationship between party identification and the vote is one with which we are familiar; from 1960, it falls
precipitously. The square of the correlations reported in figure 10.5 tells us
the proportion of variance in the vote that is explained by party identification.
The variance explained was about 50 percent in 1956 and 1960; by 1972 it
had fallen to 25 percent.

The contrast between the attitude/vote correlations and the party/vote
correlations is dramatic. The relationship between issues and the voting decision rises sharply. In 1956, the correlation between issue position and the
vote was .18. The correlation goes up dramatically in 1964 and remains
substantially above the earlier years. In the pre-1964 period a citizen's position on the issues, as measured by our summary attitude scale, had little or no
impact on the way in which he voted. Citizens on the left side of the scale
were almost as likely to vote for a Republican as for a Democrat. Citizens on
the right were almost as likely to vote Democratic as Republican. There was a
small increase in the relationship between issue position and the vote in 1960,
but the major shift seems to have come between 1960 and 1964. From 1964
on, there is a considerable association between left-right issue position and
direction of the presidential vote.

We think it important that three major changes occur during the same
time period, between the 1960 and 1964 elections. These are the increase in
consistency among attitudes themselves, the increased relationship between
attitudes and the vote, and the decreased relationship between party identification and the vote. The data suggest that the American public has been
entering the electoral arena since 1964 with quite a different mental set than
was the case in the late 1950s and early 1960s. They have become more
concerned with issues and less tied to their parties.

There is substantial controversy in the political science literature as to
what issue voting is and how one measures it. The increased correlation of
position on our issue scale and the vote is consistent with the hypothesis that
issues play a larger role in the voting decision after 1964 than before. But it is
not direct evidence that the voting choice was made with issues as one of the
criteria. We can present, however, some data on this. We have presented some
of these data earlier, though in a slightly different form. In each presidential
election study, citizens were asked to list the things they liked or disliked
about the opposing candidates. We have already seen that the frequency of
reference to political party as a reason for liking or disliking a candidate has
declined, while the frequency of reference to issues or ideological position has
risen (see above, Chapters 5 and 7). In figure 10.6 we summarize both

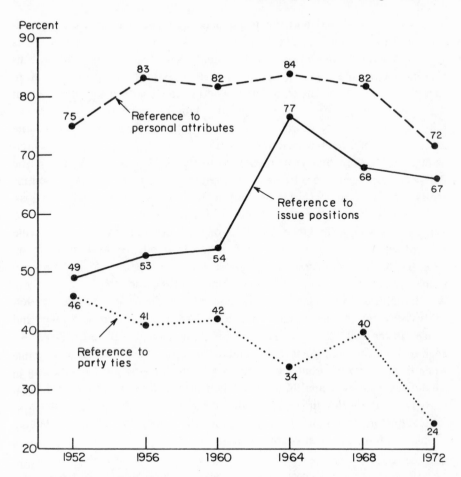

FIGURE 10.6. Frequency of evaluations of candidates in terms of party ties, personal attributes, and issue positions, 1952–1972

changes. We compare the proportion of responses that clearly refer to the candidate in party terms (that is, where the candidate is liked or disliked because of his party ties) with those responses that refer to a specific issue or issue area and add a third category of responses that refer to the personal traits and characteristics of the candidate.[9]

The data from these questions are particularly appropriate for examining the way in which the citizens think about an election. The questions are

[9] Note in examining the data presented in this figure that respondents may give more than one of these three types of responses.

completely open-ended and the respondent spontaneously lists the type of characteristics which lead him to like or dislike each of the candidates.[10]

The changing importance of party and issues in the voting decision is very clear from the data. There are sharp changes in the frequency of reference to the issue positions of candidates and to their party ties. References to the former climb; references to the latter fall. In the first three elections, references to the party ties of the candidates are slightly (about 10 percent) less frequent than references to their issue position. There is, however, a sharp change in 1964. In that year, references to the issue positions of the candidates are 43 percent more frequent than references to party ties. And the gap remains as large in 1972. Or, to look at the data somewhat differently, in 1952 almost half of the respondents mentioned party ties as a reason for liking or disliking a candidate. By 1972, only about one in five mention party. In contrast, before 1964, about half of the respondents mentioned issues. After 1964, the proportion rises to about three out of four. Again the most significant change appears to take place between 1960 and 1964.

In contrast to the data on issues and parties, the frequency of reference to the personal characteristics of the candidates remains high and relatively stable, till the 1972 election when there is some decline.[11] In short, there has been a significant change in the standards of evaluation invoked by citizens when they are asked about presidential candidates. In the pre-1964 elections, candidates were evaluated in terms of their personal characteristics and their party ties. After 1964, the party ties of the candidate receive less mention and evaluations depend more heavily on the issue position of the candidate, coupled with his personal characteristics.

---

[10] The merit of using the open-ended like-dislike questions to do this kind of analysis is argued in Repass, "Issue Salience and Party Choice," and in Lawrence, *Issue Voting and Demand Failure*. Other analyses using corresponding measures include: Angus Campbell and others, *The Voter Decides* (Evanston: Row-Peterson, 1954); Angus Campbell and others, *The American Voter* (New York: Wiley, 1960); Donald Stokes and Warren E. Miller, "Components of Electoral Decision," *American Political Science Review*, 52 (June 1958), 369–387; and Angus Campbell and Donald Stokes, "Partisan Attitudes and the Presidential Vote," in Eugene Burdick and Arthur J. Brodbeck, eds., *American Voting Behavior* (New York: Free Press, 1959), 353–371. Chapters 7, 8, and 9 use the same data differently in doing an analysis of attitudes and ideological conceptualization. For a longitudinal analysis of the vote choice using these particular data, see Donald E. Stokes, "Dynamic Elements of Contents for the Presidency," *American Political Science Review*, 60 (March 1966), 19–28.

[11] The decline in the proportion making personal references to candidates in 1972 does not mean that such personal evaluations were unimportant in that year. Quite the contrary. The decline in personal references involves largely a decline in positive references. Negative evaluations of the candidates—particularly of McGovern—were frequent and had an impact on the vote. See Arthur Miller and others, "A Majority Party in Disarray," paper presented at the Annual Meeting of the American Political Science Association, New Orleans, September 1974, pp. 53–54.

We can take these data one step further. Citizens use issues more frequently as a standard of candidate evaluation. But are those issue evaluations used as a basis of the vote? We test for the importance of issue evaluations as a basis of the voting decision in the following manner. For those respondents who mention the issue positions of one or both candidates when asked for evaluations of the candidates, we develop a score reflecting the extent to which the issue references are, on balance, favorable to one candidate over the other. (Those who do not mention issues are left out of the calculation.) Issues can be mentioned in response to four different questions: on the reasons for liking candidate A, on the reasons for disliking him, on the reasons for liking candidate B, on the reasons for disliking him. We use the fact that issues can be mentioned as a reason for liking or disliking a candidate to create our issue evaluation score. A couple of examples ought to make clear what we have done. Someone who mentions issues twice as a reason for liking candidate A and issues once as a reason for disliking candidate B has a net issue evaluation score of three in favor of A. If the respondent, on the other hand, had mentioned issues once as a reason for liking A and once as a reason for liking B, he would have a score of zero on our scale. The latter respondent uses issues as a standard of evaluation but when one looks at all the issue evaluations he gives, they do not on balance favor one candidate over the other. We developed parallel measures in relation to party references and personal references. The former measures the degree to which the references to the party affiliation of one or both candidates are on balance favorable to one of the candidates; the latter does the same for personal references.

These issue, party, and personal evaluation scores can then be correlated with the vote. In other words, we can ask whether the degree to which an individual's issue evaluations favor candidate A over B is related to the likelihood that he will vote for A rather than B. And we ask the same about party evaluation and personal evaluation. We plot these correlations in figure 10.7. Once again, the pattern in the data is quite clear. The impact on the vote of evaluations of candidates' personal attributes remains strong and relatively constant in each presidential election from 1952 to 1972. The data on the relationship between evaluations based on a candidate's party ties and the vote, on the other hand, reveal, once again, the declining salience of party in the post-1960 period. There is a drop in the correlation between 1964 and 1968 and an even more dramatic decline in 1972. Not only do citizens evaluate candidates less frequently in party terms in 1968 and 1972, but even among those who do make such party-based evaluations one cannot predict their vote on that basis as well as one could before 1964.

The pattern for issue-related references is in marked contrast. The correlations between issue evaluations and the vote remain relatively stable throughout the time period. Those who evaluated candidates in issue terms during the early years were as likely to vote in accord with those evaluations as are the issue evaluators in the later years. The difference, of course, is that there were many fewer issue evaluators in the earlier period.

The joint impact of the proportion of the electorate that uses the various evaluative criteria and the correlation between such evaluations and the vote is made apparent if we repeat the calculations reported on figure 10.7, but carry them out for all voters rather than for those who make the particular evaluation under question. In figure 10.7, for instance, we reported the corre-

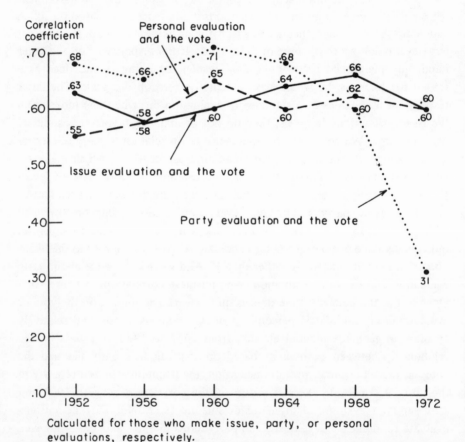

Calculated for those who make issue, party, or personal evaluations, respectively.

FIGURE 10.7. Pearson correlations of evaluations of the candidates in terms of personal traits, party ties, and issue positions with the presidential vote, 1952–1972

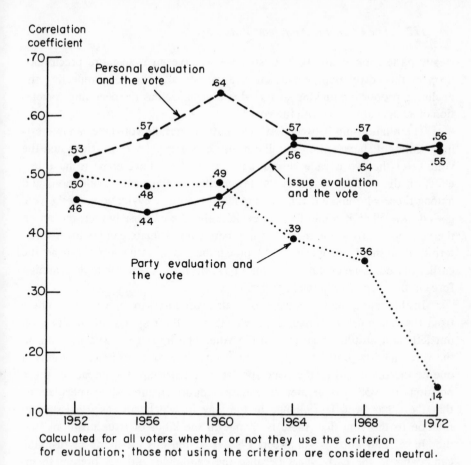

Correlation
coefficient

FIGURE 10.8. Pearson correlations of evaluations of the candidates in terms of personal traits, party ties, and issue positions with the presidential vote, 1952–1972

lation between the issue evaluation scores and the vote only for those who made some issue evaluation. In figure 10.8 we report the same correlation, but include those who make no issue evaluation in the calculation, scoring them as falling at the neutral point of the scale. The effect of this is to increase the correlation when there are many who make issue evaluations and decrease it when few use issue criteria.

The comparison of the data on figure 10.8 with those on figure 10.7 is instructive. In both figures, the correlation of personal evaluations with the vote remains relatively steady throughout, reflecting the fact that both the proportion making such evaluations and the correlation of the evaluations with the vote are steady. The correlation of issue evaluations and the vote on figure 10.8, however, goes up between 1960 and 1964, reflecting the change in the proportion using issues as evaluative standards. This contrasts with the steady pattern on figure 10.7. Lastly, we observe an even more precipitous drop in the correlation of partisan evaluations and the vote, reflecting the declining proportion making such evaluations as well as the declining correlation of such evaluations with the vote.[12]

The relationship between issue evaluations and the vote takes an interestingly different shape from the relationship between party evaluations and the vote. Over the two decade period, party evaluations have come to have less effect on the vote for two reasons: fewer citizens make such evaluations and among those who make them, the impact of the party evaluations on the vote goes down. When it comes to issue evaluations, the increase in their impact on the vote comes from the increased numbers who evaluate candidates in issue terms. If as many people thought of candidates in issue terms during the earlier period, issue evaluations would have been as potent a vote determining force in that period as in the later period.

In this sense, the relationship of issue *evaluations* to the vote also differs from the relationship of issue *position* (that is, the respondent's position on our left-right attitude measure) to the vote. The impact of issue position on the vote increases both because more citizens have coherent issue positions at one or the other end of the issue spectrum and because the impact of those positions on voting is greater. The data support an interesting speculation: that there has been less change in the way in which citizens use issues in relation to the vote than there is change in the kinds of issue positions that they have. Few citizens volunteered issues as reasons for liking or disliking candidates in the early years because the candidates did not present themselves in clear issue terms. However, for the voter who discerned some issue on the basis of which he could evaluate the candidates, the issue evaluation was as potent a force on the vote as were evaluations in later years. In contrast, the respondent's own issue position was not as potent a force in relation to the vote in the early years even among those who had coherent positions. The difference, we believe, has to do with the relationship between the voter's issue position and the positions presented by candidates.

Voters who use issues to evaluate candidates in response to the open-ended questions have selected issues important to them and on which they perceive the candidates to differ.[13] Fewer did this in early years, but those who did voted on that basis. Voters who have coherent issue positions on the left or the right, in contrast, cannot necessarily vote on the basis of those

---

[12] For a discussion of our approach in comparison with others see Appendix 2D.

[13] Repass, "Issue Salience and Party Choice," shows how issue voting is greater if one uses as the measure of issue position the issue that the respondent chooses as most important.

postions; they have to be given an issue choice by the candidate. In the earlier elections, this suggests, such choices were not offered to the public (or, at least, were not perceived by the public to be offered them). If voters in the later years vote in accord with issue position, it is because they are offered choices that allow them to do so.[14] In sum, the changes we observe appear to reflect an interaction between citizens and the choices they are offered. In the following chapter and in Chapters 17 and 18 we shall analyze this interaction more fully.

---

[14] We must add a note of caution. The data do not eliminate the alternative causal explanation: that people adopt issue positions to suit their already-selected voting choice —that is, if they prefer a candidate (for whatever reason) they will accept his issue preferences. As Richard Brody and Benjamin Page point out, it is difficult if not impossible to choose between the two causal directions with the kinds of data available. The convergence of the data from the open-ended and closed questions leads us to believe that we are observing a real increase in the impact of issue position on the voting choice. But even if the causal direction were to run the other way, we could still conclude that issues had grown in importance. At minimum, it would mean that citizens after 1964 felt greater necessity to adopt issue positions consistent with their favored candidates or were more likely to rationalize their preference for a candidate in issue terms. We think we can say something stronger than that. But even if people are rationalizing, they are doing it on an issue basis much more than used to be the case. See Benjamin I. Page and Richard A. Brody, "Policy Voting and the Electoral Process: The Vietnam Issue," *American Political Science Review,* 66 (September 1972), pp. 979–995.

11 | The Years Before Eisenhower: Looking Backward

Our interpretation of the change in the structure of political attitudes is essentially a historical one; the structure of citizen attitudes changes in good part as a function of the issues with which citizens are faced in the political process. The argument is consistent with the data we have presented but it is hard to make a more precise connection than we have made. One reason is that we cannot isolate the historical change in issues from other changes that occur at the same time. Another reason is that our time span is relatively short. We argue that the rise in issue consistency from the late Eisenhower years is the result of the rise of new issues, the fact that the issues "penetrate" into the lives of citizens, and the fact that they are presented to citizens as connected bundles of issues.

But this interpretation is somewhat weak, based as it is on a comparison of two time periods. Our argument would be stronger, of course, if we could trace similar shifts in issue coherence at other times when the issues facing the citizenry change.

Though the data analysis we have presented spans almost two decades, it still represents but a moment of American political history. Consider the increase in attitude consistency we find in 1964. Suppose we could have measured the same phenomenon well back into the nineteenth century.

Figure 11.1 presents some hypothetical results from such surveys. The solid line represents that brief period of time for which we have data from the Michigan studies; the dotted line represents some hypothetical patterns we might have found if we had a longer historical record.

Note how different would our interpretations of recent events be if we had found the pattern in figure 11.1A rather than that in B, or B rather than C. Figure 11.1A would have told us that the pattern of political attitudes found in the late 1950s—the lack of issue consistency—was the normal pattern found in the United States up till that time. The change in the early 1960s would produce a new level of issue consistency never before achieved. In contrast, the pattern presented in B would suggest that the late 1950s were a deviant moment in American political history, a time when the usually more consistent political attitudes of citizens were temporarily blurred. Finally, figure 11.1C suggests a long history of fluctuations in the extent to which citizens have consistent attitudes. The late 1950s would simply be one of many recurring low points in a cyclical pattern.

The different patterns would lead to different interpretations of the meaning of the changes from the fifties to the sixties. If we found pattern A, we might explain the growth of attitude consistency by some new feature of American political life that had not previously existed. The introduction of television or the spread of mass higher education would be the kind of explanatory factor consistent with the data. Such changes could create a population with previously unattained levels of political sophistication. The pattern in B would, on the other hand, probably lead us to explanations based on some more transient phenomenon; but again to some phenomenon not previously seen in American politics. We would look for some factor that could temporarily reduce the degree of attitude consistency normally found in the American public. An example of such a factor might be the personal characteristics of Dwight Eisenhower. He was a national hero, above politics, who tried deliberately to defuse issues. The response to such a leader might be a softening of issue positions so that issue consistency would drop. With his departure, the "ordinary" level of consistency would return.

The pattern in C would require some interpretation consistent with a cyclical rise and fall of attitude consistency. Our argument that attitude consistency is responsive to the particular configuration of issues at a particular point in time is such an interpretation. Some sets of issues lead to consistency, some do not. The fluctuation in issue consistency is the reaction to the particular issues of the day.

The three different patterns in A, B, and C would lead to different prognostications. Is the level of issue consistency reached in the late 1960s

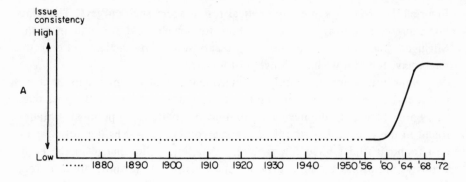

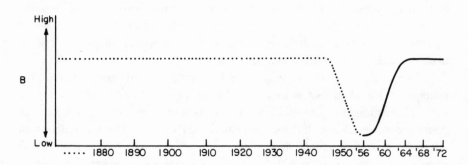

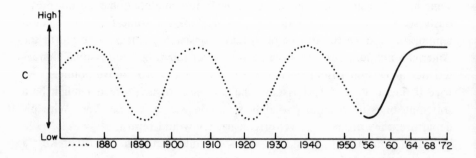

FIGURE 11.1. Hypothetical survey results on levels of issue consistency from the nineteenth century to the present

and early 1970s likely to remain with us, or are we likely to find a return to the levels of the 1950s? It is clear that one would project the lines in figure 11.1 differently into the future depending on which line one was projecting. Figure A suggests a continuation of the high level of consistency. So does figure B, though for a different reason. Figure C would suggest that consistency was due to drop sometime in the future.

The problem is, of course, that survey studies reaching back into American history do not exist. The reason our historical account begins in the mid-1950s, as we have pointed out, is that the Michigan election surveys begin then. The Gallup and Roper polls, however, have their beginnings in the 1930s, and their surveys from the late 1930s and 1940s may give us some historical perspective on the 1950s. The late thirties represent the culminating years of the New Deal, a period in which one would expect that political attitudes—particularly on domestic issues—would be more clearly structured along an ideological dimension than in the 1950s. In addition, data from the New Deal era would help us evaluate whether there was something special and transient about the impact of President Eisenhower on American political attitudes.

Though there are surveys dating back into the 1930s, there are serious problems of comparability between the earlier studies and the later ones. We have based our comparisons among the SRC election studies on the fact that the "same" questions were asked of similar samples in each of the elections. Even that base for our analysis turns out, as we have discussed, to be quite uncertain: the "same" questions often turn out to be different under closer scrutiny. When we turn to the earlier studies, we are on even less certain foundations.

Earlier studies, of course, asked different questions. The analysis of issue consistency presented in Chapter 8 was based on across-time comparisons of the intercorrelations between responses to pairs of questions, where each question in each pair comes from a different issue area: a question on integration with a question on welfare; a question on foreign affairs with one on domestic matters. But at each point in time, we had (roughly) the same set of issue items. When we look back at earlier studies we do not find such a similar set of items. Questions are asked about issues that differ from those we considered in the Michigan studies. Furthermore, the format of the questions differs somewhat. Different numbers of response categories are offered than in later studies (respondents are often offered only the opportunity to agree or disagree with a position, no middle position being suggested to them). Since the number of response categories can have an effect on the intercorrelation among items, this poses problems. In addition, earlier studies were less sensitive to the way in which wording or format could affect answers. The interview format is often such that the intercorrelation among questions could be artificially inflated due to "response-set," that is, the tendency for some respondents to answer similarly phrased questions in similar ways no matter what the substantive content of the questions. Lastly, the earlier studies used loose quota samples and had less well developed quality controls.

Nevertheless, the questions we can ask about the earlier data are important enough to warrant an attempt to answer them; they shed light on an otherwise dark landscape. Furthermore, a close study of the patterns of response in earlier years convinces us that these differences do not substantially undercut our ability to make meaningful comparisons between the data from the later Michigan studies and the earlier studies. Though we would hesitate to lean too heavily on the results to any single question, the patterns we find cannot be plausibly explained as artifacts of the data. We discuss this problem more fully in Appendix 3. Here we will present some substantive results.

For the analysis of attitude consistency we need data on a number of political issues within the same study. In addition, the issues must come from what we have considered to be different issue areas. From the many early public opinion studies we found a number that met these criteria. Some are studies conducted by the Roper poll in 1939, 1946, and 1948, and Gallup studies in 1937 and 1940. The studies offer important points of light on what otherwise would be left totally obscure.

We were able to find items that tap some of the same issue areas we used in the post-1956 studies. We do not have data on every issue area in every study, but each study allows some cross-issue area relationships to be calculated. The issue areas on which we have information are:

1. *Size of government:* Various questions are asked about government ownership of parts of the economy—the railroads, telephone, TVA. In addition, there are questions on government regulation of the economy—setting prices, regulating utilities, regulating labor-management relations. Though not identical to the set of items we have later, they appear to tap a similar set of concerns.

2. *Welfare/redistribution:* Questions are asked about the welfare obligations of the government—social security, relief for the poor, government guarantees of a minimum income or of a job. In addition, questions are asked about government programs to redistribute the wealth, in particular about the use of the income tax for this purpose.[1]

---

[1] Some domestic issues seem to straddle the "size of government" and "welfare" areas. Questions on "government-built housing for the poor" are of this sort. Such items

3. *Foreign issues:* Various questions are asked about the role of the United States in the would—about U.S. aid to other nations, about the value of U.S. involvement with other nations via free trade, about membership in international organizations, and about the degree to which this country should be "tough" with the Russians. We have considered "isolationist" answers and "tough on the Russians" answers to represent the conservative end of the policy continuum.

4. *Race relations:* The questions here are not clearly distinguishable into an integration and black welfare set as are the questions from the Michigan studies. But they do allow a consideration of the relationship between race issues and domestic economic issues. They are largely about laws that prevent job or voting discrimination. In the 1930s we have questions on a federal antilynch law.

The questions were put in the same format as those in later years. Gamma was calculated as a measure of association for pairs of issues across the several issue areas. The average gammas were then calculated for all pairs representing a particular combination of issue areas.[2]

Figure 11.2 presents the average intercorrelation among pairs of items across the two domestic economic areas: size of government and welfare/redistribution. We plot the data for 1939, 1946, 1948, and 1952. And we repeat the data presented earlier for the period from 1956 to 1973.[3] The average gamma in 1939 is substantially higher than the low figures recorded for the trio of years, 1956, 1958, and 1960, though it is not as high as the figures shown for 1964 and beyond. The figures for 1946, 1948, and 1952 show a decline from 1939 but are, nevertheless, substantially higher than the figures for 1956 through 1960.[4]

The data do not resemble the hypothetical pattern A pictured above: the low level of issue consistency found in the period from 1956 to 1960 does not appear to be a continuation of a previous "normal" pattern. Rather the data in figure 11.2 resemble our hypothetical patterns B or C—the Eisenhower

---

were omitted in calculating the relationship across the two domestic economy areas. But they were used to relate the domestic economy to the other issue areas of race and foreign policy.

[2] In most cases, we present the average gammas for a substantial number of pairs of questions. The number of pairs for a set of issues in the pre-1956 studies are listed in Appendix 3. In a few cases, we report data based on one or two pairs of questions; these instances are indicated on the figures.

[3] We leave out the "size of government" items in 1972 for reasons discussed above. It is likely that a truer picture for 1972 is provided by the .49 average gamma for domestic issues outside of the size of government area.

[4] We have, in addition, one pair of items from a Gallup study in 1940 (*American Institute of Public Opinion (AIPO)* study 181, January 10, 1940). The issues are minimum wage and government control of the banks. The gamma is .63.

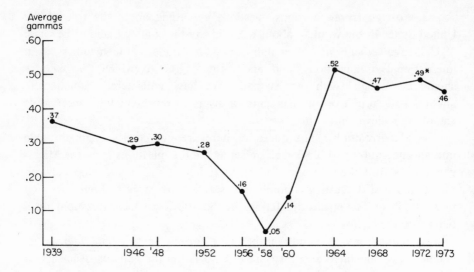

*1972 average of all domestic issues excluding size of government

FIGURE 11.2. Domestic economic issues: size of government versus welfare/redistribution, 1939–1973

years represent a low point of issue consistency between two higher points. We cannot tell, however, whether the data resemble pattern B (the Eisenhower years representing the deviant low point in a historical pattern of otherwise high levels of issue consistency) or pattern C (the Eisenhower years representing the low point of a cyclical pattern) since we do not know what the situation was before 1939.

The data make clear that there was issue consistency in the New Deal era. The level is not as high as the level attained in 1964 and beyond (though the fact that the earlier studies are not coterminous with presidential elections may lower somewhat the intercorrelations).

Figure 11.3 reports the interrelationship between the domestic issue areas (size of government *and* welfare/redistribution) and foreign policy attitudes. Unlike the situation in relation to the correlation between the two domestic issue areas, there was no apparent consistency across foreign and domestic issues in the 1939 study nor in the studies of the 1940s or of 1952. In 1939 the gamma is slightly negative (at −.10), indicating that, if anything, those who took a more left position on domestic matters were somewhat more isolationist in international affairs. But the relationship is weak. And the

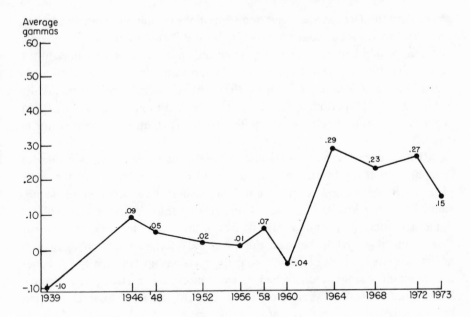

*1972 average of all domestic issues excluding size of government

FIGURE 11.3. Foreign and domestic issues, 1939–1973

relationships between foreign and domestic attitudes through the forties and fifties and up through 1960 are even weaker. After 1960, we see the rise in consistency which we have noted earlier.

The low level of consistency between the foreign and domestic issues that we find in the Eisenhower years turns out to be a continuation of the situation in the late 1930s and the 1940s. This is different from the situation in relation to domestic issues. The domestic/foreign relationship in figure 11.3 does not suggest that the fifties were a low point in a recurring cycle nor that they were a deviant period of issue inconsistency in comparison with a normal situation of consistency across the two issue areas. The amount of consistency found in the years since 1964 represents a level not previously seen—at least not since 1939 when our data series begins. The foreign/domestic relationships appear qualitatively different from those in all the earlier years for which we have data.

Next we consider attitudes on racial matters. There are a few questions on federal lynch laws in 1937 and 1940 studies that can be related to other issues. And the 1948 studies have some questions on job and vote discrimination. As can be seen from figure 11.4, pre-SRC studies reveal a moderate interrelationship between racial issues and the domestic economic ones in the years from 1937 to 1948; approximately the same as the interrelationship found in the SRC studies of 1956 to 1960. The relationship rises substantially in the 1964–1968 period. It falls a bit in 1972, but in general, the post-1964 years show a level of relationship quite a bit higher than in the years prior to 1964.

The pattern for race issues and domestic economic issues is similar in "shape" to that for foreign policy issues and domestic issues. All the years prior to 1964 show low levels of interrelationship; the years after show substantially higher levels. The level of interrelationships in the foreign policy/domestic policy pairs is not as high as that in the racial/domestic policy area: that is, the relationship between domestic and foreign policy changes from nonexistent to moderate around 1964; the relationship between racial issues and domestic economic ones changes from moderate to strong at that time. But in each case, the years from 1964 onward show a closer connection among these issues than do any of the earlier years.

Lastly we can consider some data on the relationship between attitudes on civil liberties and economic attitudes. We did not have a complete 1956–

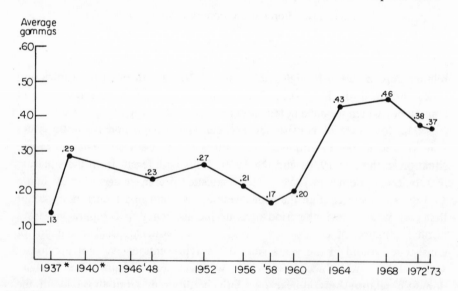

*AIPO studies, August 16, 1937, and October 28, 1937. (One pair in the former, two in the latter.)

FIGURE 11.4. Race and domestic economic issues, 1939–1973

1973 time series for these items, but did have some measures that allowed a comparison of 1956 and the 1968–1973 period. As we showed in Chapter 8, there was no civil liberties/economic issues relationship in our 1956 base period. In contrast, the late 1960s and early 1970s showed a moderately close relationship between civil liberties attitudes and domestic economic ones. What had, in 1956, been two issue realms unconnected one to the other, had become moderately connected by the late 1960s.

We have little parallel data before 1956. But in a Roper study of December 1939 a question was asked about the limits that ought to be placed on free speech. In addition two questions were asked on domestic economic issues: should the government limit income and should business profits be curbed? The average gamma between these two economic items and the free speech items was .03.[5] When we place that data on figure 11.5, we can see how similar 1956 was to 1939 in this respect. The moderately positive relationship between civil liberties issues and economic issues in the late 1960s and early 1970s represents a connection among those two issue spheres found neither in 1939 nor in 1956.

The contrast between the relationship found among domestic economic issues (that is, the relationship between size of government measures and welfare/redistribution measures) and the relationship among other sets of issues allows us to divide the time period into three seemingly distinct eras: the late New Deal period as revealed in the 1937 through 1940 studies, the Eisenhower years, and the years from 1964 on, with the late 1940s perhaps representing a transition from the New Deal era to the Eisenhower years. In the New Deal era, we find a good deal of consistency among domestic economic issues. The issues for which the New Deal stood—a stronger and more active government and greater concern for redistribution of the wealth and citizen welfare—hang together in the minds of the citizens. But aside from the structuring of public attitudes along the lines laid out by the New Deal, there is little evidence for broader attitude consistency. There is no attitudinal relationship between domestic and foreign issues, or between civil liberties

---

[5] It is interesting to note that the two economic items in December 1939 are related to each other at .35—about the same as the average of .37 reported in figure 11.2 for the March 1939 data on domestic issues. This is an impressive similarity, especially when one notes that the two economic items in December 1939 are reversed—in one the liberal answer is first, in the other the conservative answer is first—which ought to lower the relationship. In contrast, the direction of the question does not affect the relation of the free speech item to the economic ones. Where the free speech item and the economic item both have the liberal answer first, the correlation between the two is .04. Where the free speech item has the liberal answers first and the economic item has the conservative answer first, their relationship is .02. See Appendix 3 for other examples which suggest that we are not merely observing interview artifacts.

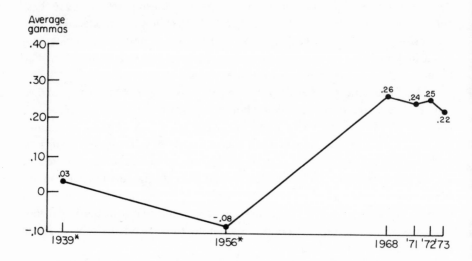

* In 1939, free speech versus limits on income and limits on business profit. For civil liberties items in 1956–1973, see table 8.2. In each case from 1956 to 1973, the civil liberties items are related to the welfare and size of government items.

FIGURE 11.5. Free speech and domestic economic issues, 1939–1973

and economic issues, and a relatively weak and inconsistent relationship between racial attitudes and domestic economic ones.

In contrast, the Eisenhower years show an across-the-board weakness of interrelationships among attitudes. Domestic economic issues do not relate to each other very strongly, nor do they relate to foreign issues, nor to free speech issues. They have a weak to moderate relation to racial attitudes. Lastly, we have the years from 1964 on. They differ from earlier years in the *degree* of issue consistency as well as in the *scope* of issue consistency. Whereas the New Deal period showed issue consistency within one set of issues, the data from 1964 to 1972 shows that that issue linkage is much more general. Domestic economic attitudes have a strong or, at least, moderate relationship to other attitudes.

The following table sums up the three time periods:

	New Deal (1939)	Eisenhower years (1956–1960)	1964 and after
Consistency among:			
Domestic economic issues	strong	weak	strong
Domestic economic and foreign issues	weak	weak	moderate
Domestic economic issues and race	weak to moderate	weak to moderate	strong
Domestic economic issues and free speech	weak	weak	moderate

(Weak relations are gammas under .20, moderate are in the .20–.29 range, strong .30 or higher.)

In sum, the New Deal era was a period in which one found substantial issue coherence. But that coherence was limited in scope to the core issues of the New Deal—government control and regulation of the economy and government commitment to welfare. Other issues were unrelated. The Eisenhower years show the decline of even those linkages across domestic economic issues. When issue consistency rises again around 1964, the domestic economic issues are linked to all the other issues of the day—foreign issues, free speech issues, race issues, domestic social issues.

Education and Issue Consistency

Let us consider one other contrast between our baseline years under Eisenhower and the late 1960s. In the former years there was a fairly sharp difference in issue consistency between those with higher levels of education and those with lower levels. In 1956, for instance, the average gamma among domestic issues was .34 for those with some college education, .16 among those who did not complete high school. This had supported the cognitive capacity interpretations of attitudinal consistency. But by 1964 the gap between the educational groups had narrowed sharply. The increase in attitude consistency was found to cut across educational lines. These data were reported in Chapter 9. We can now look backwards before 1956.

The data reported in Chapter 9 were for all domestic attitudes. In figure 11.6 we provide parallel data for domestic economic attitudes (that is, the

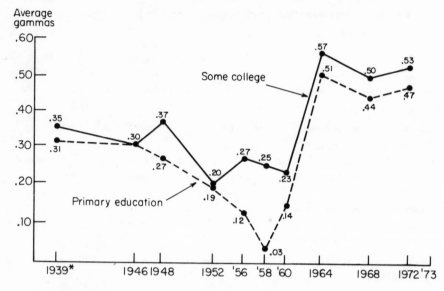

Average
gammas

* In 1939 the division is on the basis of a general interviewer evaluation of
socioeconomic status.   The division we use would appear to approximate
an educational split similar to that in other years.

FIGURE 11.6. Domestic economic attitude consistency by education, 1939–1973

average relationship between attitudes on government intervention in the
economy and attitudes on welfare) since these allow more meaningful comparisons with the New Deal era. The data for the late Eisenhower years tell a
familiar story. There is a sharp difference across educational levels in the
degree of issue coherence in 1956 and 1958. In 1958, the college educated
have average gammas of .25, those with less than a high school degree,
gammas of .03. If one considers only the data for those two years, one can see
how observers would have concluded that consistency among political attitudes was a function of education. But when, in Chapter 9, we tested the
hypothesis that the increase in attitude consistency found after 1964 was
largely a function of the increased levels of education in the mass public we
found it to be inconsistent with the data. This is apparent also in the domestic
economic attitude data for 1964, 1968, and 1972. When consistency goes up,
it goes up for those with higher and for those with lower levels of education.
In fact, it goes up *more* for those with limited education.

If we look at the pre-1956 data, we find a much less substantial gap
between the upper and lower educated citizens in terms of the consistency of
their political attitudes than was found in 1956 or 1958. In the 1952 and

1946 studies, there was no noticeable difference across educational levels. Perhaps the most interesting data are for 1939. We do not have a measure of educational level in the March 1939 survey that we have been using, but there is a measure of socioeconomic status which we have divided up so as to approximate the educational division used in the later years (1946–1973). In 1939, we find relatively little difference in consistency level across the two groups. Furthermore, it is striking that the level of consistency for those on the lower level in 1939 is *higher* than the consistency level of the upper educational group in the Eisenhower years. Those citizens categorized as "poor" by the Gallup Poll in 1939 (and whom we assume include few with college education) have more consistent attitudes than the college graduates in the Eisenhower years!

The data indicate quite clearly that the Eisenhower years were rather unusual. Not only is attitudinal consistency much lower in those years than in the ones preceding or following[6] but also the consistency gap between the more and the less educated is substantially larger than that before or after.

Issue Voting: A Retrospect

We can also consider the data on issue voting in the pre-Eisenhower years. In several studies where we have issue questions we also have questions about vote intention or past vote. The March 1939 Roper study is the first year in which we have appropriate issue questions coupled with a voting choice. The voting choice question is somewhat indirect. It consists of a question on whether FDR has outlived his usefulness, followed by another asked of those who said "no" to the first as to whether they would vote for him if he ran again. We constructed a vote measure out of these two questions. The measure is obviously different from later vote choices since the opposition candidate is not specified and the questions have some odd phrasing. But despite these cautions, the data are worth consideration.

In figure 11.7 we plot the average relationship between issues and the vote in those years where we have the relevant measures. We do this separately for four issues: welfare, government size, race, and foreign policy. The data parallel those for issue consistency, though not completely. Three different patterns are apparent. Attitudes on redistribution and welfare show moderately strong relationships with the vote in 1939. The correlations fall in

---

[6] The late Eisenhower years are lower in consistency than the following years in relation to all issues and lower than the ones preceding in relation to domestic economic issues.

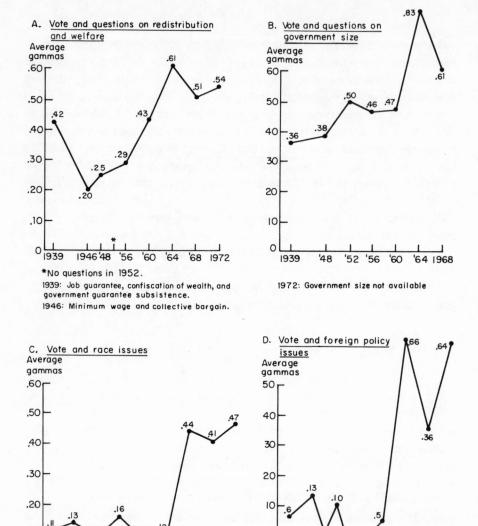

A. Vote and questions on redistribution and welfare

Average gammas

*No questions in 1952.
1939: Job guarantee, confiscation of wealth, and government guarantee subsistence.
1946: Minimum wage and collective bargain.

B. Vote and questions on government size

Average gammas

1972: Government size not available

C. Vote and race issues

Average gammas

1940: AIPO, one pair (1/10/40)
1945: AIPO, one pair (5/12/45)

D. Vote and foreign policy issues

Average gammas

1953: NORC study, three pairs (5/53)

FIGURE 11.7. Correlation of vote and issues

magnitude during the forties and fifties and rise thereafter. Attitudes on government size show a moderate relationship to the vote during the New Deal, maintain that moderate relationship during the forties and fifties, and rise thereafter. Lastly, attitudes on foreign and race matters show no vote connection from the New Deal era till the 1960s when that relationship rises as well.

The data support our interpretation of the differences between the New Deal era and the later periods. In the 1930s, the issues that were structured by the New Deal (that is, on which there was a clear choice) predicted the vote. These issues were size of the government, welfare, and redistribution. Other issues—race and foreign policy—did not form part of that bundle of issues. In the Eisenhower years, the link between issues and the vote weakens. Race and foreign policy continue to have little impact on the vote and the impact of welfare and redistributive issues falls as well. The reason for this is probably that the times were prosperous and such issues were less salient. The one issue that has a moderate relationship to the vote in the Eisenhower years is the size of government issue. In the period from the middle sixties onward, the number of issues that are linked to the vote increases (as well as the average strength of the linkage). In sum, the Eisenhower years show almost no issue voting; the New Deal years, issue voting on one set of issues; the later years, issue voting on multiple issues.

The data parallel the data on issue consistency in another way. The issue voting that appears in the New Deal era does not appear to be a function of education level. This is seen in figure 11.8 where we present the data on the correlation between the vote and issue position on matters of welfare and redistribution. Note that in the 1939 study there is little difference between those with higher education (actually higher socioeconomic level in that year) and those with lower. The former have average gammas of .41, the latter .37. During the forties and the fifties the gap between the educational groups grows, only to narrow again in the post-1964 period. The data support the interpretation that issue voting is not necessarily a result of cognitive capacity and educational level. Rather it appears to be a response to the clarity of the issues as presented to the voter.

The data on the New Deal era, we must reiterate, have to be treated with caution. The studies are not as comparable to the series of election studies from 1952 onward as are the election studies to each other. But the studies are at minimum suggestive and probably a lot better than that (see Appendix 3). They do put the Eisenhower years in clearer perspective.

In the Eisenhower years, citizens were found to have low levels of attitude consistency. There was, however, more issue consistency among the more highly educated. When we followed the SRC studies from the 1950s through the 1960s, we observed a dramatic rise in attitude consistency. And this is observed among upper and lower educated citizens, undercutting an

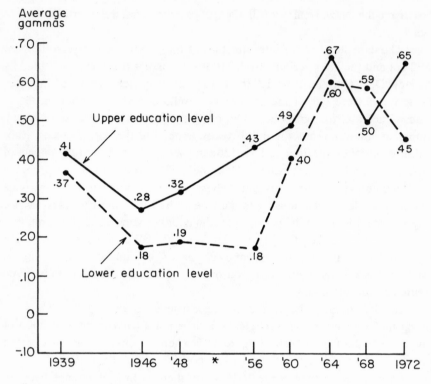

Average
gammas

.70

.67   .65

.60   .59
/.60

.50   Upper education level   .49   .50
.43   .45

.41
.40   .40

.37

.32
.30   .28

.20   .19
.18   .18

Lower education level

.10

0

-.10

1939   1946 '48   *   '56   '60   '64   '68   1972

* No questions in 1952

FIGURE 11.8. Correlations between the vote and attitudes on welfare and redistribution, by education, 1939–1972

educational level explanation of issue consistency. Indeed, the sharp distinction between the more and less educated fades quite a bit when one considers
the data for the latter years.

The studies in the New Deal years are also inconsistent with an educational level interpretation of issue consistency. In 1939, we find relatively high
levels of issue consistency (at least on domestic economic issues). The consistency level is not as high as that in the post-1964 era, but substantially higher
than that in the Eisenhower years. But the average level of education was, of
course, substantially lower in 1939 than in 1956. Furthermore, we find a
consistency level in 1939 that is similar for those high and low on the socioeconomic educational ladder.

The New Deal data also call into question another possible interpretation of the decline in educational differences after 1964—that is, that the
saturation of the public by television in the early 1960s eliminates differences

across citizen groups in their exposure to political stimuli. The absence of educational differences in 1939 could not easily be explained by the power of television to penetrate to all social levels.[7]

The most plausible explanatory factor appears to be the nature of the issues. In 1939, citizens at all educational levels were responding to a fairly clear-cut set of issues posed by the New Deal. The issues of welfare and government intervention in the economy were clearly related to each other within the New Deal program. One did not need advanced education or high intellectual skills to see the connection.[8] The issue consistency was, however, limited to those issues that formed the heart of the New Deal program. Other issues did not cohere with these.

The New Deal issues lose their salience in the Eisenhower years. They are replaced by concerns with more "distant" issues of foreign policy—distant not simply because the issues deal with our relations to other nations but because they are distant from the life space of the individual citizen. No clear cluster of issues faced the citizenry. Under such circumstances, the lack of consistency among issue positions is easy to understand. Furthermore, whatever issue consistency one finds is an intellectual matter; not a reaction to pressing political issues but a reflection of more general intellectual evaluations fostering logical consistency among beliefs. Thus consistency was found among those with higher educational levels.

The elections from 1964 onward, this suggests, represent a return to the situation in the New Deal era, when issues as presented to the public formed meaningful political clusters. However, unlike the New Deal era, the scope of the issues that cluster together is wider. In the former period, the issue cluster

---

[7] Of course, one could invoke the radio for 1939. It is likely that it did play a role then, but the radio was also available in the 1950s.

[8] A Gallup study in October 1937 enables us to divide the population more finely by economic level. Two domestic economic questions are asked: on minimum wage and on profit sharing. The relationship between these two issues, and the relationship between each and the vote, is greatest for those on relief.

October 1937 (*AIPO* study 102)

| | Gammas between: | | |
Socioeconomic classification	Minimum wage and profit sharing	Minimum Wage and the vote	Profit sharing and the vote
Average plus	.07	.48	.00
Average	.03	.34	.01
Poor plus	.30	.30	−.06
Poor	.16	.44	−.08
On relief	.32	.66	.26

centered around welfare and government intervention in the economy. Race and foreign policy were unconnected to these issues. In the latter era, race and foreign policy form part of a more general issue syndrome.

One cannot be sure why this is the case. But surely part of the explanation has to do with the fact that the issues of race and foreign policy were no longer distant from the lives of the average American. The civil rights movement (and all that accompanied it) and Vietnam took care of that. In this the saturation by television surely helped. Furthermore, much depends on whether or not the issues are presented as coherent bundles by candidates or media. In this connection it is probably not coincidental that issue consistency rises so substantially in 1964, when Goldwater offered a more coherent set of issue positions than had been previously presented—a set of positions that linked domestic and foreign policy. And the two succeeding elections also had candidates, George Wallace in 1968 and George McGovern in 1972, who offered more clear-cut issue choices than was the case in the Eisenhower years—and issue choices that covered domestic economic issues, race, and foreign policy.[9]

The nature of the issue choices offered the public also appears to be a likely explanation of variations in the amount of issue voting one finds. In the New Deal era, citizens cast issue votes in relation to those domestic economic issues for which the New Deal stood. By the fifties, those issues had faded. The times were prosperous and the candidates in 1952 and 1956 were not perceived as polarized on those issues. Nor were there any other issues to take their place. The result was that citizens did not have coherent issue positions, nor did they vote on the basis of issues. On the other hand, in the absence of new issues to push the citizenry in one direction or another, the old partisan ties forged in the New Deal era remained. And new voters entering the electorate inherited such ties. What was missing was the issue commitment that had earlier created the partisan identifications. Thus, when the first major election studies began in the 1950s they found an electorate in which habitual party ties were important, in which voters might temporarily abandon their party to vote for a popular candidate, but in which issues played little role.

The data in this chapter place the Eisenhower years in clearer focus. The New Deal created a party system in which partisan commitment and issue position reinforced each other to form the stable coalitions that emerged from that era. The partisan ties formed in the New Deal era appear to have sur-

---

[9] Benjamin I. Page and Richard A. Brody, "Policy Voting and the Electoral Process: The Vietnam War Issue," *American Political Science Review*, 66 (September 1972), pp. 979–995, provides evidence that the nature of the issue choice affects the degree to which issue voting occurs. See also Chapters 17 and 18 below.

vived into the Eisenhower years despite the fact that the issue commitments out of which those ties had originally been formed had faded. In the 1960s we see a reemergence of issues. They become more coherent, and they become more closely tied to the vote than in the Eisenhower years. In this sense, the later period comes once more to resemble the New Deal era—the curve of attitude consistency dips down for the Eisenhower years and then rises up again.

But this does not imply that the period from the 1960s onward represents a return to the New Deal party system. The issues that emerge in the sixties do not reestablish the issue commitments that had existed earlier. They are issues, as we have suggested, that cut across the parties—particularly across the Democratic party. In sum, the economic issues of the New Deal helped form the party system of that era. That system survived into the Eisenhower years despite the fact that its issue component had faded. The new issues of the 1960s have undercut that New Deal party system.

12 | Issues and the Parties: One United, One Divided Against Itself

The New Deal party system was one in which issues and party lined up together. Those in favor of an increased governmental role in the economy and greater commitment to welfare programs became committed to the Democratic party; those opposed to such programs became committed to the Republicans. In the 1960s, as we have seen, issues reemerge as important political forces: citizens have more coherent views on them, use them to evaluate candidates, and vote consistently with them. But this does not mean that the issue-based party coalitions such as those of the New Deal era will reemerge. Whether they do or not depends on the issue positions of the supporters of the two parties. If those on the left are also Democrats while those on the right are Republicans, the increased issue consistency would facilitate the development of a more issue-based party system. But if some democrats and some republicans have drifted to each pole of the issue scale, the creation of issue-based parties would be more difficult. They still could be built if there was a reshuffling of party identifiers. This would not be impossible, but it would mean a good deal of party switching on the basis of issue position—something for which we have no historical precedents.

Studies have shown that Democrats do differ from Republicans on many issues, and such differences date back to early surveys before World War II.[1] The differences have been clear, especially on the kinds of welfare and economic issues associated with the New Deal. The development of more coherent attitudes in the mass public since 1964 creates the potential for a sharper differentiation across a number of issues between the supporters of the two political parties. But does this happen? It all depends on whether supporters of a party who become more issue consistent move to the same end of the left-right scale—in particular, the Democrats to the left, the Republicans to the right.

We can use our issue position scale (described in Chapter 8) for this purpose. We have used this scale to focus on the *structure,* rather than the *direction* of citizen attitudes—that is, on the extent to which attitudes on one issue are correlated with attitudes on another, rather than the extent to which citizens are liberal or conservative. There is a methodological reason for this emphasis when dealing with the public as a whole. An analysis of changes in the consistency of attitudes is on firmer methodological ground than an analysis of the direction of attitude change over time. The structure of political opinions depends on the interrelationship among political attitudes. Such interrelationships are less sensitive to variations over time in question wording or question format than would be the marginal results to the questions.

If we were interested in the direction of opinions of citizens on political issues, we would have to deal with the problem of alterations in question wording and format during our period under investigation. Minor question changes can result in rather substantial differences in the proportion of a sample giving a liberal or conservative answer. The availability of a large number of response categories, for example, generally causes respondents to avoid choosing the extreme categories. Seemingly minor changes in the alternatives offered in an issue question can push respondents left or right in their answers. The SRC altered the form of its questions in 1964 and again in 1970 and 1972. The NORC 1971 and 1973 studies utilize a slightly different style of question. These changes have little effect on the results of our analysis of consistency.[2] But if we had tried to consider the *direction* of attitude change, the alterations in question format would have become serious obstacles.

However, we can use the scale to examine the liberal or conservative drift of *subgroups relative to the public as a whole.* With roughly parallel questions and population groups of roughly constant size, we can determine

---

[1] See Everett Carll Ladd, Jr., and Charles D. Hadley, *Political Parties and Political Issues: Patterns of Differentiation Since the New Deal,* Sage Professional Papers in American Politics, Beverly Hills, 1973.

[2] Some of the changes, however, could have an effect on the level of issue consistency, but there is evidence that this is not the case (see Appendix 2A for a discussion).

where various groups are relative to the population as a whole at any point in time and, in turn, trace changes in their relative positions. The referent of comparison becomes the distribution of opinion in the population as a whole at a given point in time. The changes in question wording and number of response categories across time have less impact since the basic comparisons are between subgroups and the population at particular points in time.[3]

In figure 12.1, we plot the proportion who fall on the far left or far right segments of our issue scale among Democratic identifiers and Republican identifiers across the various election years.[4] The proportions derive from the consistency scale "unfolded" to differentiate consistently liberal attitudes from consistently conservative ones. For each party, we plot two lines over time. The dotted live gives the proportion of identifiers with that party who hold attitude positions from the leftmost category of our issue scale. The solid line shows the proportion of identifiers who hold right views. As one reads across the figure, one moves from the 1956 data to 1972.

In 1956, 9 percent of the Republican identifiers were in the left extreme of the attitude scale, while 18 percent were in the right extreme. In other words, 27 percent of Republican identifiers had fairly consistent issue positions. Of those, those on the right of the scale outnumber those on the left by about two to one. Over the years, the proportion of Republicans who fall in the liberal end of the issue scale remains fairly steady and quite small. On the other hand, the proportion with strong right attitudes grows. In 1964, fully one out of three of the Republican identifiers falls in the rightmost category of the scale. The proportion of Republicans with strong right views falls somewhat in 1968 and again in 1972. But the Republican identifiers remain heavily tilted to the right.

The Democrats are in some sense the mirror image of the Republicans. In all years, there is a higher proportion of Democratic identifiers with left than right attitudes. In 1964 and more so in 1968 the proportion of Democrats whose attitudes place them in the outer left category of our attitude scale grows so that it is far in excess of the proportion on the right.

But there is a major difference between the parties. The Democrats tend to be more split internally than the Republicans. The ratio of Democratic liberals to Democratic conservatives is always smaller than the ratio of Re-

---

[3] Particular questions may change their meaning more drastically for one group than for another, and this remains a problem.

[4] The criterion we use is the furthest left 15 percent of the scale and the right 15 percent. The distribution of scores on the scale is calculated across all election years so that in any year there can be more or less than 15 percent in the "15 percent extremes" of the scale. Of course, any subgroup can have more or less than 15 percent in the outlying categories.

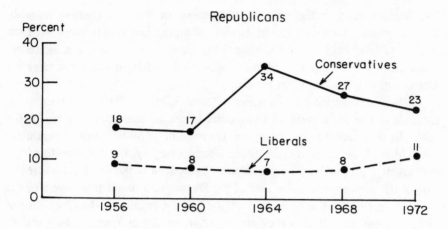

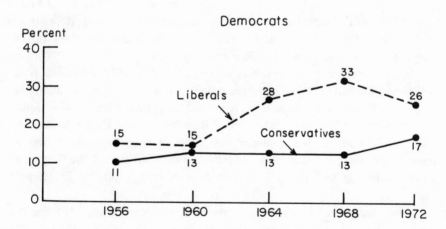

FIGURE 12.1. Proportion of Democratic and Republican identifiers who fall in the liberal or conservative extremes of the issue scale, 1956–1972

publican conservatives to Republican liberals. Consider the 1956 and 1960 years. There are two conservative Republicans for each liberal Republican. The party clearly tilts right. In the same years, there are more liberal Democrats than conservative Democrats, but only by a small margin. When the

Republicans move to the right in 1964, there are five conservative Republicans for every liberal one. But in the year when the Democrats take their most distinctive left position—1968, when 32 percent of the Democratic identifiers come from the liberal end of the scale—they outnumber the conservative Democrats only by about 2½ to one.

The most important difference is seen in 1972. There is a dramatic increase in the proportion of Democrats in the conservative extreme of the scale. In that year 17 percent of the Democratic identifiers fall in that category. More Democrats remain in the liberal category, but the growth of the conservative proportion indicates a party badly split in the ideological orientation of its supporters. Almost half of the Democratic supporters have an issue position at one or the other end of the issue continuum. But they do not cluster at one end. Rather they are found in goodly numbers at each end of the scale. In contrast, the Republicans in 1972 continue to show the distinct conservative bent they have always shown.

It is interesting to note that the major change for each party takes place between 1960 and 1964. The latter is clearly an election in which the issue positions of the two-party support groups became sharply differentiated from each other. The proportion in the far right category among Republicans doubles from 1960 to 1964, and the proportion of Democrats in the far left category almost doubles in the same period.

There is no way to confirm precisely that voters in 1964 were responding to the cues presented by the candidate, Barry Goldwater. But it is likely that his appeal, based as it was on a fairly consistent conservative position, led to a crystallization of the political views of Republicans and Democrats. In any case, the data make clear that the sharp rise in issue consistency that we uncovered in the 1964 election study reflects a drift leftward of the Democrats counterpoised against a much sharper movement rightward of the Republicans.

The change in the issue positions of the support groups for the two parties is summarized in figure 12.2. We divide the issue scale into five groups: those who are most left, moderate left, the center, the moderate right, and those in the furthest right category.[5] And we show the distribution of Democratic supporters and Republican supporters on that scale in 1956 and 1972. The reader will remember a similar comparison for the population as a whole in Chapter 8. It showed a reduction of the proportion of the populace

---

[5] The criterion used for the most right or left category is a score in the outer 15 percent of the scores aggregated across all the years. The moderate left and right represent the next 15 percent of the population from the left side and the next 15 percent on the right. The center category, thus, contains those scores that fall in the middle 40 percent of the scale.

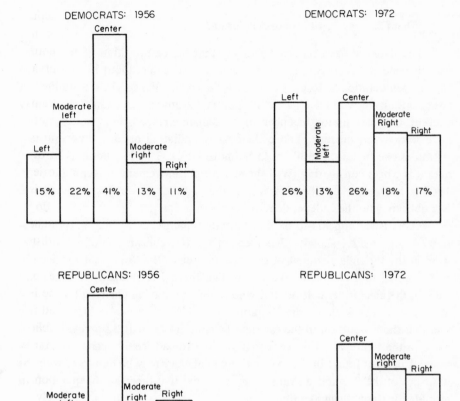

FIGURE 12.2. Distribution of Democrats and Republicans on the issue position scale, 1956 and 1972

in the center of the attitude continuum and a growth at the extremes. As one would expect, a similar change happens to each of the party support groups: in 1956, 41 percent of the Democrats and 41 percent of the Republicans are in the center of the issue scale while only about one out of four are found in the outer categories. By 1972, the center has fallen in number to 26 percent among the Democrats and 30 percent among the Republicans, while the outer categories grow. But the Republicans move more consistently than do the Democrats. As the Republican center collapses, the center of gravity moves right. When the Democratic center collapses, citizens move off in both directions. And the center of gravity is hard to find.

What Changes: Attitudes or Affiliation?

The data we have reported indicate that the composition of the parties has changed in recent years. Such a change can come about in one of two ways: Democratic or Republican identifiers can change their attitudes on issues or citizens who have particular political attitudes can change their party support. Our assumption has been that the main change is in attitudes. As we have shown, few citizens change their party affiliation once it is established. Attitudes, we believe, are likely to be more labile. Yet the alternative explanation is worth considering. Was the sharp right movement of Republicans in 1964 a movement by Republicans to the right or a movement by liberal Republicans into the Independent or Democratic camps?

The answer appears to be that attitudes change rather than party affiliation. As figure 12.1 shows, 17 percent of the Republican identifiers in 1960 were in the far right segment of our attitude scale. By 1964, that proportion had doubled to 34 percent. We can isolate those Republicans in 1964 who were in the electorate in 1960 and who report not having changed their party affiliations—that is, they were Republicans in 1960. If we take this group, we find that the proportion in the far right category in 1964 is 32 percent—quite close to the figure of 34 percent that we find for all Republicans. The additional 2 percent found in the extreme right category may be due to movement in or out of the Republican ranks; but it is clear that there has been a shift in attitude for Republican identifiers.

A similar phenomenon is found for the Democrats. The percent of Democrats in the far left category of our scale doubles from 15 percent in 1956 to 33 percent in 1968. If we consider only those Democrats who were in the electorate in 1956, and who say they have not changed their affiliation, we would find proportions liberal in each year almost identical (that is, within one percentage point) to those proportions reported on figure 12.1 for all Democrats.

Party Activists

We have compared the political views of Democratic and Republican identifiers. The Democrats represent a large and quite heterogeneous portion of the population; the Republicans a smaller and more homogeneous portion. If we wish more fully to understand the differences between the parties we must distinguish between the ordinary supporters of the party and the party artivists.

Party activists are but a minority of those citizens who identify with one or the other of the political parties. But they are a significant minority. They provide the resources for political campaigns by contributing money and time. Because of this, they are likely to be more influential in party decisions. Party leaders are likely to pay more attention to those whose contribution to party success goes beyond the vote. And the activists—because they are active— will exert greater pressure than the rank and file in the process by which candidates are chosen. They are more likely to take part in primary campaigns and to vote in primaries; they are more likely to show up at and take part in party caucuses and conventions.

All this would not make much difference if the activists were like the ordinary party supporters in their preferences. Democratic activists would be like ordinary Democrats, just more active. A party leadership that attended to the activists would not differ in its decisions from a leadership that attended to the mass of party supporters. But activists are not like the rank and file. Early studies of party activists found they tended to have more coherent issue positions than the ordinary voters, and issue positions that were more distinct across the parties. In a study conducted by Herbert McCloskey and his associates in the second Eisenhower term, convention delegates for the two major parties were compared with samples of ordinary party identifiers. The delegates were found to have more distinctive positions than the rank and file— the Democratic delegates somewhat to the left of the rank and file Democrats, the Republican delegates to the right of the Republican rank and file. In addition, the differentiation between delegates and rank and file was greater within the Republican party than within the Democratic party—the Republican delegates were further off to the right of ordinary Republicans than Democratic delegates were off to the left.[6]

As we have seen, however, the structure of public attitudes has changed. The average Democrat moved further to the left from the late 1950s to the middle 1960s and the average Republican moved even more sharply right. Do the party activists move as well? We do not have data on convention delegates, but we can differentiate our samples of the mass public into those who are quite active in political campaigns and those who are only moderately active or not active at all.[7] Our campaign activists do not occupy as high a position in the party hierarchy as do the convention delegates, but they can

---

[6] See Herbert McClosky and others, "Issue Conflict and Consensus Among Party Leaders and Followers," *American Political Science Review*, 54 (June 1960), 406–427; see also David Nexon, "Asymmetry in the Political System: Occasional Activists in the Democratic and Republican Parties," ibid., 65 (September 1971), 716–730.

[7] A campaign activist is one who engages in two or more campaign activities of the six about which the SRC asks.

give us some indication of the degree to which there has been differentiation between ordinary voters and those more active in party affairs.

In figure 12.3 we present data on the proportion of the party activists who fall in the rightmost and leftmost ends of the issue scale. We also repeat the data from figure 12.1 on the proportions of the party identifiers who are in the extreme issue categories.

The Republican group as a whole shows, as we have previously noted, a decidedly conservative tilt. A small group of Republicans (7 to 11 percent) fall in the liberal end of our scale in each year, but the proportion in the conservative end is consistently much larger. In each year it is twice as large as the liberal contingent or more. The conservative percentage rises dramatically in 1964. It falls thereafter but remains quite substantial.

The data on the Republican activists indicate that they have a conservative bent like the ordinary Republicans, only much more so. An even smaller proportion of Republican activists fall in the liberal category than among the rank and file; a larger proportion falls in the conservative category than among the rank and file. The activists change in ways that are similar to the ordinary Republicans. When the proportion of ordinary Republicans in the most conservative category of the scale doubles from 17 percent to 34 percent between 1960 and 1964, the proportion of Republican activists doubles as well from 28 percent in 1960 to 54 percent in 1964.

In general, the relationship between the Republican activists and the Republican rank and file remains fairly similar throughout the time period. The Republican rank and file tends to be on the right with the activists outflanking them further to the right. Both groups move further right in 1964 when one out of three ordinary Republicans is found in the right category and one out of two activists. During the Goldwater-Johnson presidential contest, the issue positions of Republicans crystallized in a clear, conservative direction, and the issue position of the active Republicans was even clearer.

The Democrats present an interesting constrast. In the earlier years of 1956 and 1960, Democratic activists are quite similar to the ordinary Democrats. However, there is a larger percentage of Democratic activists in both of the outlying categories of the issue scale. Indeed, in 1956 almost as large a proportion of the Democratic activists are in the most conservative category of the issue scale as are in the most liberal category. The data present a clear picture of a party with little coherent issue tendency. Democratic activists in 1956 and 1960 are more likely to have coherent issue positions than the ordinary Democrats. But the activists came in almost equal proportions from the left and the right.

The years 1956 and 1960 bracket the McCloskey study. The data are

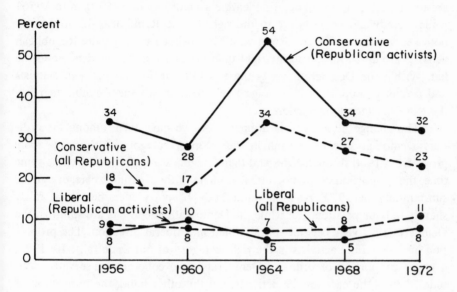

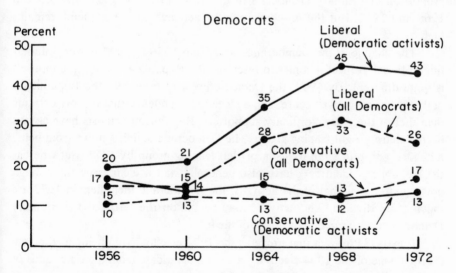

FIGURE 12.3. Proportion of Democratic and Republican identifiers and activists who fall in the liberal or conservative extremes of the issue scale, 1956–1972

quite consistent with the pattern found by McCloskey. Democratic activists are to the left of the Democratic identifiers (more so in 1960 than in 1956) while Republican activists are to the right of the Republican identifiers (in both years). But again, consistent with McCloskey's findings, the Republican activists are much further to the right than the Democratic activists are to the left. Within the Democratic party there is little distinction between activists and ordinary supporters in average issue position. In the Republican party there is a substantial distinction.

The change after 1960 is dramatic. As we have seen, among the ordinary Democrats the proportion in the leftmost category of the issue scale grows from 1960 through 1968 and then falls back a bit in 1972. At the same time, the proportion of Democratic identifiers in the rightmost category grows substantially in 1972, resulting in a body of party identifiers split fairly sharply in issue position. But while the Democratic identifiers are splitting, the Democratic activists become more unified in a liberal direction. The proportion of Democratic activists in the right category of our scale falls. By 1972, a larger proportion of ordinary Democrats have coherent conservative attitudes than is the case among activists. On the other hand, the proportion of Democratic activists in the most liberal end of the scale grows dramatically. In 1968 and 1972 over 40 percent of the activists are in that position. The proportion of ordinary Democrats in the most liberal position falls between 1968 and 1972. But the proportion of the activists on the left flank remains high.

The change in the Democratic party from 1956 to 1972 is worth underlining. In one respect it comes to resemble the Republican party; in another it is quite different. By 1972, the Democratic party resembles the Republicans in that it has an activist cadre with a clear issue tendency that is more extreme than that of the party's ordinary supporters. Republican activists have always been a sharply right leaning group. The Democratic activists move from being a divided group in 1956 to a sharply left leaning group by 1972. But whereas the Republican identifiers have also generally had a clear issue tilt, though not as extreme as that of the activists, the Democratic identifiers in 1972 are much more divided. The activists may be off on the left, but the ordinary Democrats are found on both sides of the fence.

It is this latter fact that prevents the 1972 election from being a complete mirror image of the 1964 election. In each a candidate from the outer ends of the issue scale runs—in 1964 a Republican conservative against a more centrist Democrat; in 1972 a Democratic liberal against a more centrist Republican. And in each case the activists from the party of the more extreme candidate come overwhelmingly from those with issue positions far out on the issue scale. The Republican activists in 1964 and the Democratic activists in

1972 are predominantly found at the issue extremes. But whereas the Republican identifiers were similar to the activists in 1964, if not as extreme, the Democratic identifiers were quite different from the activists in 1972. In the latter year a left-leaning group of activists presided over a much more divided party.[8]

What Changes: Attitudes, Party Identification, or Activity Level?

One note of caution ought to be mentioned in relation to the interpretation of the data in figure 12.3. A change such as that between 1956 and 1972 in the issue positions of party activists can come from any one or a combination of three changes: (a) attitudes of citizens may change; (b) party identification of citizens may change; (c) activity rates of citzens may change.[9]

When we considered the political attitudes of the ordinary party supporters we indicated that change from year to year in the proportion with coherent attitudes on the left or the right indicated attitude change, not change in the party identification of citizens. That is, if a higher proportion of Republicans has conservative attitudes in 1964 than in 1960, this means that many people who were Republicans in 1960 but did not have consistently conservative views have taken on such views. It did not mean that many people who were conservative in 1960 but did not identify with the Republican party came to identify with it.

But the situation is not as clear when we consider the proportion of party activists who take coherent issue positions on one end or the other of the issue scale. It seems fairly clear that the sharp changes in the attitudinal profiles of party activists does not result from shift in party allegiance. Consider, for instance, the Republican activists in 1960 and 1964 on figure 12.3. The change is dramatic. The proportion of activists who are conservative goes up from 28 to 54 percent, the proportion of activists who are liberal falls from 10 to 5 percent. If we look, as we did for all party identifiers, only at those

---

[8] While our data on activists are limited to citizen activists, very few of whom are likely to be real party elites, data from participants in the national democratic convention in 1972 suggest a similar ideological profile characterized and convention delegates. See Dennis G. Sullivan and others, *The Politics of Representation* (New York: St. Martins Press, 1974) and Jeane Kirkpatrick, "Representation in the American National Conventions: The Case of 1972," *The British Journal of Political Science,* 5 (July 1975), 265–322.

[9] This refers to change among those already in the electorate. In addition, new people may enter the electorate with combinations of the three characteristics listed above. Since such a high proportion of new members of the electorate have been Independents, especially in the later years, we can temporarily ignore them.

activists in 1964 who were Republican identifiers in 1960 (that is, eliminating any effect from changed identification between those two years) we see an almost identical pattern—the proportion of activists who are conservative is 52 percent and the proportion liberal is 9 percent. One can say the same thing about the shift of Democratic activists to the left in the late sixties. It is not a result of shifting party identifications.

However, the apparent change in the political profile of the activists may be due to movement of voters with different issue positions into the activist group rather than actual attitude change. For instance, when the proportion of Democratic activists with consistent liberal positions rises after 1964 it may mean that a new cadre of activists has come to the fore.

We have no information on how active the activists in one election were in the previous election or on how many of the inactives in one election were active in the previous. But we would guess that of the three characteristics— party identification, issue position, and activity rates—the first is the most stable and the last most volatile.[10] When the proportion of Democrats with right attitudes grows it is, we believe, because Democrats who had more centrist or more liberal views in the previous election have changed their attitude positions. When the proportion of Democratic activists with left attitudes grows it is, we believe, because voters with Democratic identification in the previous election (and probably liberal attitudes) move into the activist cadres.

Democrats and Republicans: The Changing Role of Political Beliefs

The data on party activists reflects, we believe, a fundamental change in the two parties. Previous data had suggested that the two parties differ in the extent to which they were "ideological." The Republicans had been the party with a more consistent ideological bent. As we have seen, Republican identifiers have been more consistently on the right than were Democratic identifiers on the left. And the Republican party activists had a more consistent and more extreme issue stance than have Democratic activists—at least through 1964.

---

[10] The fact that citizens are often active in one campaign and not in another is supported by a comparison of data from Angus Campbell and others, *The American Voter* (New York: Wiley, 1960) and from Sidney Verba and Norman H. Nie *Participation in America* (New York: Harper and Row, 1972). In the former citizens are asked about their activity in the recent campaign; in the latter they are asked about activity across several campaigns. The latter approach locates more activists, indicating that there are some who are active in one campaign but not the other.

More important than the difference between the parties in the issue positions of the identifiers and the activists was a difference between the parties in the relationship between issue position and political activity. In an earlier work on political participation, two of the present authors tried to account for the fact that Republicans with a strong attachment to their party were more active in political campaigns than were strong Democrats. This difference in activity rates was first noted in a study of political activity conducted in 1967, and was found to be the case across all of the election studies from the early 1950s through 1970.[11] In each election, the activity rate of those voters who considered themselves to be strong Republicans was substantially higher than the activity rate for the strong Democrats.

Two explanations were offered for the difference between the parties. One was that strong Republicans had higher socioeconomic status than strong Democrats. The higher levels of activity of the former merely reflected, therefore, a general tendency for those with more education or more income to higher status occupations to take a more active role in public affairs. And analysis of the data indicated that the difference in socioeconomic level did explain part of the gap in activity rates between the two groups. When we controlled for socioeconomic level the disparity in activity rate was reduced. But a substantial difference remained.

The second explanation of the difference between the Republicans and the Democrats is more germane to our present analysis. Republicans, we argued, were more likely than Democrats to be motivated to take part in political activity by their policy preferences. Our 1967 data supported the position that participation was more closely related to policy position among Republicans than among Democrats. The correlation between political activity rates and various measures of political preferences arrayed in a left-right direction was higher for Republicans than for Democrats. (The correlation between issue position and campaign activity was .26 for Republicans and .06 for Democrats.) In other words, one's issue preference related more strongly to political activity among Republicans than among Democrats.[12]

The data on the changing issue positions of party identifiers and party

---

11 See Verba and Nie, *Participation in America,* chaps. 12 and 14.

12 As one would guess, for Republicans, the political beliefs that were having this effect on participation rates were conservative in direction. The political preferences that we correlated with participation had to do with the extent to which the government has responsibility for welfare in various fields, the extent to which further efforts are needed to reduce income disparities between rich and poor in the United States, and the extent to which civil rights for blacks ought to be pursued vigorously by the government. On all these issues, strong Republicans had more conservative views than other citizens, and these views are related to their rate of political activity. For details of this analysis see Verba and Nie, *Participation in America,* p. 225.

TABLE 12.1.   Correlation between campaign activity rate and issue scale, 1956-1972

	1956	1960	1964	1967[a]	1968	1972
Democrats	.00	.00	.01	.06	.05	.11
Republicans	.11	.12	.26	.24	.12	.10

[a] Source: Calculated from Verba/Nie participation survey, 1967, National Opinion Research Center, 1967.

activists suggest that this difference between the two political parties may have been somewhat transitory. The Republican party no longer appears to be the main home of the issue-oriented activist. And if we consider the data in table 12.1 we see that the relationships found in our 1967 data do not hold up throughout the time period. In that table we report the correlations between a measure of campaign activity and a measure of issue position. The circled figures are those we have reported from our 1967 survey, figures that show a much closer correlation between issue position and activity rates for Republicans than for Democrats. As one can see, the results of our survey in 1967 are quite similar to the results found in the SRC election survey. And they are consistent with the somewhat weaker results found in the surveys in 1956, 1960, and (after our 1967 study) in 1968.[13] In all of these studies, the correlation between issue position and activity is greater for Republicans than Democrats. But it is in the 1964 study and in our 1967 study that one finds the most substantial differences between the party groups. The data suggest that 1964 was a year in which Republican activists were particularly mobilized from the ideologically more committed partisans. And our study in 1967 was probably picking up the results of that mobilization.[14] However, the data also suggest that the "ideological mobilization" of Republicans in 1964 was but an extreme example of a general pattern. The correlations between issue position and activity are stronger for Republicans than for Democrats in all the elections through 1968.

The data in 1972 differ. In that year, the correlations are similar for each party group. Political beliefs have as much effect on the activity rates of Democrats as they have for Republicans. The correlation for each party group

---

[13] Our 1967 study was actually about equidistant in time between the election studies in 1964 and 1968 since it was conducted at the beginning of the year.

[14] Indeed, our questions on campaign activity were designed to elicit reports of such activity in previous elections, so we were probably receiving reports of campaign activity in the 1964 presidential election.

is modest but similar in magnitude to the positive correlations found for the Republicans in the election years of 1956, 1960, and 1968. In other words, by 1972 we find issue position playing a similar role in each party. It appears to be one of the forces impelling partisans to take an active part in the campaign.

One Party United, One Divided

The issue positions of the supporters and activists in the two parties put some of the changes traced earlier in the size of the party groups into perspective. The Republicans, as we have seen, have come to represent a smaller and smaller proportion of the electorate. In recent surveys, less than 20 percent of the samples have identified with that party. But it has clearly become a more homogeneous party.

The Democrats, on the other hand, are larger and more split. A large proportion of the Democratic identifiers is on the left; but a substantial (though not as large) group is on the right. The party activists—at least in recent elections—have been more homogeneously on the left. But that may only exacerbate the internal split. Candidates who go for the middle to try to hold both wings of the party rank and file risk the loss of support of these activists. If these activists induce the party to nominate a candidate from their end of the issue spectrum, they may lose substantial portions of the Democratic vote. 1972, as we shall disuss in Chapter 19, was a case in point. Not that the activists from the left are necessarily the only potential activists among the Democrats. Others may exist in the center or on the right, ready to work for a candidate closer to their persuasion. But the candidate who depends on them runs the risk that they may not be there. We return to these issues in Chapters 18 and 19.

13 | The Party Coalitions

The parties that emerged from the New Deal were issue-based groups. They also were coalitions of particular demographic groups. To see what has happened to that party system we must look at the demographic composition of the parties. We have treated the American public in a simplified manner, tracing some average changes across the population as a whole. The simplification has, we believe, been useful because it has enabled us to highlight some massive changes in the electorate that cut across social groups. But politics in the United States is much more differentiated than the overview would suggest. The American public is made up of many subgroups, not all of whom respond in a similar way to the changes we have been tracing. Our habit of looking at overall tendencies has obscured these differences.

As Chapter 4 documented, changes in partisanship between the early fifties and the early seventies have been striking, but the average change analysis in that chapter masks great variation among groups. Various segments of American society have responded differently to the forces which have eroded partisanship. Some groups have remained relatively steadfast in their party affiliation, others have changed substantially.

The pattern of these changes is important. Party politics in the United States has been a group-based politics.

Each of the parties has drawn its support disproportionately from different segments of the population.[1] In recent elections, however, there is evidence that some of these bases of party support have changed. The regional strongholds of the parties are weakening: the Democratic vote has declined in the South, while it has increased in New England and in the central and plains states. Other stable bases of party support seem much less stable. Conflicts between whites and blacks or between "liberals" and "hard-hats" divide the Democratic party; and a growing liberalism among certain traditional Republican groups threatens the Republican support base.

Does this portend a major party realignment? Some commentators believe we are on the threshold of a major reshaping of the electorate; others claim we are witnessing some short-term stresses which will have little long-term effect on the parties.[2] In part, the debate is about what one means by a

---

[1] Robert Axelrod, "Where the Vote Comes From: An Analysis of Electoral Coalitions, 1952–1968," *American Political Science Review*, 66 (March 1972), 11–20; Samuel Lubell, *The Future of American Politics* (New York: Harper and Row, 1952); J. M. Allswang, *A House for All Peoples: Ethnic Politics in Chicago, 1890–1936* (Lexington: University Press of Kentucky, 1971); Richard P. Formisano, *The Birth of Mass Political Parties: Michigan, 1827–1861* (Princeton: Princeton University Press, 1971); Richard J. Jensen, *The Winning of the Midwest: Social and Political Conflict, 1888–1896* (Chicago: University of Chicago Press, 1971); Paul Kleppner, *The Cross of Culture: A Social Analysis of Midwestern Politics, 1850–1900* (New York: Free Press, 1970); Raymond E. Wolfinger, "The Development and Persistence of Ethnic Voting," *American Political Science Review*, 59 (December 1965), 896–908; Michael Parenti, "Ethnic Politics and the Persistence of Ethnic Identification," *American Political Science Review*, 61 (September 1967), 717–726; Nathan Glazer and Daniel Moynihan, *Beyond the Melting Pot* (Cambridge, Mass.: M.I.T. Press, 1963); Mark R. Levy and Michael S. Kramer, *The Ethnic Factor: How America's Minorities Decide Elections* (New York: Simon and Schuster, 1972); Eugene Burdick and Arthur J. Brodbeck, eds., *American Voting Behavior* (New York: Free Press, 1959), see the chapters by Henry W. Riecken, V. O. Key and Frank Munger, and R. Duncan Luce; Angus Campbell and others, *The American Voter* (New York: Wiley, 1960), chaps. 12–17; Angus Campbell and others, *The Voter Decides* (Evanston: Row-Peterson, 1954), chap. 5; Angus Campbell and Robert L. Kahn, *The People Elect a President* (Ann Arbor, Institute for Social Research, 1952).
The two preeminent monographs dealing with the social group and demographic correlates of party preference are Paul Lazarsfeld and others, *The People's Choice* (New York: Columbia University Press, 1954). Good historical analyses of a general sort of the social facets of the party coalitions can be found in Wilfred Binkley, *American Political Parties: Their Natural History* (New York: Knopf, 1958), and in William Nesbit Chambers and Walter Dean Burnham, eds., *The American Party Systems: Stages of Development* (New York: Oxford University Press, 1967). An exceptionally fine analysis of the formation of the New Deal coalition is David Burne's *The Politics of Provincialism: The Democratic Party in Transition, 1918–1932* (New York: Knopf, 1968).
[2] For contrast see Walter Dean Burnham, *Critical Elections and the Mainsprings of American Politics* (New York: W. W. Norton, 1970); W. D. Burnham, "American Voting Behavior and the 1964 Election," *Midwest Journal of Political Science*, 12 (February 1968), 1–40; Kevin Phillips, *The Emerging Republican Majority* (New Rochelle, N.Y.: Arlington House, 1969); Richard M. Scammon and Ben J. Wattenberg, *The Real Majority: An Extraordinary Examination of the American Electorate* (New York: Coward, McCann and Geoghegan, 1970). A nice synthesis of some of these views can be found in E. C. Ladd, *American Political Parties: Social Change and Political Response* (New York:

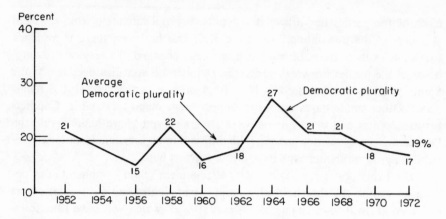

FIGURE 13.1. Plurality of Democratic over Republican party identifiers, 1952–1972

"realignment." To some, a realignment is a major change in the relative strength of the two major parties. Clearly, there has not been that kind of realignment over recent elections. As we have seen, the proportion of independents in the electorate has increased by a substantial amount: 40 percent of the eligible electorate report no partisan identification by 1974. But this has not affected the balance between the parties. The decline in the proportion of Republican and Democratic identifiers between the fifties and the seventies is approximately equal. There are about 6 percent fewer Democratic identifiers in the electorate than there were at the beginning of the 1950s and about 5 percent fewer Republicans.

The stability in the relative positions of the parties is seen in figure 13.1. The figure presents the Democratic plurality over time—that is, the proportion of Democratic identifiers in the population minus the proportion of Republican identifiers.[3] There is some variation around the average plurality of 19 percent over the twenty year period, but the data display no clear trend. The decline in mass support for the political parties has not challenged the numerical dominance of Democrats over Republicans. In this sense, there has been little, if any, party realignment.

However, there is another definition one can give to the term realign-

---

W. W. Norton, 1970). The most cosmic interpretation of the social and political change discussed by Burnham and Ladd can be found in Apter's "Introduction, Ideology and Discontent," in David E. Apter, ed., *Ideology and Discontent* (New York: Free Press, 1964).

[3] This index of percentage differences is used throughout the chapter. Formally it is: PDI = % Democrat − % Republican. Therefore, if the result is positive there are more Democrats than Republicans and when it is negative, it indicates an excess of Republicans over Democrats. Figure 13.1 presents overall data.

ment: a party realignment is a substantial change in the support that various social groups give to the political parties.[4] If a group shifts its support from one party to the other or if a group that had no particular partisan bias comes to support one of the parties, there has been an important change in the party/vote alignment. Changes of this sort have usually precipitated changes in the relative strength of the major parties—one party loses the support of one or more groups and the loss affects the degree to which the party is dominant. But a movement of social groups from one party to the other does not necessarily imply a net change in the relative strength of the two parties. Reciprocal movements could cancel each other out. The result of such group change might be a substantial change in the composition of the party coalitions but no change in the relative position of the parties.

This is what has happened in recent years. Shifts in group identification with the parties have not resulted in a change in the relative positions of the parties. Recent changes in the partisanship of various groups have, thus far, not (1) caused the demise of either of the parties (as happened in the realignments of 1828 and 1856, for example), (2) made the minority party the majority party (as happened in 1928/1932), or (3) increased the strength of the majority party (as happened in 1896). The changes, though, have been substantial. The parties now look quite different from the way they looked in the early fifties.

Parties as a Coalition of Sociodemographic Groups

The supporters of the two American political parties have been distinguished from each other by economic, religious, and national-ethnic differences. This distinctiveness is sufficiently pervasive to serve as the working politician's guide to what he must do to win elections. "From the stump . . . politicians righteously deplore any suggestion that their red-blooded constituents might be influenced by bloc-voting patterns; off the stump they find it hard to discuss strategy in any other terms."[5]

---

[4] There seems to be considerable casualness in the exact definition of realignment. Key is quite consistent in using this notion of the party bias change as the characteristic of realignment. See his "A Theory of Critical Elections," *Journal of Politics* 17 (February 1955), 3–18, and especially "Secular Realignment and the Party System," *Journal of Politics*, 21 (May 1959), 198–210. James Sundquist is a bit less careful about keeping to his explicit definition, but generally Sundquist also defines a realignment as a change in the party bias of distinct social groups. *Dynamics of the Party System: Alignment and Realignment of Political Parties in the United States* (Washington, D.C.: Brookings Institute, 1973).

[5] Quoted by Raymond E. Wolfinger from *Newsweek,* in "The Development and Persistence of Ethnic Voting," *American Political Science Review,* 59 (December 1965), 896.

What kind of sociodemographic and economic distinctions are important today? The first difference to come to mind, of course, is regionalism. The South has exhibited a strong bias for the Democratic party since the end of reconstruction and especially since the turn of the century.[6] It was only in some upland mountain counties in the South—the same counties which had opposed secession in 1860—that Republican party candidates won elections. In general, the South sent Democrats to Congress; and virtually every southern state had only Democratic governors, legislators, judges, sheriffs, and road commissioners since 1900.

Another obvious difference between the parties is found in the social and economic status of their supporters. Republicans are likely to have larger incomes, more education and higher status jobs than Democrats. Partly as a consequence of this, union members are more likely to support the Democratic party. The Democratic preference of organized labor preceded the New Deal, but the sharply pro-labor stance of the FDR administrations solidified the support of organized labor for the Democratic party. The activist and welfare oriented policies of the FDR presidency contributed mightily to the status difference in the support base of the two parties.

The Democrats differ from the Republicans in religious and ethnic terms as well. Catholics are more likely to be Democrat than are Protestants; Jews are more likely to be Democratic than are either Protestants or Catholics; and blacks are perhaps the most pro-Democratic (large) minority in the country. Further, within the religious groupings there are nationality differences. Proportionally there are more Democrats among Irish and Polish Catholics than there are among German and Italian Catholics. These religioethnic differences have deep historical roots.[7]

---

[6] We are aware of the fact that the South has supported the Democratic party longer than that. A lot of what we currently define as the South was frontier a century and a half ago and partial to Jackson's Democratic-Republican party.

[7] It is frequently believed that the pro-Democratic bias of Catholic voters dates from Al Smith and FDR. In fact, American Catholics have supported the Democratic party more heavily than the Republican party for well over a century. The nativism of the Whigs and later the Republicans pushed Catholic immigrants into the Democratic party. Consistent Democratic majorities were being delivered in Irish Catholic areas as early as 1840. Indeed, most non-English immigrant groups seemed to prefer the Democrats. The most likely reason that our awareness of the size of the Catholic contingent in the Democratic party dates from the Al Smith and the New Deal period is that it was at that point that Catholic voters—the immigrants and the children of immigrants—voted in heavy numbers for the first time. In these elections the normal Democratic bias of the group was reinforced by election-specific forces; as a consequence Catholic voters learned a preference for the Democratic party at the moment they were first mobilized into party politics. A similar process probably accounts for the markedly pro-Republican sentiments of several Protestant nationalities, many of whom came to the United States in the 1830s, 1840s, and 1850s, and entered politics for the first time when short-term forces favored

We have used these various characteristics—region, social status, religion, and ethnicity—to define various population groups that have been distinctive in their partisan bent. Ours is not an exhaustive categorization; rather it is one which singles out some distinctive groups.[8] Figure 13.2 presents the partisan tendencies of these groups in the 1950s. The horizontal dimension indicates the plurality that a group gives to one party over the other. If the group gives a percentage advantage to the Democrats it is plotted to the left; if the group gives plurality to the Republicans it is plotted to the right. A group equally divided between Democrats and Republicans is at the zero point in the center of the horizontal axis. The vertical axis indicates the proportion of the group that is independent. The lower the position of the group in that line, the greater the proportion of independents. A group that was 100 percent behind the Democratic party would be in the upper left corner, a group 100 percent behind the Republicans would be at the upper right. A group totally

---

the emerging Republican party. For a more extensive analysis of this phenomenon as it affected the 1928/1932 realignment see Kristi Andersen, "Political Generations and Partisan Change," Ph.D. dissertation, University of Chicago, 1976, and Chapter 5 of this book.

[8] The groups that are used in this and the subsequent chapter are a reduction of a more elaborate grouping of the population used in John Petrocik, "Changing Party Coalitions and the Attitudinal Basis of Alignment: 1952–1972, Ph.D. dissertation, University of Chicago, 1976, chap. 4.

The groups are based upon social status, race, religion, and region of residence. The status groups are defined by education and occupation. The number in the cell indicates the status group to which a respondent was assigned. Status group 1 is the highest and 5 is the lowest. All respondents with a farm occupation were put into a special group. When categories are dichotomized, 1 and 2 are higher status, all others are lower status.

	Profession and higher white collar	All other white collar	All blue collar jobs	Farm
Less than a high school education	3	4	5	6
A high school degree	2	3	4	6
At least some college	1	2	3	6

Region was defined as follows: Border South (Kentucky, Maryland, Oklahoma, Tennessee, Washington, D.C., West Virginia); South (Alabama, Arkansas, Florida, Georgia, Louisiana, Mississippi, North Carolina, South Carolina, Texas, Virginia); and North (all other states).

Certain combinations of these region, status, race, and religion characteristics define the groups traced through the twenty year period: (1) higher status WASPs include any white Protestant who lives in the North and is in the first or second status group; (2) middle and lower status WASPs include all other white Protestants who live in the North; (3) border South includes any white Protestant living in the border South; (4) middle and upper status native southerners includes any white Protestant living in the South who reports being raised in the region and has a status score of 4, 5, or 6; (6) all Catholics regardless of social status or region of residence; (7) all Jews regardless of social status or region of residence; (8) all blacks regardless of social status or region of residence.

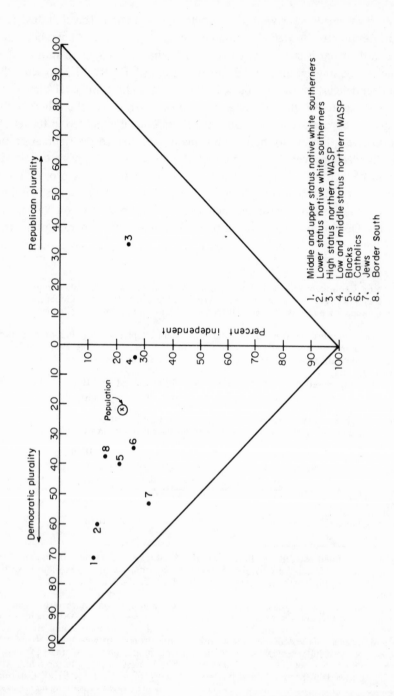

FIGURE 13.2. Partisan tendencies of selected groups, 1950s

1. Middle and upper status native white southerners
2. Lower status native white southerners
3. High status northern WASP
4. Low and middle status northern WASP
5. Blacks
6. Catholics
7. Jews
8. Border South

independent would be at the lower point of the triangle. Lastly, a group that was completely polarized, giving 50 percent to each party and having no independents within it would be in the center of the horizontal line.

The figure allows us to locate the partisan proclivities of various population groups in the 1950s. The partisan proclivities of the population as a whole is located on the graph as well so that one can compare other groups with it. Twenty-three percent of the electorate was independent during that period. Any group located below the figure for the whole electorate on figure 13.2 is more independent. The electorate as a whole gave a 19 point plurality to the Democrats. Any group to the left of them gives a larger plurality to the Democrats, any group to the right gives a smaller one to the Democrats or a plurality to the Republicans.

The location of various groups on the graph shows their partisan bent when our time period began. Consider the high status WASPs. They are not much different from the population as a whole in the proportion that is independent, but they have the clearest Republican tendency. They have many of the characteristics that distinguish Republican from Democratic supporters: they are Protestants, they have above average educations, above average incomes, and high status occupations; and they live outside of the South.

The dominant role played by region can be seen by comparing the northern WASPs with their southern counterparts—the middle and upper status white southerners. The latter group differs from the former by 60 percentage points in terms of the proportion Democratic, and gives a strong plurality to that party. The northern and southern WASPs are the most distinctive groups. But other groups have distinctive partisan profiles as well: the Jews, Catholics, and blacks are all more Democratic than the population as a whole and the Jews somewhat more independent as well.

The variety of locations of groups on the figure indicates the varied basis of party support and the distinctiveness of the party orientations of the groups during the 1950s. We can now see how these groups move. We begin with the most distinctive group.

The White Southerners

The South is no longer solidly Democratic. Presidential candidates from the Democratic party cannot rely on southern support. But the change is more than an increase in presidential Repulicanism; state and local offices are no longer a Democratic monopoly, and party identifications have changed. Figure 13.3 presents data on change in the party identification of white southerners. The three lines in the graph are the proportion of the group who are Democratic identifiers, Republican identifiers, or Independent over the period from 1952 to 1972. The 30 percentage point decline in Democratic identification is dramatic. In the 1950s the white southerners had an overwhelming preference for the Democratic party. By the 1970s white southerners were no more Democratic than the population as a whole. Where 70 percent or so were once Democrats, we now find less than half describing themselves as Democrats.

This realignment of the southern electorate is, however, only partial. The Democrats have lost, but there has not been a very substantial increase in the

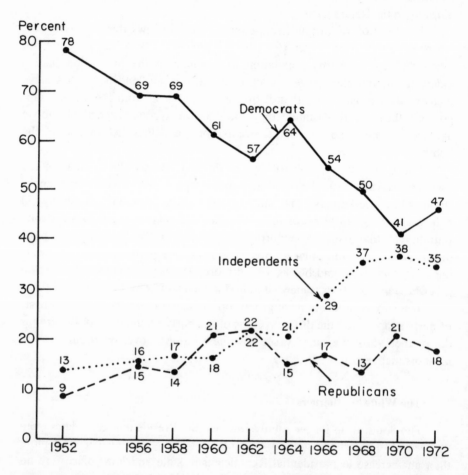

FIGURE 13.3. Party identification among white Protestant southerners, 1952–1972

rate of identification with the Republican party. The 35 point decline in Democratic identification has been converted into only a 9 point increase (roughly) in Republican identification. The major result of the decline in Democratic identification has been a rise in Independents.

The Effect of Migration

There are many reasons for the change in the South. The Republican party has courted southern voters, the Democratic party has become identified with civil rights, the South has become economically modernized, and the population of the region has changed as new people moved there. The migration hypothesis is a particularly plausible explanation for the changes. The South was unusual in the strength of its ties to the Democratic party; and, therefore, the extensive postwar migration into the region must have diluted the Democratic commitment of the area. Migration is such an obvious explanation for the partisan change of the region that it is not unreasonable to believe that it must be responsible for all of the change.[9]

The data, however, do not support this interpretation. The decline in Democratic identification has not resulted simply from migration into the South. Consider figure 13.4 which presents data for "native" southerners— that is, southerners raised in the South. The decline in Democratic identification is almost identical with that found for all southerners. There is, however, more variation by specific election among native southerners. Up to 1964 there is a slow decline in Democratic commitment, but after 1964 the drop is more precipitous. In the six years after 1964 there is a 27 point decline. There are many possible reasons for this. The increasing activism of Republican organizations in the late fifties and early sixties, the surge of civil rights activism, the courtship of the South by the national Republican party, and the pro–civil rights stance of the national Democratic party all helped to precipitate the decline in Democratic identification.[10]

The data suggest that immigration was the major cause of the decline in the southern Democracy up to about 1964, but there is no warrant for believing that it had much impact after 1964. Table 13.1 compares the proportion Democratic in the South as a whole (including immigrants) with the propor-

---

[9] The argument that change in the South comes from migrants is made by Philip Converse in "On the Possibility of Major Political Realignment in the South," in Angus Campbell and others, *Elections and the Political Order* (New York: Wiley, 1966), pp. 212–242.

[10] See especially the brilliant interpretive essay by Donald Strong, "Durable Republicanism in the South," Alan P. Sindler, ed., *Change in the Contemporary South* (Durham, N.C.: Duke University Press, 1963), pp. 119–147.

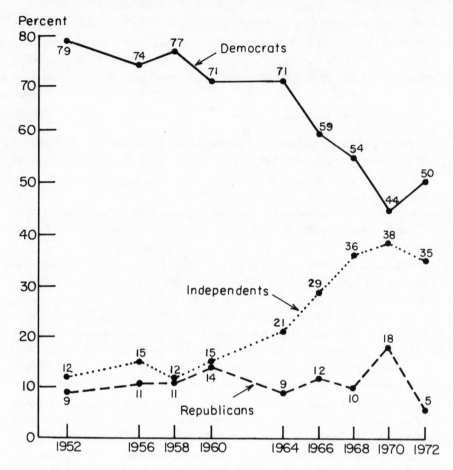

FIGURE 13.4. Party identification among white native southerners, 1952–1972

tion Democratic among native southerners (excluding immigrants) in the
Eisenhower election, in 1964, and in the early 1970s. If we compare the
Eisenhower years with 1964, we can see how much of an impact immigration
had on the declining proportion of Democrats in the southern electorate. The
figures for all southerners (including immigrants) show a drop of 9 percent in
the proportion Democratic between the fifties and 1964. If we exclude immigrants, we find a fall of only 6 percent in the proportion Democratic for the
same period. A consideration of the change from 1952/56 to 1964 supports
the view that the decline in the proportion of Democrats is due in part to the
arrival of newcomers to the South.

But compare 1970/72 with the earlier years. Even if we exclude new
southerners, we find a sharp decline in the proportion of southerners who are

TABLE 13.1. Proportion democratic among southerners, including and excluding immigrants, 1952–1972

	All southerners	Excluding immigrants
Percent Democratic in 1952/56	73	77
Percent Democratic in 1964	64	71
Percent Democratic in 1970/72	44	47

Democratic: from 71 percent in 1964 to 47 percent in 1970/72. The 47 percent for native southerners differ by only 3 percentage points from the 44 percent for all southerners. Clearly, there have been two stages in the transformation of the South. From the early fifties to the 1964 election, the majority of the change away from the Democratic party came from the migration of citizens into the South. After 1964, the native southerners changed. In overall effect, comparing the early fifties with the seventies, the decline in Democratic identification would have been almost as great (only 6 percent difference) if no newcomers had arrived. The immigration of white northerners into the South over the last few decades cannot be responsible for more than about 18 percent of the total decline in Democratic identification in the South. Had there been no immigration to the South to contribute to the decline in Democratic identification, the proportion of Democratic identifiers would still have declined 36 percent (27 percentage points).

Status Cleavage in the South

The New Deal realignment created parties differentiated along class lines in the North. In the South, such a division did not develop. There was no Republican party to attract upper status voters. Upper and lower status whites were both in the Democratic party. Economic clashes took place, as V. O. Key pointed out, within the Democratic party.

The arrival of the Republican party in the South provided the opportunity for a status differentiation between the parties. This is seen in figure 13.5 where we plot the changes in party identification for upper and lower status white southerners. As one can see, the desertion from the Democratic party is greater among upper status southerners. By the end of the time period, the proportion of Democrats among the upper status white southerners has fallen to less than 50 percent. The change is not as sharp among the lower status group.

In sum, the South moved during the two decades we have been studying

A. High status native southerners

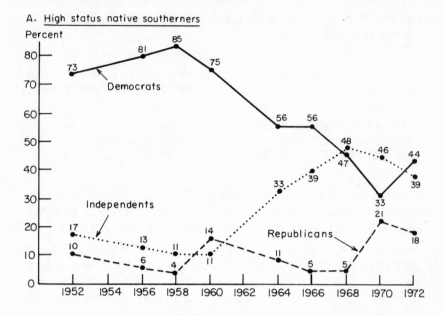

B. Low status native southerners

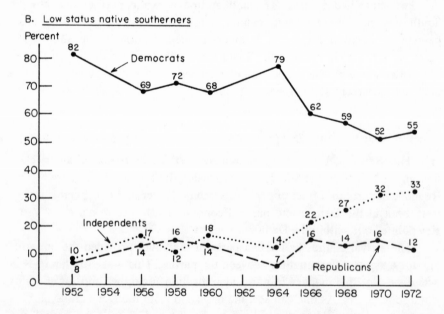

FIGURE 13.5. Party identification among high and low status native southern whites, 1952–1972

to rejoin the union. It has become a two party area. The Democratic party continues to have a strong lead over the Republican party in terms of the proportions that identify with it, but that lead is of the same magnitude as the Democratic lead for the nation as a whole. Furthermore, Democratic identifiers in the South have followed the pattern of party supporters elsewhere; they are more likely to abandon their party to vote for the opposition than in the past. This increases the competitiveness of southern elections. And as the South has rejoined the union in the development of competitive parties, it has rejoined the union in that the competition between the parties is based, at least in part, on differences in the status of their supporters.[11]

Change Outside the South: Fewer Republicans

The South was always important to the Democratic party. Southerners make up about 20 percent of the population, and they traditionally voted for Democrats. If one had removed the South from the electorate, the Democratic majorities of the past twenty years would have virutally disappeared. With the exception of the Johnson election in 1964 there would not have been a Democratic president after 1940. The loss of the Solid South, then, would seem to presage a decline of the majority status of the Democratic party nationally. This has not happened, and there is little indication that it is about to take place. The stability of the Democratic party on the national level indicates the existence of countertendencies: Democratic gains within former Republican groups or an intensification of Democratic support in normally Democratic groups.

One countertrend is the decline of Republican support among white northern Protestants.[12] The change among white Protestants in the North is

---

[11] There is little evidence that these changes have a rural/urban component. The change is greatest in the more urban areas of the South, but it does not seem to be accurate to argue that urbanization constitutes the causal phenomenon. The extent to which both higher status and youth are concentrated in the larger cities tends to be the primary explanation for the observable differences between urban and rural areas in shifts in party identification.

[12] Although it is true that socioeconomic status differentiates party support (with the less affluent being more Democratic, and the more affluent being more Republican), it is less important than ethnoreligious and regional differences. What this means for the demography of party preference is that there are greater party preference differences between ethnocultural groups of similar social status than there are between status groups of the same ethnocultural group. In the North this has meant a clear difference in party preference between white Protestants, on the one hand, and Catholics, blacks, and Jews on the other. Northern white Protestants, for example, account for about 53 percent of all Republican identifiers. There are, of course, some differences in the party preference of Protestants depending upon their social status and where in the country they live; class and region are important, but the predominant Republicanism of white northern Protestants is incontestable.

not nearly as large as that in the South, but it is considerable. Figure 13.6 presents the data for this group. Although they remain more Republican than Democrat, the relative advantage for the Republicans here is smaller in the seventies than it was in the fifties. A plurality of 43 percent of this group considered itself Republican in the early fifties. The proportion fell about ten points during the two decades.

More interesting than this overall change is the change in upper status Protestants (see figure 13.7A). Again, the data are not as dramatic as those for the South, but there is a clear erosion in Republican support in a group which had heretofore been as traditionally Republican as white southerners had been Democratic. The critical period for this group seems to begin about 1960. In 1960 the group registered the highest preference for the Republican party over the period. This peak probably results from the candidacy of a Catholic for the Democratic party. The Goldwater candidacy produces some disenchantment with the Republican party. A decline in Republican support

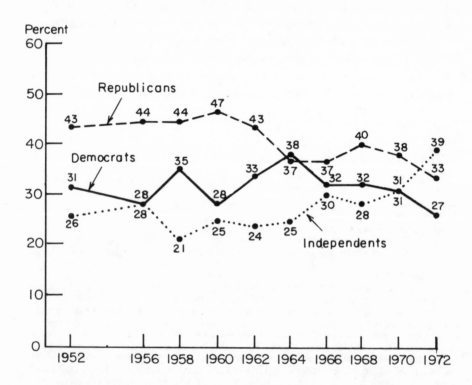

FIGURE 13.6. Party identification among northern white Protestants, 1952–1972

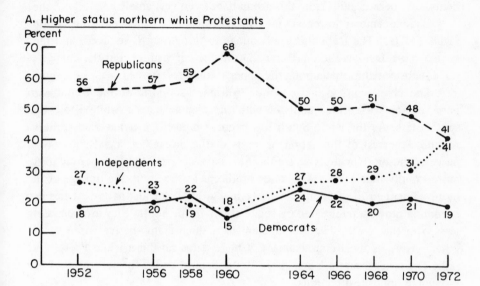

A. Higher status northern white Protestants

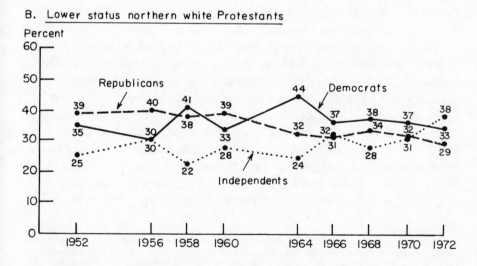

B. Lower status northern white Protestants

FIGURE 13.7. Party identification among higher and lower status northern white Protestants, 1952–1972

begins in 1964 and has been maintained. As in the South, the decline in Republican sympathies has resulted in an increase in the number of Independents. Democratic gains from this group have been very small.

Change among lower status white Protestants has been smaller (see figure 13.7B). The Republican advantage in this group is reduced, and they have a more Democratic character than in the early fifties, but the change is not as substantial as that among the upper status Protestants.

The change in northern white Protestant support for the Republican party presents a curious contrast with the change among white Protestant southerners. As the white South has become bipartisan, it has also come to resemble the rest of the nation in terms of the linkage of social status with party affiliation. Upper status southerners have deserted the Democratic party more rapidly than their lower status brethren. In the South the linkage of the more affluent to the Republican party has grown. But just as the parties are becoming more differentiated by social status in the South, they are becoming less so in the North. The Republicanism of high status native white southerners grows as the Republicanism of high status northern white Protestants falls. The latter group remains more Republican than the former; but they are moving in opposite directions.

Further Changes: More Democrats

The movement away from the Republicans of some traditional northern Protestant supporters counterbalances some of the Democratic loss in the South. There are other counterbalances. Some traditionally Democratic groups have become even more Democratic. Blacks present the most striking example. The conversion of blacks to the Democratic party dates from the middle 1930s. The conversion is a consequence of the welfare programs of the Roosevelt administration and the political recognition that his first administration accorded blacks.[13] With Roosevelt, the pictures of Abraham Lincoln were "turned to the wall" and a wholesale conversion of northern blacks to the Democratic party took place.[14] The change was slower in the South. While Republican identification averaged about 14 percent throughout the 1950s and into the 1960s among northern blacks; it averaged very close to 25 percent for southern blacks. The local Democratic party in the South

---

[13] To develop some feel for the Republicanism of at least northern blacks the reader might examine Charles Merriam and Harold F. Gosnell, *Nonvoting* (Chicago: University of Chicago Press, 1924). This change is documented in Allswang, *A House for All Peoples.*

[14] This may be one of the few instances where there was an actual conversion from one party preference to another (see Chapter 5).

was not the party of racial moderation and progress that it was in the North. Quite the contrary, the Republican party, while not actively championing the black cause, was the party of racial moderation and the opposition to the segregationist white Democratic population. A considerable portion of this Civil War Republicanism had evaporated by the middle of this century, but southern blacks remained distinctively more Republican than their northern counterparts.[15]

Figure 13.8A presents the distribution of party identification for northern blacks from 1952 through 1972. Two points are obvious in the graph. First, northern blacks were predominantly Democratic in the fifties and the decade of the sixties saw an increase in this Democratic majority. Second, Republican support among northern blacks declined from less than 20 percent to the vanishing point by the late sixties. Southern blacks change in a similar direction, but they do so at different rates and at different times. During the fifties, the Democratic dominance in this group was more limited. The rate of identification with the Republican party among southern blacks was not that different from the rate among northern blacks. What did differ was the frequency of Independents. Southern blacks apparently found the racism of the southern Democratic party too immediate and pervasive to consider themselves Democrats. This changes after 1960.

The rise of white racial militancy in the Republican party in the late fifties and early 1960s, coupled with the Goldwater campaign in 1964, pushed most black southern Republicans into the Democratic party.[16] In the early fifties about 25 percent of southern blacks regarded themselves as Republicans. In the North, in contrast, the Republican portion among blacks was under 20 percent. This difference disappears by the early seventies. By 1970, in the North and in the South, only about 6 percent of all blacks regarded themselves as Republicans. The turning point occurs between 1960 and 1964. After 1964 there is virtually no difference between northern and southern blacks in their party identification. Something less than 10 percent of blacks are Republican, a bit more than 20 percent are Independent, and the remaining 75 percent or so are Democrats.

The unanimous black support for the Democratic party has had a compound effect on the black Democratic vote because it comes at the same time

---

[15] Southern blacks were so Republican that throughout the 1950s, for example, students of southern politics often based their analyses of the southern vote on the assumed unanimous Republicanism of black voters. See Donald S. Strong, *Urban Republicanism in the South* (Birmingham: University of Alabama Press, 1956).

[16] John C. Topping, John R. Lazarek, and William H. Linder, *Southern Republicans and the New South* (Cambridge, Mass., 1966).

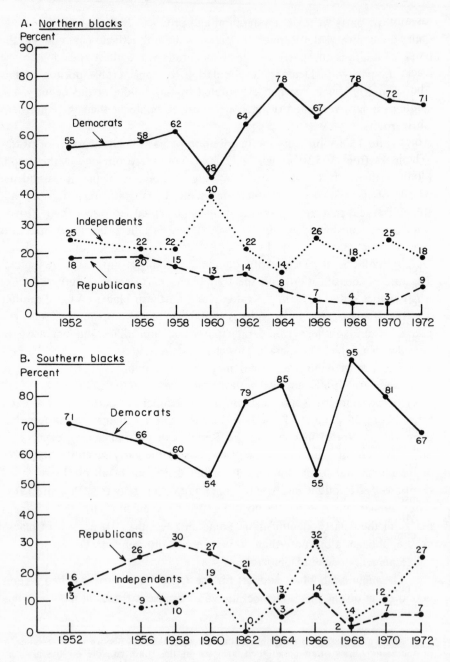

FIGURE 13.8. Party identification among northern and southern blacks, 1952–1972

as a major increase in the turnout of blacks at the polls. In the 1952/1956 period, less than half of the blacks of voting age voted, compared with over two-thirds of the whites.[17] By the early 1970s the difference between the racial groups had declined. The sharpest change has been in the South where the voting rate of blacks went from 14 to 51 percent. Southern blacks were more Republican than northern blacks in the early fifties, but this difference in their support had little impact on elections because only a small minority voted. When they became overwhelmingly Democratic they also began voting. The juxtaposition of the two changes makes them a potent force in the Democratic party.

Jews

American Jews are another minority with a traditional Democratic preference. This preference remains, but it has eroded somewhat. Jews no longer vote consistently Democratic. In addition, there has been some decline in their Democratic identification, though the movement is toward a higher proportion of Independents rather than a movement to the Republican party (see figure 13.9).

The Ethnics and the Hardhats

In the late 1960s, political commentators "discovered" the white working-class ethnics. There is no agreed definition of an "ethnic" but the term is usually applied to Catholics of Irish or southern and eastern European descent. As figure 13.10 makes clear, Catholics have become less Democratic and more Independent. But although they have recently been the target of conservative appeals, Catholics have not moved into the Republican ranks. If anything, the Catholic population has, compared with the rest of the public, become more distinctively Democratic over time. In the fifties the Democrats received from the Catholics a plurality about 10 percentage points greater than they received from the population as a whole (that is, the Catholics were 30 percent more Democratic than Republican; the population as a whole was 20 percent more Democratic). If we take an average of the years after 1964,

---

[17] This proportion is larger than the turnout reported by the Bureau of the Census. For the analysis of the causes of the discrepancy see Stanley Kelley, Jr., and Thad W. Mirer, "The Simple Act of Voting," *American Political Science Review*, 68 (June 1974), 571–572; Aage R. Clausen, "Response Validity: Vote Report," *Public Opinion Quarterly*, 32 (Winter 1968–69), 588–606.

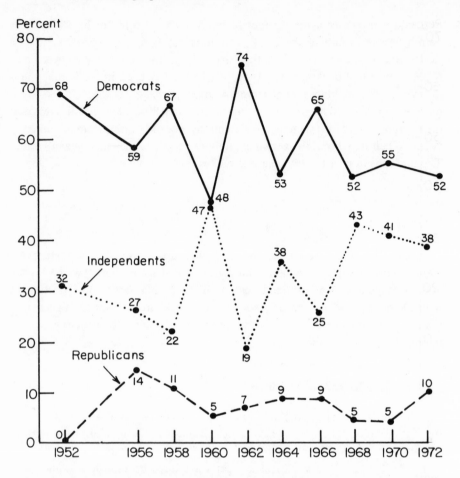

FIGURE 13.9. Party identification among Jews, 1952–1972

we find the Catholics giving a plurality to the Democrats 15 percent larger than that given by the population as a whole.

There are some variations among the Catholics: Irish and Polish Catholics are somewhat more Democratic than others. But in none of the Catholic ethnic groups do we see evidence of a desertion of the Democratic party. Upper status Catholics have moved a bit into the Independent ranks over the past two decades, but the movement has been from both the Democratic and the Republican camps—leaving the Democratic plurality unchanged.[18] In

---

[18] There is, for example, a 6 point decline in Republican identifiers among the Irish and Poles. Among high status Catholics of other nationalities the decline in Republicans is 4 points and among the lower status Catholics of other nationalities the decline is 7 points.

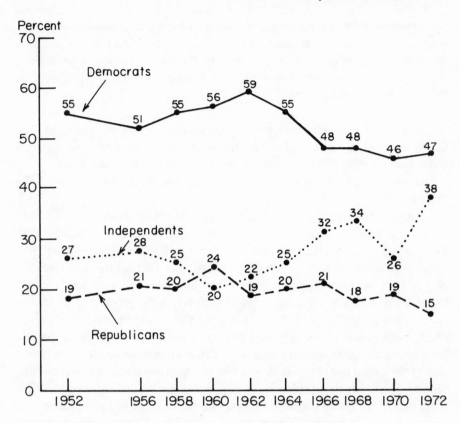

FIGURE 13.10. Party identification among Catholics, 1952–1972

short, when it comes to party identification, there is no evidence of a shift toward the Republican party among Catholics. If there is a weakening of Democratic identification among some subgroups of Catholics, the movement is into the independent category. Taking Catholics as a whole, one finds an *increase* in the Democratic plurality.[19]

The voting pattern of Catholics in contrast to their party identification is more mixed. The evidence hardly suggests an abandonment of Democratic affiliation. Catholics, like other Americans, are more prone to abandon their party when it comes to the vote than they once were. But if we compare Catholics with the population as a whole we find that lower status Catholics

---

[19] The pattern is similar for that other bulwark of the Democratic party, the union member. They have become relatively more, not less, Democratic.

have become even more distinctively Democratic in their voting behavior.[20] Among upper status Catholics, on the other hand, there is a distinctive increase in Republican voting. This may be the harbinger of change in party identification among these higher status Catholics. We cannot tell. Thus far there has been no such change.

Figure 13.11 summarizes most of the changes we have considered. The figure is similar to figure 13.2 in this chapter, where we located various groups in terms of the plurality they gave one party over the other in the 1950s.

Figure 13.11 indicates the change from the Eisenhower years to the early 1970s.

Consider the group labeled high status northern WASP. In the early fifties, the group was about 34 percentage points more Republican than Democratic and about 22 percent independent. By the early seventies, the group was about 20 points more Republican than Democratic and about 38 percent independent. The pro-Republican bias in the group has declined about 14 points. There is only a slight increase in the proportion of Democrats in the group. Most of the change results from the increase in Independents. Each group can be inspected in turn. The length and slope of the line for a group compared to any group indicates the extent to which the partisanship of the group has changed. A line which slopes down at a very steep angle, relative to the left or right length of the line, indicates that the change in the party bias of the group depends primarily on the increase in Independents. On the other hand, if the up or down angle of the line is rather shallow but the left–right movement is large, then the group is changing primarily because of equal increases and decreases in Republican and Democratic identifiers.

Figure 13.11, of course, indicates exactly what the previous graphs indicate: that most of the change in the party bias of the groups is a result of higher rates of independence in the seventies. The advantage of the summary in figure 13.11 is that the rates of change and the character of the change for each group can be compared with each other group. Such a comparison shows that southerners (those from the deep South and the border South) have changed the most, and that Catholics, Jews, and middle and lower status northern WASPs have changed the least. Only two groups have increased their preference for one of the parties. Blacks have not become more than a couple

---

[20] Union members have also persisted in their Democratic voting. A Democratic candidate for the House of Representatives, for example, can on the average expect to obtain 60 to 70 percent of the union vote, and a Democratic presidential candidate, even if he does badly, will do less badly among union members than one would expect on the basis of national figures. This has not changed over time.

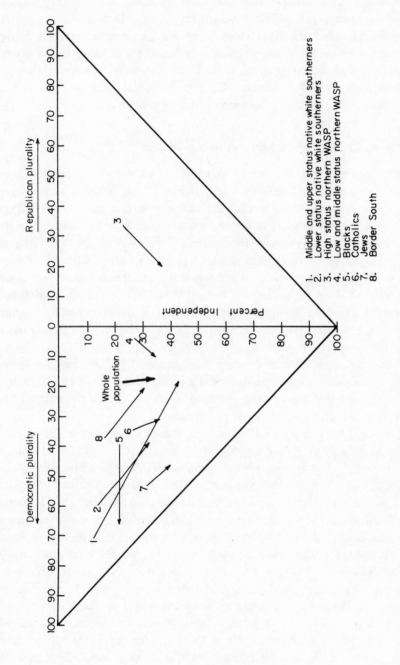

FIGURE 13.11. Party tendencies of selected groups, 1950s to 1970s (arrow begins where the group was in the 1950s and ends where it is in the 1970s)

1. Middle and upper status native white southerners
2. Lower status native white southerners
3. High status northern WASP
4. Low and middle status northern WASP
5. Blacks
6. Catholics
7. Jews
8. Border South

of percentage points more Independent since the fifties, but they have become much more Democratic. Where blacks once gave the Democratic party a 40 point advantage over the Republican party, by the seventies they are giving Democrats a 68 point advantage. Similarly, middle and lower status whites have moved from a bare preference for Democrats to a 10 point preference for Democrats over Republicans. Clearly there has been a considerable change in the partisanship of these major social groups.

Group Change and the Entrance of New Voters

The data in figure 13.11 show that there has been substantial change in the party preferences of various social groups. What is the source of this change? Our earlier analyses would lead us to expect that much of the change comes from the entrance of new voters rather than from the conversion of older voters. We can estimate the impact of new voters on the changing position of groups by comparing the change in the party affiliation of each group with the change we would have found if we had considered only those voters who were in the electorate before 1960. The bigger the difference between the actual change in the party preference of the group and the change found among older voters, the greater the impact of the new voters who enter after 1960.

Figure 13.12 reproduces the data from figure 13.11 but adds to it information which permits a comparison of the changes that occur in the group, and the changes that would have occurred if the young had not entered the electorate with such a different party preference.

The solid lines in figure 13.12 are reproduced from figure 13.11; they indicate how the party bias of a group as a whole has changed from the fifties to the seventies. The broken line, in contrast, depicts the change from the fifties to the seventies for that age cohort eligible to vote before 1960. The broken line, in other words, shows what change would have been like if young voters had not entered the electorate after 1960. The change in the party bias that is measured by the broken line is quite a bit smaller than that in the solid line. In almost every case, the addition of the young has made the group more independent and less biased toward one of the parties than would have been the case if only the pre-1960 generation voters were counted. In some cases the effects of the young are small. Among the native southern groups, the addition of the young simply gives a more pronounced result to a change which would have existed without them. For Jews, for the northern Protestant groups, and for Catholics, the entrance of the young substantially increases the amount of change in the party bias of the group.

Table 13.2 summarizes the results of this analysis. The first column reports the total percentage point change in the party identification of various groups from the fifties to the seventies.[21] The second column lists the proportion of that change which is due to the coming of age of new voters in the post-1960 elections.[22] While there are some differences across the groups, it is clear that the post-1960 generation is disproportionately responsible for the change in the party bias of each group. The major contrast in the table is

---

[21] This measurement can be best understood through the following illustration. Consider a group with the following distribution of party preference:

	The fifties	The seventies	Change: fifties to seventies
Democrat	45 percent	39 percent	−6 points
Independent	25	34	+9 points
Republican	30	27	−3 points
	100	100	

Since the shares must always total 100 percent, any decline for one category of party identification must represent an increase in the percentage associated with another. In the example above there has been a 6 percentage point decline in Democratic identifiers. a 3 point decline in Republican identifiers, and, in consequence, a 9 percentage point change in the distribution of party identification for hypothetical group—that is, 9 percentage points have been redistributed throughout the categories.

[22] The measurement of the contribution of the young to this change uses the same procedure as in note 21. Taking the same group in the fifties, we ask the question: What is the distribution of party preference in this group in the seventies without the cohort that entered the electorate after the 1960 election? The question that is being asked is what would the distribution of party identification for the group be in the seventies if the young were contributing to the change at the same rate as the old contribute to whatever change there appears to be in the data. It is not possible to alter the data for the young but it is possible to eliminate the young from the table. The distribution of party identification following this elimination of the young is of the same age cohort that appears in the data for the fifties. The observed change represents the *maturation* of the electorate as opposed to change caused by the *replacement* of the electorate by a new cohort.

	A The fifties	B The seventies excluding young cohort	B–A	C The seventies including young	C–A
Democrat	45 percent	43 percent	−2	39 percent	−6
Independent	25	28	+3	34	+9
Republican	30	29	−1	27	−3

The change among the older cohort is 3 percentage points, representing a 2 point decline in Democrats and a 1 point decline in Republicans. Including the young results in a 9 point change in the distribution of party identification for the group. The difference between the 9 percentage point change observed when the young are included and the 3 point change observed when the young are excluded is 6 points—the effect of the young on the party identification of the group. If this example group were one of the groups in table 13.2, the table would indicate that the party identification of the group had shifted 9 percentage points between the fifties and the seventies and that the post-1960 cohort was responsible for 67 percent of this change.

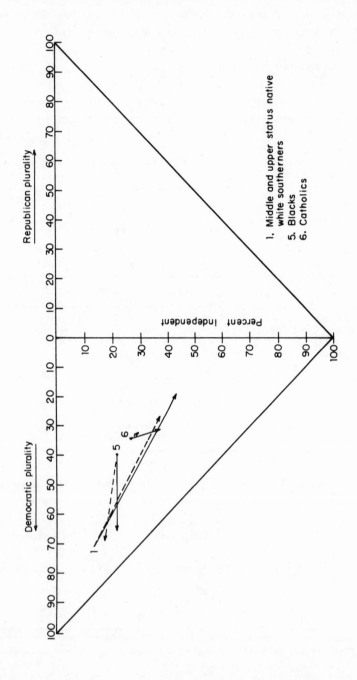

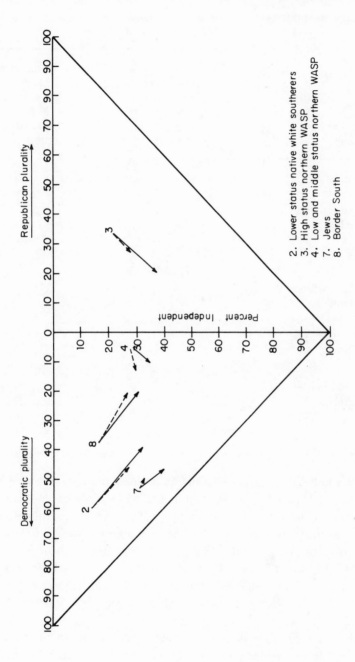

FIGURE 13.12. Party tendencies of selected groups: the impact of new generations

2. Lower status native white southerers
3. High status northern WASP
4. Low and middle status northern WASP
7. Jews
8. Border South

TABLE 13.2. Percentage point change in party identification of groups from the fifties to the seventies and proportion of that change due to new voters

Group	Total percentage point change in party identification of group	Percentage of change contributed by electors who entered after 1960
High status northern white Protestants	15	60
Middle and lower status northern white Protestants	7	57
All native southern whites	27	26
Native southern whites, upper and middle status	41	17
Native southern whites, lower status	20	35
All Catholics	9	56
High status Catholics	10	50
Other Catholics	7	71
Jews	9	78
Blacks	13	31

between the southern groups and the blacks on the one hand, and all others. In the South and among blacks less than half of the overall change is contributed by the new cohort; for all other groups, the new voters contribute more. One must remember, furthermore, that the new voters represent only about 25 percent of each group in the 1970s. This makes their contribution to the change quite disproportionate. The unique pattern among southerners and blacks is, we believe, attributable to the issue position of these groups which has affected all ages. (We will examine the extent of these pressures in the next chapter.)

The data on the various population groups indicate quite a bit of population movement from one party to the other (or into the Independent ranks). The major consequence of such movement is a decrease in party identification and a reduction in support for each party. The result is a lot of movement but no substantial change in the relative strengths of the two parties. In this sense there has been no realignment of the parties. But if one takes a realignment to mean a change in the bases of support for two parties, there has been a significant realignment.

In previous analyses in this chapter we have looked at the various subgroups and asked: To which party do they give their support? We can now look at the two parties and ask: From what social groups do they get their support?[23] Table 13.3 compares the social group profile of the parties in the 1950s with their group profile in the 1970s. Consider the Democratic identifiers. Between the 1950s and the 1970s there has been little change in the proportion of support that the Democratic party receives from Catholics. The same is the case for lower status northern Protestants. The white South, on the other hand, provided 30 percent of the Democratic support in the 1950s, but only 20 percent by the 1970s. The slack is taken up by blacks, and a bit from upper status northern Protestants and from the border South.

The shift in the sources of support for the Democratic party underscores the uneasy coalition that goes to make up that party—a subject to which we shall devote a good part of the conclusion of this book. The party is as dependent as it once was on northern Catholics and lower status Protestants. It is less dependent on southerners. But as the latter have left, blacks have come to play a more dominant role in the Democratic support. As we shall see, these changes create some important issue divisions within the Democratic party.

The Republican support groups appear to have changed as well. The most significant changes are the decline in support that the Republicans receive from middle and lower status white northern Protestants. They made up about one-third of the Republican support in the early fifties; in the 1970s they were closer to one-fifth of their support. They have been replaced by high status white southerners and, to a lesser extent by border state residents and lower status southerners. The Republican change, it would seem, has made that party more homogeneous in a status sense. The one lower status group that had provided substantial support (northern lower status Protestants) has become less important in the party, while upper status southerners have become more important.

The data in table 13.3 can be a bit misleading. The change in the proportion of a party's supporters that come from a group can result from one

---

[23] See Robert Axelrod, "Where the Votes Come From: An Analysis of Electoral Coalitions, 1952–1968," *American Political Science Review,* 66 (March 1972), 11–20, for a discussion of the distinction.

TABLE 13.3. Source of party identifiers, 1950s and 1970s

Group	Democratic identifiers			Republican identifiers		
	1950s	1970s	Deviation from expected	1950s	1970s	Deviation from expected
High status northern white Protestants	9.8	11.5	+ .5	36.1	38.1	−2.3
Lower and middle status northern white Protestants	18.9	18.3	+3.7	32.6	22.3	−2.8
Border South white Protestants	5.2	7.8	+ .8	4.2	7.7	+2.1
Southern white Protestants, middle status and above	12.4	8.6	−6.9	4.1	11.2	+6.1
Southern white Protestants, lower status	17.3	11.8	−2.7	4.1	5.4	+2.0
Catholics	20.3	20.8	− .3	12.4	12.0	− .5
Jews	5.0	3.6	− .2	.9	.8	.1
Blacks	11.2	17.7	+4.3	5.6	2.5	−4.2

of two changes—a change in the size of the group in the population and a shift in the allegiance of the group. Some of the population groups change in size over the two decades. Middle and lower status northern Protestants, for instance, were 25.7 percent of our sample in the 1950s, they are only 19.9 percent of our sample in the 1970s. The reduced role they play in the Republican party could result from the decline in their size rather than from a shift in allegiance—from demographic changes rather than political changes.

We can separate these components of the shift in party composition by comparing the contribution which a particular group makes to one of the parties with the change that would be expected after making adjustments for the change in the size of the group. If, for instance, a group were to become a larger segment of the electorate between the fifties and the seventies, we would expect—everything else being equal—that it would become a proportionally larger percent of each party. If it shrunk in size, its contribution to each party would shrink. We can then compare the change in the contribution to each party a group actually makes with these expectations. The result gives us the change in the composition of the parties due to the political changes in groups rather than their growth or decline in size.

We have added data to table 13.3 to indicate these deviations from expectation. Positive numbers mean that a group is that much more a proportion of the party than one would have predicted on the basis of changes in its size. Negative numbers mean that it is now a lesser proportion than one would have predicted.

Consider the figures for the upper status northern Protestants. They are a group that has grown in size between the two time periods (from 20 percent of the population to 22.4 percent). Because of this growth one would have expected them to represent a larger proportion of each of the parties. The +.5 percent figure for "deviation from expected" for the Democrats means that they contribute that much more to the Democratic coalition than one would expect on the basis of their growth. The figure of −2.3 percent for the Republican party means that they contribute that much less to the Republican coalition in 1972 than one would have expected on the basis of their growth. (Note that they in fact are a larger proportion of the Republican party in the 1970s than in the 1950s, but that growth is less than one would have expected on the basis of their change in size alone.)

The figures for deviations highlight the differences between the party support groups in the fifties and the seventies. The Democrats have lost support in the South, particularly from middle and upper status southerners. The Republicans have gained from them. The Democrats have gained from blacks and from middle and lower status northern white Protestants. The Republicans lose from both of these groups.

The changes in the social correlates of party identification that are described in this chapter clearly point to a realignment of the parties. In large measure, the change has resulted from the arrival of a new generation of voters who are less differentiated in their party preference than were the older members of their sociodemographic groups. As this newer cohort repopulates the social groups, the party bias of the groups has changed.

The Democratic party has become more black, less southern, and has developed a larger "silk-stocking" component. The Republican party, in contrast, has become more southern, less black, less Catholic, and relatively less of a silk-stocking and Protestant party compared to the fifties. Changes in the clientele of the parties are interesting in themselves, but more important for what they portend for the policies the parties are likely to pursue.

The Democratic party now draws almost a fifth of its support from blacks. They are crucial to Democratic dominance in general; and in some states they are the segment of the electorate that keeps the Democratic party competitive. They represent, on the other hand, less than 3 percent of the Republican support. They are likely to play a smaller role in Republican electoral calculations than in Democratic calculations.

The impact of this trend is exacerbated by the loss of a good portion of the southern electorate by the Democratic party. That conservative influence is now less potent in the Democratic party and more potent in the Republican. By replacing white southerners with black supporters the Democratic party has changed the balance of pressures it receives from racial liberals and racial conservatives. But its continuing dependence as well on northern Catholics and lower status Protestant whites implies continuing cross pressures if the racial issue continues to be a northern one.

The Republicans, on the other hand, have moved in a more consistently conservative direction. Whatever little support they had from blacks has faded, and they have lost support among lower status northern Protestants as well as from liberal WASPs in the North. In return, they have picked up southern support.

14 | Attitude Change Among Groups

Groups have occupied a central place in discussions of American politics for the entire period with which this book deals. Southerners, blacks, Jews, Catholics, and WASPs are the currency of discussions of the political beliefs of Americans. Analysts have expectations about group political attitudes no less strong than their expectations about group party preferences.[1] Because attitude expectations are assigned

We are grateful to Kristi Andersen for assistance in preparing this chapter.

[1] See Richard Scammon and Ben J. Wattenberg, *The Real Majority* (New York: Coward, McCann and Geoghegan, 1970); Kevin Philips, *The Emerging Republican Majority* (New Rochelle, N.Y.: Arlington House, 1969); Angus Campbell and others, *The Voter Decides* (Evanston: Row-Peterson, 1954); Paul Lazarsfeld and others, *The People's Choice* (New York: Columbia University Press, 1954); Bernard Berelson and others, *Voting* (Chicago: University of Chicago Press, 1954); R. Duncan Luce, "Analyzing the Social Process Underlying Group Voting Patterns," in Eugene Burdick and Arthur J. Brodbeck, eds. *American Voting Behavior* (New York: Free Press, 1959); Edward Banfield and James Q. Wilson, "Public Regardedness as a Value Premise in Voting Behavior," *American Political Science Review,* 58 (December 1974), 876–887; Angus Campbell, *White Attitudes Toward Black People* (Ann Arbor: Institute for Social Research, University of Michigan, 1971); Nathan Glazer, "Blacks and Ethnic Groups: The Difference and the Political Difference It Makes," *Social Problems,* 18 (Spring 1971), 444–461; Andrew Greeley, "Civic Religion and Ethnic Americans," *World View,* 16 (February 1973), 21–27; Lewis M. Killian, *White Southerners* (New York: Random House, 1970); Barbara Currie, "Political Beliefs Among American Ethnics," unpub-

to groups, there is merit in examining the degree to which the political opinions of these important segments of the population have changed in the past decade. In addition, changes in group attitudes might help to explain changes in the party bias of the groups.

Analyzing Attitude Change: The Overall Index

The analysis of group attitudes in this chapter uses the summary attitude index described in Chapter 8 and used for much of the analysis in subsequent chapters. As discussed in Chapter 12, the index cannot be used to deal with the direction of opinion for the population as a whole, but can be used to deal with the direction of opinion for subgroups. Since the index is standardized for the issue preferences of the population, the values assumed by a group represent its deviation from the population. Our major comparison is between the issue profile of a group in the late fifties and the issue profile of the same group at about the beginning of this decade. To obtain the fifties profile, we pool the data from the election studies of 1956 and 1960. The seventies data represent a pooling of the 1968 and 1972 studies. This averaging obscures no important variation. There are several reasons why we have pooled the data. First, several of the groups represent relatively small fractions of the population, and the pooling of data minimizes sampling error. Second, averaging the data from several studies minimizes perturbations which may result from election-specific or other short-term forces. Third, using only a beginning and end time point permits an examination of variations in opinion while maintaining a certain ease in visual comparison.

Figure 14.1 presents the distribution of the liberal/conservative attitude index by deciles for the studies comprising the 1950s time point and for the studies which constitute the 1970s time point. The solid line in the figure presents the proportion of the group in each of the deciles of the index in the late 1950s. The dashed line presents the distribution of opinions in the group for the 1970s. The low attitude consistency and absence of issue polarization that typified the public in the 1950s is reflected in the shape of the curve of the line for that period. Less than 10 percent of the population are found in the left- and right-most deciles where relatively consistent liberal or conservative views across issue domains would place the individual. There is a concomitantly greater proportion in the center deciles, indicating the predomi-

---

lished paper, 1971; Michael Parenti, "Ethnic Politics and the Persistence of Ethnic Identification," *American Political Science Review,* 61 (September 1967), 717–726; Andrew Greeley, *Ethnicity in the United States* (New York: Wiley, 1974).

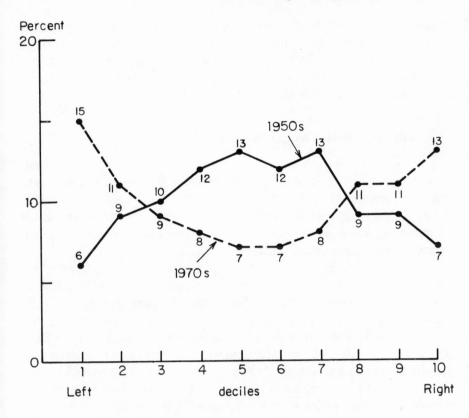

FIGURE 14.1. Distribution of population according to deciles in the liberal-conservative summary attitude index for 1950s and 1970s

nance of those with mixed or centrist political views. The substantial increase in attitude consistency and polarization through the decade which followed is just as easily seen in the dish-shaped distribution of opinions of the line for the early 1970s. Larger proportions of the population are found in the consistently liberal and conservative deciles on the extremes than are found in the more mixed attitude positions near the center of the scale. These data merely repeat what earlier analyses have shown: the public has become more polarized as issue consistency has grown.

This summary liberal/conservative attitude index will be used to compare across time the attitude profiles of each of the eight groups introduced in the last chapter. Several characteristics of the groups will be examined with the index: How liberal or conservative, relative to the population as a whole, were each of the groups in the mid- to late 1950s? How has each of the groups changed (again, relative to the population) by the end of our period of investigation in the early 1970s? Has it become significantly more liberal or conservative? Is it more internally divided or more homogeneous with regard to the issues? Finally, how does the change (if any) relate to its previously documented change in party affiliation?

Analyzing Attitude Change: The Specific Issues

The summary index has the advantage of providing a portrait of overall attitude change and most of the analysis of political opinions will be traced with this measure. However, the index has the disadvantage of masking changes on the specific issues which constitute the overall measure, and which are interesting and informative by themselves. One cannot understand group change without understanding attitudes on specific issues.

Five issues are considered: (1) opinions on racial integration in the schools, (2) opinions on government action designed to benefit blacks in particular, (3) feelings about general economic welfare programs, (4) orientations to the scope of perceived power of the national government, and finally, (5) feelings about the stance the government should take in its dealings with communist countries. The opinions of the groups on these issues are measured in the same general fashion as group opinions on the overall measure. A group is identified as liberal or conservative depending upon the proportion of liberal to conservative responses for the group compared to the proportion of liberal to conservative responses for the population. This measure allows us to gauge changes for the group between the two time periods—relative to the population as a whole, as usual. For example, consider the following figures for the school integration issue. In the 1956 and 1960 studies the population was split fairly evenly, with 1 percent more giving conservative than liberal replies to the question on the subject. In the 1968 and 1972 studies the population was 6 percentage points more conservative than liberal. In the fifties, therefore, any group that was more than 1 percentage point more conservative than liberal is considered to have a greater conservative bias than the population in general and any group that was more than 6 percentage points more conservative than liberal in the seventies is considered a conservative group. This manner of comparing the percentages adjusts for any change in the opinions of the population generally.

Throughout this chapter and several others which follow groups and individuals are classified as liberal or conservative on the basis of scores on our summary attitude index. Like all reasonable analytic labels the classification has some validity and it enables one to create order and meaning out of the patterns in the data. However, we are fully aware that the terms "liberal" and "conservative" have been given many meanings and applied in different ways than they are used here. Suffice it to say that when we use the terms liberal or conservative, we are talking about positions on this summary attitude continuum—no more and no less. In this way we hope to refrain from reifying our measure and hope that the reader does likewise.

The White South Becomes More Conservative

Figure 14.2 presents the opinion profiles of relatively low status native white southerners. Contrary to the popular image, white southerners have not always been particularly conservative. In the 1950s lower status native whites were only slightly more conservative than the population as a whole. Only a small proportion of the group is found in the two most right and two most left deciles. Fully 60 percent are found in the four center deciles. The fact that over a quarter are in the three right-most categories does indicate, of course, that lower status white southerners are more conservative than liberal. The

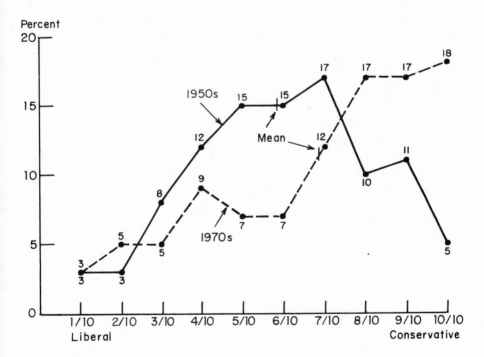

FIGURE 14.2. Liberal-conservative attitude profile of lower status native white southerners

average position of the group in the fifties is about 5.9 on the decile index placing them almost in the sixth decile, but this mean is only 0.5 farther to the right than the mean for the entire population.

The basic centrism of the group in the fifties is replaced by a pronounced rightward tilt in their political opinions in the seventies. The mean of the group on the opinion profile shifts to 6.9. The proportion of the population in the two right-most deciles increases nine percentage points and the proportion in the two left-most deciles declines 2 percentage points. As an examination of the two profiles indicates, however, these numerical shifts fail to do justice to the changes. The line that profiles the group's opinion in the fifties is essentially centrist with a slight conservative tendency. The line for the seventies indicates a loss of the center (down from 60 percent in the four center deciles to 35 percent) and a growth in the proportion in the three right-most categories. These conservatives constitute 52 percent of the group in the seventies, while they were about half as numerous in the fifties.

The source of this greater conservatism can be determined by examining the data in table 14.1, which presents the percentage deviations from the total population that indicate the relative liberalism or conservatism of the group on the specific issues. A negative number indicates that the group is more liberal than the population, while a positive number indicates it is more conservative. The slight rightward tilt of the group in the fifties is a consequence of small conservative percentage deviations for two of the individual items, school integration and size of government, coupled with the markedly more conservative position on the question of black welfare. Most of their relative conservatism is a consequence of the large deviation on that particular issue. That deviation would force the summary index even more to the right if it were not for the substantial leftward tilt of their opinion on economic welfare. To understand why the group has become more conservative one must only look at the extent to which their opinions on economic welfare

TABLE 14.1. Issue preferences on the five items summarized in the overall index: *Lower Status Native White Southerners* (percent difference index)[a]

	Economic welfare	Size of government	School integration	Black welfare	Foreign policy
1950s	−21	10	7	43	−3
1970s	15	23	18	49	1
Change	36	13	11	6	4

[a] Positive numbers indicate a conservative value or trend; negative numbers indicate a liberal value or trend.

have changed. From being 21 points more liberal than conservative on the economic welfare question in the fifties (as always, relative to the population) they are now 15 points more conservative than liberal. This 36 point shift added to an average 8 point conservative shift on the other four opinion items is sufficient to make lower status native southerners much more conservative now than they were in the late fifties.

Upper status native white southerners provide a contrast with lower status native southerners (figure 14.3). In the 1950s the mean political opinion of the group was 7.2—well to the right. A negligible proportion of the population was in the two most left deciles, indeed, less than 10 percent of the

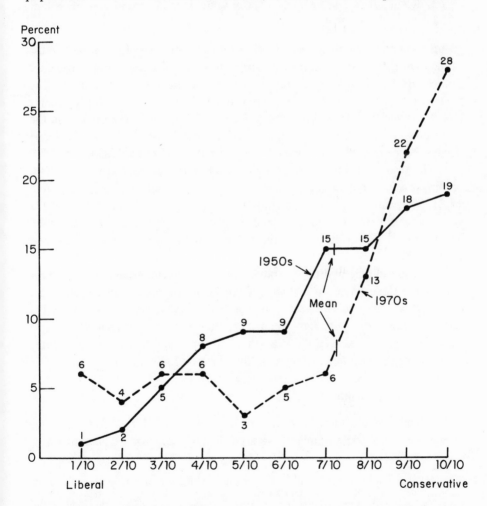

FIGURE 14.3. Liberal-conservative attitude profile of middle and higher status native white southerners

TABLE 14.2. Issue preferences on the five items summarized in the overall index: *Middle and Upper Status Native Southerners* (percent difference index)[a]

	Economic welfare	Size of government	Black welfare	School integration	Foreign policy
1950s	36	18	36	41	−14
1970s	32	26	35	39	24
Change	−4	8	−1	−2	38

[a] Positive numbers indicate a conservative value or trend; negative numbers indicate a liberal value or trend.

group is found in the three left deciles. Almost 40 percent of the population is in the two right-most categories and less than 45 percent are in the four center deciles. By the 1970s the group has become even more conservative. The mean decile position of the group shifts slightly farther to the right, the center collapses even farther, and over 50 percent of the group is represented in the two right-most deciles. Had it not been for an increase in the two left-most deciles the mean of the index would have shifted sharply to the right.

The source of this change is almost exclusively the greater conservatism of higher status native southerners on the foreign policy issues (see table 14.2). They have also become slightly more conservative on the matter of the size of government. But, on other matters, they were and remain conservative. Their foreign policy attitudes have fallen into line with this more general conservatism.[2]

Overall, middle and upper status white native southerners are conservative. While there has been a slight growth in the proportion in the left-most deciles, that increase still leaves higher status native southerners with far fewer liberals, proportionately, than there are in the nation as a whole; and the substantial increase in the proportion in the right-most deciles has completely overwhelmed any incremental liberalism on these questions.

The Border South

Whoever chose the term "border" for Kentucky, Maryland, Oklahoma, Tennessee, and West Virginia chose a particularly apt word. The contrast in

---

[2] It is worth noting that in the fifties higher status native southerners were conservative on all issues except the foreign policy item, while in the seventies they are consistently conservative on all issues, averaging more than 31 percentage points to the right of the population.

culture and politics that distinguishes the South from the North is muted in these states. They represent a transition from the conservatism of the South. Western Tennessee may have affinities for Mississippi but the politics and culture of eastern and northern Tennessee belong to the Midwest. The political history and current politics of the area reflect the fact that the southern democracy has an influence here. Events which affect the South stop here first and whatever nationalizes the South will first affect the border South.

This quality of the region shows up in the political attitudes of the population (see figure 14.4). The overall opinion profile of the region in the 1950s looked very close to the opinion profile of lower status native southerners, though on the average border southerners were a bit less conservative than the lower status native southerners. Their mean on the decile index was about 5.7 rather than 5.9. There were more people in the center four deciles (about 63 percent), but almost the same proportions in the far right and far left deciles of the distribution. Again, however, there has been a change between the fifties and the seventies, and the movement is in the conservative direction. The change is smaller than for either of the native white southerner groups, but is considerable nontheless. While less than 20 percent of border

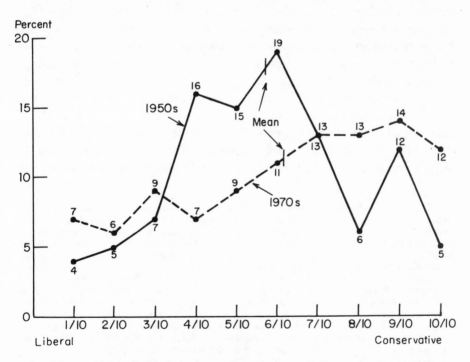

FIGURE 14.4. Liberal-conservative attitude profile of whites in the border South

TABLE 14.3. Issue preferences on the five items summarized in the overall index: *Border Southerners* (percent difference index)[a]

	Economic welfare	Size of government	Black welfare	School integration	Foreign policy
1950s	2	−26	4	31	5
1970s	3	15 (−9)[b]	10	19	−2
Change	1	41 (17)[b]	6	−12	−7

[a] Positive numbers indicate a conservative value or trend; negative numbers indicate a liberal value or trend.

[b] Percentages adjusted to reflect effects due to question wording (see footnote 3).

southerners were in the two right-most deciles in the fifties, over a quarter are there in the seventies. The proportion in the four center deciles has declined over 20 percentage points to only 40 percent. Also like the deep southerners there is an increase in the proportion of the group in the most liberal deciles, but, again, the increase is not large enough to overcome the increase in the right-most deciles and arrest the conservative shift in the group. As table 14.3 indicates, the source of this change is the much greater conservatism of the border southerners on the issue of the proper role and power of the national government. It is no exaggeration to say that the 40 percentage point shift is dramatic. Some large fraction of the greater conservatism of the border South on the issue of the size of government is a function of the change in the particular question that was asked the respondents in the later period.[3] However, not all of the change can be attributed to the measurements, so it seems reasonable to interpret the change in the overall measure as a reflection of slightly greater conservatism of whites in the border South states. Further it

---

[3] In the fifties the respondents were asked their opinion on the desirability of the national government being responsible for the operation of utilities such as electric power and for the provision of housing. (Bear in mind the significance of the TVA to the people of the upper South.) In the seventies they were asked a more general question about whether the government was getting too powerful for the good of the country. (Appendix 2 provides a more complete description of the questions.) The general theme presupposed by each form of the question probably constitutes two very different questions for the respondents. Fortunately, in 1964, when the SRC introduced the later question wording into their questionnaires, they also retained the first question. We have examined the relationship between these questions for our groups and discovered that for the Border South, at least, question differences account for about 60 percent of the change in the percentage point differences. Adjusting for question differences, border southerners have become about 17 points more conservative on the question of the power of the national government than they were in the fifties. The difference between 17 and 41 points represents, we believe, question effect.

seems reasonable to believe that the principal explanation for the change is the greater suspicion of these particular Americans of the power and scale of the national government.

While terms like "liberal" and "conservative" are subject to many different meanings there seems little question that the South has become considerably more conservative when viewed from the perspective of its profile of opinions on the five issues examined here. In this meaning of the terms "liberal" and "conservative," the deep South and the adjacent border South have come to be the most conservative groups in the entire country. Furthermore, native white southerners have, through the last decade, become more homogeneously conservative, regardless of their social status. Finally, while some portion of this change could be due to a deepening resentment of federal government intervention in the area of race, it is impossible for individuals to achieve conservative scores placing them in the eighth, ninth, and tenth deciles solely on the basis of their answers to the questions involving blacks. Racial conflict may have been the catalyst for the conservative drift in the South, but it has led to more conservative views on a wide variety of other issues, as tables 14.1, 14.2, and 14.3 indicate. Changes in opinion on non-racial issues are principally responsible for the rightward shifts of southerners.

Blacks, Traditionally Liberal, Are Now More So

In stark contrast to the growing conservative trend in the attitudes of white southerners is the liberal swing of opinion among blacks. As can be easily seen in figure 14.5, blacks held predominantly liberal attitudes on the issues in the 1950s. Twenty-five percent were in the most extreme liberal decile, and a full 65 percent were to be found in the three most liberal deciles. Moreover, the remainder of the black population was moderately liberal, with less than 7 percent of all blacks giving responses which placed them in any decile on the conservative side of the scale.

However, even with this predominantly liberal profile in the 1950s, the degree of change in political attitudes is greater for blacks than for any other group in the population. The extreme and homogeneous liberal opinion profile of blacks in the early 1970s is striking. Where we once found 25 percent in the most liberal decile, we now find 62 percent of all blacks at this point. What is more, 85 percent of all black Americans now respond to the issues in a way which places them in the three most liberal deciles.

The civil rights movement and the subsequent mobilization and politicization of American blacks during the decade of the sixties explain the leftward drift found for blacks in our society. The degree of liberal attitude

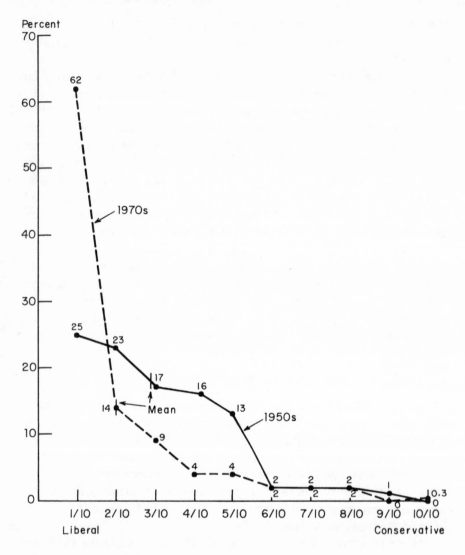

FIGURE 14.5. Liberal-conservative attitude profile of blacks

consistency across such a diverse set of issues is greater than that for any other group. In order to obtain a score on our overall attitude index that places a respondent in the left-most decile, he or she must respond to virtually all of the attitude questions in each of the issue areas with the most liberal possible response. That over 60 percent of a group should be found to have such a uniform pattern of response is an unusual phenomenon in survey data.

TABLE 14.4. Issue preferences on the five items summarized in the overall index: *Blacks* (percent difference index)[a]

	Economic welfare	Size of government	Black welfare	School integration	Foreign policy
1950s	−66	−21	−49	−37	−15
1970s	−69	−41	−74	−76	−28
Change	− 3	−20	−25	−39	−13

[a] Positive numbers indicate a conservative value or trend; negative numbers indicate a liberal value or trend.

A brief look at the individual issues in table 14.4 shows that the leftward movement of the black population has occurred not only on the issues of central importance to blacks—school integration and increased governmental attention to black problems—but on issues of foreign policy and the scope of the government as well. In the 1950s, blacks were already quite far from the rest of the population in their attitudes toward government provision of welfare services such as guaranteed jobs and medical care. Their 66 percentage point deviation from the population attitude on welfare was of far greater magnitude than any other group. By the 1970s their increasingly liberal (relative to the population) attitudes on school integration and black welfare placed them equally far from the population on these issues. Blacks also moved substantially further to the left on the issues of the cold war (13 point change) and the scope of the government (20 point change).

No other group in American society is as distinctively liberal as American blacks. Given their equally dramatic shift toward Democratic identification it is quite clear that blacks must be counted an important part of any liberal coalition.

Before turning our attention to changes in the attitude profiles of other segments of American society, it is worth reflecting on some of the more important implications in the trends of political attitudes in the white South, on the one hand, and blacks, on the other. First, it is clear (and will become even more so as we examine other groups) that these two segments of the electorate have contributed substantially to the growth and maintenance of the political polarization which has come to characterize American society. Second, these data point directly to perhaps the greatest single dilemma of the Democratic party. During the last decade, blacks, as a group, have become the most indisputably liberal group in the society in terms of their position on the central issues. At the same time, they have also emerged as the group with the single highest proportion of Democratic identifiers. During this period, the white South has become the most conservative group in America. It is edging away from the Democratic party, but it nevertheless retains one of the most Democratic biases of any group. For example, in the 1950s blacks were virtually unanimous in their agreement with the idea that the government should provide more services for blacks. This unanimity remained in the 1970s. Middle and high status white southerners made somewhat fewer conservative than liberal responses to this question in the 1950s, but by the 1970s over 60 percent fell into the conservative category, compared to 39 percent of the population and only 9 percent of blacks. The dilemma is clear: if blacks, on the one hand, and the white South, on the other, represent a major proportion of the nation's Democratic supporters, how does any party with such a polarized base maintain (in the long run or in any specific election) the allegiance of both groups? There is no easy resolution of this dilemma, but the data in this chapter indicate the severity of the centrifugal forces faced by the Democrats.

Jews, Like Blacks, Become More Liberal

Jews represent a small portion of the American population (less than 3 percent), but they have been a highly cohesive liberal bloc. In spite of a tendency toward increasing independence in the 1970s, Jews remain predominantly Democratic supporters. The predominantly liberal issue stance of Jews in the mid- and late 1950s was second only to that of blacks, and the situation appears to remain the same today (see figure 14.6). The shape of political opinion among Jews in the 1950s differs from that of the 1970s in a complex way. Over a third (36 percent) of Jews are in the left-most decile of our overall measure in the 1970s, while only 13 percent fell into this category in the 1950s. However, the percentage in the three most liberal deciles remains exactly the same, and the proportion in the three most conservative deciles shows a slight increase in the 1970s. On average, Jews have slipped leftward in relation to the political attitudes of the nation; their mean on the summary index has shifted from 4.1 to 3.7. And the modal position of Jews on the scale has moved from the third most liberal decile to the most liberal category.

But unlike blacks, whose leftward movement has been relatively consistent across all five issue areas, the change in the summary measure for the Jews masks some notable variations on the individual issues (see table 14.5). In the 1950s, Jews were only slightly more liberal than the population in their attitudes on black welfare and anticommunist foreign involvements; in both these areas they have become far more liberal than the population by the

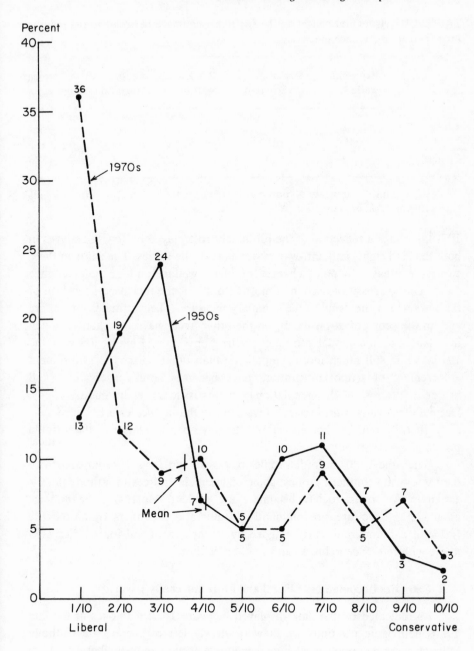

FIGURE 14.6. Liberal-conservative attitude profile of Jews

TABLE 14.5. Issue preferences on the five items summarized in the overall index: *Jews* (percent difference index)[a]

	Economic welfare	Size of government	Black welfare	School integration	Foreign policy
1950s	−31	−15	− 4	−47	− 8
1970s	−40	−19	−38	−30	−44
Change	− 9	− 4	−34	17	−52

a Positive numbers indicate a conservative value or trend; negative numbers indicate a liberal value or trend.

1970s, perhaps a reflection of the prominent role played by Jewish activists in both the civil rights and anti-war movements of the sixties. The shifts in these two issue areas—34 point change for black welfare and 52 point change on the cold war issue—account almost entirely for the increased liberalism of the Jews which shows up in the summary measure. Their attitudes on welfare and on the scope of government, on the other hand, have not changed much in relation to the modal attitudes of the population. Finally, Jews in the 1970s, while still much more sympathetic than other citizens to government enforcement of school integration, have become more conservative (and nearer to the rest of the population) on this issue since the middle 1950s. Despite these variations, in general we can say that a once clearly but moderately liberal group has become more intensely liberal, relative to the attitude profile of the larger population.

When the 1970s attitude profiles of blacks and Jews are compared with the three white southern groups, some of the main sources of attitude polarization in American society become quite evident. Moreover, the findings about Jews, who are predominantly Democratic identifiers, reinforce the image of a Democratic party plagued by strong centrifugal forces, discussed above with reference to blacks and southern whites.

Catholics Become Less Liberal and More Internally Divided

As indicated by the data displayed in figure 14.7, Catholics in the late 1950s held issue positions which were clearly left of center. But Catholic attitudes were by no means as homogeneously or unanimously liberal as those of either Jews or blacks. Approximately 35 percent of all Catholics were to be found in the three most liberal deciles, while a little over 20 percent held attitudes which placed them in the three most conservative deciles. The

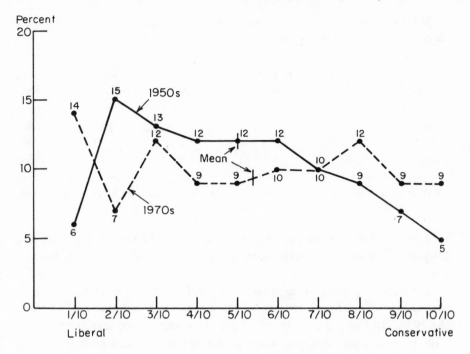

FIGURE 14.7. Liberal-conservative attitude profile of Catholics

Catholic mean in the 1950s was 5.0, which put them slightly on the liberal side of the population mean of 5.5.

The 1970s attitude profile has changed somewhat. Catholics are now evenly divided between liberals and conservatives—their mean on the summary index is 5.4. This movement indicates not an across-the-board rightward shift, but the polarization of Catholics on these issues. While the proportion of Catholics in the three most liberal deciles remains the same, the three most conservative categories grew from 21 percent to 30 percent of all Catholics.

How is this rather modest overall change reflected in changes in the Catholic position on individual issues? Catholics have become more like the population (by becoming more conservative) on welfare, black welfare, and the cold war issue; this change is even more prominent with regard to school integration (see table 14.6). Where in the 1950s Catholics displayed a liberal 16 percentage point deviation from the population on school integration, now they are only slightly more liberal than other citizens. In contrast, their growing liberalism on the scope of government issue (a 9 point change) has increased slightly their distance from the population on that issue. Thus, while the change in the relationship between group attitudes and population atti-

TABLE 14.6. Issue preferences on the five items summarized in the overall index: *Catholics* (percent difference index)[a]

	Economic welfare	Size of government	Black welfare	School integration	Foreign policy
1950s	−11	− 4	−3	−16	−3
1970s	− 4	−13	3	− 3	3
Change	7	− 9	6	13	6

[a] Positive numbers indicate a conservative value or trend; negative numbers indicate a liberal value or trend.

tudes on the issues is not nearly as great as for southerners, Jews, or blacks, Catholics have moved in both liberal and conservative directions on different issues.

We are not, however, arguing that Catholics have become a particularly polarized group, for they are less polarized than the population as a whole in the 1970s. Unlike some of the other groups, Catholics are spread across the attitude continuum, with only a few deciles in our summary scale containing much more or less than 10 percent of the Catholic population. For this reason, the impact that Catholic attitude change has had on the party system has been much less than that of southerners, blacks, and Jews.

White Protestants Outside the South: Those of Lower and Middle Status Move Right, While the More Affluent and Better Educated Polarize

Figure 14.8 displays the attitude profiles in the 1950s and 1970s of lower and middle status white Protestants outside of the South. It is clear from these data that this large segment of American society (approximately 55 percent) was characterized in the mid- and late 1950s by views which were both centrist and diverse. Forty-nine percent of this group fell in the center four deciles of the scale; the proportions on the liberal and conservative ends of the scale were equal.

Many of the characteristics of the attitude profile of this group in the 1950s remain in the 1970s. They are still a relatively moderate group composed of citizens with heterogeneous attitudes on issues. Nevertheless, there have been changes: middle America has drifted toward a more consistently conservative political view. In the 1950s, a little over 25 percent of this group took positions on the issues which placed them in the three most conservative

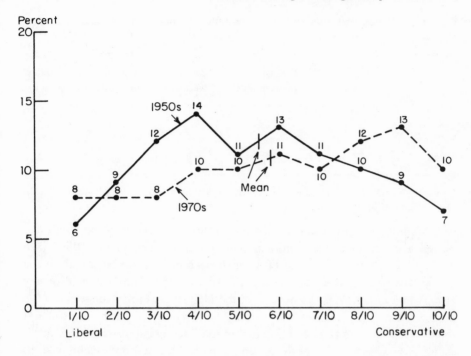

FIGURE 14.8. Liberal-conservative attitude profile of middle and lower status northern white Protestants

deciles, and an equal number were to be found in the three most liberal deciles. In the 1970s, the proportion in the three most liberal deciles has dropped a few percentage points, even though there has been a considerable growth in these categories among the population as a whole (see figure 14.1). At the same time, the proportion in the three most conservative deciles has grown from about 25 percent to about 35 percent. The increase in the relative overall conservatism of lower status northern Protestants is due almost entirely to their becoming more conservative than the population (whereas in the 1950s they were slightly more liberal) on the two issues related to race: welfare for blacks and school integration (see table 14.7). In the 1950s, they are 2 and 5 percentage points more liberal than the population on the issues of black welfare and integration; in the 1970's they are 6 points more conservative on each. Their attitudes on race have been brought into line with their relatively conservative attitude on welfare. In short, it is clear that this group has become more consistently conservative on the issues, relative to the population, though it can hardly be thought of as having an overwhelmingly conservative tone.

TABLE 14.7. Issue preferences on the five items summarized in the overall index: *Middle and Lower Status White Northern Protestants* (percent difference index)[a]

	Economic welfare	Size of government	Black welfare	School integration	Foreign policy
1950s	8	8	−2	−5	−2
1970s	5	2	6	6	0
Change	−3	−6	8	11	2

[a] Positive numbers indicate a conservative value or trend; negative numbers indicate a liberal value or trend.

Wealthy and better educated white Protestants outside of the South displayed a clear conservative bias in their political views in the 1950s (see figure 14.9). More than 6 out of 10 in this group were to be found on the conservative side of the scale (their mean was 6.3, the farthest right of any group) and in the 1950s 35 percent of the high status Protestants were in the three most conservative deciles, but only 19 percent were in the most liberal three. What appears to have happened in the intervening years is quite interesting. A large proportion of the group has moved further to the right; over 40 percent of these high status Protestants are now in the three most conservative deciles. But there has also been a substantial growth on the liberal side of the scale, particularly in the proportion of high status Protestants in the most liberal decile. 26 percent of this group is in the three most liberal deciles in the 1970s, and 13 percent are in the most consistently liberal category.

This dish-shaped distribution suggests a significant amount of opinion polarization in the group. Perhaps even more interesting is the fact that more detailed analyses suggest that among the white Protestants outside of the South, the higher up the socioeconomic ladder one goes, the larger the liberal component. Among very high status white Protestants one finds large numbers holding consistent liberal positions and large numbers holding conservative issue positions. Few are centrists.

The growth in relative liberalism in this group is most evident on the welfare issue—whether the government should aid schools, guarantee jobs, or subsidize medical care (see table 14.8). While high status white Protestants, as a group, remain more conservative in the 1970s than the population on this issue, they have moved substantially from their extremely conservative position. The proportion of this group which falls into the most liberal category on the issue of welfare almost doubled in twenty years, while the proportion in the most conservative category declined by almost 30 percent. Polarization

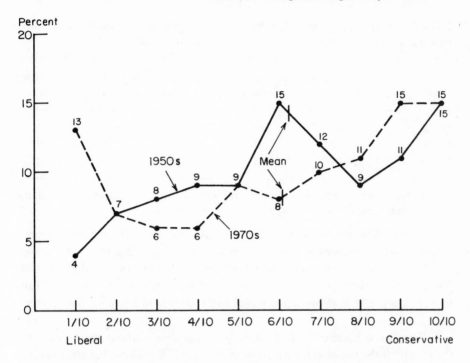

FIGURE 14.9. Liberal-conservative attitude profile of higher status northern white Protestants

on this issue, it would seem, is particularly severe. The issue of the size of the government is the only other one on which the higher status Protestants deviate substantially from the population; they are more conservative, but the size of the deviation has shifted only 4 points from the 1950s to the 1970s.

These findings are, we believe, particularly interesting and politically important because of the prominence and visibility of this group in American society. This very high status group contains many of the political and social activists in the society. That its composition should be so highly polarized in political views is not only a new phenomenon in American politics, but also one which is likely to add a rather ideological and conflictual tone to our political life.

The Effect of the Generation of the Sixties

No analysis of attitude change in these groups would be complete if it omitted a theme which was very important in the earlier analysis of party preference: the effect of the young on political opinions. Almost every Ameri-

TABLE 14.8. Issue preferences on the five items summarized in the overall index: *Higher Status White Northern Protestants* (percent difference index)[a]

	Economic welfare	Size of government	Black welfare	School integration	Foreign policy
1950s	47	17	5	−4	2
1970s	22	13	4	2	1
Change	−25	−4	−1	6	1

[a] Positive numbers indicate a conservative value or trend; negative numbers indicate a liberal value or trend.

can believes that the young hold more liberal ideas about the dominant issues than the older members of society. How different the young are from the old is, of course, a matter of dispute. Whether the young are a harbinger of a postindustrial ideology that will "green America" is open to question; but there is no doubt that the tendency of the young is to be more liberal than their elders.

The first column of table 14.9 presents the shift of the mean position of the group on the decile categorization of the index of political beliefs. Positive numbers indicate that the group has become more conservative since the late fifties and negative numbers indicate that the group has become more liberal. The first column simply summarizes the profile graphs presented above for each of the groups. It shows that upper status northern Protestants, Jews, and blacks have become more liberal since the fifties, and that every other group has become more conservative.

The second and third column permit an examination of the role of the post-1960 cohort in these changes in opinion. The second column presents the shift in opinion of the pre-1960 cohort between the fifties and the seventies. That is, the second column is similar to the cohort analysis that was pursued in Chapters 4 and 13. It is based on eliminating from each group in the 1968 and 1972 surveys all respondents who, by virtue of their age, were not eligible to vote in the 1960 election. The resulting figures show the change in attitudes of the older members of that population group—that is, those who were eligible to vote in the 1960 election. Note that in every case, with the exception of the figures for Jews and blacks, the older segment of the group has had a more conservative movement than has the group as a whole. Among the upper status northern white Protestants, indeed, we find that the older segment has become more conservative, while the group as a whole has become more liberal.

TABLE 14.9. The effect of the young on the political attitudes of the group

Group	Group change from 1950s to 1970s	Change between 1950s and 1970s of pre-1960 cohort	Effect of post-1960 cohort on group attitude change
Northern Protestants, upper status	−.18	.17	−.35
Northern Protestants, middle and lower status	.36	.41	−.05
Border South	.44	.77	−.33
Native southerners, middle and upper status	.09	.39	−.30
Native southerners, lower status	.97	1.00	−.03
Catholics	.36	.45	−.09
Jews	−.38	−.59	.21
Blacks	−.90	−.99	.09

The third column presents the impact of the younger members of the group on its attitude change. The figures indicate the movement in the average position of a group that derives from the entry into the group of the younger cohort. A positive number means that a group is that much more conservative in the 1970s than it would have been without the younger members; a negative number means that it is that much more liberal. The numbers are shifts on the decile index, so a number such as −.35 indicates a shift of over three-tenths of a decile toward the left.

With only a couple of exceptions, the data indicate that the young make each group less conservative than it would be if the old cohort alone determined group opinions. But the differences are not as simple as one might imagine. The "silk-stocking" Protestants differ from other whites in that they have become more liberal rather than more conservative since the fifties. Their greater liberalism, however, is purely a function of the relative liberalism of the younger cohort. The older members of the group have become more conservative in the seventies than they were in the fifties. They have not become as conservative as the older cohort in most other groups, but the direction of change is in the conservative and not in the liberal direction. The young in the group are so much more liberal than the old that they completely counter this rightward movement. The young push the mean for the group over three-tenths of a decile in the liberal direction. As a consequence, the mean position of the group on the opinion index does not move in the conservative direction to about 6.4, but rather in the liberal direction to about 6.1.

The effect of the young on border southerners and on upper and middle status native southerners is equally strong. In both of these groups the post-1960 cohort pushes the mean for the entire group .30 points to the left of where it would be if the older cohort alone determined the opinion preferences of the group. The other white groups are less interesting because the change is less dramatic. But an inspection of table 14.9 will show that every white group would be more conservative now than it was in the fifties, except that the young in every group are sufficiently liberal to retard the rightward shift of the population. The differences between the opinion profile of the younger and older cohorts for middle and lower status northern Protestants, lower status native southerners, and Catholics always mark the young as more liberal. The differences, however, are not large enough to affect the overall mean of these groups as much as the young have influenced the silk-stocking group, border southerners, and middle and upper status native southerners.

Blacks and Jews represent a contradiction to this general pattern. Although young blacks and Jews are much more liberal than the young of any other group, they tend to be more conservative than their elders on our measure. The difference for blacks is quite small. Moreover, the age differences among blacks are not really inexplicable. One can imagine a goodly proportion of young blacks rejecting the traditional black rights orientation measured by the race items in the index. It would not take many young blacks with a very militant position (which would be anti-integrationist) to shift the mean for all blacks.

The reversal of the age differences among Jews is less understandable. The data indicate a considerable difference between young Jews and their elders in the way they respond to the questions which constitute the index. Young Jews are less liberal in the conventional sense than their parents.

In summary, the young have played a part in the opinion changes of these groups of voters. In almost every instance, they young have made the group more liberal than it would otherwise be compared to the fifties. Few will be surprised by this finding. However, it would be incorrect to say simply that the young are generally more liberal than the old. Some groups of young voters are much more conservative than other groups of old voters. What does seem to be generally the case is that the young in each group tend to be less conservative than their elders—for example, young southerners are less conservative than older southerners, young upper status WASPs are less conservative than older upper status WASPs, and so on. But the young differ among themselves in the same way that older citizens do. Our data show differences between age groups within social categories and among similar age groups across these categories.

Issues and Party Affiliation

The previous chapter demonstrated the extent to which the characteristic party preference of these groups has changed since the early fifties. This chapter has documented equally striking changes in the opinion profiles of the same groups. Are these changes related?

At various points throughout the book we indicated that voters are more issue oriented and less party oriented in making their vote decision. Have issues played a part in changing the party bias of these groups? We would expect the answer to be affirmative. Table 14.10 summarizes the partisanship and issue preferences of the groups in the fifties and the seventies. An inspection of the table indicates that the partisanship and issue preferences of most of the groups were "properly" aligned in the fifties. Blacks, Jews, and Catholics were liberal and they were Democratic in the fifties. Northern Protestants tended to be conservative and, correspondingly, less Democratic. The relationship between party preference and issue preference was not simple, but it substantially met the normal expectation that Republicans were conservative and Democrats were liberal.

White southerners, of course, deviate from this. As a group white southerners are conservative, but they were also the most Democratic segment of the population in the fifties. Their attachment was to a regional Democratic party quite different from the liberal northern party.

Keeping in mind, then, the complex relationship between issue preference and party bias, is it possible to account for the change in the party bias of the groups with change in the issue preference of the group? Groups that have become more liberal since the fifties should have become less Republican and more Democratic. Conversely, groups which have become more conservative should have become more Republican and less Democratic. Generally, such a change appears in the summary table. The decline of Democratic strength in the South follows a greater conservatism in the region and the lessening of the Republican commitment of northern Protestants follows a greater liberalism. Blacks have become more liberal and more Democratic. For most of the remaining groups, changes in attitudes seem to be associated with a growth of independence more than a noticeable movement toward one of the parties.

These changes in attitudes, as they relate to changes in party bias, are

TABLE 14.10. Summary of the partisanship and opinion profiles of the groups in the fifties and seventies

Group	1950s		1970s	
	Issues	Party	Issues	Party
Middle and upper status native white southerners	Quite a bit to the right	Strongly Democratic	Move further right	Move away from Democratic party, more Independent
Lower status native white southerners	Moderately right	Strongly Democratic	Move further right	Move away from Democratic party, more Independent
High status northern WASP	Moderately right	Strongly Republican	Move a bit left and splits	Less Republican, more Independent
Middle and lower status northern WASP	Center	Slightly Republican	Move a bit right	More Independent and more Democratic
Blacks	Strongly left	Strongly Democratic	Move even further left	Even more Democratic
Catholics	Moderately left	Strongly Democratic	Move to center	A bit more Independent
Jews	Strongly left	Strongly Democratic	Move further left	A bit more Independent
Border South	Moderately right	Strongly Democratic	Move a bit further right and split a bit	More Independent

interesting for what they indicate about the earlier themes of the growth of issue salience and consistency. For some groups—notably blacks and upper status WASPs—the relationship between the changes is simple. For others—notably southerners—it is more complex. In the fifties, southerners were conservative and Democratic. Now, in the seventies, they are a bit more conservative and they have become less Democratic. The change is in the right direction but it starts from the wrong origin. Of course, there are good historical reasons for the conservative southern democracy, but these good historical reasons raise some doubts about the simple issue model that is used to explain partisanship and party change.

The explanation of the pattern is simply that southerners perceived the

Democratic party as more representative of their feelings about the issues than the Republican party. In some basic sense, the perception was incorrect but it was held nonetheless, and the perceived proximity wedded the South to the Democratic party. The tumultuous sixties eroded this myopic perception. As issues became more salient and politics intruded on more individuals, there was a heightened awareness of discrepancies between what the parties actually stood for as opposed to what they were believed to stand for. The consequence of this greater sensitivity to political stimuli was that groups such as southerners began to align their party preference with their existing issue preferences. There was some attitude change, but the best explanation of the change in partisanship is not these changes in attitude but the attempt of groups of voters to square their attitudes with the party preference. Although it might have gone the other way, the result of this adjustment was a change in partisanship.[4]

As a result, it is possible for a conservative group such as white southerners to engage in a wholesale abandonment of their prior party preference with only modest increments in their conservatism—at least in relation to the level of conservatism one would expect in a group before it appears to be predominantly Republican. For the same kind of reason, attitude change in other groups has not translated into great changes in party bias because there have not yet been substantial changes in the perception of the parties along these issues.

---

[4] A more complete analysis of the relationship between issue preferences, perceptions of the parties, and party identification is presented in John R. Petrocik's "Changing Party Coalitions and the Attitudinal Basis of Alignment: 1952–1972" Ph.D. dissertation, University of Chicago, 1976, chaps. 4 and, especially, 6.

15 The Sequence of Changes

Earlier we asked whether it was proper to use the late Eisenhower years as our baseline for the analysis of change. Was that not perhaps an era of abnormal calm in American politics? The data we have presented make the fact that it was such an era remarkably clear. But was the following decade—the decade of the race and urban crisis, of drugs and student unrest, of the counterculture, of the war in Vietnam—a return to "normalcy"? Perhaps the best that can be said is that the abnormal calm of the Eisenhower years was replaced by the abnormal turmoil of the 1960s (and maybe that both periods were preceded by the abnormality of World War II and before that by the abnormality of the depression—which simply suggests that the abnormal has become our normal state).

That there has been so much change in American attitudes since the 1950s appears to be a function of changes in the political situation between the 1950s and the 1960s. Furthermore, the magnitude of those attitude changes may derive from the particular sequence with which the American public was faced with political changes from the 1950s. In this chapter we want to step back a bit from the details of the various changes to consider their overall sequence.

But before doing so, we must fill in some gaps in our data and consider a few additional ways in which the public has changed in the past two decades. We will consider changes in the political activity of the citizenry, their interest and involvement in politics, and their trust and confidence in the government.[1]

Political Activity

The political activity of citizens in the 1956 election, as we have seen, was relatively low. Aside from voting, only a small minority engaged in any of the campaign acts about which the SRC researchers asked.

How have things changed since then? The answer is in figure 15.1. There we plot the average number of campaign acts reported by the respondents in each year—that is, the average number of positive answers respondents gave to the six campaign activity questions that the SRC researchers asked. In 1956, as reported in the previous chapter, the average for all citizens was

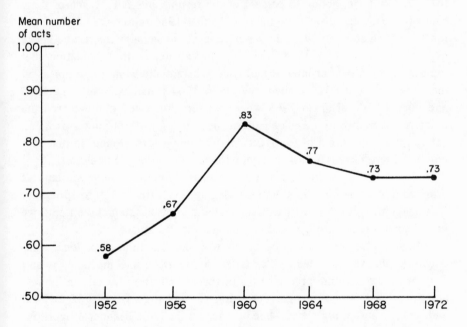

FIGURE 15.1. Mean number of campaign acts, presidential election years, 1952–1972

---

[1] In this chapter we provide only an analysis of longitudinal data concerning citizen involvement and confidence in government. For a more extensive discussion of citizen participation see Sidney Verba and Norman H. Nie, *Participation in America* (New York: Harper and Row, 1972), and Lester Milbrath, *Political Participation* (Chicago: Rand McNally, 1965).

about two-thirds of a campaign act. As figure 15.1 shows, the 1956 activity level is somewhat above the activity level in 1952, but substantially below the level in 1960. Political activity for the American public rose quite sharply between 1956 and 1960. In 1960 one finds the highest amount for the two decades. The amount of activity falls somewhat after 1960, but nevertheless remains at a level well above that for 1956.

Political Interest

In each of the presidential election studies from 1952 to 1972, respondents were asked whether they were interested in the presidential campaign. Figure 15.2 reports the proportions of the population that responded that they were "very interested" in the campaign and the proportions that said that they were "not very interested" (or not interested at all) in the campaign. In our base year of 1956, about 30 percent of the respondents fell in each of these categories. But it is clear from figure 15.2 that 1956 represented a relatively low level of interest. In 1952, the reported level of campaign interest had been higher than in 1956. And by 1960 the proportion of the population that reported a good deal of interest had risen substantially while those not at all interested had fallen. Campaign interest in 1964 remained similar to 1960 and interest rose again in 1968 when the very interested outnumbered the uninterested by two to one. The pattern suggests a growth of interest from an "abnormally" low point in 1956. But in 1972 things turn around. In that year political interest drops again—not quite to the level of 1956, but almost.

The data suggest that the level of campaign interest is quite variable. It drops to a low point in 1956, climbs to higher levels from 1960 to 1968, and falls again after 1968. But let us hold aside attempts at intepretation until we have a somewhat fuller picture of the changes that take place.

Figure 15.3 traces the proportions who pay attention to political campaigns in the various media. The data on the electronic media—TV and radio—are hard to interpret in terms of their implication for citizen interest and attention to the campaign. Television viewing soars from 1952 to 1960 and remains at that high level while reliance on the radio declines proportionately. This change reflects changes in media availability more than it reflects changes in campaign interest.

The growth of television as a source of campaign news comes at the same time as the growth in political interest seen in figure 15.2. But though it is likely that television has introduced a new dimension to campaign attentiveness, the growth of interest does not seem to be only the result of the availability of this new medium. As the second part of figure 15.3 indicates,

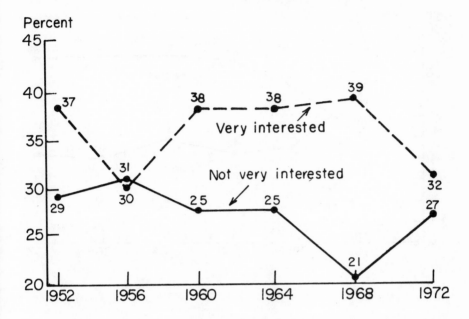

FIGURE 15.2. Interest in presidential campaigns, 1956–1972

attention to the campaign in newspapers and magazines also rose between the 1956 and 1960 elections. Since these media were always available, the increase in interest shown on figure 15.2 is likely to reflect more than the availability of television.

The measures of campaign attentiveness in the media are consistent with the measures of campaign interest. The data on newspapers and magazines suggest that 1956 was an abnormally low year in terms of campaign attention. The increase in campaign attention in newspapers and magazines that one observes between 1956 and 1960 represents a return to the levels of 1952, not the attainment of a new level of attentiveness. (The data on electronic media are not easily comparable in these terms because of the drastic changes in availability that were taking place at that time.)

Finally, one ought to note the decline in newspaper attentiveness in 1972. The decline parallels that in campaign interest reported in figure 15.1. We shall have to look more closely at 1972 shortly.

Figure 15.4 summarizes the changes in campaign interest and attention from 1956 to 1972. It plots the proportions of the population who can be categorized as "involved" and "uninvolved"—that is, those who are both interested in campaigns and attentive to them in the written media and those who are neither interested nor attentive. In 1956 roughly equal small groups of

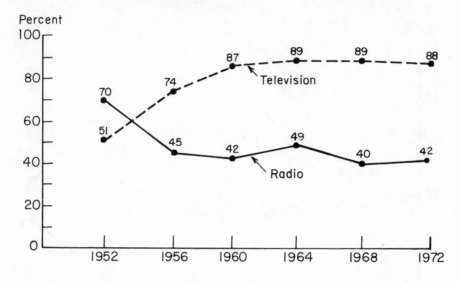

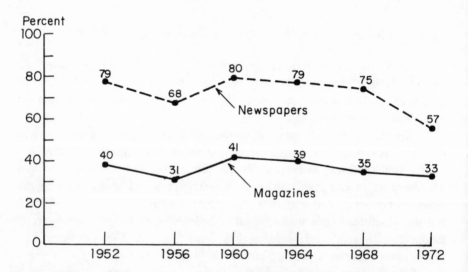

FIGURE 15.3. Attentiveness to campaign in media, presidential election years, 1952–1972

each type of citizen were found. But this represented a significant drop of involvement from 1952. By 1960 the involved outnumbered the uninvolved by about two to one, a situation that remains stable through 1968. In 1972, as we would expect from the data thus far presented, the figures return to those found for 1956.

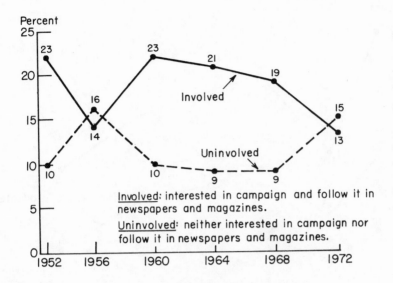

FIGURE 15.4. The involved and the uninvolved, presidential election years, 1952–1972

The data on activity, interest in campaigns, as well as the more general measure of political involvement are somewhat puzzling. In general they are consistent with other data indicating that 1956 was a year of relatively low political intensity. Activity and interest rise fairly sharply from the 1956 base point. So does attentiveness to political campaigns in the media. But though activity remains fairly close to the new levels it reaches after 1960, the measures indicating psychological involvement in the campaign fall.

As has been shown elsewhere, the change in activity rates from the Eisenhower years to the 1960s is in part explicable by changes in the educational level of the public, but only in part. Activity rates increased at a level somewhat greater than one would predict on the basis of changes in the educational level of the public.[2] On the face of it, the data on political interest would seem unrelated to changes in educational level; the up and down pattern found in the data is of course quite different from the steady educational growth. However, educational levels are related to the change in interest—though not in any simple way. Figure 15.5 reports the proportion at three educational levels of those who are high on our measure of campaign involvement. In general, the data confirm that the change in level of involvement is not simply a function of changes in the level of education in the population. If

---

[2] Verba and Nie, *Participation in America,* chap. 14.

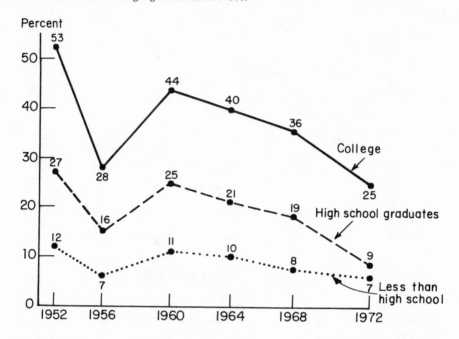

FIGURE 15.5. Proportion high on political involvement, by education, presidential election years, 1952–1972

that were the case, there would be little change in involvement levels once one had controlled for education. But during the period of greatest increase in political involvement, the period from 1956 to 1960, the involvement level of all three educational groups goes up. And during the period of earlier decline in involvement, between 1952 and 1956, the involvement level falls for all three groups. On the other hand, though educational growth clearly does not explain the changes in involvement, there are some interesting differences across educational levels. The rise and fall in involvement appears to affect the college group more than the high school graduates and the latter more than those without a high school degree. The group with less than a high school degree, for instance, changes very little in comparison with the college group. Most interesting is the fact that the fairly sharp decline in political involvement in the period after 1968 affects the college graduates the most and the lowest educational group hardly at all. Whatever it is that leads to the sharp decline in citizen involvement after 1968, it is something that more strongly affects the more educated segments of the population.[3]

---

[3] We have looked into the extent to which the changes in the level of political involvement are connected to the movement of new young age cohorts into the electorate—that

To explain the decline in political interest in the post-1968 period we can turn to the last set of characteristics whose changes we are tracing: the trust and confidence of citizens in the political system.

Confidence in the Political System

The data presented for our base year, 1958, on the degree of confidence that citizens had on the government were somewhat mixed and hard to interpret.[4] To some questions citizen replies showed a high level of confidence, to others a low level. The situation becomes clearer if we trace the degree of confidence over time.

Figure 15.6 traces the proportions of the population who reply in a nontrusting fashion to several questions. The data are consistent across all the items. Distrust in the government rose substantially between 1958 and 1972. In 1958, 18 percent of the population felt that the government was run for the benefit of a few; by 1972 57 percent took that position. On other items, the change is dramatic. The proportion saying that one cannot usually trust the government to do what is right nearly doubles, and climbs another 20 percentage points by the end of 1973. The proportion who say that there are a lot of crooks in the government rises slowly from 1958 to 1972, but the year after the 1972 election the proportion soars. The data make clear that the erosion of confidence in government that accompanied Watergate represented an acceleration—in some cases a sharp acceleration—of changes that had begun much earlier.[5]

Figure 15.7 presents data on another question, one for which data exist in 1952. Respondents were asked whether they agreed or disagreed with the statement that "public officials care much what people like me think." In 1952 about one-third thought they did not. By 1956 and 1960, the figure had fallen to one out of four Americans who felt that the government did not care what people thought. After 1960 matters begin to change. By 1972 the public was equally divided into those who think officials cared and those who think

---

is, whether the fall in involvement in 1956 or in 1972 reflects the entrance of a new group of uninvolved young citizens. In general this does not seem to be the case. When involvement levels fall from 1952 to 1956 or again from 1968 to 1972, they do so for all age groups. And when new age groups enter the electorate, they tend to have levels of involvement similar to those for the rest of the populace at the same time point.

[4] We use 1958 as the base year for tracing trust and confidence in the government, because questions on that topic begin to be used then.

[5] For a discussion of trust and confidence in government see Arthur H. Miller, "Political Issues and Trust in Government: 1964–1970," *American Political Science Review*, 68 (September 1974), 951–972, and in the same issue, a comment on Miller by Jack Citrin, "Comment: The Political Relevance of Trust in Government," ibid., 973–988.

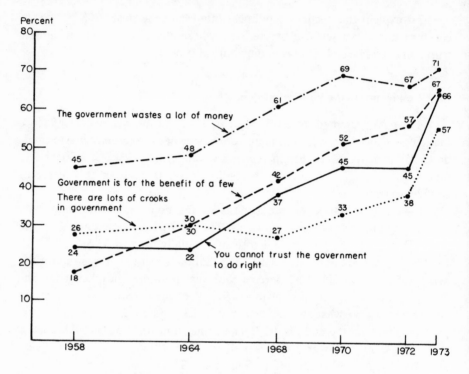

FIGURE 15.6. Confidence in government, 1958–1973

they do not. And by December 1973 the figures were 56 percent saying government officials don't care: that is, a majority now take the negative view.

Declining Confidence and Declining Interest: A Connection?

The data on the sharp decline in political interest after 1968 represent something of an anomaly. In 1972 the proportion saying that they follow the campaign in the newspapers also falls. The change is an anomaly because in other ways 1972 continues the trends of earlier years: political activity remains at the level of the previous elections and well above the 1956 level. Political beliefs become, if anything, more consistent than in the previous election year.

The solution to the puzzle may lie in a change in the meaning of the response, "I am not at all interested in politics," in 1972 from its meaning in earlier years. In the analysis of political attitudes, measures of political interest have been used to distinguish the passive, quiescent citizens from those for

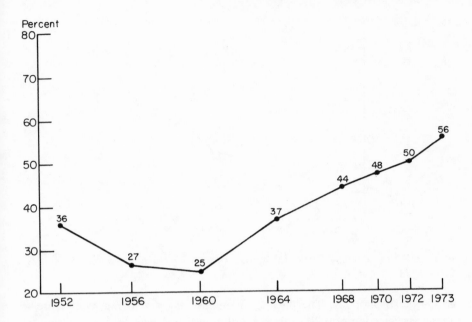

FIGURE 15.7. Percent reporting that government officials "don't care what people like me think," 1952–1973

whom politics is salient. The absence of interest meant apathy, that is, a lack of concern for or feelings about the political system. By 1972, we would suggest, disinterest in politics may mean a positive rejection of politics rather than apathetic withdrawal.

To see whether the meaning of political disinterest has, indeed, undergone such a change, we can use the questions about distrust of the government. We can divide the respondents who are uninterested in politics into two groups: those who are also distrustful of the government and those who are basically trusting. Figure 15.8 shows the proportions of the uninterested who were distrusting in 1964, 1968, 1972, and 1973. (The distrustful are those who take distrustful positions on at least three of the four trust items listed on figure 15.6.) In 1964 few of the uninterested citizens fell into the distrustful category. By 1972 the situation changed considerably; 42 percent of the uninterested citizens were distrustful. In 1973, 59 percent of uninterested citizens lacked trust in the government. The uninterested, this suggests, are composed of two kinds of citizens: those who are apathetic and those who are disenchanted, and the ratio of the latter to the former has grown substantially.

When considered in the light of the data on decreased confidence in the government, the apparent decline of political interest in the post-1968 period

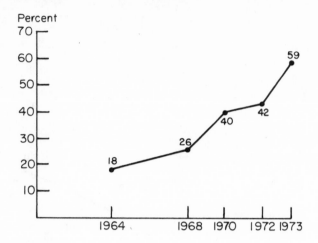

FIGURE 15.8 Percent distrustful among those who are uninterested in politics, 1964–1973

is less of an anomaly. The decline in interest appears to represent more a conscious rejection of politics than a withdrawal into more neutral apathy. In this sense the data are less inconsistent than they might seem to be with the data on the generally increasing politicization of the public during this period —a politicization manifested in its increased political activity, its increased use of issues and ideologies to evaluate parties and candidates, and its increased attitudinal consistency.[6]

The data on the increased activity rate of citizens, their generally higher levels of political involvement (with the qualification for 1972), and their increased distrust of the government indicate some further important changes in the American electorate that have to be added to the other changes we have traced in partisanship and in ways of political thinking. The public in the early 1970s was substantially different from that in the mid-1950s: it has become more involved but more alienated, it has substantially weaker ties to either of the major political parties, it has a more coherent set of issue preferences that have become more important as guides to political behavior.

---

[6] There are some interesting differences across educational groups in terms of the level of trust in the government. In general throughout the period, the less educated groups are more distrustful. As distrust grows, it grows somewhat more rapidly for those with higher education. But in 1972, those with less than a high school degree are still considerably more distrustful than the college educated. We also considered the possibility that distrust was a function of the entrance of the more disenchanted cohorts of the late 1960s, but found them quite similar to the electorate as a whole in terms of their distrust level.

The Sequence of Change: A Speculation

The sequence of these changes is most interesting. In each case, we find a threshold effect: a series of years in which one finds stability in these measures followed by a period of fairly rapid change, followed by a new relatively stable period. But the period of rapid change differs from one dimension to the other.

Consider the data in figure 15.9 where we plot the trend line for each of four characteristics of the mass public: the proportion expressing strong interest in the campaign, the proportion in the "consistent" ends of our attitude scale, the proportion of independents, and the proportion giving "distrustful" answers to several questions about confidence in government. Note the difference across the several measures in terms of the point in time when major change takes place. Interest rises between the 1956 and 1960 elections. It reaches a plateau where it remains till the plunge down again in 1972. Consistency rises between the 1960 and the 1964 election. It reaches a plateau

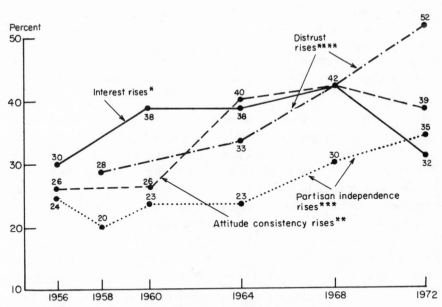

*Percent expressing strong interest in the campaign.
**Percent in the consistent one-third of our attitude scale.
***Percent Independent.
****Average percent taking distrustful position on the four trust items (see figure 15.6).

FIGURE 15.9. Thresholds of change, 1956–1972

TABLE 15.1. Timing of change in various orientations, 1956–1972

	1956	1960	1964	1968	1972
Involvement					
Interest in campaigns		sharp rise			sharp fall
Campaign activity		sharp rise			
Ideology					
Level of conceptualization		⟵ steady rise ⟶			
Issue consistency			sharp rise		
Distrust					
Distrust of government				⟵ sharp rise ⟶	
Antipartisanship					
Proportion of ' Independents				⟵ rise ⟶	
Proportion reporting vote switching				⟵ sharp rise ⟶	
Proportion alienated from parties				⟵ sharp rise ⟶	

and stays there. The increase in distrust and the erosion of party commitment begin after 1964 and move steadily upward across the next two elections.

These changes are not limited to the specific measures we plot on figure 15.9. In several instances we have multiple measures of similar phenomena. And for each measure the threshold of change is the same. Table 15.1 presents the moment of sharpest change for eight different measures. Involvement in politics may be measured by expressed interest or by rates of activity. Both go up at the same time, around 1960. The way in which citizens conceptualize political matters may be measured by the index of level of conceptualization or by attitude consistency. Both change at the same time, around 1964. And the decline of partisanship can be measured in three ways: by the proportion who are Independents, by vote switching, and by the expression of negative attitudes toward parties. Each is a different and independent measure. Each moves at the same time, beginning around 1968.

The data we have are too crude to allow us to link these changes to specific political events. But it is interesting to speculate how the various events of the sixties and early seventies may have led to this staggered series of changes. The story begins in 1956 when all is relatively quiet: politics is low-keyed, party ties firm, citizens satisfied or relatively so. Politics are, comparatively speaking, dull. As we have seen, the main issues are nondivisive ones—foreign threats.

The next four years bring an awakening of political interest and a rise in the excitement of politics. The civil rights movement begins to catch the public's attention; Little Rock brings the first major confrontation of the federal government and the states over integration. And in 1960 John F. Kennedy stimulates a new level of political interest (or, at least, brings the country out of the doldrums of the 1956 election). But though politics have become more stimulating, the issues are not divisive. They remain the issues of foreign policy well into the Kennedy administration.

By 1960 we find a public that is much more active and involved in politics than was the case four years earlier. But the structure of public attitudes has changed little. The measure of attitude consistency shows no increase in the coherence of public attitudes between 1956 and 1960. And party affiliation as a guide to voting behavior remains as strong. In 1964 we find another change; this time a sharp change in the consistency of political attitudes. By 1964, as we have seen, the divisive issue of race had moved to the forefront. And in that year, of course, the Republican party deliberately chose a candidate, Barry Goldwater, who provided a clear issue alternative. This reversed the strategy of 1952 when the Republican party, faced with a choice between a war hero with no clear issue position and a clear conservative, chose the former. It is likely that the 1964 campaign—coming when a more potent issue, race, had come to the fore, when that issue was presented by both sides as a clear liberal/conservative choice, and when the campaign was conducted before a public that was more interested in and attentive to political campaigns—led to the greater crystallization of citizen attitudes. The Kennedy years aroused citizen interest; the Goldwater candidacy crystallized the issue postions of that more interested citizenry.

The next step in the story is obvious. A more politically involved public with more coherent political views runs right into the troubles of the late 1960s. The result: a growing disenchantment with government—reflected in the sharp rise in expressions of distrust in the government. The issues of the 1960s, furthermore, do not clearly coincide with party lines; thus the parties offer no meaningful alternatives that might tie citizens more closely to them. Thus the political parties reap the results of the disaffection. Citizens come to look at the parties in more negative terms; they also begin to abandon the parties in growing numbers.

In short, 1960 and 1964 create a more interested populace with a more coherent set of political positions. Such a populace was ripe for the disillusionment associated with Vietnam, the racial crisis, and the multitude of shocks that begin in the mid-sixties. And the last step, seen in the 1972 election, is the sharp decline in interest, a phenomenon that appears to be another manifestation of the growing disenchantment with government and politics.

We would need panel data to confirm our argument. But we can look at the data we have to see if the following sequence holds: increased interest leads to increased attitude consistency (with the 1964 election as catalyst); increased consistency leads to growing dissatisfaction with the government and the parties (with the divisive issues of the late 1960s as catalyst).

Does Interest Lead to Consistency?

As we saw in Chapter 9, these characteristics are clearly connected one with another. The consistency of political attitudes was found to go up especially among those citizens who are interested in politics. These data are consistent with our sequential explanation.

Does Consistency Lead to Dissatisfaction and Withdrawal of Partisan Support?

We can take the story one step further. If our argument is correct, it should be among those with the most consistent attitudes that one finds the greatest growth of disaffection with the political process and the sharpest rejection of parties. Arthur Miller has studied this subject closely, using the SRC data files. He finds in 1970 that cynicism toward the government is most pronounced among those who have clear issue preferences on the left or on the right. His interpretation is consistent with the sequential model we have presented: "By 1970, Americans to a considerable degree had withdrawn some of their trust from the government because they had become widely divided on a variety of issues, for in the normal attempt to satisfy the greatest numbers, the government generally followed a more or less centrist policy which in reality appears to have displeased a substantial portion of the population."[7]

If we look beyond 1970, however, the situation appears less clear. Figure 15.10 reports the level of distrust for those on the left of the political

---

[7] Miller, "Political Issues and Trust in Government," p. 963.

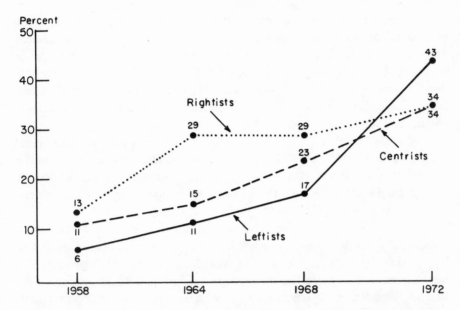

FIGURE 15.10. Perecent distrustful by consistency of political beliefs, 1958–1972

belief spectrum, in the center, and on the right. The leftists are those who score in the left-most sixth of our left-right belief scale; the rightists are those who are in the right-most sixth of that scale. On the vertical axis we plot the percentage of the group that takes a distrustful position on at least three of the four items listed on figure 15.6.

The data do show a relationship between issue consistency and distrust of the government, but not a simple pattern of growing distrust on the part of the more consistent citizens. Miller found in 1970 that leftists and rightists were both more distrustful than those in the center. But that is apparently the only year in which that happens. In the earliest year for which we have data—1958—citizens on the right are the most distrustful; those on the left are the most trusting. Between 1958 and 1964 distrust rises most among the rightists. The increase in distrust from 1964 to 1972, in contrast, comes from the leftists and the centrists, but especially from the former. The rightists remain the most distrustful through 1968. Between 1968 and 1972, distrust goes up for all groups, but for leftists the most and rightists the least. The result is that by 1972 the leftists are the most distrustful (though all three groups are less trusting in 1972 than they were in 1958).

The data do suggest that the sharp growth in distrust is related to the issue position of the citizen. But it is not simply a matter of growing distrust at both ends of the issue spectrum. Rightists have been distrustful of the government at least since the late 1950s (when we have our first measurement point). Their level of distrust does not change much, compared with the other groups. In part their position may reflect their relationship to the administration in power: under Nixon their level of distrust stays relatively steady between 1968 and 1970 (while that for the other two groups climbs sharply); and in 1972, their level of distrust falls.[8]

Was the late 1960s a period in which citizens with coherent issue positions became dissatisfied with the government because it did not carry out the policies they preferred? The data suggest that this happens on the left. If anyone has been let down by the government in that period it is the leftists. The rightists were never satisfied to begin with.

Does an increase in the coherence of political views also lead to a withdrawal from the political parties? If this were the case, one would expect to find that those citizens with more coherent views are also the ones who have loosened their party ties in recent years. In figure 15.11 we trace over time two measures of attachment to the political parties: the proportion identifying as independent and the proportion expressing generally nonsupportive views of both parties.[9] We trace these proportions for those at the left end of the issue spectrum, those at the right, and those in between.

The data do not support the hypothesis that it is the citizens from the left and the right (in contrast with the centrists) who are abandoning the political parties. The rise of the proportion of Independents is found on the left, on the right, and in the center. The same is true for the proportion who express negative views about the parties. The proportion expressing such views goes up across the political spectrum. If any group expresses less alienation from the parties it is that group at the far left of the issue spectrum rather than the centrists. But the proportion of alienated citizens goes up in that group as well.

In short, though the increase of political distrust and the weakening of party ties comes on the heels of the increase in the coherence of political attitudes, there is no clear evidence that distrust and the abandonment of parties takes place among those who have developed those coherent attitudes. On the other hand, we did find that consistency grew particularly among those who were more politically interested.

---

[8] In 1964 and 1968, when the rightists are most distrustful, there is a Democrat in the White House. In 1958, of course, there is a Republican president, but probably one perceived as to the left of those at the far right of the issue spectrum.

[9] Those considered "nonsupporters of parties" have, on balance, more dislikes than likes about both parties or more dislikes than likes about one party and no views one way or the other on the other party, or neutral views on both.

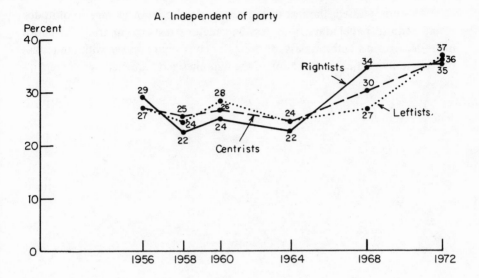

A. Independent of party

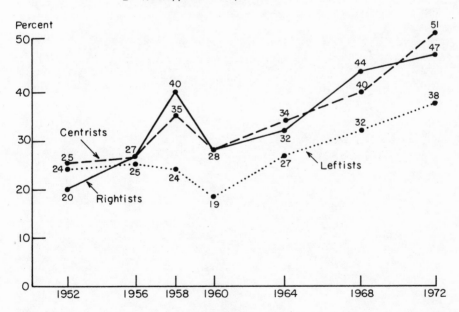

B. Nonsupporters of parties

FIGURE 15.11. Change in level of party attachment among leftists, rightists, and centrists, 1952–1972

As we suggested, the test of our sequential model of change in attitudes would require panel data. Our less satisfactory test—comparing the more interested citizens with the less, or the more consistent citizens with the less—provides only partial confirmation of the hypothesized sequence.

16 American Elections: Past and Future

The main theme of our book has been change in the American electorate. In many ways the electorate of the 1970s is different from that of the late 1950s, and the ways in which it differs from the earlier electrorate have significant implications for the future of American politics, in particular for the way in which elections are likely to be fought and won or lost in the future.

It is, of course, easier to document what has happened in the past than to predict what will happen in the future. It is clear that the party-based electoral system of the late Eisenhower years is no longer with us. But it is less clear what will replace it. The changes in the electorate are of a sort that introduce a good deal of uncertainty into the electoral process. When elections were dominated by partisan voting, one had an anchor point from which to chart deviations based on such short-term forces as the personality of the candidate or the issues of the day. The partisan vote was the "normal" vote.

The ties of partisanship provided stability from election to election as issues and candidates came and went. Without such stability, elections should turn on shorter term and, hence, less predictable forces. The outcome of an election will depend heavily on the issues and on the candidates that appear in that year. Whether the electoral system will continue in its present unstructured form or resolve into some more stable and predictable one is hard to know. Several alternative futures are possible.

1. The new concern of the citizenry with issues coupled with the coherence of their issue positions provides the potential for the development of that dream of many political scientists (and nightmare to some others): a "responsible" two-party system where parties with clearly distinguished issue positions offer the populace clear alternatives.[1]

2. On the other hand, the weakness of party ties coupled with the general discontent of the early 1970s may hasten the decline of the political parties as stabilizing forces in American politics. This might lead to a more volatile electorate willing to follow a demagogic extremist.[2]

3. Or perhaps the decline of some of the passing issues of the 1960s— Vietnam, the social and cultural issues—coupled with a renewed concern with economic welfare will resuscitate the old party alignments. Perhaps the New Deal coalition can be reconstructed out of what looks like (as we write in early 1975) the ongoing economic difficulties of the 1970s. We have documented the decline but not the demise of the party system. Parties play less of a role in determining the vote than they once did, but they still play a role. And the new Independents are not necessarily permanently Independent.

Which of these is most likely? Or is some other future in the offing? The data offer no clear answer. In part this is the case because of where we stand in a period of transition. We appear to be at the point where past ties have been loosened but new ones to replace the old have not yet started to be attached. It is clear what has ended; it is less clear what will replace it. Furthermore, we have been looking at but one side of the electoral process—the nature of the electorate and how it responds to stimuli. One of our major themes is that the electorate *does respond* to stimuli; that is, how it votes, how it decides how to vote, and how it thinks about political matters is a function not merely of some inherent social and psychological characteristics but of the issues and candidates it faces in the real world of politics.

As V. O. Key argued forcefully and as political scientists such as Gerald Pomper have recently demonstrated: how the public behaves in elections depends heavily on the choices it is offered.[3] We do not know what future

---

[1] American Political Science Association, "Toward a More Responsible Two-Party System," *American Political Science Review,* 44 (September 1950), Supplement, is the optimistic and liberal ideological interpretation of responsible parties.

[2] See Chapter 2, note 31, for references to literature on the stabilizing effect of parties.

[3] V. O. Key, *The Responsible Electorate* (Cambridge, Mass.: Harvard University Press, 1966), and see Gerald Pomper, "From Confusion to Clarity: Issues and American Voters—1956–1968," *American Political Science Review,* 66 (June 1972), 415–428, and Arthur H. Miller, "Political Issues and Trust in Government: 1964–1970," *American Political Science Review,* 68 (September 1974), 951–972.

choices will be; that is the side of the electoral process (the process of nomi-
nations, the organizational structure of the parties, and so on) we have not
been analyzing. Yet we can take the data we have to help illuminate the
future. We do know how the electorate has reacted to a variety of electoral
choices in the past. If we consider these choices carefully we may learn a lot
about how it will react to choices in the future. Thus to look forward, we shall
look backward at the set of elections we have been studying from 1952 to
1972.

A number of components may go into the electoral choice. Voters may
vote on the basis of their party affiliation; they may vote on the basis of their
issue preferences; they may vote because they like something about the candidate (his personality, his religion); or they may vote because of some acci-
dental event of the election campaign (a Watergate break-in, an Eagleton
affair). We will focus on the interaction of the first two components of the
electoral decisions: party and issues. The other components may be important
in an election (in some elections they may dominate), but it is hard to
generalize about them.[4]

Issue versus Party Voting

As we saw in Chapter 10, party voting has declined for two reasons: the
number of Independents (who cannot cast a party vote) has risen, and the
number of party identifiers who defect when they vote has gone up as well. At
the same time issue voting has increased for two similar reasons: more citizens have consistent issue positions on the basis of which they can vote; and
more citizens are guided by those issue positions in casting their vote. To see
the implication of this change we ought to consider more closely the relationship between issue voting and party voting.

Issue voting and party voting are not necessarily incompatible one with
the other. One can vote for both at the same time—if issue position and party
identification push in the same direction. Consider figure 16.1. We plot a
person's position on a liberal-conservative issue dimension (horizontally)
against his position on a party identification dimension (vertically). The figure assumes that issue positions can be simplified into the one-dimensional
liberal-conservative continuum. Whether citizens can vote for party and issue

---

[4] Angus Campbell and others, *The American Voter* (New York: Wiley, 1960), is still
the definitive examination of the multiple factors influencing vote choice. A later examination demonstrating the election-specific variability of those vote influences is Donald
Stokes, "Dynamic Elements of Contests for the Presidency," *American Political Science
Review,* 60 (March 1966), 19–28.

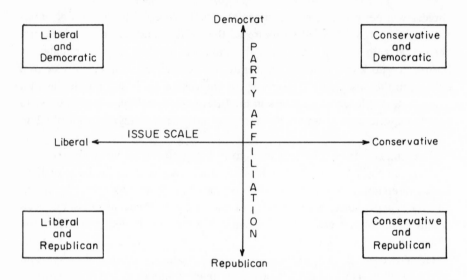

FIGURE 16.1. Issue space and party space

at the same time depends on where citizens and candidates are located on that figure.

Suppose we had issue-based parties where all those with liberal issue positions are Democrats and all with conservative issue positions Republicans (and Independents in between). If the parties offered candidates compatible with the positions of their supporters, the Democratic voters and their candidates would be in the upper left of the figure and the Republicans and their candidate would be in the lower right. Voters would then cast votes that were both party and issue votes at the same time. There would be no way to tell which kind of vote was being cast on the basis of the act itself (though one could question voters as to which they considered more important).

Alternatively, party and issue might be at odds. Suppose the Democratic party presented a liberal candidate and the Republicans presented a conservative one; but Democrats were at the conservative end of the scale and Republican voters at the liberal end. In this case, voters would have to choose between party and issue. (Or the same could happen if Democratic voters remained liberal, Republican voters conservative; but the parties "crossed them up" by nominating candidates from the opposite ends of the spectrum.)

It is important to distinguish the two circumstances above—one in which issues and party line up, the other in which they are counter to each other. If the former situation, an increased concern for issues and a greater willingness to vote on the issues reinforces partisanship. If the latter, issue voting undercuts partisanship and might lead to party realignment.

TABLE 16.1. Types of potential party and issue voters

	Belief measure		
Party	Left	Center	Right
Democrats	Potential issue-reinforced partisans	Centrist party voters or party defectors	Potential issue defectors
Republicans	Potential issue defectors	Centrist party voters or defectors	Potential issue-reinforced partisans
Independents	Potential issue-voting Independent	Unguided by issues or party	Potential issue-voting Independent

In fact, Democratic identifiers and Republican identifiers are not all in the same location on a liberal-conservative scale. Some Democrats are on the left, some on the right; and the same holds true for Republicans. If party identifiers are split this way, some conflict between issue voting and party voting becomes inevitable (unless the party can nominate a split candidate who is on both ends of the continuum at the same time—as some try to be). This distinction between issue voting that reinforces partisanship and that which undercuts it is important because it helps us understand the way in which the tendency of voters to be concerned about issues is likely to affect the party system.

Let us look at this a bit more concretely. We can array voters along our liberal-conservative issue scale: some are on the left, some in the middle, and some on the right. Voters can also be divided into Democratic identifiers, Independents, and Republicans. This gives us nine types of voters, as in table 16.1. In the upper right-hand box and the middle left-hand box we have potential defectors. In the upper left box and the middle right box we have potential issue-reinforced voters. In the center (where issues offer no guide) we have voters who can be either defectors from their party or loyalists.[5]

---

[5] Actually, centrists can vote on the basis of issues when a centrist is opposed by a candidate from the left or the right. As we shall show, this is an important aspect of issue voting (see Chapter 18), but here we will focus only on those voters whose issue positions are clear enough to place them at one end or the other of the issue scales and who have unambiguous issue guidance.

TABLE 16.2. Types and numbers of potential issue voters,[a] 1956–1972

Type of voter	1956	1960	1964	1968	1972
Potential defectors on issues (conservative Democrats and liberal Republicans)	18	21	19	19	20
Potential issue reinforced voters (liberal Democrats and conservative Republicans)	27	27	37	33	27
Potential Independent issue voters (liberal Independents and conservative Independents)	16	15	16	22	25
Total potential issue voters	61	63	72	73	72

[a] People with coherent issue positions (that is, in the most liberal or most conservative one-third of summary attitude index).

Last, we put a bottom row of categories for those with no party affiliation. These Independents can vote on the basis of their issue position if they have such a position (as do those in the lower left and lower right boxes). Issue voting by Independents, of course, does not reinforce partisanship, since they have none to reinforce.

Table 16.2 reports the actual proportions of the population across our six elections who have coherent issue positions and therefore could be issue voters. Based on the categorization in figure 16.1 we divide these voters into three groups: those who are potential issue defectors because their issue positions and their party affiliations do not line up (conservative Democrats and liberal Republicans); those who are potential issue-reinforced voters because both issues and partisanship are on the same side of the political spectrum (liberal Democrats and conservative Republicans); and those Independents whose political views place them in the consistent categories of our issue-attitude scale.[6]

As one can see, there are three distinct patterns: that in 1960 and

---

[6] The party categorizations are obvious. The issue categories are less clear. The issue index is divided into thirds by categorizing respondents in the right-most third of the index as the consistent conservatives, those in the left-most third of the index as the consistent liberals, and all others as centrists. The division is done by pooling the samples.

before, that in 1964, and that in 1972 (with 1968 appearing to be a transition from 1964 to 1972). In the elections of 1956 and 1960, slightly over 60 percent of the public are potential issue voters; the total rises to about three-quarters in the last three elections. But in 1964, the bulk of the potential issue voters (over half of that group) were potential issue-reinforced voters—that is, they had attitudes that were consistent with the direction of their party preference. By 1972, the potential issue-reinforced voters had fallen substantially in percentage, while the proportion of Independents with issue positions had increased.

The data in table 16.2 represent another way of looking at two phenomena with which we are already familiar. One is the rise in issue consistency from 1960 to 1964. The second is the increase in the proportion of the electorate who are Independent. But the data highlight the fact that party and issues are in closer alignment in 1964 than in 1972. Between 1960 and 1964, there is a sharp increase in the proportion of the electorate with coherent issue positions.[7] But the rise comes entirely from an increase in the proportion of voters for whom party and issues overlap. From 1964 through 1972, the proportion of citizens with coherent issue positions remains at the high level it reaches in 1964. But the composition of that group changes. The proportion of voters whose party and issue positions line up consistently with each other falls back to the level of 1956. On the other hand, the proportion of Independents with coherent issue positions rises. This is, of course, consistent with the fact that there are more Independents in 1972 than in 1964—the proportion of Independents in the electorate was 23 percent in 1964, 30 percent by 1972. But what is important is that the increase in the proportion of Independents consists entirely of independents with coherent issue positions. This is seen in figure 16.2. It plots the proportion of the electorate that is both Independent and has coherent issue positions and the proportion that is independent but without coherent issue attitudes. As one can see, the latter group does not grow in size. The former group grows from 16 percent of the electorate to 25 percent.

In sum, the majority of the voters with coherent issue attitudes in 1964 were voters whose issue positions reinforced their party identification. By 1972 the majority of those with coherent issue positions were either Independents or partisans whose issue position was not congruent with their party identification.

---

[7] This, of course, reflects the correlation between issue preferences and party preference. A recent longitudinal analysis can be found in Pomper, "From Confusion to Clarity," pp. 415–428.

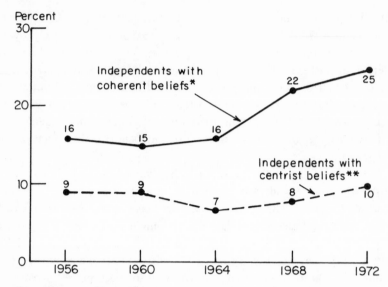

* In the most liberal or conservative third of the summary attitude index.

** In the middle third of the summary attitude index.

FIGURE 16.2. Independents with and without coherent beliefs, 1956–1972

Coherent issue positions make it possible for voters to vote consistently with their issue attitudes. But they do not necessarily do so. Some voters who have coherent issue attitudes might vote contrary to those attitudes. That is, of course, most likely among voters whose issue attitudes and party affiliation pull in opposite directions. They can remain loyal to their party. In addition Independents might vote contrary to their issue position because of the personality of the candidate or for other reasons. And even those whose attitudes and party affiliation pull in the same direction might, for one reason or another, vote in the other direction.

In figure 16.3 we take those voters who have consistent beliefs and plot the proportion who vote in the direction predicted by their beliefs. As we can see, the proportion increases sharply in 1964 and remains high afterwards. These data, of course, simply repeat what we already know: that the correlation of issue position and the vote increases sharply between the 1960 and 1964 election and remains high afterwards.

But if we take the data one step further we gain insight into the interaction of issues, party, and the vote. We can divide the party identified voters with consistent beliefs into those whose beliefs run counter to their party affiliation and those whose beliefs reinforce party position. We have just

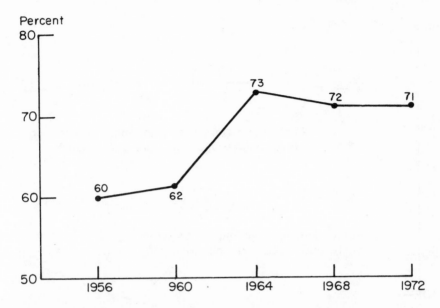

FIGURE 16.3. Proportion of voters with coherent issue attitudes who vote consistently with that position, 1956–1972 (includes partisans and independents with coherent beliefs)

considered the change in the size of these groups. We can now consider their voting behavior. In figure 16.4 we plot the proportion of each of these groups that votes consistently with its issue position. There is little change in the proportion of potential issue-reinforced voters (that is, citizens with congruent issue and party positions) who vote consistently with their issue position. Since both party and issues push in the same direction, one would expect to find few voting in the opposite direction. The proportion behaving as we would expect them to remains steadily high throughout the time period.

A sharp change, though, is found among those voters whose party and issue positions are incongruent. As one would expect, they are less likely to vote in accord with their issue positions than are those for whom issue and party push in the same direction. They have the counterpull of their party affiliation. But of this group, caught between contrary pressures, the proportion that chooses to vote in the issue direction rises substantially during the period. In the 1956 and 1960 elections, the proportion choosing the issue direction when party pulls in the other direction is 22 percent and 24 percent respectively. In 1964, the issue voters rise to become 36 percent of the group. The proportion rises again in 1968, and by 1972 almost one out of two of this group chooses the issue direction over the party direction.

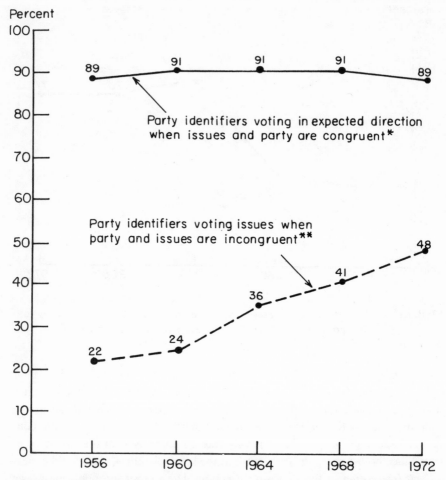

Percent

FIGURE 16.4. Proportion of two types of party identifiers who vote consistently with their issue position, 1956–1972

In figure 16.5 we plot the proportion of Independents with coherent issue positions who vote along the lines their issue positions would indicate. In 1956, Independents were as likely to vote counter to their issue preferences as they were to vote in accord with their issue positions. The proportion

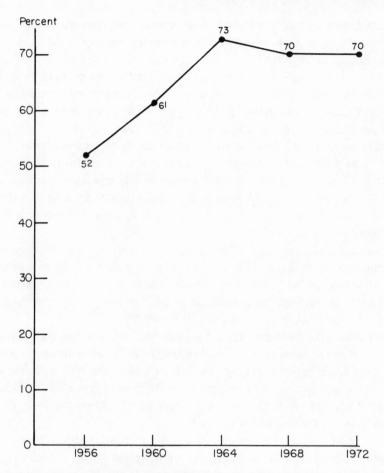

FIGURE 16.5. Proportion of Independents with coherent issue positions who vote consistently with their issue position, 1956–1972

voting in accord with issue position grows in 1960 and more so in 1964. It remains relatively high after that. In other words, not only are there more Independents with coherent issue positions in 1972 than in 1956, those with such positions are much more likely to vote along the lines of their issue position.

The data add to our understanding of the differences among the various elections. When issue coherence rises between the 1960 and the 1964 elections it lines up with party affiliation. The main source is the rise in the proportion of the electorate with coherent issue positions that reinforce their partisan inclinations. This is a group that overwhelmingly votes as one would predict on the basis of the joint force of issues and party. That they are so numerous increases substantially the relationship between issues and party. And that they vote as they do adds to the joint relationship of the former two characteristics to the vote.

From 1964 to 1972, on the other hand, the overlap between party and issues as an influence on the vote slumps. There are several components of that slump. One is the decline in the proportion of citizens whose issue positions reinforce their party affiliation. In 1972 those voters who have congruent issue and party characteristics are as likely to vote in the expected direction as were their counterparts in 1964, but there are fewer of them. In contrast, the number of Independents who have coherent issue positions rises in 1972. They are no more likely to vote consistently with their issue positions than were the Independents with coherent issues in 1964, but there are more such Independents in 1972.

Finally, we can consider these voters whose issue position is incongruent with their party affiliation. They are only slightly more frequent as a proportion of the electorate in 1972 than in 1964. But whereas they overwhelmingly voted party in this conflictual situation at the beginning of our time period, they are as likely to vote issues as party be the 1970s.

In sum, issue voting in 1972 does not reinforce partisan commitments for three reasons: because fewer citizens have issue attitudes and party affiliations that are congruent; because more issue voters are Independents; and because those citizens who are caught between opposing pressures from issue commitments and party affiliation vote more frequently on the basis of the former than was the case in 1964 or earlier.

The data we have been considering help us understand the phases summarized in Chapter 15. We found a different threshold for the several changes we have been studying. The period between 1960 and 1964 is the threshold for the rise of attitude consistency and issue voting. Partisanship, on the other hand, changes somewhat later; for most measures of partisanship, the decline comes after 1968. Figure 16.6 illustrates the lag between the two changes by comparing the voting behavior of partisans with that of citizens with coherent issue positions. As one can see, the proportion of those with coherent issue positions who vote consistently with their issue position rises between 1960 and 1964. But the proportion of partisans voting as their partisanship would indicate falls only after 1964.

The reason that the rise in the proportion of citizens voting in accord with issue positions is not matched by a decline in the proportion of citizens voting in accord with their party identification is explicated in figure 16.7. There we break apart the two groups plotted in figure 16.6. Those two groups are not mutually exclusive, for some citizens vote simultaneously in accord

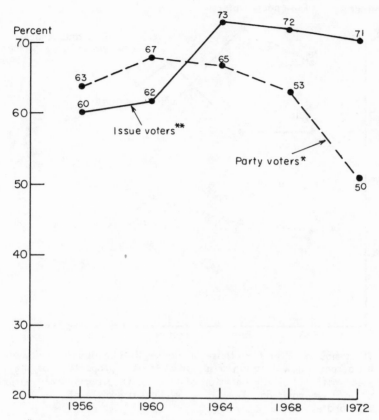

* Proportion of those with a partisan identification who voted
  consistently with that identification.
** Proportion of those with coherent issue position who vote in
  accord with that issue position (includes partisans and
  Independents with coherent positions).

FIGURE 16.6. Party voting and issue voting, 1956–1972

with issues and party. In figure 16.7 we show the proportion of the electorate that falls in this "reinforced" group whose vote is consistent with both party and issues. We compare this group to the proportion of the electorate who can be considered "pure party voters" and the proportion who are "pure issue voters." The pure party voters vote in accord with their party identification but *not* in accord with their issue position (either because they have no coherent issue position or because they have such a position but it is incongruent with their partisanship and they choose party over issues). The pure issue voters vote in accord with their issue position, but *not* with their party identification

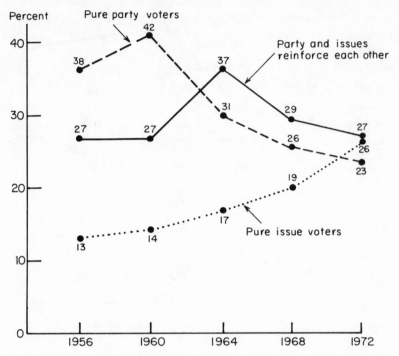

These figures differ from those on figure 16.6 because we calculate the percentage voting in particular ways as a proportion of the electorate, not as a proportion of those with a party identification or an issue position. The figure provides a profile of the electorate.

FIGURE 16.7. Issue voting, party voting, issue and party voting, 1956–1972

(either because they are Independents who have no party identification or because they have incongruent issue and party positions and vote the former).

From 1960 to 1964 there is a decrease in the pure party voters. But it is matched by a rise in the reinforced proportion who vote both party and issues simultaneously. Only after 1964 does one see a decline in the proportion of voters voting in accord with party. Between 1964 and 1972 the proportion of voters who vote issues and party simultaneously and the proportion of voters who vote party but not issues fall by 9 and 7 percent respectively. At the same time the proportion of voters who abandon party to vote their issue position rises.

Issues, Party, and the Vote: A Decomposition

The complex interaction among issue position, party affiliation, and the vote can be summarized through a decomposition of variance. The analysis enables us to separate the percent of the variance in the vote that is directly attributable to party identification from that directly attributable to attitudes on political issues. In addition, the technique permits us to identify the proportion of the variance in the vote that stems from the effect of these two factors working together. This "shared" component of the variance can be directly attributed neither to party identification alone nor to political attitudes alone. Rather, it reflects the joint effect of the two forces when they reinforce each other.

The results of the analysis are in figure 16.8[8]. In 1956 and 1960, approximately 45 percent of the variance in the presidential vote is uniquely

---

[8] There is no agreed upon statistical method for identifying and decomposing the variance in a multiple regression equation containing independent variables that (a) are correlated and (b) have no specified causal ordering. The technique which we utilize to establish the proportion of the explained variance in the direction of the presidential vote in each year attributable (1) uniquely to partisan identification, (2) uniquely to the attitudes on the issues, or (3) to their inseparable joint effects (or commonalities) is variously known as "flip-flop regression," "analysis of shared effects," or "analysis of commonalities." See Jae-on Kim and others, "Voter Turnout Among the American States: Systemic and Individual Components," *American Political Science Review,* 69 (March 1975); *Statistical Package for the Social Sciences, Second Edition* (New York: McGraw-Hill, 1975), pp. 389–392; and Fred N. Kerlinger and Elazar J. Pedhazur, *Multiple Regression in Behavioral Research* (New York: Holt, Rinehart and Winston, 1973), pp. 297–305.

The problem which requires a decomposition of the variance into these three components is the presence of significant numbers of individuals who are liberal Democrats or conservative Republicans (earlier referred to as "reinforced partisan voters"). It is impossible to determine for these individuals which of the two variables is responsible for their voting choice or to establish a casual priority. The notion of "commonality" or "shared variance" enables us to talk about the *combined* effects of these two forces.

To partition the variance, a step-wise regression procedure is used, specifying two equations. In the first equation, party identification is brought in first; the attitudes are stepped-in next, and the increment in the squared correlations between step 1 and step 2 is thus obtained. This process is then repeated with the second equation, which forces in the attitude index on the first step and brings in party identity on the second. One again, the increment in squared correlations between step 1 and step 2 is noted. This procedure yields (for each independent variable) the "most" conservative estimate of its *unique* contribution to the direction of the presidential vote. These unique contributions are added together, and the sum is subtracted from the total squared correlation obtained when both variables are present in the equation. Because the independent variables are positively correlated to at least some degree in each year, the sum of their direct effects will always be less than this squared correlation. This difference is the joint effect, shared variance, or (as Kerlinger and Pedhazur put it) "commonality." In years when the two independent variables are highly correlated, this shared variance is large—provided both independent variables are strongly correlated with the vote. In verbal terms, this reflects the presence of a large number of liberal Democrats and conservative Republicans who cast their votes on the basis of both of these consistent forces.

In figure 16.9, the decomposition of the variance into three components is expressed as a percent of the total variance explained by the two independent variables. Each year's total explained variance (that is, the denominator) is located at the bottom of the figure under its appropriate year. This standardization relative to the total variance explained enables us to compare the *relative* importance of the three sources of variation, even though the total amount of variance explained differs substantially from election to election.

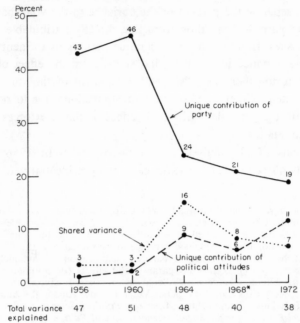

FIGURE 16.8. Percent of variance in presidential vote uniquely attributable to party identification, to political attitudes, and to their shared component, 1956–1972

attributable to party identification, with a minuscule 1 to 2 percent of the variance directly traceable to the citizen's position on the issue scale. In addition, only 3 percent of the variance in the vote is attributable to the joint impact of party identification and attitudes. It is easy to see why the early election studies concluded that party identification was the prime force in American voting behavior and that issues played a negligible role. In 1964, however, there is a rather dramatic shift in the weight of these forces. The direct contribution of party identification drops from 46 percent in 1960 to 24 percent in 1964. The independent contribution of beliefs rises sharply. In 1960, it explained about 2 percent of the variance in the vote; in 1964, 9 percent. The most dramatic increase, however, is in the joint impact of party and issue position on the vote. The percent of shared variance jumps from 3 percent in 1960 to 15 percent in 1964.

The data for 1964 indicate that party was still important. If one adds the variance that party shares with issues to that directly attributable to party alone, one finds partisan affiliation continuing to play a prime role. But what declines between 1960 and 1964 is the independent role of party. What grows most noticeably is the reinforcing effect of party and political beliefs. Issues grow in importance, but in 1964 they work along with partisanship.

The relative role of party affiliation and political beliefs changes again between 1964 and 1972—almost as much as it does between 1960 and 1964. For one thing, the independent effect of party identification falls further. In contrast, there is another significant jump in the independent impact of political beliefs. Finally, the amount of variance attributable to the two forces together falls back to a level only marginally above that if 1956 and 1960.

The data in figure 16.8 highlight the shift in the role of our two forces: party and issues. The 1956 and 1960 presidential elections appear to have been dominated by habitual partisan loyalties. Partisanship alone accounts for almost 50 percent of the variance in the presidential vote. Positions on issues play almost no role. The year 1964 brings a decline in pure party voting. In that presidential election and the two subsequent ones, habitual party attachments play a reduced role. And from 1964 onward, political issues play a growing role in determining the direction of the vote. There is, however, a major difference between the 1964 and the 1972 election. In 1964, partisan loyalty and issues appear to be reinforcing factors for a large portion of the citizenry, with liberal Democrats voting for the Democratic candidate and conservative Republicans voting for the Republican candidate. This is precisely what the high percentage of shared variance means.

The pattern for 1972 is very different. Beliefs now appear to be an *independent* force in determining the direction of the vote. A much smaller proportion of the impact of issues stems from their joint impact with party identification. At the same time, the direct impact of party identification seems to take a further decline—though it still has important independent effects. As we indicated earlier, the data show the decline not demise of party effects. Nevertheless, 1972 clearly represents a further loosening of the electorate from its reliance on partisan attachments.

Issue-based voting and party-based voting are not, in any simple way, opposites. As the former rises in frequency, the latter does not necessarily decline. Party and issue voting reinforced each other in 1964. Under such circumstances, issue coherence furthers the differentiation between the two political parties and increases the likelihood that citizens will vote consistently with their party affiliation. Conversely, issue position can lower the impact of partisanship on the vote if it pulls the citizen in a direction different from that of his partisan inclination. This happens more frequently in 1972.

But even when, as in 1964, issue position appears to reinforce partisanship, it changes the nature of the relationship between partisanship and the vote. In the pre-1964 elections, pure party voting predominates. Partisan voting is essentially habitual voting (or perhaps voting reinforced by a favorable image of the candidate's personal qualifications).

Party voting in 1964 appears to be based much more on issue differentiation between the parties. The two-party support groups face each other across an issue divide: conservative Republicans on one side, liberal Democrats on the other. Habitual party ties may also hold the party groupings together and add an impetus to the vote. Indeed, where the two—issue orientation and party identification—line up together, it is hard to distinguish the one from the other as a force determining the vote. But the party groupings in 1964 are clearly issue-based collectivities.

A party system such as that in 1964 is quite different from that of the Eisenhower years. But such a clear differentiation between the political parties does not last very long. By 1972, as we have seen, the Democratic electorate is no longer lined up clearly on the left. Many more voters are in incongruous positions, with issues pushing one way, partisanship the other. And in such circumstances we can differentiate the relative impact of party and issues. Forty-eight percent of the citizens who were faced with such contrary pressures vote in the direction they are pushed by the issues. This is still a minority, but a much larger one than the 20 or so percent who chose the issue alternative in the elections of 1956 and 1960.

The years 1972 and 1964 differ in another way. Not only do we find that partisans are more likely to be pulled away from their party by their issue position, we also find an increase in the proportion of Independents in the electorate. And these Independents add to the issue component of the vote. Not only are they more numerous than in 1964, they also are more likely to have coherent issue positions and to vote consistently with those positions. In this way they increase the proportion of the electorate for whom issues play a more important role than party.

17 | Candidates and the Electorate

The crucial transition year for the elections we have been studying is 1964. That is the year when the public becomes more issue oriented and when its issue positions develop a coherence they did not previously have. At the same time citizens begin to vote consistently with their issue positions. It is the year when partisan commitment begins to erode. Pure party voting—that is, a vote for the candidate of the party with whom one identifies even if that vote is not in accord with one's issue inclination—declines. Most important of all, 1964 appears to be a threshold. The changes that come in that year persist.

But 1964 is a year of change in another respect. Barry Goldwater runs on the Republican ticket as a candidate offering the American public a choice rather than an echo. He takes an issue position further from the center of the issue continuum than that taken by candidates preceding him. And in the next two presidential elections, other candidates run who occupy issue positions not in the center of the issue continuum. In 1968, the "issue outlier" is George Wallace with a position far to the right of center; in 1972, George McGovern takes a position at the left of the issue space. In each of the elections from 1964 through 1972 the outlying candidate is opposed by a candidate who takes a more central position on the issue space—in 1964 Johnson occupies a more centrist position; in 1968 we assume that both Nixon and Humphrey were closer to the center than was Wallace; and in 1972 Nixon was closer to the center than McGovern.

If we were to try to assign the various candidates in the elections we have been studying to positions on an issue scale similar to that which we have used to place the citizenry, we might assign the candidates to positions as in figure 17.1 In the elections before 1964, both candidates would likely fall within the center third of our issue position scale. From 1964 onward there would be a candidate whose position on the issues placed him in the left or right segment of the issue scale, while his opponent (or opponents, as in 1968) would be in the center.

The characterization of the elections in terms of the location of the candidates on the issue scale used to categorize the public is speculative. We do not know, in any precisely measurable way, where the candidates stood on a general left-right issue scale. Nor do we know—what may be more important for our purposes—where the public perceived the candidates as standing.[1] However, in a few cases we can compare the public's issue position with the perceptions of the public as to the location of the candidates on those same issues. In 1972, citizens were asked to place themselves on seven-point scales on a number of issues. The positions can be arrayed from left to right. In figure 17.2 we present several of these scales: attitudes on government guarantee of jobs, on increasing taxes on the rich, on strategy for Vietnam, on the legalization of marijuana, and on urban unrest. We also record the proportion of the population falling at each of the seven points on the scale. Using these percentages we can divide the population into those in the left third of the distribution on each issue, those in the center third, and those in the right third (or the nearest approximation that the distribution of percentages allows to a division into equal thirds).

In addition, citizens were asked to place Nixon and McGovern on these various issue scales. We have placed the average response for the two candidates on the scale. These figures tell us where, on average, the public perceived the two candidates to stand on the respective issues.

In all of the cases, Nixon's average position falls in the center third of the issue preference scale. In three out of five of the cases, McGovern falls clearly in the left segment of the population. On one of the issues on which he falls in the center third—tax increase for the rich—he falls much closer to the border of the left position than Nixon falls close to the border of the right

---

[1] For an analysis of candidate position see Benjamin R. Page, *Choices and Echoes in Presidential Elections,* forthcoming.

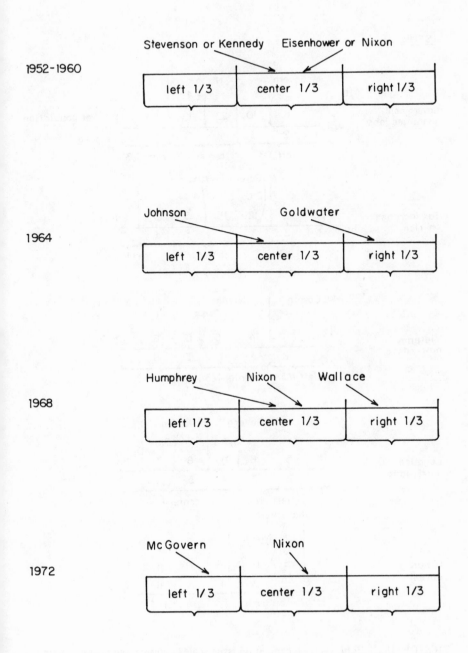

FIGURE 17.1. Hypothetical issue stances of the candidates, 1952–1972

ISSUE

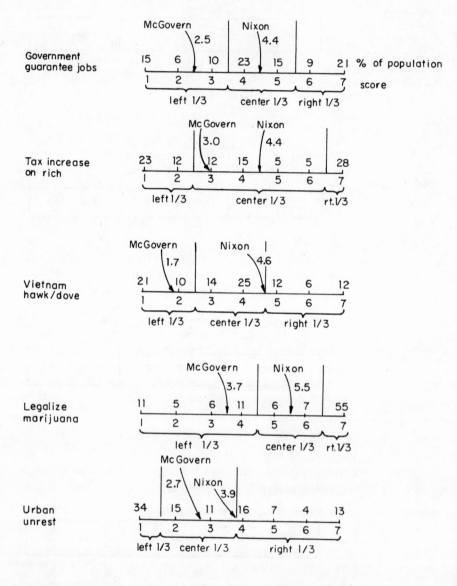

FIGURE 17.2. Public self-placement on issue scales and average position assigned to candidate, 1972

position. Only on the urban unrest issue does McGovern appear closer to the middle of the issue preference scale than does Nixon. It is clear that if we were to take an average of the positions assigned to McGovern and to Nixon, we would find the former to be perceived by the public to be an outlying candidate with policy positions to the left of the public as a whole, while Nixon would be firmly established in the middle.[2]

The existence of a candidate like McGovern (or Goldwater or Wallace) creates a greater issue distance between the alternative candidates. And such distance should foster issue voting. When both candidates are close to each other in issue space—as in elections between two centrist candidates—there is less reason to expect issue voting. Citizens may have one candidate who is perceived to be closer to them on the issues, but the relative closeness will be slight. It may not be enough to overcome the pull of other forces such as party.

As we have seen, since 1964 many more are voting consistently with their issue position, the most dramatic change being in the proportion voting their issue position when it is incongruent with their partisan affiliation. Does this result from the new structure of citizen attitudes and the new relationship between their attitudes and their behavior? Or is it largely that a new set of alternatives has been offered to the American public?[3]

Citizen attitudes become more coherent at the same time as the relationship between issue positions and the vote increases. And both of these changes in the citizenry appear in 1964—the first election with a clear outlying candidate. This makes it hard to separate the effect of one change from that of the others. Ideally one would want to see how the American public in the 1950s—given the weaker structure of political attitudes then and their weaker relationship to the vote—would have reacted to a choice involving an outlying candidate whose political position was far from the center of the political spectrum. Conversely, one would want to see how the public after 1964 would react to a choice between two centrist candidates, given the new coherence of political attitudes and their connection with the vote. Would they react as did the public in the 1950s to a choice between two centrist candidates?

---

[2] As Page points out, however, many people may have misplaced McGovern. On specific issues, he was not as far to the left as the public believed. *Choices and Echoes in Presidential Elections.*

[3] Each element is important. See Duncan Black, *The Theory of Committees and Elections* (Cambridge: Cambridge University Press, 1957); Anthony Downs, *An Economic Theory of Democracy* (New York: Harper and Row, 1957).

We may be able to approximate such a circumstance through our mock election studies. In a survey conducted for us by the National Opinion Research Center in 1973, we presented our samples with a series of mock elections. How would they vote, we asked, if the 1976 election were being held now, and————were the Democratic candidate and————were the Republican candidate? They were asked about five pairs of candidates: McGovern vs. Goldwater, Humphrey vs. Percy, Kennedy vs. Percy, Humphrey vs. Reagan, and Kennedy vs. Reagan. The pairings were chosen to provide us with a variety of types of choice. The McGovern/Goldwater choice was intended to provide a choice between two candidates each with a position far from the center of the issue scale. The Humphrey/Percy choice was intended to provide two candidates closer to the ideological center, as was the choice between Kennedy and Percy. The Humphrey/Reagan and the Kennedy/Reagan races were intended to reproduce the pattern of the 1964 election with a centrist Democrat opposing a Republican candidate from the right of the ideological spectrum.[4]

The mock elections are hardly ideal experiments. We are not sure that the candidates in fact occupy the position on the issue scale we assume that they occupy.[5] The clearest cases appear to be the McGovern-Goldwater race with two outlying candidates, and the Humphrey/Percy race with two comparatively centrist candidates. In addition, the mock elections take place outside the context of an actual election. The positions of candidates were by no means salient to the respondent. How they would react in the midst of an election cannot necessarily be predicted by our results. We did phrase our question in such a way that the respondent could easily respond that he "did not know enough about the candidates to judge." That alternative was explicitly suggested as a possibility. And many respondents took that option.[6]

---

[4] In the winter of 1973, when the NORC survey was conducted, these candidates appeared to be the most reasonable pairings. Neither the Nixon nor Agnew resignations had taken place, and Gerald Ford was still a congressman from Michigan.

[5] We are also not convinced that our electorate sees the "elections" as we see them. Each candidate in each pairing is not equally known, and this could affect choice even when those who do know both candidates place them on the same ideological ground that we did in designing the pairings. For discussion and for some similar mock elections, see Benjamin I. Page and Richard A. Brody, "Policy Voting and the Electoral Process: The Vietnam War Issue," *American Political Science Review,* 66 (September 1972).

[6] The proportion who reported an inability to choose between the candidates ranged from a high of 41 percent in the Humphrey-Percy pairing to a low of 16 percent in the Kennedy-Reagan pairing. The exact question was: "If the 1976 election were being held now (December 1973), and *Hubert Humphrey* were the Democratic candidate and *Charles Percy* were the Republican candidate, who would you vote for? Or perhaps you *don't know* enough about them now to make a choice?" They were then asked, for the remaining four pairs: "What if (the appropriate name) were the Democratic candidate

This, we believe, improves the validity of our data. We preferred to have the election choice made by respondents who had some notion of who the alternative candidates were and what they stood for, even if this meant that many respondents were nonvoters in the election. Our goal is not to predict the election outcome, but to see the functional relationship between issues and partisanship on the one hand and the vote on the other. Our assumption is that the nonvoters, if they became better informed about the candidates, would choose on the same basis as did those who made a choice.

We wish to use the mock elections to answer the following questions: How would the post-1964 public with its higher level of issue coherence respond to an electoral choice involving two relatively centrist candidates? Would it respond as did the less issue-consistent public of the 1950s to the centrist choices offered then and vote on the basis of party affiliation rather than issue position? Or would it respond like the public in 1964, 1968, and 1972 when outlying candidates were in the field and vote more frequently on the basis of issue position?

We can explain our mock election experiments by putting them into the framework of the three components of change we have been discussing: the increase in the number of citizens with coherent issue positions; the strengthening of the functional relationship between issue position and the vote; and the kind of candidate choice offered the public. Our independent variable is the candidate-choice component. We vary that by offering the respondent different mock election choices. The dependent variable is the functional relationship between issue position and the vote. And the third component—the level of issue coherence in the public—is held constant. As we have seen in Chapter 7, the 1973 study revealed a population with a level of issue consis-

---

and the Republican candidate were (the appropriate name)?" The results of the mock elections were:

		Don't know enough	Wouldn't vote
(1) Humphrey 30%	Percy 22%	41%	7%
(2) Goldwater 34%	McGovern 36%	20%	10%
(3) Kennedy 44%	Percy 27%	24%	5%
(4) Humphrey 43%	Reagan 30%	19%	8%
(5) Kennedy 51%	Reagan 27%	16%	6%

The rather high proportion of voters who reported in the first pairing that they didn't know enough about the candidates to make a selection is at least partly a consequence of the fact that the question was asked first and that the voters were explicitly given the option to report that they didn't know enough.

tency quite similar to the high levels found in all the studies from 1964 onward. In this sense, the sample in our 1973 study can be taken to represent the public of the post-1964 period, a public with much more coherent issue positions.

Our experiment would be invalid, however, if the coherence of political attitudes were inextricably intertwined with the nature of the choice offered the electorate. As we have pointed out, it may well be that the rise in issue coherence around the 1964 election is in part the consequence of the choice offered the public at that time. If issue coherence results from exposure to candidates with positions near the ends of our issue scale and does not exist without such exposure, it becomes meaningless to ask how an issue-coherent public such as that in our 1973 study would react to centrist candidates. If there were no outlying candidates, their issue positions would not be coherent.

However, we do not believe that issue coherence and the availability of candidates from the issue extremes are totally dependent one on another (though they may be related). As we have shown, when issue coherence rose in 1964, it reached a new level that was maintained across the remaining election studies. The effect of Goldwater—if it was the effect of Goldwater—remained into other elections when he was not running. More important, we find the same high level of issue consistency in nonelection years—in our NORC studies in 1971 and 1973—when there was no electoral choice to give issues their coherence. The point is that the new levels of issue coherence may result from the particular candidate choice offered the electorate after 1964. But it appears to be a long-term consequence of that choice. Issue coherence does not appear in response to the specific stimuli of an election and then fade away when the campaign ends. It thus becomes meaningful to ask how the public—with its post-1964 structure—would react to candidates who were not like those of the 1964, 1968, and 1972 elections.

Let us begin with the most distinctive pattern change since the 1964 election: the growing proportion of voters who when faced with incongruity between their issue position and their partisan affiliation vote on the basis of the former. As we saw in the previous chapter the proportion of voters who choose issue over party when the two conflict rose from 22 and 24 percent in 1956 and 1960 to 48 percent in 1972. Table 17.1 repeats these data for the six elections from 1956 to 1972 and compares them to the data for the mock elections in 1973.

The data offer strong evidence that the nature of the choice offered the citizenry affects the functional relationship between issue position and partisan identification on the one hand and the vote on the other. When the public is offered a choice of two outlying candidates—McGovern vs. Goldwater—

TABLE 17.1. Issue voting in real and mock elections, 1956–1972

Among those whose party affiliation is incongruent with their issue position	Real election					Mock election, 1973				
	1956	1960	1964	1968	1972	McGovern/Goldwater	Humphrey/Percy	Kennedy/Percy	Humphrey/Reagan	Kennedy/Reagan
Percent who defect from their party to vote their issue position	22	24	36	41	48	44	24	24	32	27
Percent who stick with their party	$\frac{77}{100}$	$\frac{80}{100}$	$\frac{65}{100}$	$\frac{59}{100}$	$\frac{52}{100}$	$\frac{56}{100}$	$\frac{76}{100}$	$\frac{76}{100}$	$\frac{68}{100}$	$\frac{73}{100}$

the frequency of issue voting is high. In that mock election, 44 percent of the voters whose issue position is incongruent with their party affiliation vote consistently with the former. The 44 percent figure is quite close to the figures found for the real elections from 1964 to 1972—it is, in fact, halfway between the figures of 41 percent and 48 percent for 1968 and 1972. On the other hand, when the candidates are more centrist—as in the Humphrey/ Percy race or the Kennedy/Percy race—the proportion who defect from their party's candidate to vote on the basis of their issue position falls to 24 percent, a proportion quite similar to that found in the elections of 1956 and 1960. In the early elections, when party identification was the key to the vote, three out of four voters in our incongruent party and issue position stuck by their party identification when it came to the vote. In 1973, when we gave the public a choice that was supposed to maximize party choice and minimize issue differences, a similar proportion of three out of four voters choose the partisan alternative.

The two elections involving Ronald Reagan fall somewhere in between the other elections. When Reagan runs against Humphrey, the proportion who vote on the issues is 32 percent—fairly close to the figure for the real election in 1964 (the real election to which the Reagan/Humphrey choice is probably most analogous). The Reagan/Kennedy race, on the other hand, produces a proportion of issue voting about halfway between the pattern of the pre-1964 elections and the pattern for the elections from 1964 onward.[7]

The comparison between the real and mock elections is even clearer if we consider all voters in either the left or right category of our issue scale. These consist of those voters with issue positions incongruent with their party identification, voters with congruent issue and party positions, and Independents who are not in the center of the issue scale. Table 17.2 reports the percentage of that combined group who vote in ways that are consistent with their issue position. For the real elections we see data already familiar to us (see figure 16.4). The breaking point is between the 1960 and 1964 elections. In the earlier elections, the proportion of those with a coherent issue position who vote on the basis of that position ranges from 60 percent to 62 percent. After 1964, the percentage is consistently over 70 percent.

If one compares these data to the mock elections, one finds similar variation among the latter elections. The election with two outlying candidates (McGovern vs. Goldwater) is similar to the elections from 1964 through 1972 in terms of the proportion of voters who vote for the candidate consis-

---

[7] The high level of party voting in the Kennedy–Reagan race is due to the ability of Kennedy to hold on to conservative Democrats. It is clear that there are a lot of candidate effects involved here, not merely issues and party.

TABLE 17.2. Proportion of voters with coherent issue positions voting consistently with that position, in real and mock elections, 1956–1972[a]

Real election		Mock election	
1956	60	McGovern-Goldwater	74
1960	62	Kennedy-Reagan	70
1964	73	Humphrey-Reagan	69
1968	72	Humphrey-Percy	62
1972	71	Kennedy-Percy	66

[a] The figures are the percentages voting consistently with their issue position from three groups combined: partisans with incongruent issue positions (the defectors), partisans with congruent issue positions (the reinforced), and Independents on the left or right.

tent with their issue position. And the proportion is similar for the two elections with one outlying candidate—the Humphrey/Reagan race and the Kennedy/Reagan race. On the other hand the centrist contest between Humphrey and Percy produces a proportion of issue voting among those with a coherent issue position quite similar to that in the pre-1964 period. The Kennedy/Percy race, on the other hand, falls in between the two types of elections for reasons that are not completely apparent to us, but probably have a lot to do with personal appeal.

The data in tables 17.1 and 17.2 support the position that the functional relationship between issue position and the vote is in good part a reflection of the choices offered the public. Despite the increase around 1964 in the proportion of the populace that has relatively consistent political attitudes, the populace in recent years does not look that different in terms of the proportion of those with such consistent attitudes who would vote on issue grounds. If the proportion of those with issue positions who vote consistently with that position appears to have risen from the pre-1964 elections to the ones from 1964 onward, the main reason appears to be the nature of the choice offered. If a more centrist set of candidates had been offered after 1964, the public would likely have reacted as it did in the earlier elections.

This does not mean, though, that issue voting is no more important after 1964 than before. Remember the distinction between the proportion of the electorate with consistent issue positions (the pool of potential issue voters) and the proportion of that group that votes on the issues. The latter component of the electoral process does not appear to have changed from the early to the late elections (if one controls for the nature of the candidate choice).

But there is a larger pool of citizens with consistent issue positions. Thus even if a centrist candidate were to run in the post-1964 period, the proportion of issue voters in the electorate would be larger, because the pool of potential issue voters would be larger—this despite the fact that the proportion of that pool choosing the issue-congruent alternative would not be different from the proportion in earlier years.[8]

Our mock elections in 1973 are by no means perfect experiments. By providing an election alternative like that offered the electorate before 1964, we do not reconstruct the electoral atmosphere then, but only simulate one aspect of it. The ideal experiment would be to take the society as it existed in one or the other of the presidential years and to run various pairs of candidates in a real campaign setting. But we have neither the time machine, the resources, nor the constitutional authority to do so. Thus we must stick to our mock elections.

The data do indicate that the new role of issues in the elections since 1964 is, in good part, a reaction to the nature of the candidates offered. If the public is faced with candidates distinguished from each other on the basis of the issues, it will vote on the issues. If the public is offered a more centrist choice, the vote will depend much more heavily on partisan identification.

---

[8] This can be illustrated by a comparison of the Humphrey–Percy "centrist" mock election in 1973 and the "centrist" real elections of 1956 and 1960. The Humphrey–Percy contest was similar to the earlier real elections in terms of the proportion of potential issue voters who voted consistently with their issue positions. The average voting that way for the early elections is 61 percent; the figure for the Humphrey–Percy contest is 62 percent. But in 1956 and 1960, 65 percent of the electorate had coherent issue positions. In 1973, 75 percent of the electorate had coherent positions. This means that about 40 percent of the electorate in 1956 and 1960 were issue voters—they had coherent positions and voted consistently with them. In 1973, we find 47 percent to be issue voters.

18 | Issue Voting: A Further Analysis

A simple but important theme runs through much of this book: the public responds to the political stimuli offered it. The political behavior of the electorate is not determined solely by psychological and sociological forces, but also by the issues of the day and by the way in which candidates present those issues. If candidates offer clear issue alternatives, voters are more likely to make political issues a criterion for electoral choice. In this sense the public does respond to candidates who offer a choice rather than an echo. But unfortunately for the candidate who offers the choice, the public seems to choose the echo. In 1964, it was Goldwater who offered the clear issue alternative; in 1972 it was McGovern. And each went down to defeat to the more centrist candidate.

The electoral defeats of Goldwater and McGovern resulted from a complex combination of forces, not merely from their issue positions. As we showed in Chapter 16, issue voting has increased, but by no means does it explain all of the voting decision—even in elections such as 1964 and 1972 that were heavily issue oriented. Party still plays an important (though diminishing) role. And, as figures 16.2 and 16.3 of Chapter 16 make clear, personal evaluations of the candidates are still significant components of the electoral decision—roughly as important as issue evaluations even at the height of issue importance. Goldwater and

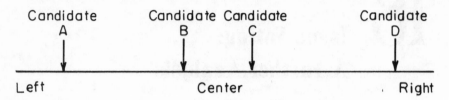

FIGURE 18.1. Candidates on left-right issue space

McGovern lost in part because of who they were (or who they were perceived to be) as well as because of what they stood for (or were perceived to stand for).

However, their issue positions were important. As we have seen, issue voting was particularly central in the 1964 and 1972 elections. Spatial analysis of voting would predict that the candidate who establishes a position far from the center of the population on an issue scale will do less well than a candidate closer to the center—in those cases when citizens decide their vote on the basis of political issues. This is illustrated in figure 18.1. Assume that we can meaningfully array citizens along a single left-right continuum (which our data indicate is a more reasonable though still simplifying assumption after 1964). Assume also that voters are equally distributed along the continuum (which is the case for the issue scale we have been using).[1] It is clear that if voters vote for the nearest candidate, the candidate nearest to the center gets more votes. If, for instance, a left outlying candidate such as candidate A runs against a candidate slightly to the right of center such as Candidate C, more voters are close to C than A. The same is true if a right outlying candidate such as D runs against a slightly left of center candidate such as B. In each of these contests—A running against C or B running against D—we would expect a lot of issue voting, and we would expect the issue voting to go against the outlying candidate.

If A runs against D, we would also expect a good deal of issue voting, but it ought not to favor one candidate over the other. Lastly, if B runs against C, there ought to be little issue voting, nor should the benefit of what issue voting there is go to one candidate rather than the other.

In the previous chapter we considered the amount of issue voting and have seen our expectations borne out. When A runs against C (McGovern v. Nixon) or B runs against D (Johnson v. Goldwater) we found substantial

---

[1] This is so simply because we have been dividing the scale into equal thirds in terms of numbers of respondents or, as in this chapter, into equal tenths. A more realistic array of issue positions would be a bell shaped curve. This of course would make the position of an outlying candidate even worse.

issue voting, as we did when A runs against D (in the McGovern-Goldwater mock election). On the other hand, when two centrist candidates ran (as in 1956 or 1960 or in several of the other mock elections), there was less issue voting. In this chapter we want to look at the direction of issue voting: which candidate benefits?

Figure 18.2 presents some hypothetical voting patterns for various kinds of election contests. On each graph we plot on the vertical axis the proportion of the vote going to the Democratic candidate (whom we assume also to be the more left of the candidates) and on the horizontal, the respondent's position on the left-right scale. Assuming that respondents vote in accord with their issue position, one would expect the following patterns.

A. In section A of figure 18.2 we present the hypothetical result of a contest between a right-wing outlying candidate and a candidate slightly to the left of center. If the spatial expectations are correct, issues should play a major role. But more issue voting ought to go to the centrist candidate. The right-wing outlying candidate should do well with voters close to his end of the scale. But as one moves toward the center of the scale, votes ought to shift quickly to the centrist candidate. The centrist ought to dominate the votes near the center of the scale as well as the votes of those to the left of center. Those voters on the far left of the issue scale are not particularly close to the centrist candidate but they are much closer to him than to the rightist. The centrist should hold their vote quite well, if only because voters are strongly motivated to vote against the right candidate.

B. Section B is the mirror image of section A. When a left outlier runs against a candidate slightly to the right of center we expect the opposite to happen. The left outlier should do well only with those voters at the left extreme of the issue scale. His vote should fall off quickly as one moves toward the middle. The centrist candidate should hold voters from the middle as well as the right end of the scale.

C. Example C pits two outliers against each other. There is a lot of issue voting. But such an election is more balanced, with each candidate likely to hold those voters at his own end of the issue scale. They divide the voters in between.

D. Example D plots the expectation for a contest between two centrists. Issue position ought to play less of a role, as is seen from the flatness of the line.

We can compare these expectations to the voting data we have for various elections. We do this by dividing our respondents in each election year into equal tenths on the left-right issue scale. Thus we can compare the vote of those in the left-most decile of the issue scale with those in the next decile

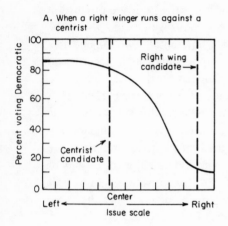

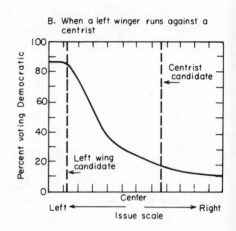

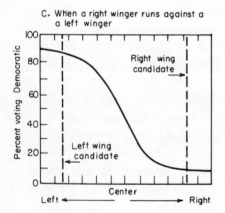

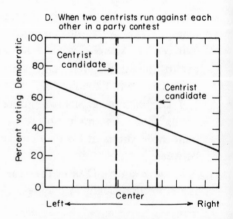

FIGURE 18.2. Some hypothetical voting patterns

and so forth all the way across to the right-most 10 percent. On figure 18.3 we show the proportion of the electorate voting for the Democratic candidate in each of five elections. Three of the elections offer a pair of candidates similar to those in the hypothetical examples A, B, and C, respectively, in figure 18.2, and two elections offer candidates resembling those specified in example D.

A. Section A of figure 18.3 reports the data on the 1964 election. It resembles the hypothetical pattern on figure 18.2 quite closely. Goldwater dominates only among those voters in the far right decile of the electorate; he gets 76 percent of their votes. But as one moves toward the center his vote falls off sharply. He receives a majority of the vote from the next decile, but not from any other group. Johnson, in contrast, gets about 60 to 70 percent of the vote from the next four deciles as we move left and over 80 percent of the vote from the left four deciles. In sum, issues appear to play a major role, and they tilt the electorate away from the right outlier.

B. The 1972 election is an almost perfect mirror image. McGovern dominates among those voters in the left-most decile of the electorate getting 76 percent of their vote, but he gets a majority only of that group and the one next to it. Nixon gets between about 60 to 70 percent of the next four deciles, and 70 percent or more of the four right deciles.[2]

C. The next example is our mock election between McGovern and Goldwater. Unlike the "unbalanced" elections of 1964 and 1972, the mock election is balanced with two outlying candidates running against each other. And the result is much more balanced. Each of the outlying candidates holds on to the voters at his own end of the scale—each gets over 70 percent of the vote of those voters in the three deciles closest to his end of the scale. The four center deciles divide their votes. McGovern gets over 60 percent of the two deciles to the left of the center point while Goldwater gets 60 percent or more from the two deciles to the right of the center point.

D. The last two examples are the centrist (party dominated) elections of 1956 and 1960. They differ quite sharply from the other examples. For one thing, the lines are much flatter, indicating a lesser relationship between issue position and the vote in those elections. For instance, the furthest left and right deciles on the issue scale do not differ as much in their vote as in the other elections. In 1964, there is a 74 percentage point spread between the

---

[2] James A. Stimson reports a similar assymetrical result for the 1972 election. Using a seven point liberal-conservative scale, he finds Nixon receiving two thirds or more of the vote in the three right categories and the center category; McGovern receives two-thirds or more only in the left two categories. James A. Stimson, "Belief Systems: Constraint, Complexity and the 1972 Election," *American Journal of Political Science,* 19 (August 1975), 393–418.

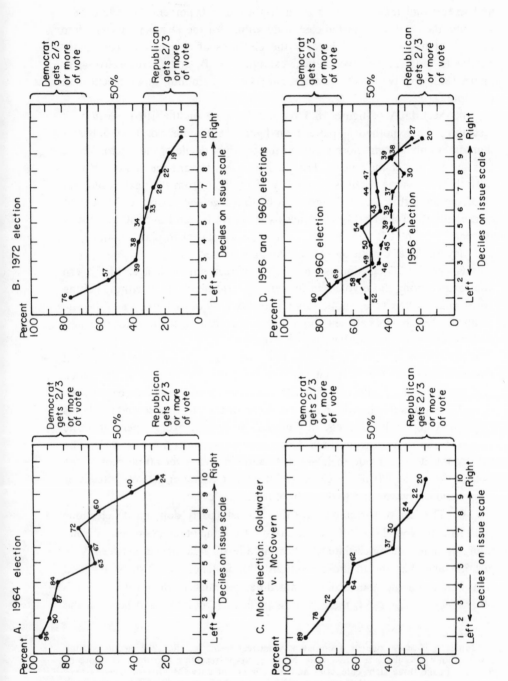

FIGURE 18.3. Percent voting Democratic by position on left-right issue scale

proportion voting Democratic at the left extreme of the scale and at the right extreme, in 1972, there is a 66 point spread, and in the mock election between McGovern and Goldwater there is a 69 point spread. But in the 1960 election the difference between the left and right deciles is 53 percent, and in 1956 it is only 32 percent.

The 1960 election is more balanced than the 1956 election: Kennedy gets 80 percent of the vote from the far left group, Nixon 73 percent from the far right group. In the 1956 election, Eisenhower gets 80 percent of the far right group but Stevenson gets only 52 percent of the far left group. It is unlikely, though, that this is due to the issue position of Eisenhower compared with that of Stevenson. As the relative flatness of the line indicates, issues play relatively little role in 1956. The tilt toward Eisenhower is—as these data suggest and other analysis confirm—much more a matter of his personal appeal.[3]

In sum, the data in figure 18.3 support the expectations derived from a spatial analysis of the vote. Issues play a role in an election of one or both of the candidates takes an outlying position on the issue scale. If each candidate takes a position at the opposite end of the issue spectrum, the election is "balanced" and they divide the vote—the leftist candidate taking most of those votes to the left of the scale; the rightist taking the right votes. But if one candidate is close to the center, while the other candidate is closer to the extreme, more voters find themselves closer to the centrist than to the outlier, and the vote tilts in favor of the former.[4]

---

[3] The comparison between the 1956 election and those in 1964 and 1972 is important. If we had only compared 1964 and 1972 with the more "balanced" elections in 1960 and the mock Goldwater–McGovern election, we would have been comparing two landslide victories (1964 and 1972) with two close contests (1960 and the mock election). The difference in the pattern of issue voting might be due to the difference in closeness of outcome rather than vice versa—that is, the imbalance in the issue voting might be due to the popularity of the centrist candidate not to his centrist position. The 1956 data are for another election with a landslide winner. The pattern of the issue vote is quite different when the victory is based on nonissue criteria.

[4] As Chapter 17 made clear, the differences among the elections that we see on figure 18.3 reflect differences in the choices offered the electorate. The two-party dominated elections (1956 and 1960) in section D take place before the change in issue importance around 1964. But if the public were given a party dominated choice after that, it would in all likelihood respond with a voting pattern similar to that in 1956 or 1960. Consider the results of the 1973 mock election that appears to be most party dominated, the choice between Humphrey and Percy. The accompanying figure (see p. 326) reports the percentage voting Democratic in each of the deciles of our issue scale.

The pattern is quite similar to the 1956 and 1960 elections. The Democratic candidate garners more than two-thirds of the vote only in the far left decile, the Republican only in the far right. Across the rest of the scale , the vote is more evenly divided. The flatness of the relationship is strikingly similar to the relatively flat lines found in section D of figure 18.3. (The Kennedy–Percy race produces a similar pattern, but one shifted in a Democratic direction, as Kennedy generally does better than Humphrey in a race against Percy.) *(footnote continued)*

It is interesting to note that this imbalance of the vote in favor of the centrist does not take place among voters at the issue extremes. Among those voters who are in the far right or far left categories of our issue scale, the centrist does not have a particular advantage. (But, it must be stressed, neither does he have a particular disadvantage!) Johnson loses almost all the votes of those voters in the far right decile of the issue scale, but he makes up for this

---

Footnote 4 continued

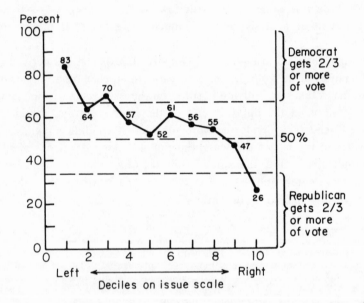

Percent voting Democratic in a Humphrey-Percy race by position on left-right issue scale

In a similar manner, we can recreate the Republican loss in 1964 by running a centrist Democrat such as Humphrey in a 1973 mock election against Ronald Reagan (see p. 327). The pattern is remarkably similar to that for the 1964 election as seen in figure 18.3, section A. Humphrey wins two-thirds or more of the vote in the four left deciles, over half the vote in the next three, and almost half in the eighth decile toward the right. Reagan does well only in the two right-most deciles, and gets over two-thirds of the vote in the right-most decile. (A Kennedy–Reagan race produces almost the same result.)

(footnote continued)

by winning almost all the votes of those in the far left. Nixon, in 1972, balances his loss among the far left voters with an impressive vote from the far right. It is only when one moves to more center deciles that the imbalance in favor of the centrist appears.

We can illustrate this in figure 18.4. There we compare the proportion of

Footnote 4 continued

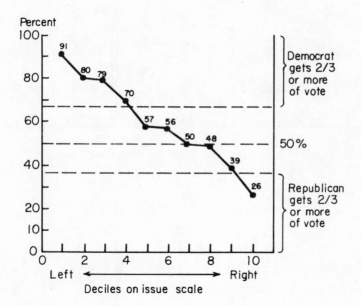

Percent voting Democratic in a Humphrey-Reagan race by position on left-right issue scale

These similarities between our mock elections and the real elections that parallel them are, we believe, quite striking and make our results quite convincing. The issue scale we use in 1973 is based on somewhat different questions from those in the studies of the real elections (and the latter scales differ as well from year to year). The particular candidates differ, though they are similar in ideological position. In 1973 we ask hypothetical choices. In the real elections we are dealing with real vote intentions or reports of actual votes. That such similar patterns appear out of such poor data is most encouraging.

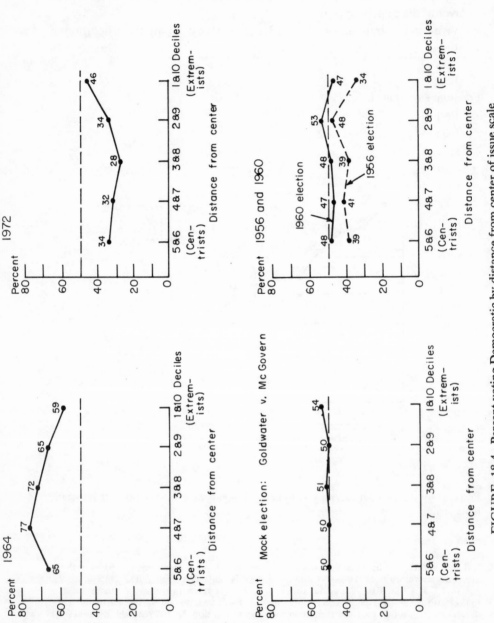

FIGURE 18.4. Percent voting Democratic by distance from center of issue scale

the vote going to the Democratic candidate among voters at various distances from the center of the issue spectrum—regardless of direction. We combine the fifth and sixth deciles of the issue scale to give us the centrists, the fourth and seventh to give us the group one step further to the extremes, and so on till we reach the extremists from deciles 1 and 10. Those nearer the extremes are the citizens with more consistent attitudes in either a left or right direction. As one can see from figure 18.4, the imbalance in favor of the centrist candidate tends to be greater near the center of the scale. In 1964, Johnson receives a majority from voters in all of the groups, but his majority is smallest among those in the outer categories of the issue scale. This reflects the balance noted earlier: what Johnson gains at the issue extremes from the leftists is balanced by a loss in votes among the rightists. Toward the center of the issue scale, Johnson's gains from those on the left are not balanced by losses on the right, and he does better.

The 1972 election is, as usual, the mirror image. When we look at the vote distribution of those at the left or right extreme of the scale, it is quite balanced: McGovern gets 46 percent, Nixon gets 54 percent. But as one moves closer to the center of the scale, the imbalance in favor of the centrist becomes quite apparent.

The mock election contrasts with the imbalanced ones. Because it is a balanced election the gain in votes that McGovern gets from leftists at any distance from the center of the issue continuum is balanced by losses of rightists to Goldwater in that group. As we can see, the two outlying candidates divide each of the groups equally.

Last, we consider the pattern for the two elections with relatively centrist candidates: 1956 and 1960. In 1960, Nixon and Kennedy divide the vote fairly equally in all of the groups. In 1956, Eisenhower wins a preponderance of the vote in each category. But the important point is that there is no clear relationship between the distance of a group from the center of the issue spectrum and Eisenhower's success. If anything, the imbalance is greater at the extreme end of the issue scale—just the opposite of the 1964 and 1972 patterns. The contrast with the pattern for 1964 and 1972 is important. All three elections—1956, 1964, and 1972—are landslides. But they are different kinds of landslides. In 1956, all issue groups—whether near the center of the issue scale or near the end—tilt toward Eisenhower. In 1964 and 1972, the data indicate that issue positions play a major role in how much of an imbalance there is for one candidate over the other.[5]

---

[5] We have not looked at the 1968 election from the point of view of issue space because of the complexity of the three-way race among Humphrey, Nixon, and Wallace. In

Party versus Issues

We can get further insight into the impact that issues have on the vote if we break the data in figure 18.3 down by party. On figure 18.5 we plot the proportions voting Democratic among Democrats, Republicans, and Independents at various points on the issue continuum. The data allow us to see the joint effect of issue position and party.

---

the accompanying figure we plot the proportion of Democratic vote found at various points on the issue scale. The pattern resembles that in 1972. Humphrey keeps over two-thirds of the vote only in the far left category. He loses over two-thirds of the vote in all five deciles to the right of center. The reason appears clear: he loses votes to Nixon and Wallace. If the opposition had been a right wing outlier such as Wallace, we might have expected a pattern such as that in the 1964 election. But Humphrey's opposition was a relatively centrist Republican and a rightist maverick Democrat. Thus there is a lot of issue voting (Humphrey gets only 14 percent of the vote from the far right decile but 78 percent from the far left decile) because there is an outlying candidate in the field. But the result is not the imbalance in favor of the Democrat found in 1964. Those voters who want a far right alternative can find one, and those who want a moderate right one can do so as well. This tilts the election away from the Democratic candidate.

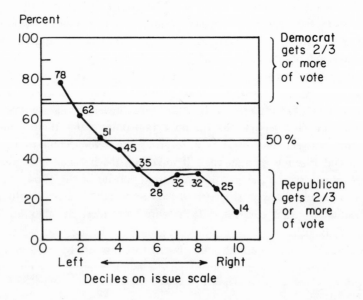

Percent voting Democratic in 1968 by position on left-right issue scale

The years 1964 and 1972 remain essentially mirror images of each other. Issues play a major role, but in each case they tilt the various party groupings in the direction of the centrist candidate.

Consider those voters whose party and issue position is not congruent— the Republicans at the liberal end of the issue continuum and the Democrats at the conservative end. In as issue-oriented race such as 1964 or 1972 we have seen that a good proportion of these voters leave their party to vote in accord with their issue position. But in each of these two elections, the centrist candidate is more successful in pulling such issue defectors from the opposition party than is the outlying candidate. In 1964, Johnson captures half or more of the vote from the four left deciles of Republicans. Goldwater does not obtain a majority from any of the Democratic groups. In 1972, it is Nixon who does better. He captures a majority of the vote from four out of five deciles of Democrats to the right of center, and he gets a strong majority from the two right-most deciles. On the other hand, McGovern does not break into the Republican ranks at all. Even among the left-most Republicans, he gets only 12 percent of the vote. In this the 1972 election differs from the 1964. Goldwater almost manages to pull a majority of the Democratic vote from the far right decile. McGovern does much worse with left Republicans.

The clearest evidence of the imbalance in the elections is seen in the middle two deciles of the issue scale. In 1964 Johnson does much better in holding centrist Democratic supporters than does Goldwater in holding Republican ones. If we combine the two center categories (deciles 5 and 6) we find that Johnson gets 96 percent of the vote of the centrist Democrats. Goldwater does less well; he gets 81 percent of the vote from the centrist Republicans. In 1972, the advantage is to Nixon. He gets 90 percent of the centrist Republicans, while McGovern gets only 50 percent of the centrist Democrats.

In sum, the party groups behave as one would expect for a spatial interpretation. The centrist candidate captures votes from the supporters of his opponent's party when those supporters are on the centrist's side of the issue scale or in the center. But the outlying candidate does less well in pulling votes from the opposition. Goldwater captures a majority of the Democratic vote only in the far right decile of the issue scale, and McGovern cannot break into the Republican vote at all.

We find a similar imbalance among the Independent voters. In 1964, Johnson captures about two-thirds or more of the vote from those Independents in the left and center of the scale. In fact, he does well among all Independents except those in the far right decile. Only among that far right group does Goldwater dominate the vote. In 1972 it is the opposite. Nixon

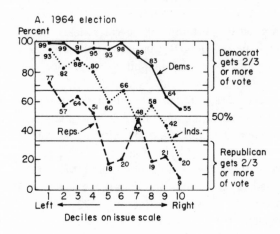

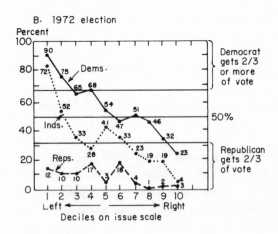

FIGURE 18.5. Percent voting Democratic by party affiliation and position on left-right issue scale

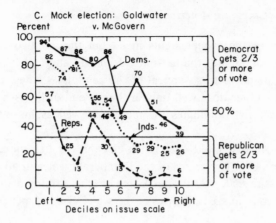

C. Mock election: Goldwater v. McGovern

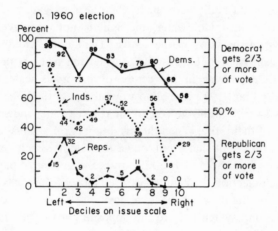

D. 1960 election

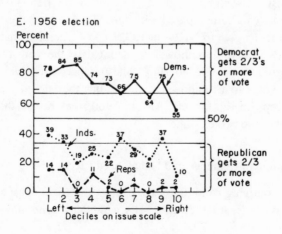

E. 1956 election

gets a majority of the Independents in all but the left two categories, and McGovern only dominates the left-most decile. In short, the 1964 and 1972 data illustrate the asymetrical appeal of the candidates when a centrist faces an outlier. The outlier does well only at the far end of the issue spectrum on his side. The centrist dominates the middle as well as his own end of the scale.

The McGovern v. Goldwater mock election is much more symmetrical. McGovern keeps over two-thirds of the Democratic votes in all of the left five deciles of the issue scale; Goldwater keeps over two-thirds of the Republican votes in all of the right six categories of the scale. The Independents split their votes fairly evenly.

The balance of the election is seen clearly if we look in the center of the issue scale. McGovern did badly with those middle groups when he ran against Nixon; Goldwater did badly with them when he ran against Johnson. When McGovern runs against Goldwater, the split is not as uneven. McGovern takes 68 percent of the votes of the centrist Democrats; Goldwater takes 78 percent of the centrist Republicans. Or consider the group with least to guide its vote: the Independents in the center of the issue scale. The outlying candidates in 1964 and 1972 lose almost two-thirds of the votes of this group. Goldwater gets 34 percent of the vote of the centrist Independents; McGovern gets 36 percent of their vote. When the two outliers run against each other, on the other hand, they split that group down the middle: each gets 50 percent. The two elections in 1956 and 1960 illustrate the impact of party in contrast to issues. In each election the candidates keep most of the votes of those from their own party no matter what the issue position. In no case does as much as one-third of a group switch over to the opposite party. The one exception is the far right decile of Democrats in 1956; it gives 45 percent of its vote to Eisenhower. But Eisenhower's ability to capture 45 percent of these right-wing Democrats can be compared with the 77 percent of the vote that these far right Democrats give to Nixon in 1972. The 45 percent that the conservative Democrats give to Eisenhower is identical to the vote they give to the much less popular Goldwater in 1964. The Independents give the preponderance of their votes to Eisenhower in 1956, but they do this across all issue categories except on the far left. And in 1960, they divide their votes fairly equally except at the two extremes.

Issue Voting in Balanced and Unbalanced Elections

When an outlying candidate runs against the more centrist candidate he appears to lose votes to the latter. His candidacy generates a lot of issue voting but it goes against him. He loses more voters on the basis of his issue position than he gains. This is clear from the data we have just displayed. We can summarize the situation by considering several types of voter we considered in the previous chapter: (1) voters for whom issues and party are incongruent (liberal Republicans and conservative Democrats), (2) voters for whom party and issues are congruent (liberal Democrats and conservative Republicans), (3) partisans who have centrist political attitudes, and (4) Independents who have coherent political views on the left or on the right. Each of these groups can cast an issue-based vote. The first group must defect from its party to do so. The second group sticks to its party affiliation when it votes its issue position. The centrists can also vote their issue position if the contest is between an outlier and a centrist; the latter being closer to them in issue terms. And Independents can vote their issue positions.

With each of these four types of voters, the outlying candidate does less well than does the centrist. In table 18.1 we divide the population into the three broad issue groupings we have used earlier—those in the left third of our issue scale, those in the center third, and those in the right third. This gives us three groups: liberals, centrists, and conservatives. We then divide them on the basis of party affiliation.

In the first section we have those voters whose partisanship and issue positions are incongruent—liberal Republicans and conservative Democrats. And we give the proportion of that group that defects from its party to vote their issue position. In 1964, when the outlying candidate was on the right, the defections are away from the Republican party: 63 percent of the liberal Republicans defect in contrast with 28 percent of the conservative Democrats. In 1972, when the outlier is on the left, the opposite happens: 64 percent of the conservative Democrats defect, but only 10 percent of the liberal Republicans. The difference in the defection rates between liberal Democrats and conservative Republicans can be taken as an index of the extent to which issue defection favors one candidate rather than the other. We place that number below the defection rates for liberal Republicans and conservative Democrats. The larger that number, the greater the imbalance in the degree to which defectors come from the Democrats rather than the Republicans. (If the figure for the difference is positive, it reflects an imbalance favoring the Democrats; if negative it favors the Republicans.) As one can see, there is a fairly large difference of 35 percentage points between the two defection rates in 1964, a difference favoring the Democrats, and an even larger difference of 54 percentage points between the two defection rates in 1972, a difference favoring the Republicans.

We present parallel data for the symmetrical mock election between

TABLE 18.1. Issue voting in 1964, 1972, and the mock McGovern-Goldwater election

	1964	1972	Mock election McGovern-Goldwater
Voters who defect from their party to vote their issue position			
Percent of liberal Republicans voting Democratic	63	10	33
Percent of conservative Democrats voting Republican	28	64	48
Difference	+35	−54	−15
Voters whose party and issues reinforce each other			
Percent of liberal Democrats voting Democratic	96	81	88
Percent of conservative Republicans voting Republican	84	97	93
Difference	+12	−15	− 5
Partisans with centrist views who defect from their party			
Percent of Republican centrists voting Democratic	30	11	14
Percent of Democratic centrists voting Republican	5	46	30
Difference	+25	−35	−16
Independents voting issue position			
Percent of liberal Independents voting Democratic	89	55	71
Percent of conservative Independents voting Republican	58	83	72
Difference	+31	−28	− 1

McGovern and Goldwater. The contrast between 1964 and 1972 on the one hand and the mock election is clear. In the mock McGovern/Goldwater election, there is a somewhat higher rate of Democratic than Republican defection, but the difference between the two defection rates is much smaller than in the real 1964 or 1972 elections. In the mock election the difference is 15 percentage points. The difference for the 1964 election is more than twice this amount; for the 1972 election more than three times this amount.

The contrast between the elections when Goldwater and McGovern run against centrists and the mock election when they run against each other is striking. When Goldwater runs against a centrist in 1964, 63 percent of the liberal Republicans defect to the centrist Johnson. When he runs against McGovern, only 33 percent of that group defects. Conversely, 64 percent of the conservative Democrats defect when McGovern runs against a centrist in 1972. He only loses 48 percent of the conservative Democrats when he runs against Goldwater.

In the other three sections of table 18.1 for the other types of issue voters the pattern holds: there is an imbalance in the issue voting rates that favors the centrist candidate in 1964 and 1972; there is less imbalance in the mock election than in the 1964 and 1972 elections.

In section 2 of table 18.1 there can be little imbalance because such voters almost unanimously vote for the choice that reflects their party and issue direction. But there still is some imbalance favoring the centrist. Johnson holds on to the votes of 96 percent of the liberal Democrats in 1964, Nixon holds an almost identical percentage of the conservative Republicans in 1972. Goldwater and McGovern do not do as well with their "natural" supporters: Goldwater gets the votes of 84 percent of the conservative Republicans in 1964; McGovern gets 81 percent of the liberal Democrats. Again, the situation is less unbalanced in the mock election between McGovern and Goldwater. In the mock election the difference between the candidates is about one-third the difference in 1964 and 1972.

The story is the same for the centrist defectors. More centrists defect from their party to vote for the centrist candidate than defect to vote for an outlier. The difference between the proportion of centrists defecting to an outlying candidate and the proportion to a centrist is substantial in elections with such an asymmetrical choice—25 percentage points in 1964, 35 percentage points in 1972. The imbalance between the defection rates of centrists from the two parties is half that amount in the mock election.

The issue-voting Independents also follow their issue inclinations to a centrist rather than an outlier. When Goldwater ran against Johnson, he received 31 percent less of the vote of conservative Independents than Johnson received of the vote of the liberal Independents, and McGovern does

TABLE 18.2. Proportion of voters with coherent issues positions voting consistently with that position, in 1964, 1972, and the mock McGovern-Goldwater election

	1964	1972	McGovern-Goldwater
Percent of liberals voting Democratic[a]	91	59	77
Percent of conservatives voting Republican[b]	57	82	71
Difference	+34	−23	+ 5

[a] Includes liberal Democrats, liberal Republicans, and liberal Independents.

[b] Includes conservative Republicans, conservative Democrats, and conservative Independents.

about as badly vis-à-vis Nixon. McGovern receives 28 percent fewer votes from liberal Independents than Nixon receives from conservative Independents. But when McGovern runs against Goldwater, there is no difference in the proportion of liberal Independents who vote consistently with their issue position and the proportion of conservative Independents who do. Each candidate draws an almost identical proportion of those Independents who agree with them on the issues.

The situation is summed up in table 18.2. There we report the proportions of all voters with coherent positions on the issues (either liberal or conservative) who vote consistently with that position. The data represent thus a summary of the data for partisans and for Independents. In the two unbalanced elections, where an outlying candidate runs against a centrist, there is a wide difference between the proportion of liberals voting Democratic and the proportion of conservatives voting Republican. And in each election, the difference favors the centrist candidate. But in the more balanced mock election there is little difference between the proportion of liberals voting Democratic and the proportion of conservatives voting Republican.[6]

---

[6] If we were to present similar data to that in tables 18.1 and 18.2 for the 1956 and 1960 elections we would find that the 1960 data look like the McGovern–Goldwater contest. Issue voting (whatever little there is) does not favor one side or the other. In 1956, the data resemble those for 1972. The various kinds of voting patterns favor Eisenhower —he gets substantially fewer of the votes of liberal Republicans than Stevenson loses of conservative Democrats; he keeps more conservative Republican votes than Stevenson keeps liberal Democrats; and he does better with the centrists and the Independents as well. In this sense, the 1956 election is "unbalanced" as are the 1964 and 1972 elections. But as the data presented above in figures 18.3 and 18.4 make clear, the unbalance has little to do with issue position, but more to do with the personal appeal of Eisenhower.

The conclusion seems obvious: if you want to win, nominate a candidate close to the center. Or, if you must nominate a candidate far from the center, hope that the other party does so as well. Then you will have a fighting chance.

The voting patterns shown on figure 18.3 clearly suggest that Goldwater and McGovern were hurt by the fact that they were perceived to be far from the center of the issue spectrum. The contrast with the 1956 election adds support to this conclusion. Stevenson lost badly in 1956 but not for issue reasons. The particular shape of the curves on figure 18.3 for the 1964 and 1972 landslides compared with the curve for the 1956 landslide highlights the importance of issues in the former two elections.

However, perhaps the conclusion that a candidate of the left or of the right cannot win is too simple. We are reluctant to draw such a firm conclusion. For one thing, we hesitate to end a book whose main theme is that the public changes with new issues and new candidates with a firm prediction of what can or cannot be done in American politics, especially when issues are changing so rapidly.

There are, however, other reasons more weighty than academic caution that make us hesitiate to draw the conclusion that only centrists can win. One reason for the reluctance to draw this conclusion is that issue position, though it has grown in significance, is not the only force affecting the vote. As we saw in Chapter 16, the personal characteristics of the candidates continue to play an important role. Here again 1956 is relevant. It indicates that there are several ways to lose an election, of which issue extremism is but one.

Analysis of the 1972 election shows that though issues played a major role in determining the vote, the personal assessments of the candidates had the largest impact on the voting decision.[7] Furthermore, the personal evaluations of Goldwater and McGovern by the public as a whole were much more negative than the evaluations of any other candidates from 1952 to 1972. Miller and his associates use the open-ended questions on the Michigan surveys to determine the balance of negative to positive statements about the candidates. Only Goldwater and McGovern were, on balance, viewed negatively, and they were viewed quite negatively.[8]

These negative personal evaluations of the two outlying candidates cannot explain the pattern of vote against them as seen in figure 18.3, since that figure obviously illustrates the existence of an issue component to the voting

---

[7] Arthur H. Miller, Warren E. Miller, Alden S. Raine, and Thad A. Brown, "A Majority Party in Disarray: Policy Polarization in the 1972 Election," paper prepared for the Annual Meeting of the American Political Science Association, New Orleans, September 1973, p. 67.

[8] Ibid., p. 55.

choice. But the negative personal evaluation may be linked to the perceived issue extremism of the candidate. They were seen not only as candidates with positions far from the mainstream opinions in the electorate but as candidates who held those positions in a manner that did not inspire confidence. If a candidate were to come along who held similar positions but who was perceived to be a more competent conservative or a more competent liberal, the negative results might not be as severe.[9]

A second reason why we are reluctant to draw the conclusion that a candidate of the left or of the right cannot win is that the important variable appears to be the *perception* by the public of the location of the candidate. Citizens vote against candidates perceived to be far from them on the issue scale. But there is no simple one-to-one correspondence between the actual position of a candidate and his perceived position. The public does appear to be able to locate fairly accurately candidates who take clear positions on the issues.[10] But where candidates take ambiguous positions, the public has trouble locating them on issue scales. And even for candidates whose position is clear, placement may not be accurate. There is evidence, for instance, that a "halo effect" may apply—George Wallace was seen as a candidate of the right on some issues where he had not taken a particularly conservative position.[11] It is our impression that Goldwater and McGovern were perceived as outlying candidates by a large proportion of the public. But it is by no means certain that other candidates with similar positions would have been perceived to be as extreme in their views. In part, the perception by the public of Goldwater and McGovern may be the result of a successful campaign by their opponents to so characterize them.

A candidate with a good deal of personal appeal might be successful even if he or she were from fairly far out on the issue scale. The personal appeal would allow the candidate to "rise above the issues." Voters might choose on the basis of preference for personal qualities. Or an appealing candidate may be seen as closer to the center than is, in fact, the case, just as an unappealing candidate may be seen as further from the center. In the American political context—where the center is the preferred position—com-

---

[9] Of course, it may be that the positions close to the issue extremes will be considered by the public to be per se evidence of incompetence. If this is the case, the extremist would always be considered the less competent candidate.

[10] Benjamin I. Page and Richard A. Brody, "Policy Voting and the Electoral Process: The Vietnam War Issue," *American Political Science Review*, 66 (September 1972), 993, and H. T. Reynolds, "Rationality and Attitudes Toward Political Parties and Candidates," *Journal of Politics*, 36 (November 1974), 1000ff.

[11] Reynolds, "Rationality and Attitudes."

petence and centrism may be perceived to be the same thing, as may incompetence and extremism.

We can illustrate how a candidate can rise above the issues on the basis of personal appeal by considering some mock elections in which Edward Kennedy takes part. He has often been mentioned as a candidate who, if he ran, could unite the disparate wings of the Democratic party—this despite issue positions that might not be far from the McGovern positions.

We ran mock elections between Kennedy on the one hand and Percy and Reagan on the other. Kennedy does quite well in holding the vote of the right wing of the Democratic party. Data for these elections are reported in figure 18.6, part A. As in the previous figures, we report the proportion of the vote going to the Democratic candidate. The data are for Democratic voters only. As one can see, Kennedy holds the bulk of the Democratic voters all across the issue spectrum. He does slightly better with the far right of his party when he runs against Percy than against Reagan (and slightly better with the far left of his party when the opponent is Reagan rather than Percy). But the general pattern is one of party loyalty among the Democratic voters.

Compare part B of figure 18.6, where we present similar data on McGovern's performance among Democrats. Kennedy receives 76 percent of the vote of the Democrats in the farthest right decile when he runs against Reagan; McGovern receives 39 percent of that group when he runs against Goldwater in our mock election. Similarly, Kennedy receives 81 percent of vote of that group when he runs against Percy, compared with the 22 percent McGovern received running in 1972 against Nixon. In sum, a candidate who can invoke personal appeal may be able to hold voters from all across the issue spectrum.

The last reason for caution as to the proper implication from our analysis has to do with the issue positions of the American public. As we have seen (in figure 8.5), the public has been moving away from the center of the issue continuum toward the extremes. The result is that a candidate who might have been an issue extremist in one year may be less of one in another year. The public moved out from the center after 1960. Goldwater and McGovern, nevertheless, still outflanked the bulk of the public. But continued movement in one direction or another by the public may convert extreme positions on the part of candidates into more centrist ones.

If the public polarizes—abandons the center and moves equally to left and to right—the advantage still may rest with a more centrist candidate, though the advantage will be less than it would be where the public itself was centrist. But if the public's movement is predominantly in one direction rather than another, the "center" of the population moves and the optimum candi-

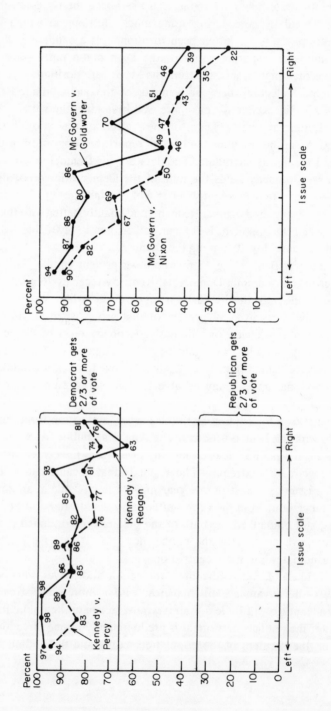

FIGURE 18.6A. Percent of Democrats voting for Kennedy when he runs against Reagan or Percy

FIGURE 18.6B. Percent of Democrats voting for McGovern when he runs against Goldwater or Nixon

date position moves in that direction as well. Our method of presenting the issue positions of the public in this chapter obscures possible movement on the part of the public. We divided the public into deciles (from left to right) based on the distribution of attitudes in the year under analysis. If the public moved left or right (or polarized) it would not affect the distribution of voters on those figures. But it would mean that a candidate's position relative to the population would move closer to the center. In other words, a candidate who takes a position far from the bulk of the population does badly. But if the public moves left or right, a leftist or a rightist may no longer be as far from the center of gravity of the electorate.

We can illustrate this point by considering two issues for which we have similar attitude measures in 1968 and 1972. In each of those years, respondents were asked to put themselves on seven-point scales—one was a Vietnam hawk-dove scale, the other a scale on urban unrest running from a preference for social reforms to a preference for maximum perservation of law and order. In figure 18.7 we report the proportions of the population that fell on the various positions of these scales in 1968 and 1972. We also indicate the average placement given by the public to McGovern in 1972. It is clear that the public moves left on both the Vietnam scale and the urban unrest scales between 1968 and 1972. The result is that McGovern's 1972 position, which was to the left of the public in that year, would have been even further to the left of the populace in 1968. In 1972, about 79 percent of the public was to the right of McGovern on the Vietnam scale. If he had held the same position in 1968, 87 percent would have been to his right. The urban unrest scale is a better illustration of how an outlier can move toward the center. In 1968, McGovern's position would have placed him to the left of about two-thirds of the public; by 1972 he is only slightly left of the center of the issue distribution.

The point is that the candidate who outflanks the public is likely to lose. But if the public shifts its center of gravity left or right, what was once an outlying position may become a more mainstream position. From this perspective, the evidence for a leftward drift of the public in recent years (see Chapter 8) is significant. It means that candidates who might have been left outliers in earlier years will be closer to the mainstream now. Furthermore, candidates can also move the public one way or the other on the issue scale. Our impression is that in 1964 and 1972 the outlying candidates affected the issue positions of the public, though not probably to their net advantage. They polarized the electorate rather than moving the center of gravity closer to them. Other candidates might be more successful in moving the center of the

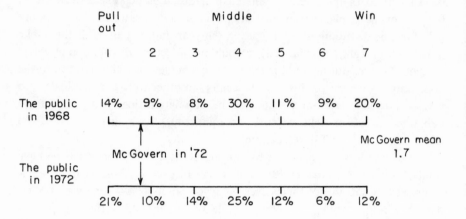

Vietnam attitudes

Pull out		Middle				Win
1	2	3	4	5	6	7

The public in 1968

| 14% | 9% | 8% | 30% | 11% | 9% | 20% |

McGovern in '72

McGovern mean 1.7

The public in 1972

| 21% | 10% | 14% | 25% | 12% | 6% | 12% |

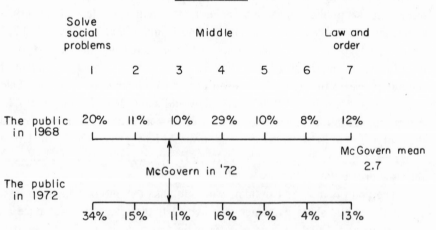

Urban unrest

Solve social problems		Middle				Law and order
1	2	3	4	5	6	7

The public in 1968

| 20% | 11% | 10% | 29% | 10% | 8% | 12% |

McGovern in '72

McGovern mean 2.7

The public in 1972

| 34% | 15% | 11% | 16% | 7% | 4% | 13% |

FIGURE 18.7. McGovern in 1968 and 1972

issue distribution closer to them. In this way a candidate may redefine the issue space into which he falls.

Our demonstration that issue voting does exist and does hurt the candidate far from the center of the issue spectrum does not imply as much rigidity in campaign alternatives as it might at first glance seem to imply. There are many alternative futures.

19

From the Past to the Future: Some Speculative Conclusions

The Party System and Continuity in the Late 1950s

The American party system in the 1950s supplied a good deal of continuity to American politics in a number of ways. For the individual voter, partisan identification provided a guide to the vote that was applicable election after election. Candidates and issues came and went, but the parties were continuing institutions (or, at least, symbols) and one could vote on the basis of identification with them. The continuity of partisanship, furthermore, extended across generations. In the late 1950s, a high proportion of new voters simply inherited the partisan affiliation of their parents. Though citizens might deviate from their party to vote for a popular candidate like Eisenhower, their identification remained intact, they were guided by their affiliation in nonpresidential elections, and they usually returned to their party's nominee for president in the next election.

Partisan affiliation provided continuity for the electoral system as well as for the individual voter. Short-term electoral forces moved the voting population away from a straight party vote, but the vote oscillated around a baseline provided by partisan identification. This stability in the electoral system was manifested as well in the fact that the parties had fairly stable demographic bases. The coalition of population groups supporting each party was heterogeneous, but with the exception of the South, there was a fairly distinct class basis to each of the parties—a class basis that carried over from the party reshuffling of the New Deal period. The impact of the party system can be exaggerated. The parties were not well organized institutions in the European sense, party identification only imperfectly predicted the vote, and the party coalitions were quite loose. Nevertheless, the party system provided a good deal of continuity.

Continuity Broken

This is no longer the case. Party decomposition—to use the phrase of Walter Dean Burnham who has traced the historical trend most effectively[1]— is illustrated in many ways by the data compiled in this book. Citizens are less committed to the political parties. The Independents represent the largest group in the society, a bit larger than the proportion of the population that considers itself Democratic and twice as large as the proportion that considers itself Republican. Furthermore, even among those with a partisan identification, the ties of partisanship are much weaker. Voters have become more likely to desert their party to vote for the opposition candidate in both national and local elections; and citizens in general are dissatisfied with the performance of the political parties, including their own. At the same time, the electorate has developed a more coherent set of issue positions and uses those issue orientations as guides in voting. The result is that voters in presidential elections are more likely to vote for a *candidate* on the basis of the candidate's personal characteristics and/or the candidate's issue positions than they are to vote on the basis of long-term commitment to a political party.

These changes on the part of the voter are paralleled by changes in the political parties and in the way elections are conducted. Party organizations have grown weaker; they are less relevant as electioneering institutions than they once were, especially on the presidential level. Presidential campaign organizations are created anew for each election. They represent the personal entourage of the candidate rather than a continuing partisan institution. The mass media have become the most important channels of campaign communication, the parties are less important.

Election choices in such a system have less continuity. The individual candidates are more independent of party;[2] they run on the basis of their own

---

[1] See Burnham's *Critical Elections and the Mainsprings of American Politics* (New York: Norton, 1970) and his more recent "American Parties in the 1970's: Beyond Party?" in Louis Massel and Paul M. Sacks, eds., *The Future of Political Parties, Sage Electoral Studies Yearbook,* vol. I (Beverly Hills: Sage Publications, 1975), pp. 238–277.

[2] Though this varies from candidate to candidate. Some are more identified with party than others. See Gary Orren and William Schneider, *Democrats versus Democrats* (Stamford, Conn.: Greylock Publishing Co., 1976).

characteristics and programs, not as representatives of continuing party institutions. Insofar as this is the case, electoral choice can no longer be retrospective. Voters are less able to vote on the basis of past performance (as V. O. Key and others have argued they did), since the candidate cannot be held responsible for what others in his party have done while in office—unless, of course, the incumbent is the candidate. Issue voting becomes, at least potentially, prospective voting. If voters vote on the basis of issue considerations it has to be in expectation of future performance on the part of the candidate.

Party decomposition is also seen in the weakening of the traditional bases of support for the two parties. As we have seen, there has been a good deal of reshuffling of the electorate. This has had a mixed effect on the class composition of the party support groups. In the South, class differences between Democrats and Republicans have become more pronounced; in the rest of the nation they have become less so. In each case, however, major components of the stable support bases of each of the parties has weakened. The Democratic party cannot rely on the South or the northern working class. The Republican party no longer can rely as heavily on the Protestant upper middle class.

The breakdown of some of the traditional bases of party support is paralleled by a split within the two parties between the active and the inactive supporters. Those active in the Republican party are more conservative than the Republican rank and file (this has been so for quite a while); those active in the Democratic party are more liberal than the Democratic rank and file (this is more recent). The result is that in both parties the activists are more likely to be issue oriented and less likely to be organizationally committed. They are attached to particular candidates, not to the party as an institution. Thus, what appears as a growing emphasis on candidates and issues rather than party among the public at large is even more strongly felt among the activists.

These changes add up to an "individuation" of American political life. Membership in a population group no longer predicts political behavior very well; region, class, religion are still associated with party affiliation and the vote, but not as closely as they once were. Nor does party affiliation predict political behavior well; fewer have such affiliation and fewer of those with affiliation follow it. The individual voter evaluates candidates on the basis of information and impressions conveyed by the mass media, and then votes on that basis. He or she acts as an individual, not as a member of a collectivity.

The result of all these changes is the decline in continuity that we have cited. Elections turn more on the short-term forces in the election—the candidates and the issues as they come across to the electorate through the media.

This may or may not mean a more responsive electoral process; it is certainly likely to mean a less predictable electoral process.

The unpredictability is made greater—and more serious—by two other changes that we have charted: the electorate has become more and more dissatisfied with the political process while at the same time becoming somewhat more active and involved in that process. The result is, we believe, a much more volatile electorate. It is a "mobilized" population—active and involved —but a populace with weaker institutional ties. To understand the nature of this volatility we should look at its origins.

The Source of Party Decomposition

Our analysis suggests that the fundamental changes in the American electorate have two origins: changes in the issues of the day and changes in political generations.

The Issues

One of our major conclusions is that the American public responds to political issues. Attitudes on specific issues can be quite volatile, as one learns from studying the Gallup and Harris polls. But underlying such volatility one can also find long-term tendencies of the public to move in one direction or another. There is evidence for instance that the public has drifted significantly in a liberal direction on a number of social and economic issues over the past two decades.

In addition, the public's views as to the trustworthiness and responsiveness of the American political system also changes in response to events. The erosion of public satisfaction with government is in good part a reaction to such issues as Vietnam, racial conflict, and Watergate.

These changes in political attitudes are hardly surprising. But it is somewhat more surprising that the public was responsive to the issues of the political world in the *way* in which it thought about politics, not merely in *what* it thought on specific political matters. As we traced the transformation of the American public, we found that a substantial change in the structure of belief systems had occurred. Political attitudes became more coherent after the Eisenhower years. Citizens began to evaluate candidates and the parties in terms of the issue positions they presented. And this new issue coherence and concern for issues was translated into a greater connection between issue position and the vote.

When we looked back to the 1930s, we found that citizens had coherent political beliefs on the set of political issues defined by the New Deal and they voted in accord with such beliefs. Issue coherence in the late 1960s, however, differs from that in the 1930s. In the later period the coherence of political attitudes ranges across a wider number of issues.

The most plausible explanation of this change is that citizens respond to the issues in the political arena. More precisely, they respond to the issues as those issues are structured for them by parties and candidates. In the 1930s, the New Deal program made clear the connection between welfare measures and government control over the economy. These issues then were connected with each other in citizens' minds and, in turn, the more coherent issue positions influenced the vote. In the 1950s, there was no such clear-cut bundle of issues. Starting in 1964, on the other hand, candidates emerged who provided the citizens with clearer issue choice. As our mock election analysis indicated, the type of choice presented to the citizen played an important role in determining the criteria used in the voting choice.

The mock election analysis highlights an important distinction. The consistency of issue attitudes that appears after 1964 may be a response to the Goldwater candidacy; the continued high level of consistency, however, does not appear to be dependent on the specific election choice. We find a high level of issue consistency during the presidential years of 1964, 1968, and 1972, when there were relatively clear issue choices. But we find a similar level of issue consistency in studies conducted during nonpresidential years. In other words, citizens have come to think about issues more consistently no matter what the specific electoral stimulus.

On the other hand, the extent to which such issue positions are converted into a voting choice appears to depend quite directly upon what choice is offered the public. Despite the fact that the 1973 sample that takes part in our mock elections manifests the same high level of issue coherence that has typified voters since 1964, they cast a party-oriented vote when presented with candidates who offer little issue alternative. The data suggest, in other words, that the public will cast an issue vote, but only if it is given a meaningful issue choice. The changing nature of political issues and how those issues are presented explains the substantial change one finds in the basic characteristics of the electorate since the Eisenhower years. The political world has changed and the American electorate has responded to that change.

The rise of new issues does not necessarily imply a decline in importance of political parties. New issues can reinforce existing party affiliations when the parties take alternative stands on the issues and those stands are consistent with the positions of their supporters. We have seen evidence for this in the 1964 election. Or new issues can create new partisan commitments if the parties take alternative stands that are not consistent with the positions of all their current supporters but the populace changes its affiliation to fall into line with party positions. The new issues that arose in the 1960s have not led to this type of realignment. The issues that loosened party ties were racial conflict and Vietnam, capped off in recent years by Watergate. These issues caused substantial discontent. They led the public to turn against the political parties and against the political process more generally. But they led to no new partisan alignments. Vietnam was not an issue that clearly differentiated one party from another, and the racial issue split the majority party. Watergate had more partisan identification. But its major effect seems to have been a rejection of government and politicians. The result of the new issues is weakened commitment to parties and politics, not reconstituted commitments.

Political Generations

In the midst of these many changes, however, we find some points of party continuity. Oddly enough, one of the stable anchor points for the American public remains party identification—something that has been declining rapidly. The decline is seen if one looks at the public as a whole, but it is less apparent among those voters who had established partisan identifications before the shocks of the 1960s. These established party supporters may be dissatisfied with their political party and more willing to vote against its candidates than they once were, but they remain relatively firm in their party identification. The fact that their identification was established at a time when the party system was not under strain and had sufficient time to become deeply ingrained seems to provide an immunity for voters against the challenges to the party system that have emerged in recent years.

Fundamental changes in the partisan division of the electorate appear to depend upon the entrance of new age groups into that electorate. Established identifications are slow in changing. A new pattern of party identifications appears when new voters enter the electorate with partisan commitments different from those held by the previous generation. The massive shift of the American electorate in the 1930s depended upon new voters—voters who came of age in the 1930s or voters who had come of age earlier but who had not yet voted. In the late 1960s, the decay of party affiliation results from the arrival of a new generation of voters. But the new generation has not taken up a new affiliation.

It takes more than a new generation of voters to change the partisan alignment of the electorate. One needs as well some new set of issues that pushes them into a partisan commitment different from that of the previous generation. New voters enter all the time. At each presidential election about 8 percent of the electorate is new—that is, they were too young to vote in the previous presidential election. If no new stimuli push them in a new direction, they will replicate the partisanship of the existing electorate.

Consider the cohorts who entered the electorate in the 1950s. The old issues that had led their parents to identify with the Democratic or Republican parties were no longer as salient. The depression was over and the social reforms of the New Deal were generally accepted by both parties. But no new issues took the place of the old ones. As a result the entering voters followed the partisan identifications of their parents, but without much commitment to the issue positions that had formed their parents' identifications. Under such circumstances, it is little wonder that the 1950s were a period in which habitual party ties were everything and issue positions played very little role.

In short, an entering generation of voters is *available* for alignments different from those of the earlier generations. But the available population is moved in a new direction only when a new issue force pushes them that way. Otherwise, the inertia of habitual partisanship is communicated from generation to generation.

The fact that change in party alignment comes from new voters entering the electorate would appear to limit the magnitude of such change. In any election, only a small proportion of the electorate is new. More substantial change might come gradually over a number of elections if some new issue remained a steady force for an extended period of time and affected each entering group of voters. There would, however, seem to be little potential for a sudden large-scale realignment in a "critical" election.

But, there can be a good deal of variation in the size of the population available for a new partisan alignment. For one thing birth rates vary, making for variation in the size of the cohort entering the electorate. One of the reasons for the substantial change in the 1930s and for the substantial impact of new voters in the late 1960s is that in each case one has a fairly large cohort of new entrants.

In addition, the available population can accumulate across a number of elections. Our analysis of the late 1930s suggested that a large number of voters came of age in the 1920s but did not vote. They were mobilized by the New Deal in the 1930s and, along with the young voters just entering the electorate in the thirties, they provided the great increase in the size of the electorate that in turn created the Democratic majority.

In a similar manner, there has been an accumulation of an available electorate in recent years. As we have seen, about half of the entering voters since the late 1960s have joined the electorate as Independents. Nor have they taken on a party identification in subsequent elections. Thus we have had almost a decade in which unaffiliated young voters have been accumulating. By 1974, 14 percent of the electorate were voters who came of voting age after the 1964 election and had no party affiliation. That represents a substantial available population.

Furthermore, the new young members of the electorate—like the available population in the 1930s—are not only Independent, they are also likely to be nonvoters. Less than 50 percent of those under twenty-four voted in 1972 compared with a 66 percent turnout among those over thirty. In short, there is a large population with little political experience—a nonimmunized population—whose allegiance has yet to be captured by any political movement.

The Future: A New Alignment, Continuing Decay, or What?

A politics of individuation, where neither demographic characteristics nor partisan ties guide the vote and where a particularly large proportion of the electorate is young, nonimmunized, and available, is an unpredictable politics. It does not have the continuity of a system in which clearly defined population groups have stable attachments to one or the other of the political parties. However, certain similarities between the present and the era of the New Deal realignment—particularly the large size of the available electorate —raises the possibility that the present individuated system will be replaced by a new party alignment which will give the polity the continuity it once had. Can such a new alignment be formed? If so, what will it look like?

The scenarios for a new majority coalition are many: a new Republican majority based on the white middle class heartland coupled with an affluent but disaffected white working class; a new conservative majority of similar composition but not tied to the Republican party; a new liberal coalition of the affluent intelligentsia and the least well-off members of society; a "real" majority of middle Americans; a reconstruction of the New Deal coalition based on common economic interest.[3] We believe that some of these groupings represent plausible coalitions. But they are likely to be temporary coalitions of voters around a particular candidate. They are less likely to form the basis of a new, stable party system.

---

[3] An excellent discussion of these alternatives with some arguments as to why they are not convincing scenarios is found in Everett C. Ladd, Jr., with Charles D. Hadley, *Transformations of the American Party System: Political Coalitions from the New Deal to the 1970's* (New York: Norton, 1975), chap. 1.

There are a number of reasons why a new partisan alignment is unlikely to emerge from the present system. One reason lies in the nature of the issues facing the country compared with those during the New Deal era. As we have seen, the issues that helped cause the decline of the party system were not such as to foster the emergence of a new party system. Vietnam, racial conflict, and Watergate created hostility on the part of the public to government, politicians, and parties in general.

The shocks of Vietnam, race, and Watergate have now been followed by the shocks of inflation and unemployment. Inflation hits all social groups; unemployment strikes more heavily at particular groups (blacks and the young). But what unemployment lacks in scope of impact it makes up for in intensity of impact on those who experience it. Furthermore, white collar and professional unemployment is widespread enough so that it is an issue across all social groups.

These new issues add to discontent and to the lack of confidence with government. Such discontent becomes more volatile because of changes in the populace. The current populace is less acquiescent and more concerned about political issues than the populace of the 1950s. Though these economic issues—particularly unemployment—are the kind which we have traditionally associated with partisan alternatives (after all, the New Deal coalition grew out of that issue), the parties have not as yet established clear alternative positions on these issues. Even if they did—the Democrats as the full employment party, the Republicans as the anti-inflation party—it would not be easy to rebuild the Democratic coalition. The class basis of the parties has been severely diminished and the issue of race cuts across the economic divisions. (Despite this, one cannot rule out such a return to the earlier party alignment.)

Furthermore, our analysis of the voting decision suggests that candidates face a dilemma. A new coalition may depend on the ability of a candidate to take a strong and clear position, a position that will draw the available voters to him. On the other hand, we have found that such a candidate may run the risk of losing a large proportion of the electorate if the opposing candidate can establish a position closer to the center. We have cautioned against generalizing too strongly from that part of our analysis. It may well be that an economic downturn would move the public far enough to the left in their preferences for economic policies that they would welcome a candidate who establishes a strong position at that end of the issue scale. Or, conceivably, the crisis might move the public to the right. If the crisis moves the American public toward one or the other extreme of the issue scale, outlying candidates may become more viable.[4] Our spatial analysis, however, does suggest that the candidate who wishes to establish a clear position for radical change has a complex task indeed.

In addition, the task of creating a new political coalition may be made more difficult by the disjunction between candidate and party that character- izes recent presidential elections. Parties are long-standing institutions, candi- dates come and go. But there is a closer connection between the public's issue positions and the candidates than there is between issue positions and the parties. The parties have not captured the new issue divisions within the pub- lic. A candidate may come along around whom a new coalition of voters can be created. Such a candidate may attract a large proportion of the available pool of Independent voters. But can such a voting coalition be translated into a more permanent set of partisan attachments?

It is likely to be difficult to convert support for a particular candidate into a more lasting party identification as was done in the 1930s. For one thing, the support bases of the two parties are quite diffuse. A candidate who can appeal to all the many groups within one of the parties, particularly within the diverse Democratic party, may not be a candidate with a strong enough position to mobilize the available unidentified voters to his side. On the other hand, if a candidate takes the strong position necessary to draw the available new voters back into a party, he is likely to lose many of those already attached to his party.

This problem is compounded by the way presidential campaigns are organized. The national party organizations have never been strong but now they appear to be weaker than ever. In each election a new organization is created around the particular candidate, and the major information source is the nonpartisan mass media. The result is that it is difficult to translate sup- port for a particular candidate into more general support for a party.

All in all, we see little prospect for the emergence of a new party system from the disarray of the present system. If there is a critical realignment going on now it is one, to quote Walter Dean Burnham, "that works not through, but athwart the traditional major parties, and which cumulatively dissolves them as channels of collective electoral action."[5]

If no new party system emerges, what will emerge? Perhaps the current system of individualistic voting choice between ad hoc electoral organizations mediated by television will continue into the indefinite future. But even if this

---

[4] Or to put it more precisely, the outlying candidate will cease to be as much of an outlier because the populace will move out toward his position.

[5] Burnham, "American Parties," p. 258.

is the case, as we think likely, it is hard to say what kind of system it will be in terms of such fundamental political values as effectiveness of decisions, responsiveness to the public, and continuity of an open political process.

In his monumental work on politics in the one-party South, V. O. Key, Jr., described some of the consequences of the absence of effective political parties. His description seems particularly apt as a conclusion for this book:

> In many instances the battle for control of a state is fought between groups newly formed for the particular campaign. The groups lack continuity in name—as exists under a party system—and they also lack continuity in the make-up of their inner core of professional politicians or leaders. Naturally, they also lack continuity in voter support which, under two-party conditions, provides a relatively stable following of voters for each party's candidates whoever they may be.
>
> Discontinuity of faction both confuses the electorate and reflects a failure to organize the voters into groups of more or less like-minded citizens with somewhat similar attitudes toward public policy . . . Under a system of fluid factions . . . the voters' task is not simplified by the existence of continuing competing parties with fairly well-recognized, general-policy orientations. That is, this party proposes to run the government generally in one way; the opposition, another. Factions that form and reform cannot become so identified in the mind of the electorate, and the conditions of public choice become far different from those under two-party conditions. The voter is confronted with new faces, new choices, and must function in a sort of state of nature.
>
> . . . It is impossible to have even a fight between the "ins" and the "outs." The candidates are new and, in fact, deny any identification with any preceding administration. Without continuing groups, there can be no debate between the "ins" and "outs" on the record . . . The candidates are, as completely as they can manage it, disassociated from the outgoing administration. The "outs" cannot attack the record of the "ins" because the "ins" do not exist as a group with any collective spirit or any continuity of existence . . . In an atomized and individualistic politics it becomes a matter of each leader for himself and often for himself only for the current campaign.[6]

We do not suggest that the political situation in U.S. national politics can be equated with the extreme factionalism of the South at the time of Key's analysis. Parties still exist and the majority of the electorate identifies with one or the other of the major parties. Yet the tendency is in the direction of the kind of factionalism Key found to characterize the South. And the more

---

[6] V. O. Key, Jr., *Southern Politics in State and Nation* (New York: Vintage Books, 1949), pp. 302–304.

the polity moves in that direction, the more may we expect the consequences Key found for the South.

There is one striking difference, however, between southern factional politics and the new candidate-based political coalitions we see emerging. Southern politics, as Key describes it, was issueless. The factions formed around personalities, not around common issue concern. The candidate-centered coalitions that now appear to be replacing parties as the basic electoral organization are often based on issue agreement, though personality also plays a role.

A politics of issue-based factions with a more sophisticated electorate may be more responsive to public preferences than was the factional system in the South. Yet it takes more than a sophisticated electorate willing to vote on political issues to make for a responsive political system. There must be some set of political structures to provide issue choices and to convert the votes of citizens into a government. The American parties never did this very effectively. They are even less efficacious now. We may be entering a post-partisan era. What politics will be like under such a system is unclear.

20 | Epilogue 1976

The American electorate has changed dramatically in the past two decades. Some of the changes have been a response to the stimuli offered the public in particular elections. For example, the relative importance of partisanship versus issue position in determining the vote appears to depend upon the nature of the choice offered to the public by the candidates in a presidential race. But other changes in the electorate are more enduring; they are only partly a response to the changing cast of would-be presidents. Declining partisanship, for instance, cannot be traced to the particular set of candidates facing the electorate in any election. There is probably some relationship between the two, but the roots of the decline lie in such long-term trends as the decreasing influence of party organizations, the increasing importance of the mass media, the new structure of political campaigns, as well as the general malaise that accompanied the intense problems and conflicts of the late 1960s. At the same time, the public itself has changed over the past two decades. It is a younger and better educated public whose composition is vastly different from that of the electorate of 1952. Almost 55 percent of the eligible electorate in 1976 was too young to vote in 1952.

Determining which changes in the electorate are long term and secular and which are responses to the idiosyncrasies of the election years is not an easy task. One almost needs the ability to experiment with the American public: to present different publics with different electoral choices. The analyses in Chapters 17 and 18 rest upon such experiments. Respondents were presented with mock elections to see how the choice they were offered affected the criteria they used in deciding how to vote. Mock elections as voting experiments have their limitations. They are artificial and offer limited stimuli. Fortunately, the Constitution mandates a real electoral experiment every four years. Like all natural experiments, the presidential election is not ideal. It does not enable us to separate the various components of change in the electorate. Too many things go on at once to allow us to isolate cause and effect very precisely. Nevertheless, the 1976 election represents an excellent opportunity to trace further the changes in the American electorate, and in doing so to sort out those changes that are a response to the particular election from those that are derived from long-term trends in the society or in the nature of the electorate.

The 1976 election also represents a challenge: Can the methods and themes developed above adequately explain what happened in 1976? This epilogue, written three years after finishing *The Changing American Voter,* looks at the 1976 election using the analytic tools developed for studying the elections from 1952 to 1972. We do not attempt a full account and explanation of the 1976 election; rather we use it to bring our analysis beyond 1972 and to test our general contention that the nature of the choice affects the behavior of the electorate. In bringing our various time series through the 1976 election, we shall not present a full review of each series—how and why we measured what we did. We refer the reader back to the main body of our book for that purpose.

The 1976 Election as an Echo

Voters respond to the choice they are offered. What kind of choice were they offered in 1976?[1]

"For myself and for our nation," Jimmy Carter began his inaugural address, "I want to thank my predecessor for all he has done to heal our land. In this outward and physical ceremony we attest once again to the inner and spiritual strength of our nation. As my high school teacher, Miss Julia Coleman, used to say, 'We must adjust to changing times and still hold

---

[1] There are several histories of the 1976 election. One of the better ones, which has a wealth of material on the primary races and the thoughts and behavior of the candidates and their advisers, is Jules Witcover, *Marathon: The Pursuit of the Presidency, 1972–1976* (New York: Viking Press, 1977).

to unchanging principles.' " In Carter's words one can almost see an echo of a much earlier call for a "return to normalcy."[2]

It is difficult to imagine Barry Goldwater, George Wallace, or George McGovern conveying the spirit of Carter's remarks had they won their respective presidential elections. They were outliers, insurgents, interested less in returning to a "standard" state of affairs than in breathing life into dreams that frightened many of their fellow citizens. Their campaigns had been divisive and the things for which they stood (or were perceived to have stood) were not a part of the standard agenda of disagreements that separate Democrats from Republicans and constitute the "normal" issue positions of our presidential candidates.

The Carter-Ford campaign might have pursued divisive themes. The machinations of the FBI and the CIA, abortion, the Equal Rights Amendment, marijuana and drugs, and the treatment of Vietnam-war deserters and draft evaders sporadically bubbled to the surface. But neither candidate embraced these highly symbolic issues in a way that provided their contest with strong moral or cultural cleavages. Carter seemed more willing to rehabilitate draft resisters and military deserters, but it was clear that he would institute a program which seemed to forgive, but not forget, thereby not leaving himself vulnerable to resentment that might arise over "coddling" the unpatriotic. Similarly, though he refused to join Ford in calling for a constitutional amendment to overturn the Supreme Court's abortion decision, he noted that he was personally opposed to abortion and unwilling to use federal funds to pay for them. Both had wives who supported the ERA and children who admitted to using marijuana, making it difficult for many to choose between them on these issues.[3]

The disagreements in 1976 hewed closely to traditional party-line divisions. In their platform the Republicans emphasized inflation, budget reduction, and reliance upon the private sector. The Democrats, in contrast, worried about unemployment, which they regarded as the direct responsibility

---

[2] Carter's inaugural address is reprinted in Gerald Pomper and others, *The Election of 1976: Reports and Interpretations* (New York: David McKay, 1977).

[3] This description of the election is drawn from several sources. Various issues of the *Los Angeles Times* and the *Christian Science Monitor* provided summaries of the candidates' positions during the campaign. Witcover, *Marathon,* and the chapter by Henry A. Plotkin, "Issues in the 1976 Presidential Campaign," in Pomper and others, *The Election of 1976,* were also valuable sources on the issues discussed in the campaign. Benjamin I. Page's work, *Choices and Echoes in American Presidential Elections* (Chicago: University of Chicago Press, 1978) was used not only for material on the 1976 election but also as a source book for the issue distinctiveness of candidates in previous elections, especially 1960 and 1972.

of government. Their platform promised that the welfare system would be expanded and made more generous.

The candidates emphasized similar themes throughout the campaign. However, they did not sharpen their points of disagreement. Though Carter indicated that he was more favorable to public service employment than was Ford, he expressed many reservations about when and how extensively the government should become the employer of last resort. His support for national health insurance was also qualified. Further, while his more supportive disposition toward blacks was virtually unquestioned, Carter was noticeably reticent about indicating what specific programs or policies he had in mind. He opposed mandatory busing programs designed to desegregate public school systems; and his support for open housing did not extend to any federal action beyond laws which specifically banned discrimination.

There were differences that marked Carter as more liberal than Ford, but the major debate between them was less over goals than over who was more competent to achieve them. The candidates' campaigns seemed to play down issues. Following polls which indicated that voters were interested in the character of their candidate, the Ford campaign stressed personal qualities. The Carter organization was also willing to trim its issue stand and "stick to the themes—competence, leadership, idealism, getting the country moving again."[4]

The McGovern-Nixon campaign had been starkly different. The candidates, or at least one of them, attempted to stake out a highly visible issue position. McGovern presented himself as a candidate with a distinctive point of view. "I'm not," he insisted, "going to betray my principles or my convictions . . . [or] . . . depart from the principles and convictions that we've taken to the people in primaries all across the country."[5] The Nixon campaign eagerly joined in the effort to tell all who would listen about McGovern's "extremist" positions.

The data in figure 20.1 illustrate the extent to which the 1976 election was an "echo" compared to the "choice" of 1972. In both years the public was asked to place the candidates and the political parties on seven-point issue scales. Figure 20.1 averages the data for three economic issues (government guarantee of jobs, taxing the rich, and health insurance), three social issues (equal rights for women, crime, and the legalization of marijuana),

---

[4] Martin Schram, *Running for President 1976: The Carter Campaign* (New York: Stein and Day, 1977), p. 309.

[5] Quoted in Page, *Choices and Echoes,* p. 141.

and three racial issues (busing, government aid to minorities, and urban unrest). It also presents the placement of the parties and candidates on a liberal-conservative scale.

The public's location of the two political parties provides a benchmark for their location of the candidates. Several features stand out. On each of the sets of issues, McGovern outflanks his party by being located further left, while Nixon is placed at the same position as is the Republican party or somewhat closer to the center. In contrast, in 1976 both candidates fall at or within the outer boundaries defined by the party location. If we think of the public's location of the parties on these issue scales as delimiting the normal range of issue competition in America, both of the 1976 candidates lie within that standard range of disagreement, while McGovern was outside of that range. In sum, the 1972 election pitted a relatively centrist candidate against an outlier on the left, while the 1976 election was a more balanced contest between two centrists.

It is interesting to note the relative stability of the perceptions of the parties compared with the perceptions of the candidates. The parties are placed roughly in the same place in 1972 and 1976. Furthermore, the distance between the parties is about the same in the two years, despite the fact that the candidate distance is only half as great in 1976 as it was in 1972. The stimuli that changed between the two elections were clearly the candidates and not the parties.

The ambiguity of candidate issue positions, the coincidence of issue differences with normal partisan cleavages, and the focus upon broad "themes" and personality in 1976 are reminiscent of earlier elections before the advent of the polarizing candidacies of Goldwater, Wallace, and McGovern. Does this mean that we should expect the electorate of 1976 to revert to earlier characteristics? Will the changing American voter change back again? One would hardly expect a complete return to the earlier behavior. If there is a reversion to earlier patterns, it should, according to the argument developed above, be confined to those aspects of electoral behavior that are sensitive to the nature of the candidate choice offered. We have argued that candidates such as Goldwater, Wallace, and McGovern affected the ways in which voters conceptualized the electoral choice, the coherence of their political attitudes, and, above all, the extent to which issue positions, rather than party, affected the vote. In the absence of an outlying candidate, we would expect voters to see candidates less in issue terms, to have less coherent attitudes, and to vote with less concern about their issue preferences.

Yet one would not expect a complete change back to the patterns of the

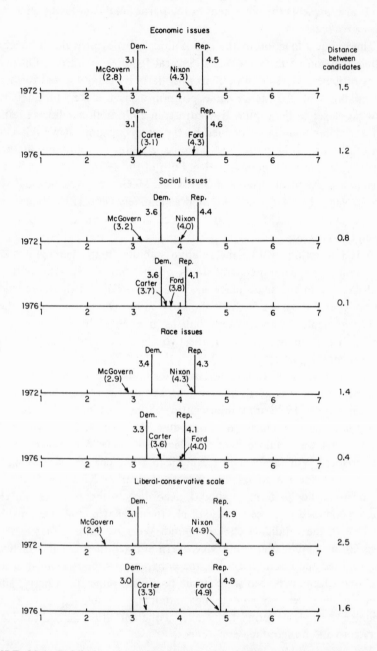

FIGURE 20.1. Public location of parties and candidates on issue scales, 1972 and 1976

fifties. Too many other things have changed. The turbulent politics of the sixties are behind us; but memories may linger on.

Partisanship in 1976

One of the most dramatic and significant changes in the years from 1952 to 1972 was the decline in the level of partisan commitment of the American electorate. The erosion of partisanship was manifested in numerous ways: a decline in the proportion with a partisan identification, increased split ticket voting, increased disaffection with the parties. In part, this erosion may be connected to the change in the nature of the candidates: candidates such as Goldwater and McGovern drove voters across party lines to vote for the opposition and may have thereby weakened the party ties of the defecting voters. But the return to centrist candidates in 1976 would not be expected to reverse the antiparty trend completely.

For one thing, the erosion of party commitments has sources other than the nature of the candidate choice offered the electorate—for example, the weakening of party organizations, the rising campaign importance of television, the nature of the political issues of the sixties that cut through party lines, and the general political malaise of those years that led to disaffection with many institutions. In addition, though Ford and Carter did not offer a clear issue choice, neither did they offer a partisan oriented choice. Neither candidate stressed party ties. Each in his own way played up his independence from the previous administrations of his party. Each stressed the desire to heal prior wounds and correct prior abuses. Neither intended to do so by reconstructing the political parties.

The 1976 data show little evidence of a change back to an electorate with more partisan commitments. There is, perhaps, a decrease in the movement away from parties but little evidence of movement back. The increase in the proportion of the electorate without partisan identification that began in the 1960s peaks at 40 percent in 1974 in the aftermath of Watergate. By 1976, the proportion Independent falls to 37 percent,[6] a figure, however, well above the earlier level of partisan independence.

---

[6] Some have denied that the proportion of Independents has increased as much as this analysis indicates. We believe that the redefinition of the Independent category that has permitted some to find a smaller increase is unwarranted. See Petrocik, "The Changeable American Voter: Some Revisions of the Revision," paper presented at the Annual Meeting of the American Political Science Association, New York, 1978. For more on Independents and the declining attractiveness of the parties among voters see Herbert Weisberg, "Towards a Reconceptualization of Party Identification," paper delivered at the Annual Meeting of the Midwest Political Science Association, Chicago, 1978.

It now seems clear that the precipitous decline in Republican identifiers to 18 percent was a short-lived response to the fall of Richard Nixon. With time—and apparently it did not take much time—the Republicans who felt compelled to deny their sympathies for the GOP during the height of Watergate have returned. Republican identifiers seem to have stabilized at 22 or 23 percent. Democrats have declined slightly from their 1972 strength to about 40 percent.

The persistent weakness of partisanship shows up in other measures as well. Split ticket voting remained high in 1976, and the balance of positive to negative evaluations of parties (see figure 4.7) continued to show a decline. The proportion that can be categorized as "positive partisans" falls another 4 percentage points to 41 percent. The proportion giving nonsupportive responses when asked about their feelings toward the parties increased a like amount to 55 percent. The "feeling thermometers" used in the Michigan election studies to measure the affect Americans feel toward various individuals and institutions also give evidence of a much weaker attraction for the parties than earlier. Even those who consider themselves to be strong partisans rate their own party lower in 1976 than did strong partisans in 1964, 1968, or 1972.

Perhaps the most important indication of the trajectory of partisanship is found in the data on the partisan affiliation of various age cohorts. Figure 20.2 traces the proportion found to be Independents in various cohorts recorded in figure 4.8. The cohorts which entered the electorate before the erosion of party support remain about as committed as they ever were to the parties. There is no change in the proportion of Independents among the established voters of 1952. A slight decrease in the proportion of Independents among the new voters of 1952 is balanced by an increase in the proportion among the new voters of 1960. Most interesting is the fact that the later cohorts remain as nonpartisan as they were four years earlier; half of the new voters of 1972 are still Independent. And the proportion of Independents in the new age cohort entering the electorate in 1976 is close to 50 percent.

In sum, the erosion of partisanship in the American public appears to have slowed, but there has been no return to the level of partisan commitment that existed in earlier years. Fewer citizens identify with one party or the other, ticket splitting is more common, and most Americans have negative views of the parties. The advent of two centrist candidates in 1976 does

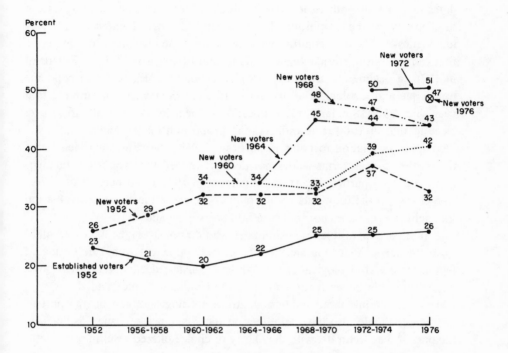

FIGURE 20.2. Proportion of Independents by age cohorts, 1952–1976

not appear to have restored the American political parties to their former place.

Conceptualization and Issue Consistency

The more polarized election choices offered the American electorate from 1964 through 1972 affected the way in which the public conceptualized politics. One consequence appeared to be that the public became more likely to evaluate candidates and parties in terms of issue position and ideology. In addition, the issue positions of voters became more coherent—that is, the relationship among issue positions on different subjects increased, indicating more consistency among attitudes. In the absence of a polarizing choice in 1976, we would expect the public to return to earlier models of thinking, to conceive of the candidates less in issue and ideological terms and to have less coherent issue positions.

Figure 20.3 traces the proportion of the public that describes the candidates in terms of both issues and ideological labels (called "ideologues" in the figure) and the proportion that uses only ideological terms (the "near-ideologues"). The data confirm our expectation. The proportion of the public that can be considered ideologues falls from 19 percent in 1972 to 7 percent in 1976, a decline almost to the level of 1960. In 1976, fewer respondents used issue and ideological terms to describe candidates than in any election year since 1960. Similarly, the proportion of near-ideologues falls to a level close to that of 1960. Interestingly, the proportion of ideologues and near-ideologues in relation to political parties—that is, the percentage describing the parties in such terms—does not decline. Indeed the proportion of ideologues vis-à-vis parties rises from 22 percent in 1972 to 35 percent in 1976.[7] The change in the candidate choice appears to affect the terms of evaluation for candidates but does not spill over into party evaluations.

It appears plausible that candidates who do not stress the issue and ideological distances that separate them from their opponent would be evaluated less in issue and ideological terms. We have suggested, however, a less obvious relationship between the nature of the candidate choice and the way in which voters think about politics. A strong ideological stand on the part of candidates should also have an effect on the coherence of issue positions on the part of the electorate, with the clarity of choice offered resulting in greater issue consistency in the minds of voters.

The 1976 election is a convenient test case for this interpretation. The candidates were more centrist. The population was as well educated—indeed better educated—than in the years from 1964 to 1972 (the change in the educational attainment of the electorate being a rival explanation of the increase in consistency). And the issue questions asked in 1976 were identical in format to those asked in the election studies from 1964 to 1972 (the change in question format between 1960 and 1964 being another rival explanation of increased attitude consistency).

The data for 1976 appear to support our assessment of the impact of nonideological candidates on issue consistency. The average correlation among the five standard issues for which we have a full-time series (racial integration, social welfare, black welfare, the size of the national gov-

---

[7] It is not clear why the proportion of voters who fall into the ideologue category when it comes to evaluation of parties should rise so much. We may speculate that the 1976 election was heavily influenced by "old" issues—essentially economic issues—that have traditionally differentiated Democrats from Republicans. The issue and ideological difference between the parties is clearer in such an election than it would be in an election dominated by social or cultural issues, when the party position is not as distinct.

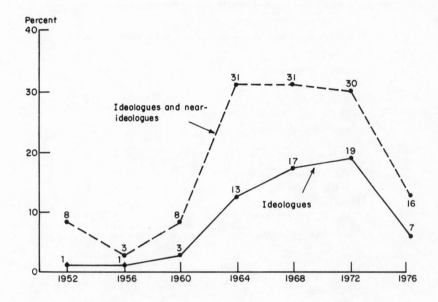

FIGURE 20.3. Ideological evaluation of candidates, 1952–1976

ernment, and our relations with communist countries) is substantially below the level of the period from 1964 through 1972. Table 20.1 presents the gamma association measures. The average gamma is about .26 (.28 if one uses the absolute value of the gamma between the size of government and cold war items), with domestic items slightly more correlated with each other and slightly less correlated with the cold war items. The decline in issue consistency since 1972 is seen graphically in figure 20.4, which reports three different gamma averages for the period 1956 to 1976. The correlations reach their apogee during the 1964 through 1972 era. Although the decline of the correlations in 1976 does not reach the level of the 1950s, it is, nevertheless, substantial.[8]

---

[8] Whether the electorate was ever as consistent in their responses to these issues as is shown here for 1964 through 1972 has been a matter of considerable debate. The SRC/ CPS election studies changed the format and, in a couple of instances, the content of these questions for the 1964 election study. Since the correlation among these items increased substantially in the 1964 data, many scholars have attributed virtually all of the change to measurement factors rather than to the substantive variables emphasized throughout this book.
The analysis upon which the competing interpretation rests appears in George Bishop and others, "Change in the Structure of American Political Attitudes: The Nagging Question of Question Wording," *American Journal of Political Science,* 22 (May 1978), 250–269; George Bishop and others, "Effects of Question Wording and Format on

TABLE 20.1. Level of attitude constraint in 1976
(average gammas between issue spheres)

Welfare/	
black welfare	.46
Welfare/	
integration	.34
Welfare/	
size of government	.27
Welfare/	
cold war	.16
Black welfare/	
integration	.46
Black welfare/	
size of government	.27
Black welfare/	
cold war	.19
Integration/	
size of government	.37
Integration/	
cold war	.16
Size of government/	
cold war	−.11

The weakening of the relationship among the five issues we have traced since the fifties has been paralleled by a decline in the association of these issues with the newer social issues—drugs, urban unrest, crime, and radical political activity—that were such a centerpiece of the political turmoil of the

Political Attitude Consistency," *Public Opinion Quarterly* (forthcoming); George Bishop and others, "The Changing Structure of Mass Belief Systems: Fact or Artifact?" *Journal of Politics*, 40 (August 1978), 781–790; Alfred J. Tuchfarber and George F. Bishop, "Trends in the Structure of American Political Attitudes, 1956–1976: Change or Stability?" paper presented at the Annual Meeting of the Midwest Political Science Association, Chicago, 1978, and George Bishop and others, "Questions About Question Wording: A Rejoinder to Revisiting Mass Belief Systems Revisited," *American Journal of Political Science*, 23 (February 1979), 187–192. All of these papers by Bishop and his colleagues present the same basic data and argument. The rejoinder cited last is slightly different from the others.

Somewhat different work has been done by John L. Sullivan, James E. Piereson, and George E. Marcus, "Ideological Constraint in the Mass Public: A Methodological Critique and Some New Findings," *American Journal of Political Science*, 22 (May 1978), 233–249, and "The More Things Change, the More They Remain the Same: The Stability of Mass Belief Systems," *American Journal of Political Science*, 23 (February 1979). Gregory Brunk has addressed the same concerns in his "The 1964 Attitude Consistency Leap Reconsidered," *Political Methodology* (1979), 176–186. Hugh L. LeBlanc and Mary Beth Merrin treat the data in a slightly different way, but they also question

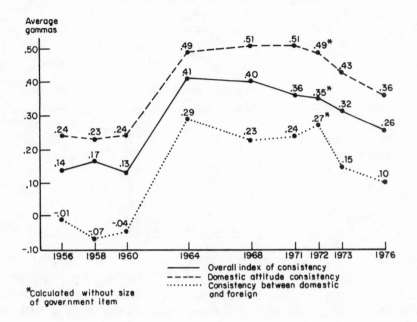

FIGURE 20.4. Changes in attitude consistency, 1956–1976

late 1960s and early 1970s. Table 20.2 presents the correlation of the five standard issues with the newer social issues in 1976. (The data in this table are similar to those in tables 8.2 through 8.4.) Again, the values are lower. The only correlations that persist at their 1972 level are those with the mari-

---

the extent to which issue consistency has increased. See "Mass Belief Systems Revisited," *Journal of Politics,* 39 (November 1977), 1082–1087. Another critique appears in Eric R. A. Smith, "The False Measures of the Levels of Conceptualization," paper presented at the Annual Meeting of the Pacific Chapter, American Association for Public Opinion Research, Lake Arrowhead, Calif., 1979.

We have attempted to answer these criticisms in Norman Nie and James N. Rabjohn, "Revisiting Mass Belief Systems Revisited: Or, Why Doing Research Is Like Watching a Tennis Match," *American Journal of Political Science,* 23 (February 1979), 139–175; John Petrocik, "Comment: Reconsidering the Reconsiderations of the 1964 Change in Attitude Consistency," *Political Methodology,* 5 (Winter 1978), 361–368; and John Petrocik, "The Changeable American Voter: Some Revisions of the Revision," paper presented at the Annual Meeting of the American Political Science Association, New York, 1978, a revised version of which will appear in *The Electorate Reconsidered,* ed. John C. Pierce and John L. Sullivan (Beverly Hills, Calif.: Sage Publications), forthcoming.

This epilogue provides particularly important data for the debate. Despite constant questions in the 1972 and 1976 surveys, the average intercorrelation among the items dropped off considerably in 1976. This decline is consistent with our expectation. We

TABLE 20.2. Association of five standard issues with
social issue items and civil liberty items (average gammas)

	Marijuana	Urban unrest and rights of criminals	Rights of radicals
Welfare	.18	.30	.13
Black welfare	.27	.36	.12
Integration	.23	.28	.07
Size of government	.01	.05	.03
Cold war	.28	.22	.20
Mean 1976	.19	.24	.11
Mean 1970s	.19	.31	.26

juana question. Responses to queries about urban unrest and criminal rights are less correlated with the five issues in 1976 than they were four years earlier; and questions about how radicals and potential subversives should be dealt with are dramatically less correlated with the five issues in 1976. In the latter case, though, the questions have been changed and that may affect the results.

The Meaning of an Issue: The Size of Government Question

Another way to document the responsiveness of the public to the political climate is with the size of government issue. Our analysis suggested that respondents read different meanings into the question depending upon the

---

assume that attitude consistency responds as much to the political context as it does to individual psychological properties. The different candidates and a vastly different political atmosphere in 1976 explain the lower correlations, just as more ideological candidates and a more heated political context after 1960, we believe, precipitated greater issue consistency. Our substantive explanation accounts for the increase and the decline in the correlations. The methodological argument explains the increase, but it does not have any provision for the downward trend of 1976. Unless there is a measurement change that has been overlooked, the artifact explanation for the data in Chapters 8 and 9, while plausible, is not sufficiently supported to dislodge our thesis.

Furthermore, our argument on the change in 1964 is based not only upon a change in the level of issue consistency but also upon a number of changes in other measures not affected by variation in format. In particular, the change in the types of answers given to open-ended candidate and party evaluation questions—a change that is coterminous with the issue consistency change—corroborates our belief that a real change took place in 1964. Both issue consistency and the open-ended answers change back again in 1976. Finally, as we shall see, the pattern of issue voting also changes in a similar manner. Thus, our argument as to the reality of change does not depend on any single measure.

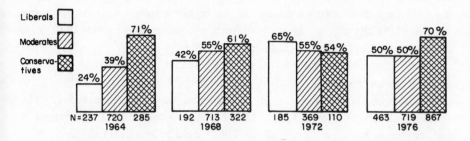

FIGURE 20.5. Proportion saying the government is too big among liberals, moderates, and conservatives, 1964, 1968, 1972, 1976

issues of the day. This is possible because the question on size of government is notably vague with regard to the issue the respondent is being asked about. When first asked in the 1950s and early 1960s, the question about the size and power of the federal government appears to have been interpreted as referring to the proper role of the national government in directing the economy and ensuring the welfare of individual citizens. Conservatives agreed that the government was "too big for the good of the country and the individual citizen," while liberals denied that the government was getting too big.

By the end of the 1960s, and certainly in the 1972 election, "big government" had acquired some new interpretations. The rise of the "social issue" and a heightened concern with domestic order caused many to see the question as a probe about government spying and the erosion of civil liberties. The responsiveness of the electorate to this redefinition of the substantive meaning of a particular question is illustrated by the data presented in figure 20.5. Before 1972, conservatives were more likely than liberals to see a threat in big government. In 1972, the pattern reversed. By 1976, however, agitation over civil liberties and domestic dissent receded. As partisan quarrels focused upon unemployment, inflation, and medical services, the more typical relationship between one's self-identification as a liberal or conservative and the size of government question reasserted itself.

Involvement and the Political Context

Neither methodological nor individual psychological explanations seem to account for the oscillation in issue consistency documented here. The social context seems a more persuasive reason for the shifts. There is an interesting feature of this change that requires some investigation. What kind of citizen is most influenced by the transformation from quiescent politics in the fifties, to turbulence in the late sixties, to the echo of 1976? In particular, it would be interesting to see whether the highly involved citizens are more influenced by the change in context from an outlier election in 1972 to a centrist contest in 1976 than those less involved in politics.

One might expect either to be more affected. The involved are more sensitive to the nature of political stimuli in the environment. If the public responds to the cues sent out by candidates, the more involved citizens should pick up such cues faster. On the other hand, one might expect a greater change among the uninvolved. They would be less likely to have developed stable ways of looking at politics and, therefore, might respond more fully to the stimuli coming from the political environment.

Table 20.3 contrasts the responses of involved and uninvolved citizens in the 1972 and 1976 elections. The top part of the table shows the proportion of those respondents who used issues to evaluate candidates in 1972 who also used issues to evaluate candidates in 1976. It is among the involved citi-

TABLE 20.3. Consistency over time in issue mentioning and in issue coherence, involved and uninvolved citizens

Of those mentioning issues in 1972:	Level of involvement	
	Involved	Uninvolved
Percent mentioning issues in 1976	70	52
Percent not mentioning issues	30	48
	100	100

	Percent remaining at same level of consistency in 1976	
	Involved	Uninvolved
Consistency level in 1972		
Very consistent	63	26
Moderately consistent	58	41
Slightly consistent	54	41
Inconsistent	43	49
Others (centrists and no opinion)	20	47

zens that one finds continuity between the two elections in issue mentioning. The fall off in issue mentioning is greater among uninvolved citizens. Among the involved respondents, 70 percent of those who mention issues in 1972 also mention issues in 1976. Among the uninvolved, the corresponding figure is 52 percent.

The bottom half of table 20.3 presents parallel data on issue coherence. The table shows the proportion of citizens with varying levels of issue consistency in 1972 who maintained a similar level in 1976. The most interesting categories are the groups that were very or moderately consistent in 1972. Among the involved citizens, a much higher proportion continues to have consistent attitudes in 1976 than is the case among the uninvolved.

The conclusion seems to be clear: the more involved citizens tend to see politics in issue terms or to have coherent political attitudes, and this way of thinking about politics is relatively impervious to political context. This is not to say that they are not susceptible to cues from the political environment. The absolute level of issue mentioning and issue coherence goes down between 1972 and 1976 for involved as well as for uninvolved citizens. But relative to the uninvolved, the involved change less between the two elections. Their way of viewing politics seems more internalized, less affected by the climate of the moment. Clearly, candidates who pose distinct issue choices have a greater effect on the modes of political thought of those citizens who are the most marginal in their political involvement.

The Determinants of the Vote in 1976

If the choice of candidates has an effect, we can expect to find the most direct impact on the individual's vote. As we have argued, the nature of the candidate choice affects not only the specific choice made by the voter but also the criteria that go into that choice. As we moved from the late 1950s across the more polarized elections that began in 1964, we found a dramatic change in voting behavior: voting on the basis of party affiliation declined; voting on the basis of issues increased. If the change was due to the changing cast of characters in the elections from 1964 onward, we should see a reversion to earlier patterns in 1976. We would, however, not expect a complete return to the electoral patterns of the pre-1964 races, for too many long-term changes have intervened. In particular, partisanship has not returned to the level of the earlier era.

In general, 1976 conforms nicely to our expectations. Party voting appears to have had a resurgence, coupled with a decline in the significance of issues. Consider, for example, those voters who have issue positions and party identifications that are incongruent—that is, they are either liberal Republicans or conservative Democrats. How do they vote? Do they follow party or their issue position? As figure 16.4 indicated, only 22 percent of this cross-pressured group voted their issue position in 1956; by 1972 the proportion had risen to 48 percent. In 1976, however, the proportion choosing issues over party fell to 29 percent—not quite back to the level of 1956 but well below the proportions for the elections between 1964 and 1972.

Figure 20.6 provides a more general picture of the relative potency of issues and party affiliation in affecting the vote. It brings up to 1976 the analysis of the contribution of party and issues to the voting choice, and shows the estimates of the unique contribution of each as well as the shared contribution of party and issues to the vote.[9] Several important differences appear between the 1976 election and the previous three elections. In the first place, the unique contribution of issues to the voting choice declines precipitously. The unique contribution of issues had peaked in 1972; in 1976 it falls back to the low point of the time series in 1956 and 1960. The shared variance of party and issues remains about the same in 1976 as in the previous two elections. But the total impact of issues (the unique contribution of issues plus that which it shares with party) is smaller in 1976 than in any election since 1960.

The trend line for the unique contribution of party affiliation to the voting decision also shows a reversal in 1976. The figure climbs well above the level of the previous three elections. However, it does not rise to the level of the 1956 and 1960 elections in which the unique contribution of partisanship appears to have dominated all other criteria.

The analysis in figure 20.6 is based on a comparison of the potency of one's party identification and one's position on our issue scale in predicting the vote. An alternative approach to measuring the relative impact of party and issues on the vote is to see the extent to which the criteria used by respondents in response to open-ended questions about the candidates predict their vote. When asked to evaluate the candidates, respondents can mention the candidate's personality, party affiliation, or issue positions as a reason for liking or disliking the person. In figures 10.7 and 10.8 we compared the correlation between evaluations based on each of the three criteria and the vote.

---

[9] For a discussion of the technique see pages 303–305 above, especially footnote 8, p. 303. This thesis is pursued in Petrocik, "The Changeable American Voter." A more complex analysis of the effect of candidates on issue voting, which rests on spatial analysis and social judgment theory and illustrates the ability to predict the shape of the slope between issue preference and the vote, appears in Petrocik, "Levels of Issue Voting: The Effect of Candidate Pairs in Presidential Elections," *American Politics Quarterly* (forthcoming).

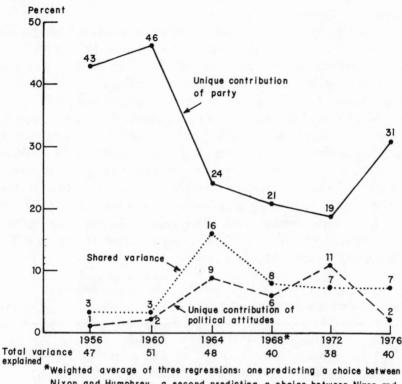

FIGURE 20.6. Percent of variance in presidential vote uniquely attributable to party identification, to political attitudes, and to their shared component, 1956–1976

The purpose was to see which was a better predictor of the vote.[10] Those measures, carried through to 1976, tell a story consistent with that reported in figure 20.6: the effect of issues goes down, the effect of party goes up. The correlation between issue evaluations and the vote was .55 in 1972; by 1976 it had fallen to .45—a figure almost identical to those from 1952 through 1960 (see figure 10.8). The correlation between party evaluation and the vote had plummeted to .14 in 1972; it rose substantially to .38 in 1976. However—and in this too the data are parallel to the data in figure 20.6— the rise in the relationship between party-based evaluations and the vote does

---

[10] For a fuller description of this approach see above, pp. 169–173.

not bring that figure back to the level found for the 1952–1960 elections, when the correlation was around .50.[11]

Thus, the two different ways of looking at the criteria for voting come to the same result: a substantial decline of issue voting in 1976 to levels reminiscent of the pre-1964 elections coupled with a rise in party voting. The fact that we obtain the same result using two different measurement techniques bolsters our conviction that we have located a real change.

The 1976 election, however, does not represent a full return to the pre-1964 elections. Issues lose their power over the vote, but party recovers only some of its power. In addition to the fact that the ability of party affiliation to predict the vote does not return to the level of those earlier elections, the proportion of voters with a party affiliation—that is, voters for whom party *can* play a role in their voting choice—also remains lower than in the earlier years. In the earlier elections, over 75 percent of the electorate reported a party identification; in 1976 the figure was 63 percent. On the other hand, 1976 appears to represent a fuller return to the earlier elections from the

TABLE 20.4. Proportion of potential party and issue voters and relationship of party and issues to the vote

Year	Potential party voters (percent of voters with party identification)	Unique contribution of party identification to vote[a]	Potential issue voters (percent of voters with coherent issue positions)	Unique contribution of issues to vote[a]
1956	76	43	61	1
1960	77	46	63	2
1964	77	24	72	9
1968	71	21	73	6
1972	65	19	72	11
1976	63	31	61	2

[a] Percent of variance in presidential vote uniquely attributable to party or issues. See pages 302–306 for the derivation of these numbers.

---

[11] The data reported are for all voters, whether or not they use the criterion for evaluation. Those not using a criterion are considered neutral. These data parallel the data on figure 10.8. If we apply the analysis only to those who use a particular criterion (as we do on figure 10.7) we find a similar result. The figures for 1976 are .54 for the relationship between issue mentions and the vote and .55 for the relationship between party mention and the vote. The relationships with personal mentions remain the same across the years.

perspective of issue voting. Not only is issue position as weak a predictor of the vote in 1976 as in the earlier elections, but the number of voters with issue positions coherent enough to allow them to vote on that basis reverts in 1976 to the level of the pre-1964 elections. The proportion of respondents who are "potential issue voters" (see table 16.2) fell from 72 percent in 1972 to 61 percent in 1976—the identical percentage as in 1956. Table 20.4, which summarizes these changes, presents the proportions who could vote on the basis of party or issues as well as the relationship between party affiliation or issue position and the vote. Party remains weaker in 1976 than in the early elections: the proportion available to vote party is as low in 1976 as in 1972. The effect of party on the vote among those with an affiliation is higher than in 1972 but is not back at the pre-1964 level. When it comes to issues, 1976 more fully resembles the earlier elections both in terms of the number of voters who can vote on the basis of issues and the likelihood that those who have an issue position will vote on the basis of it.

Figure 20.7 provides a useful summary of the changes in the electorate from the early years through 1976, a summary that takes into account the proportion of the electorate having coherent issue positions, the proportion

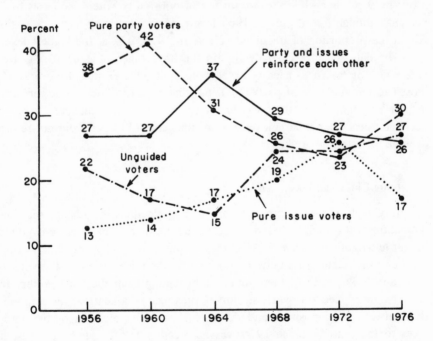

FIGURE 20.7. Issue voting, party voting, issue and party voting, unguided voting, 1956–1976

with a party identification, as well as the extent to which those characteristics affect the vote. The data are similar to those in figure 16.7, with one more category of voters added to make the typology complete. There are four types of voters in figure 20.7: pure party voters, who vote party either in the face of contrary issue position or in the absence of a coherent issue position; pure issue voters, who vote on the basis of issues either in the face of an opposite party affiliation or in the absence of party identification; reinforced voters, whose party and issue positions push in the same direction and who vote accordingly; and unguided voters, who have neither party affiliation nor coherent issue position to guide their vote or who, when party and issue both push in one direction, perversely vote in the other.

The rise in importance of issue voting and the decline of habitual party voting is apparent as we move across the elections to 1972. From 1964 through 1972, the proportion of pure issue voters increases in each election while the proportion of pure party voters as well as the proportion of rein- forced voters decline. In 1972, the electorate is divided into about equal quarters in terms of our typology.

In 1976, we see a dramatic change. The proportion of pure issue voters drops by 9 percent while the proportion of pure party voters increases by 7 percent—though not to the pre-1964 levels. Most interesting, perhaps, is the rise in the proportion of unguided voters. In 1976, it is at the highest level.

The data reflect a clear decline in the importance of issue voting. But voters do not return to a party-based vote as it once existed. Before 1964, most had the guidance of party. In 1964, that began to fade, to be replaced in part by guidance on the basis of issues. In 1976, the guidance of issues declined as each candidate moved toward the center. But party did not return again to its full pride of place.

Issue Choice and Issue Voting

In Chapter 18 we compared a number of elections in order to see how the nature of the choice offered affected the vote of citizens at various points on our left-right issue scale. In elections in which two centrist candidates run, we found the relationship between position on the issue scale and the vote to be relatively flat, with neither candidate benefiting from the issue voting. In an unbalanced election, when an outlier runs against a centrist, the relation- ship between issue position and the vote is stronger, and the outlier loses votes to the centrist. Since 1976 was an election between two centrists, it should resemble the pre-1964 elections in the impact of issues, and it should resemble 1960 more than it resembles the 1952 and 1956 elections. Though the two 1950s elections were contests between two centrists, they were affected as well by an imbalance in the personal popularity of the candidates that was not the case in 1960 or 1976.

Figure 20.8 presents the relationship between position on the left-right issue scale and the proportion voting Democratic in 1976. It compares that election with 1960 and (for contrast) with 1972. The similarity between 1976 and 1960 is quite striking. The lines have an almost identical slope and in most categories the lines are within a few percentage points of each other. In each election, almost all points fall within the central section of the graph, where neither party dominates the vote. In contrast, 1972 shows a stronger relationship between the issue position of voters and their vote, and the outcome is more unbalanced.

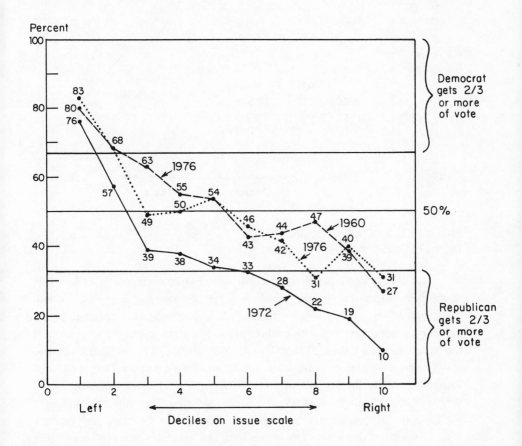

FIGURE 20.8. Percent voting Democratic by position on left-right issue scale, 1960, 1972, 1976

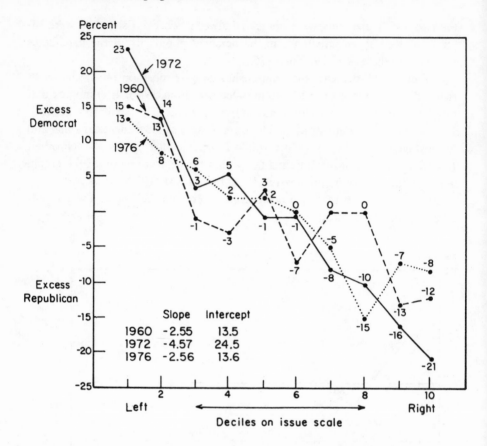

FIGURE 20.9. Residual Democratic vote by position on left-right issue scale, 1960, 1972, 1976

The difference across these elections is made even clearer in figure 20.9, which presents the relationship between issue position and a residual Democratic vote. The residual vote represents the Democratic vote reduced by the defection rates associated with each contest. The data reflect the deviation of the vote associated with a liberal or conservative issue position, over and above the liberalism or conservatism associated with being a Democrat or a Republican. The figures are positive if being liberal causes a Democratic vote, negative if being a conservative causes a Republican vote. If the figures are close to zero, issues are causing little or no deviation from the vote one would expect on the basis of partisanship. The residuals for 1960 and 1976 are virtually identical. The residuals in 1972 are substantially larger. A regression of the residual vote measure on the belief categories shows similar regression slopes for 1960 and 1976 (-2.55 and -2.56, respectively) but a larger one for 1972 (-4.57).

The 1976 election, thus, is a useful validation of the models of electoral choice presented in Chapter 18. It fits very closely with the model of an election between two centrists in which issues play a relatively weak role in the vote.[12]

Issues, Parties, and the Vote

The data are consistent with the general view that the public responds to the nature of the choice offered by the candidates. Jimmy Carter and Gerald Ford offered the public a choice that was less polarized than the choice in recent elections. The public responded by viewing the candidates less in terms of issues or ideology and by voting less on the basis of issue position. In the absence of issue cues, voting in conformity with party affiliation increased. The result is in many ways an election that resembles those of the pre-1964 era, particularly the election of 1960.

The match, however, is far from complete. Ford and Carter, by underplaying the issue distance between them, conducted an election campaign that returned issue voting to the pre-1964 level. But they did not bring partisanship back to the prominent position it occupied as a determinant of the outcome of the early elections. Party voting went up in 1976 but did not return to its pre-1964 level. And in other ways partisanship was weaker in 1976 than it had been in the earlier years. That the positions taken by the two candidates would change the trend in issue voting but leave the tendency toward party erosion unchanged makes a good deal of sense. Candidates set the issue agenda for an election. They have less control over those long-term changes in American politics that have weakened the political parties. Furthermore, the candidates made no attempt to resuscitate the parties: neither came on as a strong partisan or attempted to appeal to party symbols.

If voters chose in ways that were in conformity with their partisan iden-

---

[12] A novel and competing theory of issue-directed choice appears in George Rabinowitz, "On the Nature of Political Issues: Insights from a Spatial Analysis," *American Journal of Political Science*, 23 (November 1978), 793–817. Rabinowitz does not see issue voting proceeding from calculations by voters about their specific positions and those of the candidates. In his view, voters are disposed to support liberal or conservative candidates depending upon whether they are liberals or conservatives. Voters categorized in the far left or right of an index are not necessarily more liberal or conservative; rather, such voters are simply more likely to find issues salient. As one moves to the center of the index, therefore, issue voting drops off because the liberalism or conservatism of the voter is not so salient that it cannot be displaced by some other criterion for choosing a candidate. Rabinowitz's idea places fewer demands on the data (and, of course, on voters) than the spatial model upon which this analysis rests.

tifications, it may have been because there were fewer forces to push them away from such a vote rather than because there was a positive pull on the basis of party identification.

The Electoral Coalition: Group Support in 1976

The change in the party coalitions that became so noticeable in the 1960s continued in 1976. Many observers believe they saw a resurrection of the New Deal party system in Carter's candidacy. As a southerner with liberal credentials on the issue of race, he seemed uniquely qualified to reassemble the battered and warring elements of the Democratic coalition. As a born-again Christian, he had a potential religious appeal that previous Democrats had lacked. When Carter won the South and most of the big states and their cities with a campaign in which unemployment, taxation, and inflation were paramount issues, the old Democratic coalition seemed to have regained robust health. The prescient observers who had predicted the reknitting of the coalition seemed vindicated. The old issues were back, as were the traditional electoral college votes.[13] Carter's vote was nearer the normal Democratic vote than any presidential election since 1944.[14]

But to assume that the election of 1976 represented a resurgence of the New Deal coalition would be a mistake.[15] The Democratic party won in 1976 with a different coalition from the party of the New Deal. The coalition that elected Jimmy Carter displayed all of the differences from the New Deal coalition that our analysis of the 1960s realignment (see Chapter 13) would lead us to expect.

The New Deal built a Democratic majority out of the white South,

---

[13] T. Nicholson and J. Doyle, "Old Coalition," *Newsweek,* November 15, 1976, p. 29; Harry Bernstein, "Election Shows Labor's Return to Democrats," *Los Angeles Times,* November 4, 1976; William Schneider, "Democrats Got Their Act Going Again," *Los Angeles Times,* November 7, 1976. In commenting on the 1976 election, Ladd and Hadley write that "American electoral politics can once again be understood in the framework made familiar during the Roosevelt era." Everett C. Ladd with Charles D. Hadley, *Transformations of the American Party System,* rev. ed. (New Fork: Norton, 1978), p. xxv.

[14] The first results of the SRC/CPS election study are reported in Arthur H. Miller and Warren E. Miller, "Partisanship and Performance: 'Rational' Choice in the 1976 Presidential Election," paper presented at the Annual Meeting in the American Political Science Association, Washington, D.C., September 1977. See also Arthur H. Miller, "The Majority Party Reunited? A Summary Comparison of the 1972 and 1976 Elections," in *Political Parties and Elections in an Anti-Party Age,* ed. Jeffery Fishel (Bloomington, Ind.: Indiana University Press, 1978).

[15] See Pomper and others, *The Election of 1976,* pp. 79–82, for a brief analysis of aggregate data which illustrate the divergence of the Carter vote from that which characterized previous Democratic presidential coalitions.

Catholics (through big city party organizations), blacks, Jews, and union members. While white northern Protestants were not absent, especially if they were union affiliated, the Democratic vote among northern WASPs who were not union members was small. In the 1948 election, perhaps the last election of the New Deal era, almost 85 percent of Truman's vote was cast by southern whites, Jews, blacks, Catholics, and union members.[16] Southern whites gave 78 percent of their ballots to Truman, Catholics cast a 64 percent Democratic vote, 70 percent of the votes of union members went to Truman, and blacks and Jews were also strongly Democratic, 90 and 88 percent Democratic, respectively. The Truman vote among northern Protestants lacking union affiliation averaged 31 percent, and it was lower among upper

TABLE 20.5. Comparison of Democratic vote in the 1948, 1950s, and 1976 elections (percentage voting Democratic in each group)

Group	1948	1950s[a]	1976
Northern white Protestants			
High status	24	9	30
Middle status	26	20	36
Low status	40	28	49
White southerners			
Border State			
Middle status	60	57	33
Lower status	55	40	49
Deep South			
Middle status	77	51	39
Lower status	90	57	54
White Catholics			
Polish and Irish	63	59	53
Other nationalities			
Upper status	55	50	42
Lower status	70	52	62
Blacks	90	72	95
Jews	88	79	73
Union members	70	55	61

[a] The 1950s averages the Democratic vote of the groups for the 1952, 1956, and 1960 presidential elections.

[16] Published studies of the 1948 election are scarce. The SRC study done in 1948 was small and unable to support very extensive analyses of voting patterns. All of the analysis of the Truman vote and the 1948 election in this chapter rests upon the recalled 1948 vote of respondents in the 1952 election study.

TABLE 20.6. Social group composition of Democratic and Republican voting coalitions, 1948, 1950s, and 1976[a] (percentages)

| | DEMOCRATIC VOTERS | | |
	1948	1950s[b]	1976
WASPs	16	15	21
Southern whites	19	22	17
Catholics	17	17	19
Blacks	8	7	15
Jews	6	7	4
Union members	27	27	22
Other	7	5	2
	100	100	100

| | REPUBLICAN VOTERS | | |
	1948	1950s[b]	1976
WASPs	49	42	38
Southern whites	7	18	24
Catholics	13	11	15
Blacks	1	2	1
Jews	1	1	1
Union members	17	17	15
Other	11	9	6
	100	100	100

[a] Voters are placed in the highest category on the list into which they fall—for example, a southern white, Catholic union member is categorized as a southern white.

[b] The 1950s averages the Democratic vote of the groups for the 1952, 1956, and 1960 presidential elections.

status WASPs. Even the candidacies of Eisenhower and Kennedy did not disturb the coalitions substantially. Attracted by Eisenhower and repelled by Kennedy, Dixie still cast a majority of its votes for the Democratic ticket; and Jews, Catholics, and blacks, though buffeted by the tides of electoral fortune, were identifiably Democratic in 1952, 1956, and 1960.

The 1976 election represented a contest between two substantially different coalitions, as table 20.5 shows. Just over 43 percent of white southerners supported Carter, a pale reflection of a history of over 70 percent support for Democratic candidates. Catholic support for the ticket was ane-mic. Only a bare majority—53 percent—voted for Carter. The Democrats did well among only three traditional members of the New Deal coalition: blacks (95 percent), Jews (73 percent), and union members (61 percent). Jimmy Carter won the election because turnout among blacks made their 95 percent support more significant and because northern WASPs are now more Democratic.

Table 20.6, which contrasts the social group coalitions that cast Demo-cratic and Republican votes in 1948, in the 1950s, and in 1976, illustrates that the changed party bias described in Chapter 13 is not transitory. Jimmy Carter's winning coalition is not the traditional Democratic coalition. When we compare the 1950s to 1976, we see the proportion of northern WASPs in the Democratic camp increased by 40 percent, blacks increased by 117 per-cent, and southern whites declined by a quarter. There are corresponding changes in Ford's support compared to earlier Republicans. Carter was not able to reassemble the old coalition. The issues which have undermined it—issues such as race—make that difficult.[17]

Conclusion: The Changeable American Voter

The Changing American Voter grew out of an interest in assessing the contextual variables that influence individual-level behavior patterns. We wished to look closely at something of which scholars were becoming in-creasingly aware: "eternal" verities about political behavior can be time bound, reflecting some short-term properties of the political system. With our time-aided perspective we would disavow any intention of creating a por-trait of a new, "changed" American voter. Rather, we have found a change-able and perhaps highly maleable voter. It is not an equivocation to conclude that the American voter has and has not changed over the last two and one-half decades.

The preceding data portray an electorate whose political attitudes and behavior have changed. In the 1960s, voters began to be more issue con-scious and less partisan than they had been. Some of the apparent change may have been inflated by measurement artifacts; not all of it can be traced to methodological variables. But there is probably not a new American voter. It is unlikely that the voter has changed from one stable and normal state to a new stable and normal state. Instead, the image of the voter as a stable

---

[17] Chapter 9 of Petrocik, *Party Coalitions* (forthcoming) presents an analysis of the impact of race issues on the party coalitions—southern whites in particular—as an illus-of an issue whose partisan balance changed in recent years.

creature with a limited repertoire of responses to political events has been undermined. The original emphasis on inherent psychological characteristics of voters requires revision in the light of the changes we have observed. Yet that does not mean we have a new, much more politicized voter—though there have been changes in this direction.

Voters are probably not dramatically more or less ideological now than they were in the recent past. The increases in issue consistency and in the proportion who used ideological terms to evaluate political stimuli reflected changes in the nature of politics during the 1960s. Similarly, the surge of issue voting in the late 1960s and early 1970s, while not wholly independent of the greater politicization of the population, clearly reflected a change in the type of candidate presented to the electorate. The presidential elections of 1952, 1956, and 1960 presented few burning issues to the public and the candidates went out of their way to emphasize the person or the party they represented.[18] In contrast, polarizing issues were the stuff of the 1960s, and the candidates emphasized them. The limited data from the 1930s that were presented in Chapter 11 give good reason to believe that a similar analysis of the electorate in earlier periods would have presented a picture similar to that of the 1960s.

In short, the behavior of the voter is strongly influenced by the prevailing political context. The lower levels of issue consistency, the weaker correlation of issue preferences with the vote, and the resurgence of the correlation of partisanship and the vote in 1976 point to the variable nature of mass behavior and attitudes. This oscillation also points to a need to understand better how the electorate is influenced by the political context. Future elections—and further analysis of past elections— should allow us to continue to study this process.

---

[18] See Page, *Choices and Echoes.*

Appendices

Index

Appendix 1

THE DATA

The ten election studies conducted by the Survey Research Center/Center for Political Studies (SRC/CPS) at the University of Michigan from 1952 through 1972 provide the bulk of the data analyzed in this book. These data are distributed by the Inter-University Consortium for Political Research (ICPR), located at the Institute for Social Research at Ann Arbor, Michigan.

The SRC/CPS surveys are multistage, area probability samples to the household level. Full technical descriptions of the samples, exact question wording, coding conventions, interviewer instructions, and study codebooks are available as SRC publications.

In addition to the Michigan election studies, we have used data from two national surveys conducted under our direction at the National Opinion Research Center (NORC) at the University of Chicago. Unlike the Michigan samples, the 1971 and 1973 NORC studies are multistage, area probability samples to the block level, with the final-stage samples based on the block-quota technique. Complete information about these samples can be obtained from NORC.

The following table presents the number of unweighted interviews in each of the ten Michigan studies and the two NORC surveys, along with the year and month of the field work.

	Year	Cases
*Michigan Election Study of	1952	1899
	1956	1762
	1958	1450
	1960	1181
	1962	1297
	1964	1834
	1966	1291
	1968	1673
	1970	1694
	1972	2705
NORC Amalgam Survey of March	1971	1500
December	1973	1489

* Studies were conducted in October and November of each election year.

Appendix 2A

THE ISSUE QUESTIONS EMPLOYED IN THE ANALYSIS OF ATTITUDE CONSISTENCY

The exact questions employed to index attitudes in each of the issue domains are listed below by theme and by year.

1. Social welfare

a. Employment

(1956, 1958, 1960) "The government in Washington ought to see to it that everybody who wants to work can find a job. Do you have an opinion on this or not?" (Agree strongly—disagree strongly)

(1964, 1968) "In general, some people feel that the government in Washington should see to it that every person has a job and a good standard of living. Others think the government should just let each person get ahead on his own. Have you been interested enough in this to favor one side over the other?"

(1972) Same as 1964 and 1968. "Where would you place yourself on this scale?"

b. School aid

(1956, 1958, 1960) "If cities and towns around the country need help to build more schools, the government in Washington ought to give them the money they need. Do you have an opinion on this or not?" (Agree strongly—disagree strongly)

(1964, 1968) "Some people think the government in Washington should help towns and cities provide education for grade and high school children; others think that this should be handled by the states and local communities. Have you been interested enough in this to favor one side over the other?"

(1972) Not asked.

c. Medicare

(1956, 1960, no question asked in 1958) "The government ought to help people get doctors and hospital care at low cost. Do you have an opinion on this or not?" (Agree strongly—disagree strongly)

(1964, 1968) "Some say the government in Washington ought to help people get doctors and hospital care at low cost, others say the government should not get into this. Have you been interested enough in this to favor one side over the other?"

(1972) "There is much concern about the rapid rise in medical and hospital costs. Some feel there should be a government insurance plan which would cover all medical and hospital expenses. Others feel that medical expenses should be paid by individuals, and through private insurance like Blue Cross. Where would you place yourself on this scale, or haven't you thought much about this?"

d. NORC 1971 welfare questions

"Some people think that the government should support any family that doesn't have enough money to live on, even if the father is working. Look at Card F. They would be at point 1. Other people think that, no matter how poor a family is, they should take care of themselves. They would be at point 7. Still other people have an opinion that falls somewhere in between. Where would you place yourself?"

"Some people think that the government should use all its resources to eliminate poverty in this country. Look at Card K. They would be at point 1. Others think the government has already done too much about poverty. They would be at point 7. And others have opinions that fall somewhere in between 1 and 7. Where would you place yourself?"

2. Black welfare

(1956, 1958, 1960) "If Negroes are not getting fair treatment in jobs and housing, the government should see to it that they do. Do you have an opinion on this or not?" (Agree strongly—disagree strongly)

(1961 and 1968) "Some people feel that if Negroes (colored people) are not getting fair treatment in jobs the government in Washington ought to see to it that they do. Others feel that this is not the federal government's business. Have you had enough interest in this question to favor one side over the other?"

(NORC 1971) "Some people think that the recent attempts to improve conditions for blacks in America should be speeded up. Look at Card E. They would be at point 1. Others think that these efforts should be slowed down; they would be at point 7. And those who have other opinions would be somewhere between 1 and 7. Where would you place yourself?"

(1972) "Some people feel that if black people are not getting fair treatment in jobs the government in Washington ought to see to it that they do. Others feel that this is not the federal government's business. Have you had enough interest in this question to favor one side over the other?"

3. School integration

(1956, 1958, 1960) "The government in Washington should stay out of the question of whether white and colored children go to the same school. Do you have an opinion on this or not?" (Agree strongly—disagree strongly)

(1964, 1968, 1972) "Some people say that the government in Washington should see to it that white and Negro children are allowed to go to the same schools. Others claim this is not the government's business. Have you been concerned enough about this question to favor one side over the other?"

(NORC 1971) "Some people believe that the government should do whatever is necessary to see to it that blacks can buy homes in white neighborhoods. Look at Card I. They would be at point 1. Others feel that the government should stay out of it altogether. They would be at point 7. While others have opinions somewhere in between. Where would you place yourself?"

4. Size of government

(1956, 1958) "The government should leave things like electric power and housing for private businessmen to handle." (Agree strongly—disagree strongly)

(1960) "The government should leave things like electric power and housing for private business to handle. Do you have an opinion on this or not? (If yes) Do you think the government should leave things like this to private business?"

(1964, 1968, 1972) "Some people are afraid the government in Washington is getting too powerful for the good of the country and the individual person. Others feel that the government in Washington is not getting too strong for the good of the country. Have you been interested enough in this to favor one side over the other?"

(NORC 1971) No parallel question.

(1972) "Some people are afraid the government in Washington is getting too powerful for the good of the country and the individual person. Others feel that the government in Washington is not getting too strong. Have you been interested enough in this to favor one side over the other?"

"What is your feeling. Do you think the government is getting too powerful or do you think the government is not getting too strong?"

(1973) "Some people think that the government in Washington is trying to do too many things that should be left to individuals and private businesses. Others disagree and think that the government should do even more to solve our country's problems. Still others have opinions somewhere in between. Where would you place yourself?"

5. Cold war

(1956, 1958, 1960) "The United States should keep soldiers overseas where they can help countries that are against communism. Do you have an opinion on this or not?" (Agree strongly—disagree strongly)

(1964, 1968, 1972) "Have you been paying any attention to what is going on in Vietnam? (If yes) Do you think we did the right thing in getting into the fighting in Vietnam or should we have stayed out?

"Which of the following do you think we should do in Vietnam? Pull out of Vietnam entirely, keep our soldiers in Vietnam but try to end the fighting, or take a stronger stand even if it means invading Vietnam?" (These questions were combined into a single index. See Appendix 2B.)

(NORC 1971) "Some people think we should withdraw completely from Vietnam right now; other people think we should do everything necessary to win a complete military victory; and others have opinions somewhere in between. Look at this card. If you think of the people who support an immediate withdrawal at point 1, and the people who support complete military victory at point 7, and those who have other oinions as somewhere between 1 and 7, where would you place yourself?"

6. Civil liberties

(1956) "The government ought to fire any government worker who is accused of being a communist, even though they don't prove it." (Agree strongly—disagree strongly)

(1968) "There are many possible ways for people to show their disapproval or disagreement with governmental policies and actions. I am going to describe three such ways. We would like to know which ones you approve of as ways of showing a dissatisfaction with the government, and which ones you would disapprove of . . . How about taking part in protest meetings or marches that are permitted by the local authorities? Would you approve of doing that, disapprove, or would it depend on the circumstances? . . ."

(1971) "There are a lot of ways that people can try to influence what the government does. We are interested in knowing what you think of some of these ways. Do you think people should be allowed to hold peaceful demonstrations to ask the government to act on some issue?" (Always—never)

(1972) "There are many possible ways for people to show their disapproval or disagreement with governmental policies and actions. I am going to describe three such ways. We would like to know which ones you approve of as ways of showing dissatisfaction with the government, and which ones you disapprove of. . . . How about taking part in protest meetings or marches that are permitted by the local authorities? Would you approve of taking part, disapprove, or would it depend on the circumstances?"

"Some people feel that after the Vietnam war is over, the government should declare an amnesty—that is, men who left the country to avoid the draft should be allowed to return without severe punishment. How do you feel? Do you think the government should declare an amnesty after the war?"

7. Social issues

a. Crime and urban unrest

(1968) "There is much discussion about the best way to deal with the problem of urban unrest and rioting. Some say it is more important to use all available force to maintain law and order—no matter what results. Others say it is more important to correct the problems of poverty and unemployment that give rise to the disturbances. And, of course, other people have opinions in between. Suppose the people who stress the use of force are at one end of this scale—at point number 7. And suppose the people who stress doing more about the problems of poverty and unemployment are at the other end—at point number 1. Where would you place ———— on this scale? Which does he stress more?"

(1971) "Now about the problem of unrest and rioting in cities, some say it is more important to correct the problems of poverty and unemployment that cause the disturbances. These people would be at point 1. Others say that it is more important to use all available force to keep law and order—even if some people get hurt. They would be at point 7. And those who have other opinions would be somewhere between 1 and 7. Where would you stand on this scale?"

"Some people think that the government should be much more careful to protect the rights of suspected criminals. They would be at point 1. Other people think that the government has gone much too far in protecting the rights of suspected criminals; they would be at point 7; while other people have an opinion that falls somewhere in between. Where would you place yourself?"

"The police should be allowed to search meeting places of radical groups even though the police don't have search warrants." (Agree strongly—disagree strongly)

(1972) "Some people are primarily concerned with doing everything possible to protect the legal rights of those accused of committing crimes. Others feel that it is more important to stop criminal activity even at the risk of reducing the rights of the accused. Where would you place yourself on this scale, or haven't you thought about it much?"

"There is much discussion about the best way to deal with the problem of urban unrest and rioting. Some say it is more important to use all available force to maintain law and order—no matter what results. Others say it is more important to correct the problems of poverty and unemployment that give rise to the disturbances. Where would you place yourself on this scale, or haven't you thought about it much?"

(1973) "Some people think that the government should be much more careful to protect the rights of suspected criminals. Other people think that the government has gone much too far in protecting the rights of suspected criminals. Where would you place yourself?"

"Some people think that in order to protect itself, the government should be allowed to spy on anyone who is a member of a radical group even though that person may not have broken the law. Others think that under no circumstances should the government be allowed to do this. Where would you place yourself?"

b. Life style

(1971) "Some people think that anyone who wants to smoke marijuana should be allowed to do so. They would be at point 1. Others think that no one should be allowed to smoke marijuana; they would be at point 7 and those who have other opinions would be somewhere between 1 and 7. Where would you place yourself?"

"Now I want to ask you about some groups in America. I'd like to know your feelings about these groups. For example, here's a card with the name of a group on it. Now, here's a larger card with five boxes. Each box represents a different type of feeling. Here's how it works. If you don't know too much about a group, or don't especially like or dislike them, you should place the card in the middle. If you like the group, or feel favorably toward them, you would place the card at 1 or 2, depending on how much you like them. On the other hand, if you dislike the group or don't feel favorably toward them, then you would place the card on the right side at 4 or 5, depending on how much you dislike them."

(1973) "Some people think that the use of marijuana should be made *legal*. Others think that the penalties for using marijuana should be set *higher* than they are now. Of course, others have opinions somewhere in between. Suppose the people who want the use of marijuana made legal are at point 1 on this card and the people who think penalties for its use should be set higher than they are now are at point 7. Where would you place yourself?"

A Special Note on the Cold War Attitudes

We define the dimension labeled "cold war" as the degree to which the citizen adopts a tough versus a conciliatory attitude toward the Soviet Union and other communist states. We therefore use military policy questions, rather than questions on such things as trading with communist countries or dealing with them in political matters, to index foreign policy attitudes. For the years 1956 through 1960, the cold war dimension was represented by a single question on the desirability of sending American soldiers to help foreign countries that are against communism.

In the Michigan election surveys for the years 1964 through 1972, two questions were used to measure attitudes on the cold war: (1) whether the United States should become involved in the Vietnamese war and (2) the policy the respondent would prefer once the United States was in the war. To obtain a single measure of orientation to the cold war issue, the answers were combined to categorize the respondent as: (1) approving of American intervention in the war and wanting the United States to pursue a policy of military victory or (2) believing the United States should never have become involved and (at the time of the survey) believing the United States should immediately end its military involvement in Vietnam. Between these extremes there were three intermediate categories containing those respondents who gave a more mixed pattern of opinions. In our analysis, we treated these as a single intermediate category.

Recoding the Questions and the Treatment of Missing Data

The analysis of issue consistency based on the gamma correlation measures excluded respondents who were coded as: (1) having no opinion on the question, (2) unable to decide between the alternatives offered, or (3) otherwise giving no response to the question. This procedure was followed on a question-by-question basis, so that a respondent was included in the computation of gammas for all pairs of questions for which there were valid responses.

The gamma correlation coefficient is particularly sensitive to two characteristics of variables: (1) the number of categories in each of the variables being correlated and (2) the presence of extreme marginal distributions, particularly at the high or low end of the distribution. In general, as the number of categories of the variables being correlated increases, gamma decreases. For example, if a matrix of gammas is computed among survey items with five response categories, the average gamma in the matrix will be smaller than would be the case if the five categories were recoded into three categories prior to the calculation of the coefficients. In instances when variables have less than 15 percent of the responses in either the high or the low category, gamma becomes very unstable, producing an atypical reading on the degree of association. Because the number of response categories differs at several points, and because there are instances of at least some skew in distributions, all items were recoded into three categories for all years, and the conventions used for recoding attempted, as far as possible, to overcome extreme marginal distributions.

The questions asked in the years 1956 through 1960 were asked in the form of Likert scales, with five response categories ranging from strong agreement to strong disagreement. In certain instances, the marginals were sufficiently balanced so that it was possible to recode the questions in a way that ignored whether the agreement or disagreement was mild or intense. The questions recoded under this convention were: employment, school integration, size of government, and cold war. The recoding procedure was as follows:

agree strongly ——————————————→ liberal response
agree ————————————————————
neutral ————————————————————→ centrist response
disagree ——————————————————
disagree strongly ————————————————→ conservative response

The distributions on the remaining questions in the 1956 and 1960 studies (federal aid to schools, medical care, and black welfare) were sufficiently skewed in the liberal direction to cause us to use a slightly different recoding procedure to achieve a more balanced set of marginals. The procedure utilized in this case was as follows:

agree strongly ─────────────────────→ liberal response
agree ───────────────────────────→ centrist response
neutral ──
disagree ───────────────────────→ conservative response
disagree strongly ─

Following these two conventions, responses to all of the questions were recoded into three categories: liberal, centrist, and conservative, with no variable having less than 20 percent of the responses in any category, and few, if any categories having more than 40 percent.

In 1964 and 1968, the SRC changed the question format into a dichotomous choice, with a center category containing only those respondents who suggested an intermediate answer or rejected both alternatives. Fortunately for our analysis, none of the questions display an extreme skew in the marginals, and while the frequencies in the central category are often small, this has little impact on the gamma coefficient.

Two types of questions were employed in the 1972 study—questions of the dichotomous type, similar to those used in 1964 and 1968. These were not recoded. Others were in the format of seven-point scales. These were recoded by placing the three most liberal categories together, by letting the middle point on the scale (category 4) represent the centrist position, and by combining the remaining three categories as the conservative position. The recoding scheme is as follows:

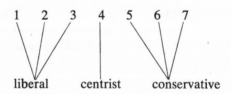

The 1971 and 1973 NORC studies also used seven-point scales. In general, the above procedure was followed. In a few instances, marginals were sufficiently skewed to require us to deviate from this pattern. When this was the case, the rule used was to produce, as nearly as possible, a measure with three categories with about a third of the nonmissing responses in each category, without doing total violence to the implicit meaning of the numbers.

The civil liberties and social issue questions were asked in a variety of formats over the years. As with the questions in the five major issue domains, questions in these areas were recoded into three categories before the gamma coefficients were calculated. The recoding conventions attempted to equalize the marginal distributions.

Most of the civil liberties questions have the following response categories: "approve," "disapprove," and "depends on the circumstances." These did not have to be recoded. In 1956 the question on firing suspected communist workers was recoded so that the responses "agree strongly" and "agree" were in one category, "it depends" and "disagree" in a second, and "disagree strongly" in the third.

Among the social issue questions there was a similarly worded question asked in 1971 on whether the police should be allowed to spy on anyone who is a member of a radical group. The recoding for this question, which had four possible responses, placed both "disagree" categories and both "agree" categories together.

The remainder of the social issue questions, in 1968, 1971, 1972, and 1973, were asked in the form of seven-point scales. Some of them could be recoded by combining the three most liberal categories, leaving the middle category, and combining the three most conservative categories, as in the scheme above. At times, the response patterns were so skewed that we had to deviate from this pattern. Again our rule of thumb was to produce three categories which divided the respondents approximately equally.

Appendix 2B

THE SUMMARY INDEX OF ATTITUDE CONSISTENCY AND LIBERAL-CONSERVATIVE OPINION

The summary index of political opinion is built from the questions in the five main issue spheres given in Appendix 2A: (1) social welfare, general; (2) social welfare, specifically for blacks; (3) school integration; (4) size of government; and (5) the cold war. The summary index appears in the analysis in several different forms. First, it appears in "folded" form, as a measure of attitude consistency. In this format, the measure is used to assess changes through time in the proportion of the population having consistent attitudes, whether liberal or conservative. Second, the index is used in "unfolded" form in several places in the book in order to create a scale running from liberal to conservative. In some places, the respondents are classified on this measure in three basic categories (liberal, moderate, and conservative); at other times, finer distinctions are made, and respondents are classified according to their score on the index into five or ten classes, according to their degree of liberal or conservative inclination.

The Scale Construction

Unlike the analysis using gammas, the summary index was built using the original coding categories for the questions. "Don't know" responses are coded as middle answers. The questions for each of the five issue domains were then standardized, using the Z-score transformation. (For the social welfare domain, which always contained more than one question, the several questions were standardized, summed, and restandardized.) These standardized measures were subjected to a principle-component analysis. A summary score for each respondent was obtained by multiplying the factor loading for each standardized item by its respective standardized score. This was repeated for

TABLE A.1. Unstandardized factor scores used to build the summary measure of political opinions

Year	Size of government	Black welfare	School integration	Economic welfare	Foreign policy
1956	.45567	.76241	.60398	.67566	.02071
1958	.28632	.81597	.74606	.56860	.05784
1960	.37823	.75315	.69295	.64512	.00055
1964	.63676	.77081	.66827	.68813	.09169
1968	.55787	.75259	.74998	.75993	.15068
1972	[a]	.76620	.75872	.63900	.43357

[a] Deleted in this year. See Chapter 8 for a discussion of these deletions.

each of the five issue domains. The sum of these five products provides the value for the individual on the opinion index. This mode of combination produces a summary index for each year with a mean of zero and a variance which reflects the overall correlation among the items. The standard deviation of this measure for each year will be approximately equal to the eigenvalue for the factor analysis. A larger standard deviation (eigenvalue) indicates a greater correlation among the items. Across the years, therefore, the change in the standard deviation of the summary measure indexes the fact that there is more constraint in the sixties and seventies than in the fifties. An increasing standard deviation also indicates that more individuals are found at the extremes of the continuum because they give consistently liberal or conservative answers. Table A.1 presents the factor scores for each issue domain in each year. Figure A.1 presents the standard deviation of the principal component of each year.

Each respondent has a score reflecting the consistency with which he answered the questions and whether he answered them in a liberal or conservative manner. Respondents with large positive scores are consistently conservative; respondents with large negative scores, consistently liberal. A score near zero indicates either that the individual was responding primarily by choosing middle alternatives or that his conservative answers were balanced by his liberal answers to the questions. There are, therefore, two types of centrists with zero scores in this measure: consistent moderates and cancelling centrists. There is no way to sort out these types of centrists.

Because of the sample design of the 1970 study and because of a lack of questions in the years 1952, 1962, and 1966, the studies from these years are not included in the analysis.

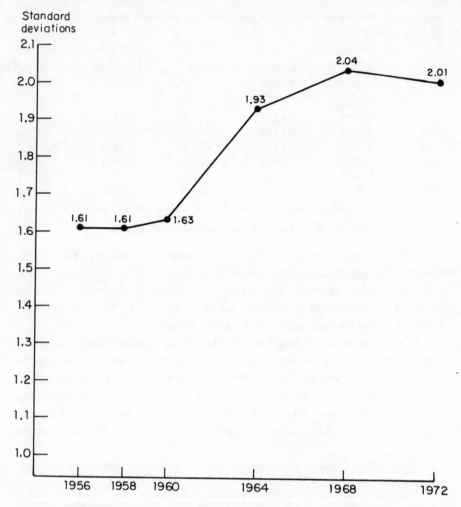

FIGURE A.1. Standard Deviation of the Factored Belief Index

Appendix 2C

THE LEVELS OF CONCEPTUALIZATION

The "levels of conceptualization" measure relies heavily upon descriptions in *The American Voter;* Converse, "The Nature of Belief Systems in Mass Publics"; and an unpublished paper by Theodore Anagason, "Ideology in the American Electorate: 1952–1972," Department of Political Science, University of Rochester, December 1972. However, our measure is fundamentally different from that in *The American Voter* in that we use coded responses rather than an evaluative reading of the interview protocols.

The measure is based on open-ended codes for responses to eight questions which ask the respondent to report what he/she likes and dislikes about the parties and candidates (The Party and Candidate Master Codes). In most years, the SRC coded five responses to each of the eight questions. We use only the first three responses to each question because in the 1972 election study only three responses were coded and we were concerned that this difference might bias the results when 1972 was compared with the earlier years.

The construction of the measure was done in two stages. The same procedure was followed for classifying the responses to parties as was used for classifying the responses to candidates, though two separate measures were developed. These categories and the codes on which they are based are as follows. It should be noted that the coding categories were changed substantially in 1972. The second set of numbers in each group (those in parentheses) represent the categorization of the 1972 codes.

1. *Explicit ideological responses.* Codes where the words "liberal," "conservative," "socialist," "liberal/conservative wing," and so forth appear. The code categories are: 260, 261, 262, 263, 264, 270, 271, 272, 280, 281, 282, 871, 872 (0162, 0163, 0164, 0531 through 0536, 0811, 0812, 0815, 0816 through 0819).

2. *Implicit ideological responses.* Codes using the terms "big business," "big government," "government intervention," "social reform" or "social change," "liberty v. government," "states rights," or mentions of government activity in the context of definable public policy orientation. The codes are: 150, 151, 210, 211, 220, 221, 222, 230, 231, 250, 265, 266, 267, 268, 391, 392, 284, 120, 121, 130, 131 (0605, 0606, 0805 through 0810, 0827, 0828, 0902, 0903, 0904, 0906, 0907, 1209, 1210).

3. *Group reference.* Any code in which is mentioned an evaluation of a party or candidate in terms of perceived policy toward or treatment of a specific group or class of people. Codes include: 440 through 446, 451, 453, 454, 493, 600, 601, 615, 616, 617, 620, 633, 640, 650, 660, 670, 671, 690, 692, 710 through 799 (0942 through 0945, 0965, 0966, 0967, 1201, 1202, 1205 through 1208, 1211 through 1297).

4. *Policy reference.* An evaluation of a party or candidate in terms of perceived position on a specific issue or category of issue, such as unemployment, welfare, education, housing, civil rights, conservation, law and order, gun control, foreign policy, or war. The codes are: 291, 300 through 303, 310, 320, 330, 340 through 348, 390, 400, 410, 420, 421, 422, 431 through 437, 455, 460, 461, 470 through 489, 490 through 493, 500 through 599, 873, 874, 982 (0509 through 0520, 0813, 0814, 0820, 0821, 0823, 0824, 0900, 0901, 0905, 0908 through 0933, 0946 through 0964, 0968 through 0997, 1101 through 1197, 0936 through 0941).

5. *Nature-of-the-times.* Responses that principally describe general needs such as the need for a change or the need to avoid a depression or refer to the existence of hard times or good times, jobs, prices, honest government, personal gains or losses, and such. The codes are: 349 through 355, 360, 370, 380, 499, 913, 100 through 115 (0703, 0704, 0705, 0706, 0934, 0935).

6. *Party mentions.* Responses referring to party loyalty or partisanship. These codes are: 010 through 090, 800 through 870, 880, 890, 891, 273, 274, 283 (0001 through 0097, 0101 through 0161, 0165, 0167, 0168, 0197, 0211, through 0297, 0303 through 0310, 0313 through 0316, 0500 through 0508, 0541, 0542, 0597, 0601 through 0604, 0720).

7. *Nonpolitical responses.* Any mentions of personal qualities of candidates or personal influences, as well as nonresponses such as "don't know." This is a residual category; any code not mentioned above is included here.

The seven response categories listed above were used to create seven types of respondents ranging from "apolitical or nature-of-the-times" respondents at the bottom of the level of conceptualization scale to "ideologues" at the top. The combinations of responses that form the basis of the categorization are listed below. Respondents were assigned to the highest category on the scale that their responses allowed.

The Levels of Conceptualization

Apolitical or nature-of-the-times responses:

These respondents consistently gave nonpolitical responses ("I like Eisenhower," "my husband is a Democrat"), or nature-of-the-times responses. Those unable to answer the question were also coded here.

Party responses:

Any vague reference to party moves a respondent out of the apolitical nature-of-the-times category. A party response might be: "I've always been a Democrat," "The Republicans are the better party," or "Ike's a Republican."

Group benefit responses:

A respondent is moved into this category if his mentions the benefits a particular group will be given or denied, that is, "Democrats do more for the working man like me."

Issue references:

A respondent is placed in this category if one or more of his responses pertain to a particular issue.

Group benefits and issues:

A respondent is moved into this category if his evaluation of the parties or candidates involves references to both group benefits and issues.

Near ideologues:

Respondents are placed in this category if they offer at least one explicit or implicit ideological mention but fail to give any issue responses or group benefit responses.

Ideologues:

Respondents are put into this category only if they make at least one implicit or explicit ideological mention and also make some reference to issues and group benefits.

Appendix 2D

OPEN-ENDED EVALUATIONS
AND THE VOTE

There is currently considerable debate among researchers on electoral behavior as to how much of an increase in issue voting is revealed by analyses of open-ended evaluation measures. Analysts agree that these measures show a significant decline in party voting.[1] However, some find more evidence for an increase in the role of personal candidate evaluations as a determinant of the vote than evidence for an increase in issue voting. The year most under dispute is 1972. The debate is complicated and involves the proper operationalization of the measures as well as the appropriate statistical methods. Conflicting results seem to derive from three sources: (1) the number and type of categories of evaluation, (2) whether the analyst combines the evaluations of candidates and parties into a single measure or treats them separately, and (3) whether effects are measured by examining standardized or unstandardized coefficients.

The following is a description of our procedures and how they relate to the procedures used by others.

(1) *The basic categories.* Several analyses of the open-ended evaluation questions use the Stokes six factor model.[2] This model uses six categories of

---

[1] Eugene Declercq, Thomas L. Hurley, and Norman Luttbeg, "Voting in American Presidential Elections: 1952–1972," *American Politics Quarterly,* 3 (July 1975), 222–246; Samuel A. Kirkpatrick, William Lyons, and Michael R. Fitzgerald, "Candidates, Parties and Issues in the American Electorate: Two Decades of Change," ibid., pp. 247–283; Samuel L. Popkin, John W. Gorman, Charles Phillips, and Jeffrey A. Smith, "What Have You Done for Me Lately? Toward an Investment Theory of Voting," *American Political Science Review,* forthcoming; and Michael R. Kagay and Greg A. Caldeira, "I Like the Looks of His Face," paper presented at the Annual Meeting of the American Political Science Association, San Francisco, September 1975.

[2] Popkin and others, "What Have You Done for Me Lately?" Kagay and Caldeira, "I Like the Looks of His Face"; and Kirkpatrick and others, "Candidates, Parties and Issues."

response: references to personal characteristics of the Democratic candidate, to personal characteristics of the Republican candidate, to domestic issues, to foreign issues, to group benefits, and to the party as a manager of the nation's affairs. These categories criss-cross the basic three-way distinction that concerns us among issue, party, and personal characteristics. The six components, furthermore, are highly intercorrelated making it more difficult to isolate statistical effects. Our three-category model contains less ambiguity in coding and allows simpler analysis of effects.

(2) *Combining candidate and party evaluations.* The open-ended evaluation questions are about the two main parties as well as the presidential candidates. Most researchers follow Stokes's original model and combine both sets of evaluations. We believe that the use of party evaluations makes it difficult to estimate the relative weight of factors in the voting choice. In the first place, parties and candidates are quite distinct objects of evaluation and have, according to our data, become more distinct over time. Second, we are attempting to explain the presidential vote, which is a choice between candidates rather than between parties. Last, and most important, our main goal is to assess the relative importance of party, personality, and the issues in relation to the vote. If one combines the evaluation of candidates with the evaluation of parties this becomes very difficult. People can meaningfully evaluate a candidate in all three terms. They cannot evaluate a party in terms of itself or in terms of personal characteristics.[3]

(3) *Standardized v. unstandardized regression coefficients.* We use both standardized and unstandardized coefficients (see figures 10.6, 10.7, and 10.8). However, most of our conclusions are based on standardized coefficients because of our concern with the variance in the vote explained by each of the three factors. We use the unstandardized coefficients only to establish the total effect of slope and proportion for each factor. The analysis with results most distinct from ours uses only the unstandardized B's.[4] While the slope may be higher for personalities than for issues in the 1972 election it does not necessarily follow that the scatter around that slope is less. In general this type of causal analysis is better done with standardized measures of the proportional reduction in variance type.

---

[3] See Kirkpatrick and others, "Candidates, Parties and Issues," pp. 271–272. They separate the candidate and issue evaluations and find that the role of evaluations of the parties in terms of domestic issues has decreased in relation to the vote in 1972, but the role of candidate domestic issue evaluations remains high.

[4] Popkin and others, "What Have You Done for Me Lately?"

Specific Procedures

The three candidate evaluation measures were created by a simple count of the number of references to party, personality, and issues given in response to questions about the respondent's likes and dislikes of the main presidential candidates. Three separate variables were created, corresponding to the three main divisions of evaluation. The following outline presents the actual numerical categories from the master codes included under each of the dimensions, the number of responses utilized, and examples of the types of response categories.

I. ISSUE MENTIONS

These codes cover general support or nonsupport on issues and favorability of policies for certain groups. Examples of categories used were:

Stand on urban, welfare, and poverty problems.

Liberal. More liberal than other Democrats.

Will stop communism abroad.

Good for the middle class.

A. *Democratic candidate*
   1. 1952–1968: 5 possible responses
      Codes 401–792, 911, 913, 970–979, 985
   2. 1972: 3 possible responses, Form I
      Codes 601–697, 801–1297
B. *Republican candidate*
   1. 1952–1968: 5 possible responses
      Codes same as for Democratic candidate.
   2. 1972: 3 possible responses
      Codes same as for Democratic candidate.
C. *Wallace:* 1968, codes 403–789, 913, 970–985

II. PERSONALITY MENTIONS

These codes cover the general experience and abilities of the candidate, his character and background, and his general personal attractiveness. Examples of categories used were:

Good man. Well qualified for the job.

Dependable, reliable, trustworthy.

Strong man, decisive.

Above politics, not a politician.

Not a leader. No leadership ability.

Good speaker. Like his face.

A. *Democratic candidate*
1. 1952–1968: 5 possible responses
Positive mentions: codes 10–391, 900–902, 981, 986
Negative mentions: codes 10–391, 900–902, 981
2. 1972: 3 possible responses, Form I
Positive and negative mentions: codes 201–497, 701–797
B. *Republican candidate*
1. 1952–1968
Positive mentions: codes 10–391, 900, 901, 981, 986
Negative mentions: codes 10–391, 900–902, 981, 983, 986
2. 1972
Same as for Democratic candidate.
C. *Wallace:* 1968
Positive mentions: codes 011–390, 810, 811, 841, 901, 986
Negative mentions: codes 011–390, 841, 842, 901–903

III. PARTY MENTIONS

These codes cover the candidate as a representative of his party or in relation to other Democrats. Examples of categories used were:
He's a Democrat (Republican), the party nominee.
He's a real Democrat (Republican).
Connections with other party leaders.
Represents liberal (conservative) wing of the Democratic (Republican) party.

A. *Democratic candidate*
1. 1952–1968: 5 possible responses
Positive and negative mentions: codes 800–895
2. 1972: 3 possible responses, Form I
Positive and negative mentions: codes 500–597
B. *Republican candidate*
1. 1952–1968
Positive and negative mentions: codes 800–896
2. 1972
Same as for Democratic candidate.
C. *Wallace:* 1968, codes 800, 812–830, 860, 870, 890

The directional measures of candidate evaluation (along the dimensions of issue, personality, and party) were created by the following method. The same issue codes as those outlined above were used. However, to obtain a directional measure, we:

(1) summed the positive mentions of a given candidate on a given dimension,

(2) summed the negative mentions of a given candidate on a given dimension,

(3) subtracted the negative mentions from the positive mentions. (If 1 and 2, above, were both zero, 3 was considered a missing value. This yielded a summary evaluation measure for each candidate on issues, personality, and party.),

(4) subtracted Republican candidate evaluation measure from Democratic candidate evaluation measure.

This produces an evaluation of the Democratic candidate relative to the Republican candidate. Positive values mean that the respondent rated the Democratic candidate higher than the Republican candidate, and vice versa for negative values. If either or both of the initial variables had missing values (3, above), the overall summary evaluation (4, above) was also considered to be missing.

Appendix 3

COMPARING THE EARLIER POLLS
WITH THE MICHIGAN STUDIES

Comparison of the levels of issue consistency found in the Michigan studies with those found in the earlier Gallup and Roper polls involves comparison of different sets of questions. This can invalidate the comparison in several ways. For one thing, the difference in the content of the questions may affect the results. The particular set of questions asked in one year may generate a level of consistency quite different from the level one would find if questions asked in other years had been asked. For instance, perhaps we would have found little consistency between size of government items and welfare items in 1939 if we had asked the same set of questions asked in 1956. To avoid the problem, we used almost identical items in our analyzes from 1956 to 1972. But for the comparison with earlier studies we must face the problem. Another source of difficulty derives from possible changes in the question and interview format. Let us consider substance and then format.

Substantive Problems

The problem is that we do not have the same questions in the pre-1950s studies that we have from 1956 on. But a good deal of evidence suggests that the difference in the level of consistency is not due to the substance of the particular items about which we ask. For one thing, the issue areas we have isolated in the 1939–1948 data appear on the face of it to be comparable to the issue areas used in the Michigan studies. A comparison of the individual items listed at the end of this Appendix and the items listed in Appendix 2A will show that this is the case.

Furthermore, as the matrix of relationships among individual pairs of items for the various years makes clear, the average gammas reported for any year do not mask widely differing individual gammas. In most cases, the individual pairs are similar to the average relationship. The year 1939 is an excellent case. The average gamma for the size of government/welfare-redistribution issue areas is .38. This is based on twenty-eight pairs of relationships between four quite different welfare/redistribution items and seven government-size items. These relationships range from a high of .50 to a low of .27. Thus, none of the relationships in 1939 is as low as the average relationships in 1956, 1958, or 1960 (.16, .05, and .14 respectively). Clearly the magnitude of the interrelationships is more a function of the time period than of the particular questions.

Another example may be relevant. In 1948 our measures are based on three separate studies, in July, August, and September of that year. The specific measures used for the various issue areas differ from study to study. Yet interrelationships found in the three separate studies are quite similar, again suggesting that the characteristic that counts is the time period, not the specific content of the questions. Table A.2 reports the data in those cases where we were able to compare average gammas based on three or more individual gammas across two or more of the three 1948 studies. This turns out to be possible largely for relations between the vote and issues. The relationships are quite stable across the studies.

Format Problems

There are three possible format problems that would make the data from the earlier period less comparable to those from later: response set, changes in coding categories, and the treatment of third party candidates.

1. *Response set.* Many questions have a format that could easily generate response set: for example, a series of similarly worded questions in which all the "agree" answers are in the same ideological direction. We have attempted to minimize this problem by eliminating from our analysis the most blatant examples of this phenomenon—that is, we do not report interrelationships across items that are very similarly worded, adjacent to each other on the questionnaire, and about similar matters. (For instance, the studies have strings of questions on whether the government "ought to own railroads," "ought to own natural resources," and so on.)

In addition, it is possible to consider the items we have used from the perspective of the potential response set. The average gamma of .38 between size of government and welfare/redistribution items was based, as we have pointed out, on twenty-eight individual paired intercorrelations. Half of these

TABLE A.2. Average gammas, three 1948 studies

	All respondents	Lower education	Upper education
Vote and domestic issues			
July 1948	.31	.23	.38
Aug. 1948	.29	.21	.37
Sept. 1948	.30	.22	.40
Vote and foreign affairs			
July 1948	−.03	.11	−.04
Sept. 1948	−.02	.08	−.02
Party identification and domestic issues			
July 1948	.23	.14	.26
Aug. 1948	.20	.22	.23

intercorrelations were between questions that had a similar format and were adjacent to each other in the questionnaire. The other half were between questions separated in the questionnaire and with a different format. If response set is the cause of the high relationship between size of government items and welfare/redistribution items, this should result in larger gammas between those items that are similar in format than between those that are different.

If we take the gammas based on questions with a similar format, we find they range from a low of .29 to a high of .48 and average .38. If we take the gammas based on differently formated pairs, we find that they range from a low of .27 to a high of .50, and average .36. The difference is negligible.

Another approach to the estimation of the impact of response set would be to compare gammas based on "reversed" items (where the liberal answer was the first answer in one item, the conservative answer the first answer in the other) with gammas based on questions where the same political direction was the first alternative in each case. Unfortunately, there are not too many such cases (which is one reason why we were concerned about response set to begin with).

The data we report for 1939 are based on the March 1939 study by Roper. There is variation in format, as we have seen, but no reversal of response order. However, in the Roper study of December 1939 (where there are only a few issue questions), one pair of questions fits our purposes. One question has to do with the desirability of limiting personal income, another with the amount of profit businesses ought to be allowed to earn. (Since these two items do not fall into our two domestic issue areas, we have not used them in our analysis of domestic economic issues.) The responses to the questions are reversed: that is, a liberal answer is the first alternative to one of them, a conservative answer the first alternative to the other. The gamma between them is .35, quite similar to the average gamma of .37 found for all domestic economic issues in the March 1939 data. The similarity across the two studies in the same year adds to the credibility of the 1939 data.

In the September 1948 study we find more examples. All the questions about welfare/redistribution matters were asked in such a way that the liberal position was the first answer. Of the three items on size of government, one had the liberal answer first, the other two had the liberal answer second. If response set is a major source of contamination, the gammas between items with a similar direction should be larger than those between items with a different direction. As table A.3 indicates, there is some tendency for similar direction in format to generate larger gammas, but a relatively slight one. The average gamma for pairs where the direction of response is the same is .33, the average for reversed pairs is .29.

Using the data in 1946 we can try a more stringent test. In that year we have one pair of items from the same issue area but where the direction of response is reversed. We can compare that with a pair of items from different issue areas where the questions are in the same direction. We should find a stronger relationship among items from the same issue area but with different

TABLE A.3. Reversed and nonreversed gammas, September 1948

	Size of government		
	Same direction items:	Reversed direction items:	
Welfare/redistribution items	Power of federal government	Gov't. regulate business	Gov't. regulate auto industry
Minimum wage	.33	.24	.26
Government guarantee living standard	.28	.21	.26
Government help the poor	.31	.34	.36
Government responsibility for welfare	.38	.32	.30
Average	.33	.29	

format than we find between the items with similar format from different issue areas. The comparison is as follows:

Same format, different issue area (government regulate collective bargaining and government provide social security) .18

Different format, same issue area (government provide social security and guarantee minimum wage) .23

The data are in the expected direction if our hypothesis is that substance rather than format is dominant. The difference, however, is not as great as one might expect. It certainly does not eliminate the existence of a response set phenomenon.

2. *Coding categories.* In order to make the items comparable and because gamma is particularly sensitive to degrees of freedom, all the items in the 1956–1972 studies were handled in a uniform way. Each item was trichotomized into positive, neutral, and negative answers, and "don't know" answers were omitted. This treatment was not always possible in the pre-1950s studies. In a number of cases, there were only positive, negative, and "don't know" response categories. No middle category existed. We had either to treat the question as a dichotomy in order to eliminate the "don't know" responses as was done with the SRC studies, or we had to put the "don't know" responses into a middle category in order to place the item into a trichotomous format. It was clear from a comparison of the two approaches that the latter caused less distortion. Gammas calculated on dichotomies are substantially higher than gammas calculated on trichotomies.

The conservative solution seemed to be to create trichotomies out of dichotomous questions by placing the "don't know" responses into a middle category. For consistency we placed "don't know" responses into the middle category even in those cases where there were already three response categories. This makes our handling of the pre-1950s data similar to the approach used for the later years in that the questions are all trichotomized. But it is inconsistent with the post-1956 data in that the "don't know" responses are included in the middle category.

We can, however, test whether this has a major effect on the results by looking at those paired relationships where we do have three response categories for each of the items. They can be handled in the exact manner as the later analyses—trichotomized with "don't knows" eliminated—and those relationships compared to gammas calculated for the same pairs of items with the "don't know" responses included as a middle category.

Table A.4 compares some gammas calculated with the "don't know" responses eliminated and some calculated with the "don't know" responses placed in the center category. The comparison shows that the differences in

TABLE A.4. Gammas calculated with and without the "don't know" responses

	Gamma calculated with "don't know" responses in middle category	Gamma calculated with "don't know" responses omitted
1939 data		
Government ownership of railroads and ownership of hospitals	.48	.52
Government ownership of railroads and vote	.39	.41
Government ownership of natural resources and free trade	−.06	−.04
1946 data		
Government build housing and job discrimination	.21	.22
1948 data		
Government help the poor and government regulate auto industry	.34	.36
Government help the poor and government regulate savings banks	.35	.36
Government relate auto industry and U.S. in international organizations	−.03	−.07
Minimum wage and U.S. in international organizations	.10	.00

the results are relatively trivial. Placing the "don't know" responses in the middle category reduces the gamma a bit, but rarely by much. Our impression is that our handling of the number of response categories tended generally to provide conservative results. But it does not seem to have much effect on the data.

3. *Third party candidates.* One problem in estimating the relationship between the vote and the issues is the handling of third party candidates. The issue arises in 1948 with the existence in the race of (the other) Wallace and Strom Thurmond. Vote intention was asked in all three studies. But in two studies (July and August), it was possible to distinguish only the Truman from the Dewey vote, with everyone else in a middle category. In September, we could isolate the various votes.

Table A.5 compares the gamma between issues and the vote for two different ways of handling the vote in September 1948:

(1) Truman versus Dewey with all others placed in the middle.

(2) Truman versus Dewey with Wallace (and the handful of Norman Thomas voters) assigned to the Truman category and Thurmond assigned to the Dewey category.

It is clear that the assignment of the left third party candidates to the left and the right candidate to the right increases somewhat the ideological polarization of the vote. But the results remain similar. In calculating the average gamma between the vote and issues across the three 1948 studies we used the somewhat more polarizing measure in September where it was available and the less polarizing measure in July and August where the more potent

TABLE A.5. Issues and the vote, September 1948

Issue	Vote measured with third party candidates in middle	Vote measured with third party candidates on left or right
Minimum wage	.20	.22
Government guarantee living standard	.28	.32
Government help poor	.28	.33
Government responsibility for welfare	.24	.27
Power of Federal government	.44	.46
Government regulate auto industry	.34	.37
Government regulate business	.36	.39
Average	.31	.34

measure was unavailable. The slight inconsistency between September and the other two months has minor effects. If we had used the less polarizing measure consistently across all three studies we would have found an average gamma for domestic issues and the vote of .29 rather than the .30 we report.

Appendix 4

CHANGING PARTY IDENTIFICATIONS: EVIDENCE FROM THE 1956–1960 PANEL

Support for the stability of party identification is found in Converse's analysis of the 1956–1958–1960 panel data. Partisanship was the most stable of attitudes over time.[1] Recent papers have called this presumed stability into question.[2] These recent papers show that a large minority of respondents do not report the same party identification over time. Some of the change is attributed to measurement instability. Another substantial part of the change, however, is attributed to actual change in the party identification of voters. The issue raised by these reports is important to the analyses that we present in several chapters of this book. For this reason it is important to examine the matter. This appendix presents some data from the panel studies conducted by the Survey Research Center in the late fifties; from the 1960 election study which asked the party identification question in both the pre- and postelection waves of the study; and from a study done at the National Opinion Research Center in 1973.

In each case we have more than one measurement of partisanship for each respondent. In each case we find many respondents who are not cate-

---

[1] The original data on the stability of party identification as an attitude can be found in Chapter 7 of Angus Campbell and others, *The Voter Decides* (Evanston, Ill.: Row, Peterson, 1954) and in Chapter 7 of Angus Campbell and others, *The American Voter* (New York: Wiley, 1960). See also, Philip Converse, "The Nature of Belief Systems in Mass Publics," in David E. Apter, ed., *Ideology and Discontent* (New York: Free Press, 1964).

[2] The most widely known articles which call into question the stability of the index of party identification are: Edward C. Dreyer, "Change and Stability in Party Identification," *Journal of Politics*, 35 (August 1973), 712–723; Douglas Dobson and Duane A. Meeter, "Alternative Markov Models for Describing Change in Party Identification," *American Journal of Political Science*, 18 (August 1974), 487–500; and Douglas Dobson and Douglas St. Angelo, "Party Identification and the Floating Vote: Some Dynamics," *American Political Science Review*, 69 (June 1975), 481–490.

gorized the same way on the seven-point index of party preference each time. A cross-tabulation of the 1956 and 1960 responses of the members of the SRC panel study indicates that only about 57 percent of the respondents have exactly the same partisan commitment in both years. A comparison of the 1956 to 1958 and the 1958 to 1960 responses of members of this panel study gives an average of only 61 percent making exactly the same responses to the party identification questions. Finally, the 1960 study, which asked the party identification questions only a few months apart (once in the preelection wave and later in the postelection survey), shows that only about 59 percent of the respondents gave the same answer twice. From these data it would seem that the revisionists are correct, that party identification is less resistant to short-term fluctuation than we have believed in the past. On the other hand, these percentages rely upon the full seven-point version of the index which distinguishes individuals on the basis of strength of identification as well. Most of the fluctuation that appears in the use of the seven-point index is movement from strong to weak identification or vice versa; or between independence and weak identification. Of the average 41 percent variation in the partisanship index, about 20 points is change in the strength of commitment to the parties; about 17 percent of the change is movement from some identification to independence (or the other way around); and only about 2 per-

TABLE A.6. Consistency in party preference for responses separated by different lengths of time (percentages)

	4 year panel		2 year panel		3 month panel		NORC experiment	
Consistent:	76		82		79		89	
Dem. to Dem.		40		44		40		39
Ind. to Ind.		44		13		13		30
Rep. to Rep.		22		25		26		20
To Independent:	8		7		7		5	
Dem. to Ind.		4		4		6		3
Rep. to Ind.		4		1		1		2
From Independent:	11		9		7		4	
Ind. to Dem.		7		5		4		2
Ind. to Rep.		4		4		3		2
Switch:	3		2		2		.6	
Dem. to Rep.		1		1		1		.1
Rep. to Dem.		2		1		1		.5

cent of the change is movement from Democrat to Republican or Republican to Democrat.

As table A.6 indicates there is impressive stability in the index of party identification if one deals with Democrats, Independents, and Republicans, and ignores the intensity of the partisanship. About 80 percent of the respondents report the same partisanship when they are reinterviewed. The proportion of consistent partisans is similar whether the reinterviews are taken four years later, two years later, or only a few months later.

What can be said about the 20 percent of respondents who do not make consistent replies when asked about their partisanship? The answer is that it depends upon what can be considered a baseline against which to measure differences. The most reasonable baseline would seem to be the NORC survey done in 1973. In that study several experiments were conducted as to the effects of question wording. One of the experiments involved the measurement of party identification. The last column of table A.6 is based on a cross-tabulation of responses to two different versions of the partisanship question. (The two questions and the cross-tabulation between them are on table A.7.) The difference in question wording is small. It seems reasonable to believe that it is not responsible for the different answers given by some respondents. Since the questions were asked about thirty minutes apart it is highly unlikely that any real change in partisanship took place between them. That being the case, differences in the answers reflect the shortcomings of the measure and

TABLE A.7. A comparison of responses to party preference questions asked 30 minutes apart (percentages)

		Generally speaking, do you usually consider yourself a Republican, a Democrat, an Independent, or what?			
		Dem.	Ind.	Rep.	
In politics, as of today, do you consider yourself a Republican, a Democrat, or Independent?	Dem.	39.2	2.3	.5	43.0%
	Ind.	3.0	30.1	2.4	35.5
	Rep.	.1	1.5	20.1	21.7
		42.3	33.9	23.0	100

the inattentiveness of respondents. By comparing the consistency of responses to the NORC questions with the consistency of responses in the SRC panels it should be possible to estimate the change that takes place in party identification over short periods of time. The biggest difference between the NORC study and the several SRC data sets is in rate of movement into and out of independence. On average, 16 percent of all respondents move into or out of independence in the various waves of the SRC panels. The NORC study finds about 9 percent moving into or out of independence. The difference—7 percent—is probably a good estimate of the real change that is occurring there.

If we look at the category of switching party identification, we find that less than 1 percent of the respondents in the NORC study change from Democrat to Republican or Republican to Democrat. If that 1 percent figure accurately estimates the amount of measurement error, then about 1.5 to 2.5 percent of the electorate in fact changes its party identification in a two to four year period. This figure is very close to the estimates of switched party identification found in responses to retrospective questions about party identification in the SRC surveys.

Index